Statistical Approaches to Measurement Invariance

Statistical Approaches to Measurement Invariance

Roger E. Millsap

Arizona State University

Routledge
Taylor & Francis Group
New York   London

Routledge
Taylor & Francis Group
270 Madison Avenue
New York, NY 10016

Routledge
Taylor & Francis Group
27 Church Road
Hove, East Sussex BN3 2FA

Library of Congress Cataloging-in-Publication Data

Millsap, Roger Ellis.
   Statistical approaches to measurement invariance / by Roger E. Millsap.
      p. cm.
   Includes bibliographical references.
   ISBN 978-1-84872-818-9 -- ISBN 978-1-84872-819-6
   1. Psychometrics. 2. Psychology--Statistical methods. 3. Psychological tests.
   I. Title.

BF39.M554 2011
150.28'7--dc22   2010045367

Visit the Taylor & Francis Web site at
http://www.taylorandfrancis.com

and the Psychology Press Web site at
http://www.psypress.com

To the memory of my parents,

Max and Lillian Millsap, and to Michele

and our children Mason, Laura, Simone, and Aiden.

Contents

Preface

The origin of this book lies in a conversation with William Meredith that happened around 1985 at the University of California, Berkeley. Responding to a question of mine about a chi-square test for item bias, Bill described the properties of the test and then noted, almost as an afterthought, that the test was "not really diagnostic" for item bias. His point contradicted what I thought I knew about this test for item bias. This single conversation led us to work on developing general conditions for the diagnostic value of any method of bias detection that relied on observed-score matching. We also developed conditions to determine when observed-score matching procedures would lead to the same conclusions as procedures based on latent variable modeling. By the time we were ready to publish some of this work, it was clear to me that the problem of bias detection was much more complex than I had previously believed.

Over the last 20 years, I have worked on aspects of the bias detection problem in psychology, always returning to the problem eventually in spite of other research obligations and interests. One reason for my fascination with the detection problem is that it remains only partially solved. Fundamentally, while we have detection methods that work under limited circumstances, we have no completely general method for detecting bias in psychological measures that works across all of the many measurement conditions encountered in psychology. Instead, we have a collection of approaches that apply under specific conditions and assumptions, and that may not function well when these conditions or assumptions are violated. A further problem is that it is usually hard to verify some of the assumptions that are needed in practice for many of the detection methods. It is undeniable, however, that substantial progress has been made in the last 20 years in the development of new methods for bias detection and in enhancements to existing methods.

I have written this book with several goals in mind. The first goal is to acquaint the reader with the broad set of statistical procedures currently used to approach the problem of detecting measurement bias. A second goal, which follows upon the first, is to provide the necessary background material so that readers can place the many detection procedures in context. Toward that end, the book devotes considerable space to describing the measurement models that underlie psychometric practice. I have also included some theoretical results that subsume many types of detection procedures, showing their strengths and limitations. Finally, I hope that the book will inspire more researchers to become involved in bias detection research. The problem of detecting bias in psychological measures is a difficult one, and it represents a significant challenge to measurement in psychology. In addition to the detection problem itself, the measurement bias problem has implications for the use of tests in many domains as predictors or as tools for making decisions about people. The last chapter of the book explores these implications for the use of tests in prediction and for the related problem of bias in prediction.

The intended audience for this book consists of researchers and students who wish to understand the array of available procedures for detecting bias in psychological measurement. The problem of measurement bias arises in many research settings, ranging from applied research in employment or educational testing to the use of tests or questionnaires in experimental studies with multiple groups. I hope that the book will serve as a useful reference for researchers in all of these settings. The book is intended to also serve as a resource for students who want to learn more about psychometrics, particularly in relation to the problem of measurement bias as a challenge to the validity of measurement. To benefit from the book, a student should have an understanding of basic probability and statistical theory, along with some knowledge of regression.

The overall structure of the book can be described as follows. Chapter 1 presents some basic information about the definition of measurement bias and how the book will examine this topic. Chapter 2 reviews the measurement models used in psychometric theory. Emphasis is placed on latent variable models, with introductions to classical test theory, factor analysis, and item response theory, along with the controversies associated with each. Measurement invariance and bias in the context of multiple populations is defined in Chapter 3. Chapter 4 describes the common factor model for continuous measures in multiple populations and its use in the investigation of factorial invariance. It examines identification problems in confirmatory factor analysis along with estimation and fit evaluation and provides an example using WAIS-R data. The factor analysis model for discrete measures in multiple populations with an emphasis on the specification, identification, estimation, and fit evaluation issues is addressed in Chapter 5. An MMPI example is also provided. Chapter 6 reviews both dichotomous and polytomous item response models emphasizing estimation methods and model fit evaluations. The use of models in item response theory in evaluating invariance across multiple populations is then described in Chapter 7, including an example that uses data from a large-scale achievement test. Chapter 8 examines item bias evaluation methods that use observed scores to match individuals and provides an example that uses the same achievement test data from the previous chapter. Finally, the book concludes with Chapter 9, which discusses the implications of measurement bias for the use of tests in prediction, as in educational or employment settings.

Acknowledgments

I am deeply indebted to the many individuals who have helped shape my thinking about the material in this book and who have contributed their time and resources to helping with its development. Three individuals in particular gave the manuscript a close reading and provided highly useful advice: Howard Everson, Steve Reise, and Mark Reckase. Many current and former students have provided assistance and feedback at various stages: Oi-man Kwok, Myeongsun Yoon, Soyoung Lee, Margarita Olivera-Aguilar, Kimberly Blackwell, Heining Cham, Stefany Coxe, Amanda Gottschall, Jessie Wong, Michael Thomas, Jeremy Biesanz, Antonio Morgan-Lopez, Thomas Uttaro, Sandra Hartog, Adam Carle, Ross Taylor, Ruth Diones, Tina Xenos, and Caroline Rodriguez. I am also strongly indebted to the many colleagues who have influenced the development of my thinking on invariance: Niels Waller, Jack McArdle, John Nesselroade, John Horn, Rebecca Zwick, John Tisak, Keith Gregory, Howard Terry, Laura Sands, Bruce Bloxom, Alberto Maydeu-Olivares, Siek Toon Khoo, Paras Mehta, David Rindskopf, Rod McDonald, Sam Green, Marilyn Thompson, Stephen du Toit, Keith Widaman, Barbara Byrne, Herb Eber, Michael Neale, Charles Reichardt, Wayne Camara, Larry Stricker, Dan Bauer, Chris Hertzog, David Kaplan, Todd Little, David Lubinski, Ozzie Morera, Ken Bollen, Tenko Raykov, Dan Ozer, Alan Gross, Maria Pennock-Roman, Joel Lefkowitz, Robert Thorndike, David Thissen, Lynne Steinberg, William Stout, David Flora, Robert MacCallum, Michelle Langer, Carol Woods, Jim Steiger, Bruno Zumbo, Bengt Muthén, Linda Muthén, Gerhard Fischer, Denny Borsboom, Jelte Wicherts, Frans Oort, Steven Osterlind, Fritz Drasgow, and Ed Rigdon. Throughout this project, I have benefited from the strong support of my colleagues in the Quantitative Psychology doctoral program here at Arizona State University: Steve West, Leona Aiken, David MacKinnon, Craig Enders, Sandy Braver, George Knight, and Christian Geiser. It has been a joy to work with these professionals on a daily basis. My colleagues at the Prevention Research Center at Arizona State University have strongly supported my work as well and deserve my thanks: Irwin Sandler, Sharlene Wolchik, Nancy Gonzales, Anne Mauricio, Tim Ayers, and Darya Bonds. Jenn-Yun Tein at the center has been especially helpful throughout the years of this project. I must also thank my editors at Routledge/Taylor & Francis: Debra Riegert, Andrea Zekus, and Erin Flaherty, who have been consistently helpful and patient throughout the long creation of this book. All of the above individuals have shaped this book in various ways, but I take full responsibility for any shortcomings in the final product.

This book would never have come about without the influence of my graduate advisor, Bill Meredith. I owe Bill a profound debt of gratitude for his patient mentoring and inspiration. Bill passed away in 2006. I hope that he would have approved of this book (though I can imagine that he would have thought it could have been shorter).

Finally, I must thank my wife, Michele, for her support and encouragement throughout the writing of this book. Thanks for keeping my focus on what is really important: our children Mason, Laura, Simone, and Aiden.

1

Introduction

This book is about measurement in psychology. It is addressed to researchers who want to study strategies for detecting bias in measurement, and who want to understand how these strategies fit in with the general theory of measurement in psychology. The methods to be described are statistical in nature, in line with the statistical nature of the models used in psychometrics to relate scores on tests to underlying psychological attributes. On the assumption that the reader may be unfamiliar with the details of these models, we will devote considerable space to describing them. The decision to include this material is motivated partly by the goal of making the book reasonably self-contained. An understanding of bias detection methods within item response theory (IRT), for example, is difficult to achieve by simply focusing on the detection methods themselves without first understanding the models and practices in IRT. A further motivation for including the material on measurement models is the conviction that bias detection methodology, while statistical in nature, is best understood through the psychometric perspective. In other words, while one can approach the topic as simply another application of statistics, in doing so one can easily forget what motivates the entire topic: inaccuracy in psychological measurement.

What Is Measurement Invariance?

The idea of measurement invariance is best introduced by analogy with physical measurement, as physical analogies have long played a role in the development of measurement theories generally (Lord & Novick, 1968). Measurement invariance is built on the notion that a measuring device should function in the same way across varied conditions, so long as those varied conditions are irrelevant to the attribute being measured. A weight scale, for example, should register varied weights across objects whose weights actually differ. We would be concerned, however, if the scale produced different weight readings for two objects whose known weights are identical, but whose shapes are different. In this case, shape is a condition that is varying, but this shape condition is known to be irrelevant to actual weight for this pair of objects. After more study, if we consistently find that the scale gives different weight readings for objects with different shapes but identical known weights, we would conclude that something is wrong with our scale. The scale is producing biased weight readings as a function of shape. We would also say that the scale violates measurement invariance in relation to shape: across objects whose weights are identical but whose shapes differ, the scale produces weight readings that vary systematically with shape.

In psychological measurement, a test or questionnaire that is designed to measure a given attribute should reveal differences among individuals if those individuals actually differ on the attribute. A scale designed to measure depression should show differences among individuals whose depression levels vary, for example. On the other hand, we should not find that the test produces different results for people who are identical on the attribute, but who might differ on other, less relevant, variables. For example, among a group of males and females who are identical in their depression levels, we should not find that the test gives consistently different results for males and females. If we do find that the test functions in this way, we would conclude that the test violates measurement invariance in relation to gender and that the test shows measurement bias in relation to gender.

Chapter 3 will address the definition of measurement bias in depth, but it is useful to consider some general aspects of this topic now. As defined here, bias in measurement is equivalent to systematic inaccuracy in measurement. This inaccuracy is replicable, in contrast to the essentially random errors of measurement that determine the reliability of a test. A test that is reliable may, or may not, be biased. An unreliable test may still yield unbiased measurement in an average sense across repeated measurement. In contrast, a biased test may be highly reliable, yet may consistently provide inaccurate measurement even when the average of many repeated measurements is considered.

Accepting this preliminary point of view, how can we know whether a measuring device is biased? In physical measurement, one might use the device repeatedly on the same object and then compare these results to the results produced by another device that is known to be more accurate (though possibly more expensive and time-consuming to use). In the weight example, one could find a group of objects whose weights are effectively known because they have been measured using more sensitive and accurate devices than the device being studied. In psychological measurement, however, this strategy is often impractical. Repeated measurement of the same individual using the same test will not often be possible without either creating boredom and fatigue or inducing real change in the individual through learning and memory. Furthermore, "gold standard" measures that are known to be free of bias and to be highly reliable do not exist in most areas of psychological measurement. The detection of bias in psychological measurement is a difficult problem for these reasons.

This book will focus on a particular aspect of the bias problem, which is bias that is related to a person's membership in a group. For example, a cognitive test item may be solved correctly at a higher rate among males than females. If this finding is replicated across large samples of males and females, we may conclude that the higher rate of correct answers for males is a feature of the population of males and females and is not a result of sampling error. If males score systematically higher on the item than females, is this fact evidence of bias in the item? One answer to this question is "yes," because the item systematically produces higher scores for males than females. In other words, systematic score differences between groups are evidence of bias, according to this viewpoint.

The above viewpoint confuses two different concepts, however: systematic group differences in scores on the item, and systematic inaccuracy in scores on the item. In the example, the higher rate of correct answers for males constitutes a group difference in scores but does not necessarily constitute systematic inaccuracy. Inaccuracy exists if the score on the item does not reflect the examinee's actual status on the attribute being measured. If two examinees truly differ on this attribute, an accurate test should produce different scores for the two examinees. By the same argument, if males and females differ on average on the attribute, an accurate test should yield different scores on average for males and females. Hence, the gender difference in average item scores has multiple interpretations. The gender difference could reflect a real difference on the attribute, or it could fail to reflect any real difference on the attribute. If you believe that no real gender differences are possible, you must then believe that the test item is biased: the item is systematically inaccurate in relation to gender.

In most areas of psychological measurement, we cannot know with certainty whether the groups being compared are actually different on a given psychological attribute. The only data available on such questions are the data at hand, or previous research with the same or similar measures. Once the question of bias is raised, trying to answer the question by simply documenting group differences in item scores is futile. For example, it may be true that (a) the groups do differ systematically on the attribute being measured, (b) the test item yields scores that systematically differ across groups, yet (c) the test is biased. This situation would arise if the test item produced score differences across groups that were systematically too large or too small. If the possibility of real group differences on psychological attributes is accepted, it becomes impossible to detect bias by simply looking at group differences in item scores. Something more is required.

How can we make any progress in deciding whether the test item is biased? The first step is to work with a definition of measurement bias that goes beyond group differences in item scores. The definition of bias that is accepted widely now relies on the *matching principle* (Angoff, 1993). This principle leads to the definition of an unbiased test or item. Consider any two individuals from different groups (e.g., one male and one female) who are identical on the attribute(s) being measured by the test item. We say the item is unbiased in relation to these groups if the probability of attaining any particular score on the item is the same for the two individuals (Lord, 1980; Mellenbergh, 1989). The matching idea enters into this definition in the requirement that the two individuals be identical or matched on the attribute(s) being measured. It is essential that we compare individuals from different groups who are matched, rather than randomly chosen pairs of individuals. A biased test item is then defined as one in which the probability of attaining any particular score differs for the two individuals in spite of the matching. In other words, the score on a biased item will depend not only on the attribute being measured but also on the group membership of the individual under consideration.

Several points should be noted about the definition of bias just described. First, the two individuals who have been matched on the attribute being measured may still achieve different scores on the test item in a particular occasion of measurement, even when the item is unbiased. Psychological measures are seldom perfectly reliable, and the two individuals may receive different scores due to this unreliability. Second, if we consider group differences in item scores in the general population without matching on the attributes, we may again encounter systematic group differences in item scores even though the item is unbiased. Group differences in item scores for the unbiased item reflect the actual magnitudes of differences on the attribute being measured. For this reason, the finding that a test produces systematic group differences in scores is ambiguous as long as no attempt is made to match individuals across groups.

At this point, anyone who has closely read the above definition of measurement bias may ask the next big question: If we must match individuals on the attribute being measured before trying to detect bias, how can this be done? After all, we do not actually know the individual's status on the attribute. If we knew the individual's status, we would not need the test item and we would know whether the item is biased.

This book is about the various answers to the matching question, and the statistical methods that have been built on these answers. In the process of explaining the answers, it will be necessary to review some portion of the theory of psychological measurement. Without this theory as background, the reader will have difficulty understanding the various strategies adopted in pursuit of bias detection. In this review, we will emphasize the unity underlying the various latent variable models used in psychometrics, but we will also not minimize the perplexing problems that have arisen in psychometric theory. Psychometrics as a separate discipline is around 100 years old as of this writing, but it is a work in progress. Basic questions still loom, such as the problem of rigorously establishing a unit of measurement for psychological scales (Michell, 1999), or how test validation should be understood (Borsboom, 2005). The problem of bias detection itself is another example. It is hoped that by the end of this book, the reader will have gained some knowledge about strategies for bias detection, but also that the reader will appreciate the difficulties involved in bias detection and in psychological measurement generally.

Is Measurement Bias an Important Problem?

It is fair to ask why we should be concerned about bias in psychological measurement. For many researchers involved in applied settings, concerns about bias in measurement have already been effectively settled: There is little or no bias in measurement in tests used to make important decisions about people (Hunter & Schmidt, 2000; Jensen, 1980; Neisser et al., 1996; Sackett, Borneman, & Connelly, 2008; Sackett, Schmitt, Ellington, & Kabin, 2001). This sense that the question of bias is settled rests on several lines of evidence. Methods for detecting measurement bias have been around for decades (for an early review, see Berk, 1982), and so we might expect the bias question to have been thoroughly investigated by now. Major educational testing companies routinely use statistical methods to screen for item bias in relation to ethnicity or gender (Holland & Wainer, 1993). Inexpensive and statistically well-grounded methods for detecting item bias are available (Dorans & Holland, 1993). Furthermore, it has been argued that whatever measurement bias may be present has little impact on the use of tests in prediction or selection (Neisser et al.; Sackett et al.). This conclusion is partly based on the many empirical studies that have examined group differences in regressions or correlations between tests and criteria and have not found major differences (Schmidt & Hunter, 1998).

Although it is true that methods for detecting measurement bias have been around for decades, the methods that were in use prior to the mid-1980s had flaws that were not recognized until relatively recently. Early factor analytic approaches relied on exploratory methods that were inefficient and only considered limited aspects of factor structure (see Millsap & Meredith, 2007, for a review). The shift to confirmatory factor analytic methods in the 1980s initially failed to consider mean structures as part of the model, now recognized as an essential part of any test of factorial invariance (Gregorich, 2006). Whereas methods for bias detection based on IRT have been known for some time, software for actually conducting these analyses, apart from those based on the Rasch model, has been slow to develop. For example, the MULTILOG program (Thissen, 1991) has been the only program for evaluating likelihood-ratio (LR) tests of item bias under a variety of IRT models, but this program requires many computer runs for a single test. The IRTLRDIF program (Thissen, 2001) makes this process much more efficient but is a recent development. An alternative approach for item bias analyses is to use confirmatory factor analytic software that will handle discrete measures, as found in item data. The extension of such software to handle discrete measures is another recent development, however, and its dissemination for general use has been hindered by a general lack of knowledge about how these models should be specified and identified (Millsap & Yun-Tein, 2004).

Apart from latent variable methods such as factor analysis or IRT, a variety of methods that condition on observed scores to achieve matching across groups have been in use for some time. Early chi-square and ANOVA-based methods are now known to be flawed (Camilli & Shepard, 1994). The Mantel–Haenszel (MH) method is a great improvement and was available by the end of the 1980s (Holland & Thayer, 1988). This method is used by major testing organizations to screen for item bias on a large scale. The MH method has known weaknesses however (see Chapter 8). Logistic regression methods can address some problems in the MH approach, but other problems remain. The development of observed-score methods for items with polytomous response formats has been slow. Finally, some hybrid methods that integrate latent variable and observed-score approaches are now available, but these are also relatively recent developments (Jiang & Stout, 1998; Raju, Van der Linden, & Fleer, 1995). We can conclude that although methods for bias detection have been available for decades, for much of this history, the methods in use have had significant weaknesses that are now known. The stronger methods have had limited use due to both the scarcity of efficient, comprehensive software and the general lack of awareness about the methods among researchers.

Although statistical methods for studying measurement bias are difficult and may have had flaws historically, regression and correlation methods for predicting various criteria from test scores are well understood and widely used. As noted above, the lack of group differences in regressions or correlations between tests and criteria has been cited as evidence that measurement bias, if it exists, does not have any practical impact. This argument was taken seriously 30 years ago (see Jensen, 1980), but it should not be taken seriously now. The truth is that a test may show identical regressions when it is used to predict a criterion measure across multiple populations, even though substantial measurement bias exists in the test (Borsboom, Romeijn, & Wicherts, 2008; Millsap, 1997, 1998, 2007). The distinction between measurement bias and predictive bias is obscured by claims that "test bias" can be detected through scrutiny of group differences in the regression of a criterion measure on the test. While "test bias" has at times been equated with group differences in these regressions (Cleary, 1968), the presence or absence of such differences is not diagnostic for measurement bias.

The issue of bias in measurement has traditionally been viewed as primarily one of fairness and equitable treatment. This outlook arose in the context of high-stakes educational and employment testing, where decisions based on biased test results could unfairly penalize or stigmatize an entire group of people. Without question, the ethical and moral dimensions of bias in measurement are important. The issue of measurement bias has another side that receives less attention: the scientific use of bias detection methods as tools for understanding psychological measurement. When a test item is found to function differently depending on the examinee's group membership, questions are raised about what the item is actually measuring. One option in such cases is to get rid of the item, a choice that is often taken in applied settings. A different option is to try to understand why the bias exists. Ordinarily, item bias is unanticipated, and the post hoc search for an explanation of the bias can be difficult. A different strategy is to generate hypotheses about the sources of the bias and then test these hypotheses by strategically selecting items to manifest hypothesized biases. Bias detection methods are then used to evaluate whether the expected bias is found. This type of research has been attempted but is uncommon (Roussos & Stout, 1996a; Scheuneman, 1987). Another strategy would be to experimentally manipulate the attribute measured by the test in a way that could be detected using bias detection methods. The idea here is that a treatment might alter the relationship between scores on the test and the underlying attribute being measured. This effect would then be detected using bias detection methods, with the groups being randomized treatment and control groups. The literature on alpha–beta–gamma change in organizational research (Millsap & Hartog, 1988; Riordan, Richardson, Schaffer, & Vandenberg, 2001) is an example of this type of research. Although uncommon at present, this strategy seems to be a potentially interesting approach whenever a treatment is intended to induce deeper levels of change.

About This Book

Terminology and Notation

A few comments on the use of terminology related to measurement bias are needed. A good portion of the literature on measurement bias has used "differential item functioning" (DIF) to refer to "item bias," with the latter being an older term. The logic of the change to using DIF in place of item bias is that the use of "bias" has a negative connotation, implying that there is some inherent flaw in the item itself, and also that this flaw entails unfairness or prejudice (Angoff, 1993). In actual fact, an item showing "bias" may have no particular structural problem or flaw, and so the DIF terminology confines itself to the statistical finding of different performance for the item across groups. To give an example, an achievement test item may be clearly worded, may be free of any offensive language, and may be relevant to the area of knowledge being tested, yet the item may show bias in the sense of yielding systematically different scores for different groups after matching on the underlying attribute. The source of this bias may be differential exposure to a particular area of the curriculum, with this differential exposure also being related to group membership. It is argued that the DIF terminology is more neutral than "bias" and that the use of DIF calls attention to the differential performance of the item without erroneously implying that the item itself is poor.

A problem with the use of "DIF" to refer to this phenomenon is that the terminology draws attention away from the question of what the item may be measuring, and whether there is any systematic inaccuracy in the item as a measure of something. Bias denotes inaccuracy. The Oxford English Dictionary, 1989 (OED) defines "bias" as "a preponderating disposition or propensity." The general notion is one of a person or thing that acts in a certain way regardless of conditions. Applied to a test item, a biased item is one that is inaccurate in the sense of providing information that does not reflect actual conditions, or the actual state of the individual being measured. The use of the phrase "measurement bias" connotes systematic inaccuracy in a test or item as a measure of something.

Shealy and Stout (1993b) suggest that the phrase "DIF" be used when we do not have a firm understanding about whether the examinees being compared have truly been matched on the target attribute that the test or item was designed to measure. The term "bias" would be used when we do have confidence that the examinees have been matched on the target attribute. I think that this distinction is the correct view of the situation. The extent to which a proper matching is achieved in bias detection will be a constant issue throughout this book. The methods to be described are not particularly useful scientifically unless we have at least some understanding about what the test items might be measuring. For example, if we cannot have confidence that some of the items under study are actually measuring the targeted attribute(s), we cannot really begin the process of detecting bias. The DIF terminology exists as a device for separating the statistical phenomenon (group differences that remain after attempted matching) from questions about what the explanation for the phenomenon might be. If the analysis is conducted for scientific reasons, however, we are interested in explanations, or at least proximal explanations.

In this book, we will define "measurement bias" in a way that reflects a focus on measurement. An important concept in this definition is the idea of a target attribute or set of attributes that the test is designed to measure. We will use the word "bias" with the understanding that it denotes systematic inaccuracy in the test or item as a measure of the targeted attribute. Clearly, this approach forces the researcher to be careful about what is considered the targeted attribute. This push is appropriate: if the researcher is unable or unwilling to clearly define the targeted attribute, efforts to detect "bias" are probably premature. More research is needed on what is being measured. The concern for the targeted attribute may lead the researcher to conclude that the "attribute" is in fact multiple attributes, and that a multidimensional conception is needed. It is also true that under this conception, an item may be "biased" for one targeted attribute but not biased for a different attribute. The purpose of the test plays an essential role in setting the stage for any analysis of bias.

As will be seen, much emphasis is placed in this book on different types of measurement models. A measurement model is a statistical model that relates scores on an observed measure to scores on one or more latent variables. Historically, different measurement models have evolved at different times and have led to notational conventions that vary across models. For example, the literature on IRT has almost always used the Greek letter θ to represent the latent variable. This symbol is almost never used for this purpose in the factor analysis literature, however. These different notational practices convey the idea that different models are being described. These apparent differences are illusory in some cases. We know that for dichotomous items, well-known models in IRT such as the normal ogive model are equivalent to single-factor models for dichotomous indicators (Lord & Novick, 1968). The varying notational practices add complexity to an already complex subject.

This book is based on the idea of an essential unity underlying all latent variable models, an idea that is hardly new (Borsboom, 2005; Holland & Rosenbaum, 1986; Lord & Novick, 1968; McDonald, 1999). To reinforce this idea, we will use the symbol W (or $\mathbf{W}$ in the multivariate case) to represent the latent variable in both the factor analytic and item response theoretic models to be considered here. The use of "W" in place of "θ" may be an uncomfortable choice for researchers who use IRT exclusively. The use of a common notation will smooth the transition between measurement models and will permit a general treatment of latent variable theory that is not tied to particular model exemplars. The decision to approach the topic of measurement bias from a general latent variable perspective, rather than through a single type of model such as IRT, is motivated by the need to accommodate many different forms of testing, in many different contexts. The methods described in this book are meant to apply to any form of psychological testing that involves individuals responding to test items. Methods will be described that can apply to either dichotomous or polytomous response formats, when either a single latent variable underlies the items or multiple latent variables are present. The latent variables themselves are not limited to cognitive variables, but may include noncognitive variables such as attitudes, personality dimensions, emotional states, or clinical variables. The diversity of potential applications demands a general approach to latent variable theory, as discussed in Chapter 2.

Contents and Scope

The next eight chapters may be read in order or may be read selectively as determined by the specific interests of the reader. A brief synopsis of each chapter will help the reader to see the overall plan for the book and to decide which chapters will be of interest.

Chapter 2 describes the general features of the measurement models used in psychometric theory. These models are broadly characterized as latent variable models, although it is true that classical test theory deviates from this definition to some extent (Borsboom, 2005). Emphasis is placed on the common framework that underlies the different latent variable models. Brief introductions to classical test theory, the factor analysis model, IRT, and latent class models are given. Some ongoing problems or controversies in these models are described in the final section of the chapter. Most of the material in this chapter will be familiar to readers who have already studied psychometric theory. Readers with limited prior exposure to psychometrics should read this chapter.

Chapter 3 formally defines measurement invariance and bias in the context of multiple populations. The definition of "multiple populations" is itself considered at some length, followed by definitions of various forms of measurement invariance. Consideration is also given to the idea of a "target" latent variable as the basis for defining invariance. The use of observed scores as the basis for matching individuals in investigating bias is described at length. Some theoretical conditions under which observed-score matching will be equivalent to methods that achieve matching via latent variables are described. This chapter contains a mixture of material that will be familiar to readers with training in psychometrics and material that will probably be new to such readers. Most readers should read this chapter before going on to later chapters.

Chapter 4 describes the common factor model for continuous measures in multiple populations and its use in the investigation of factorial invariance. Factorial invariance is defined and related to the more general notion of measurement invariance. Extensive discussion is given to the identification problem in confirmatory factor analysis. Estimation and fit evaluation are each discussed. Various levels of factorial invariance are then described, leading to a sequence of models to investigate when studying factorial invariance. An example using data on the Wechsler Adult Intelligence Scale-Revised (WAIS-R) is given to illustrate this sequence. An appendix to the chapter gives results on the impact of selection on factorial invariance, a topic whose origins lie in the early twentieth century. This chapter is useful for readers who wish to study factorial invariance in real data. Some of the material will be new even to readers who are familiar with factor analysis (e.g., the appendix on selection theory).

Chapter 5 addresses the factor analysis model for discrete or ordered-categorical measures in multiple populations. In most cases, test item scores are best viewed as discrete rather than continuous measures. The factor analysis model can be reformulated to be appropriate for such measures, but the multiple population extensions of this model are not yet widely understood among most researchers. This chapter focuses on the specification, identification, estimation, and fit evaluation issues for this model. Attention is also given to the definition of invariance within the model, and the issues that this definition must address. The sequence of models that is typically of interest in evaluating invariance is described. An example is given that uses Minnesota Multiphasic Personality Inventory (MMPI) item data. This chapter will be of interest to readers who wish to apply confirmatory factor analysis to item-level data in studies of invariance.

Chapter 6 provides a general review of models in IRT. Models for both dichotomous and polytomous item response scales are described. Estimation methods are also described, with the emphasis being on conditional maximum likelihood and marginal maximum likelihood methods, along with some description of Bayesian approaches. Model fit evaluation is discussed at some length, divided into methods appropriate for the dichotomous versus polytomous items. The topic of the number of latent variables underlying the set of items is addressed in the context of both parametric approaches (e.g., factor analysis) and nonparametric approaches (e.g., DIMTEST). The material in this chapter will be familiar to readers who have studied IRT. Readers who are less familiar with these models and would like to learn more should read the chapter.

Chapter 7 covers the use of models in IRT in evaluating invariance across multiple populations. Different forms of item bias are first described in the context of item response functions. LR tests of item bias are next described for different models in IRT. Research on the use of LR approaches is reviewed. Tests of item bias based on Wald statistics are then discussed. Problems of parameter linkage in such procedures are described. Effect size measures for item bias are also described. An example of the use of IRT to investigate item bias is given, using data from a large-scale achievement test. The material in this chapter may be familiar to the reader who has used IRT to study item bias, but at least some of the material is likely to be new.

Chapter 8 covers the large class of item bias evaluation methods that use observed scores to match individuals. These methods are diverse, but they share at least one feature: no explicit assumptions about latent variables are required. Each method is described, along with research on the use of the method. Separate consideration is given to methods for dichotomous and polytomous items. Random-effects models for item-level bias are also discussed. Finally, the SIBTEST method and related procedures are described as hybrids of latent variable and observed-score methods. This chapter is likely to contain at least some new material for most readers, particularly in sections that relate some of the theory from Chapter 3 to the performance of observed-score methods. An example concludes the chapter by applying IRT to the data used in Chapter 7.

Chapter 9 addresses the implications of measurement bias for the use of tests in prediction. Group differences in the predictive properties of tests have been of long-standing interest in applied settings, as in educational or employment settings. The relationship between measurement bias and bias in prediction is described here, beginning with the definition of predictive invariance that parallels the earlier definition of measurement invariance. Results on the relationship between the two forms of invariance are first given for the case of linear regression and the common factor model. More general results that would apply in nearly all measurement and prediction situations are then described. The material in this chapter will be new to most readers.

There are a number of topics that are related to issues of measurement invariance but are not covered in this book. First, the evaluation of invariance or bias in rating data is not covered. Rating data arise when a group of individuals (the raters) provides ratings of other individuals (the rates) on multiple attributes. Ratings of this sort are common in psychology. For example, a group of clinicians may rate a set of individuals who are undergoing therapy. Measurement bias in this context is potentially complex, given that it can be examined as a function of the rater groups, the ratee groups, or the interaction between the two. Second, the invariance of psychological measures across time in longitudinal measurement is not covered. To some extent, this topic can be handled using existing invariance methods and does not require special procedures. The literature on this topic is considerably smaller than the literature on the multiple population case, but it remains an important application for invariance methods. Third, the area of person-fit or appropriateness measurement is not addressed in any depth. This topic is related to the approaches presented here, but does not consider explicit groupings of individuals as a function of demographic or other variables. The focus in this book is confined to bias as a function of explicitly defined groupings.

2

Latent Variable Models

An understanding of statistical methods for bias detection in psychological measurement can begin with the types of models that historically have guided thinking about measurement in psychology. These models are broadly characterized as latent variable models. A latent variable model expresses the probabilistic relationship between observed measures (e.g., test scores) and one or more latent variables. Latent variables are unmeasured influences on observed measures as defined within a theory about the phenomena under study. Latent variable models vary widely in form and purpose. When the intent of the latent variable model is to justify the use of the observed variables as measures of the latent variables, the model is described as a *measurement model*. A familiar example of such a model is the common factor model, which has been used in psychological measurement for over 100 years (Spearman, 1904). This chapter focuses on the nature of the measurement models used most often in psychological measurement, with emphasis on fundamental features shared by nearly all of these models.

General Features

To begin the description of the models, we must first suppose that there exists a single population of individuals on whom measurements are to be taken. We denote this population as Π. Measurements are to be taken on samples of examinees from this population. For now, we will not dwell on how this population is defined. This definitional question will have critical importance in Chapter 3 when we consider extensions to multiple populations. Any measurement model is potentially limited in its range of applicability across diverse examinee groups. Within this chapter, we avoid this issue by assuming that there exists some population of examinees for whom a measurement model is appropriate. Samples of examinees will be assumed to be simple random samples from this population.

A key feature of any measurement model is an expression for the conditional probabilities of various outcomes for the observed measures, given the scores on the latent variables. To illustrate, let $\mathbf{X} = (X_1, X_2, ..., X_p)$ be a vector of scores on p observed measures, such as scores on p test items. Let $\mathbf{W} = (W_1, W_2, \ldots, W_r)$ be a vector of scores on r latent variables believed to underlie $\mathbf{X}$. We will regard both $\mathbf{X}$ and $\mathbf{W}$ as random variables, with $\mathbf{X}$ being unknown prior to measurement and $\mathbf{W}$ being generally unknown even after measurement. Some or all of the latent variables correspond to the target latent variables for which the observed variables were designed. If the observed variables $\mathbf{X}$ are items on a test of high school algebra, we expect $\mathbf{W}$ to include the latent variable (or possibly multiple latent variables) "knowledge of high school algebra," for example. The set $\mathbf{W}$ may also include latent variables that are *not* part of the intended purpose of the test. An example of such a nuisance latent variable would be "skill with multiple-choice tests" if the algebra items were multiple-choice items. We return to this important distinction between target and nuisance latent variables below.

Returning to the measurement model, this model will specify

$$P(X_1, X_2, \ldots, X_p | W_1, W_2, \ldots, W_r) = P(\mathbf{X} | \mathbf{W}). \tag{2.1}$$

Here, $P(A|B)$ is understood to be the conditional probability function for A given B. The conditional probability in Equation 2.1 will be denoted the *measurement response function* (MRF) for $\mathbf{X}$ in relation to $\mathbf{W}$. This general label will be used whenever the nature of the measured variable $\mathbf{X}$ is left unspecified. When $\mathbf{X}$ consists of a vector of test item score variables, the function in Equation 2.1 for an individual item will be denoted as an *item response function*, consistent with common usage. In most measurement applications, the elements of $\mathbf{X}$ can be regarded as discrete and bounded. The nature of the scale for $\mathbf{W}$ will vary but it is often regarded as continuous. Scale considerations for $\mathbf{W}$ are discussed below.

Before proceeding further, we must consider the meaning of the probability statement provided by the MRF. When we say that examinees with scores $\mathbf{W}$ on the latent variables have a certain probability of giving a response $\mathbf{X}$, what does this statement mean? Psychometric theory does not provide a definitive answer to this question. Instead, several alternative viewpoints exist, each of which entails some difficulties (Holland, 1990; Lord & Novick, 1968). The "random sampling" viewpoint (Holland) locates the source of the probability in the random sampling of examinees from the population Π or a subpopulation defined on Π. On this view, the MRF refers to the probability of sampling an examinee who provides a specific set of responses on $\mathbf{X}$, given that the examinee belongs to the subpopulation whose latent variable scores are $\mathbf{W}$. Equivalently, we can view the MRF as giving the proportion of that subpopulation who would provide the set of responses $\mathbf{X}$ if measured. No attempt is made here to model an individual examinee's response behavior probabilistically.

Each examinee is regarded as having a fixed score on **X** and **W**, with the MRF giving the probability of sampling examinees with certain score patterns.

A second viewpoint is the "stochastic examinee" perspective, which regards examinee response behavior as inherently uncertain. A common way of motivating this view is to imagine repeating the measurement of **X** on the same examinee many times. Even if we assume that the examinee's score on **W** is fixed throughout this process, it is easy to imagine that the observed scores **X** will vary over occasions. This theoretical account draws upon the analogy of physical measurement in which, for example, a substance is weighed repeatedly on a scale, generating a distribution of weight values centered at the "true" value. The stochastic examinee account thus locates the source of probability in the MRF in the individual examinee. We can view the MRF as a statement about the expected or "long-run" response behavior of an examinee with a particular value on **W**.

Neither of these viewpoints is wholly satisfactory, and it is not clear which view provides the most useful basis for measurement. The random sampling viewpoint seems incomplete in ignoring the plausible uncertainty associated with repeated measurement. On the other hand, repeated measurements of the sort envisioned in the stochastic examinee view are seldom if ever done in practice. As a result, the stochastic examinee view can be criticized as having little factual basis on which to choose a particular form for the MRF. The appropriate view in a given case may also depend upon the nature of the variable being measured. We might expect scores on a motor skill task or scores on a physiological variable to display an inherent variability over repeated occasions for a fixed **W**. This variability is less plausible for a math test, at least insofar as guessing is not a factor in performance. Many of the results in this book can be conceptualized within either view of the MRF. More detailed consideration of the appropriate view will be engaged as the need arises.

In addition to the MRF in Equation 2.1, the measurement model may specify the unconditional or marginal distribution for the latent variable **W**. This distribution is the distribution of **W** in the target population under study. Let $g(\mathbf{W}) = g(W_1, W_2, ..., W_r)$ be this distribution. For $r > 1$, $g(\mathbf{W})$ is a joint distribution. If **W** is continuous, $g(\mathbf{W})$ can be viewed as a joint density function for **W**. Because **W** is not directly measured, assumptions about the form of $g(\mathbf{W})$ are not empirically testable in any direct sense. We return to this problem below.

Combining the form of the marginal distribution for **W** with the MRF in Equation 2.1, an expression for the marginal distribution of **X** when **W** is continuous is

$$P(\mathbf{X}) = \int_{W_1} \int_{W_2} ... \int_{W_r} P(\mathbf{X} \mid \mathbf{W}) g(\mathbf{W}) dW_1 dW_2 ... dW_r, \qquad (2.2)$$

where the limits of integration are defined by the ranges of the elements of **W**. An expression for $P(\mathbf{X})$ in the case of a discrete **W** is easily developed by replacing the integration with summation over the range of **W**. The distribution in Equation 2.2 is the marginal distribution of **X** in the target population. This marginal distribution can be studied empirically, leading to fit evaluation procedures for measurement models that compare model-based values for $P(\mathbf{X})$ against real data.

The latent variables **W** are unobserved, and this fact raises questions about how such variables should be empirically studied and understood. Psychological measurements have historically been based on, or provided justification for, notions of underlying psychological attributes such as general intelligence, multiple aptitudes, personality dimensions, or attitudes. Measurement models provide a convenient formal language for describing relations between these hypothesized attributes and observed measurements. The models also incorporate what is known empirically about the measurements under study. For example, a measurement model may include features that would account for guessing behavior on multiple-choice test items or for the largely positive correlations found among batteries of cognitive tests. Measurement models are neutral, however, with regard to many questions of interest about the latent variables **W**. To what extent is a person's status on **W** potentially alterable through interventions or training? This question is of great interest both scientifically and practically, but different answers to this question do not necessarily lead to different measurement models.

The foregoing description of latent variable models provides a general probabilistic structure, but further restrictions on the model are needed if it is to have any practical or scientific value. The next three sections describe the types of restrictions that have been considered for latent variable models. These restrictions can be grouped under three headings: restrictions on the dimension of **W**, restrictions on the conditional associations among the elements of **X**, and restrictions on the functional form of $P(\mathbf{X}|\mathbf{W})$.

Model Restrictions

The Dimension of W

A measurement model specifies a value for r, the number of latent variables in **W**. In some applications, this value is itself a focus of investigation, as in the use of exploratory factor models. Even in this case, however, the analysis proceeds by fitting a series of factor models, each of which is conditional on a specific value for the number of factors. It is therefore accurate to say that all latent variable models assume that there exists a fixed number of latent variables in **W**.

Most of the measurement models used in practice assume that $r = 1$. This unidimensional case includes most current applications of item response theory (IRT) and the earliest common factor model (Spearman, 1904), which assumed a single common factor along with as many unique factors as measured variables. Unidimensionality is a plausible condition when the measured variables **X** have been designed as measures of an attribute that has been studied empirically and has appeared to be unitary. For example, **X** may represent a vector of test item scores for a set of arithmetic items, all of which are similar in content. The latent variable W is then conceptually identified with the attribute that is thought to determine performance on **X**, such as skill in arithmetic. In this book, we will denote the latent variables that are the intended attributes to be measured by **X** as the *target* latent variables $\mathbf{W}_t$, with dimension r_t. Here $\mathbf{W}_t$ may be vector valued, with $r_t > 1$, although in most applications only a single target latent variable will be considered.

While **X** may have been designed to measure the target latent variable, in practice there may be one or more additional latent variables that influence scores on **X**. These additional latent variables may represent unwanted or unanticipated influences on test performance. For this reason, these additional latent variables are denoted *nuisance* latent variables (Kok, 1988). We will represent the nuisance latent variables as possibly vector-valued variables $\mathbf{W}_n$, with dimension r_n. Considering the target and nuisance latent variables together, the total set of latent variables underlying **X** is thus $\mathbf{W} = (\mathbf{W}_t, \mathbf{W}_n)$, with dimension $r = r_t + r_n$. To illustrate, scores on the arithmetic items may be partly determined by the examinee's reading skill, especially if the items are story problems. Here reading skill influences performance as a nuisance latent variable, assuming that reading skill is not the target latent variable to be measured by the arithmetic test. As a different example, scores on a measure of extroversion may be influenced by social desirability. The individual's tendency to respond in a socially desirable manner becomes a nuisance latent variable.

From the above discussion, it should be clear that the definition of target and nuisance latent variables depends on the intended meaning for the measures **X**. In the arithmetic example, the reading skill latent variable may no longer be viewed as a nuisance variable if the test is intended to measure "arithmetic skill with real-world problems," a target latent variable that is likely to be multidimensional. Here "real-world problems" would include problems that are posed in realistic settings and that may use verbal or written language to convey the nature of the problem. A minimum level of reading skills might be essential in solving such problems, rendering the reading skill latent variable as part of the cluster of target latent variables.

The target/nuisance distinction is central to the question of measurement bias because bias is sometimes explained via a theory about nuisance variables that influence performance in different ways for different groups (Ackerman, 1992; Camilli, 1992; Mellenbergh, 1989; Roussos & Stout, 1996; Shealy & Stout, 1993a). The view here is that if **X** is truly unidimensional, any systematic group differences on **X** should be solely a function of group differences on the target latent variable. If bias in **X** is defined by group differences that remain after controlling for the target latent variable, the presence of bias would seem to imply that one or more nuisance latent variables affect scores on **X**. The role of nuisance latent variables in the definition of measurement bias will be further discussed in Chapter 3. Theories about nuisance variables certainly provide reasonable explanations for measurement bias in many contexts, but such theories may not be the only explanations for measurement bias across all settings. The literature on stereotype threat (Steele & Aronson, 1995; Wicherts, Dolan, & Hessen, 2005) provides an example of a source of potential measurement bias that may not be best conceptualized as due solely to nuisance latent variables.

The wide variety of potential nuisance latent variables in psychological measurement raises the question of whether any set of measured psychological variables **X** can be truly unidimensional. Ultimately, this question is an empirical one, but skepticism on the question is commonplace (Harrison, 1986; Humphreys, 1984; McDonald, 1981; Stout, 1990). Acknowledging the unreality of exact unidimensionality, one may still be convinced that a unidimensional model provides a good working approximation. The goal then becomes one of assessing the adequacy of this approximation, and a large literature exists on this topic (Hattie, 1985; McDonald & Mok, 1995; Nandakumar & Stout, 1993; Stout, 1987).

The assertion that a single latent variable underlies **X** should ideally be tested with only minimal additional assumptions involving the form of the MRF. We know, however, that if we eliminate any assumptions about the form of the MRF, it is always possible to construct a single latent variable for **X** that also implies local independence for the elements of **X**. This construction is always possible as long as **X** assumes a finite number of possible values (Suppes & Zanotti, 1981), a requirement that is true for most psychological test items. The implication of this fact is that unidimensionality can be tested only in conjunction with some restrictions on the form of the MRF, as considered later. For example, if **X** consists of a set of dichotomous test items, the hypothesis that $r = 1$ can be considered in conjunction with the requirements of conditional independence and monotonicity of the MRF (Holland & Rosenbaum, 1986). Taken together, these assumptions place testable restrictions on the data. Further assumptions are typically adopted in practice, such as a specific parametric form for the MRF. As further restrictions are added, however, the tests of fit for the resulting model are no longer simply tests of the unidimensionality assumption, but rather are tests of the entire measurement model.

An important point to realize is that the fit of a unidimensional measurement model for the measured variables **X** does not, by itself, establish that **X** is measuring W_t, the target latent variable. The fit of the model supports the existence of a single latent variable underlying **X**. The interpretation of the latent variable as the target latent variable or as a nuisance variable must rely on additional considerations, such as item content, previous research, or relevant theory. The process of construct validation will accumulate evidence to support the interpretation of the latent variable (Campbell & Fiske, 1959; Messick, 1989).

Conditional Associations

The measured variables in **X** are considered together because we believe that they are jointly related to one or more latent variables. In other words, we believe that the variables in **X** are measuring something in common, although there may be more than one common influence. How do these common influences affect the statistical associations among the measured variables? Measurement models usually restrict these associations. In fact, empirical regularities in these associations motivated some early measurement models such as the common factor model (Spearman, 1904).

Two types of associations among the measured variables can be distinguished: those that are *conditional* given **W** and those that are *unconditional* in relation to **W**. The conditional associations are determined by restrictions on the MRF in Equation 2.1. These restrictions determine how the measured variables are related within examinee groups that are homogeneous on **W**. Traditionally, measurement models have strongly restricted these associations. This severity is due to the notion that the latent variable **W** must "explain" the associations among the measured variables. Within a group of individuals who are homogeneous on **W**, meaningful associations among the measured variables should disappear. The latent variable accounts for all of the statistical relations among the measured variables.

The unconditional associations among the measured variables are determined by $P(\mathbf{X})$ in Equation 2.2. These associations are represented, for example, by the ordinary correlation matrix for the measured variables. These associations are a function of two influences: the conditional associations just described and the associations among the latent variables in $g(\mathbf{W})$. When $r > 1$, the measurement model may restrict the associations among the latent variables or may leave them unrestricted. The most familiar example of this idea arises in the common factor model in which the common factors may be taken as orthogonal (uncorrelated) or oblique (correlated) in exploratory factor analysis. We will focus on the conditional associations among the measured variables in what follows.

Conditional Independence

The simplest restriction for the conditional associations among the measured variables in **X** is to require conditional independence. Under conditional independence (also known as "local independence"), the MRF in Equation 2.1 factors into the product of the separate conditional probabilities as

$$P(\mathbf{X}|\mathbf{W}) = P(X_1, X_2, \ldots, X_p|W_1, W_2, \ldots, W_r) = \prod_{j=1}^{p} P(X_j|W_1, W_2, \ldots, W_r) \quad (2.3)$$

for all $W_1, W_2, \ldots, W_r$. We can understand conditional independence as follows. Suppose we identify a group of people who are identical on their scores on **W**. Within this group, scores on the measured variables **X** may vary across individuals. But under conditional independence, the p measured variables are mutually independent within the group: knowledge of scores on X_j carries no statistical information about scores on X_k for $j \neq k$. In this sense, the latent variables **W** "account for" all of the associations among the observed measures. If we consider the general population in which individuals differ on the latent variables **W**, we can find nonzero associations among the measured variables **X**. Under conditional independence in Equation 2.3, these associations only exist when scores on the latent variables **W** are varying across individuals.

Conditional independence rules out forms of item relationships that are sometimes encountered in testing, unless additional latent variables are admitted to account for such dependencies. For example, item correlations due to similarity in wording between items (apart from similarity in meaning) are prohibited. Item correlations that are attributable to a shared stem or stimulus are also prohibited. An example of a shared stimulus is the typical reading comprehension item set, in which a group of items refer to the same reading passage. Unique features of the passage may induce associations among the items that are irrelevant to the hypothesized latent variable. For examples, see Wainer and Thissen (1996).

In some cases, it will be possible to achieve conditional independence by redefining the measured variable. Instead of modeling individual test items, for example, one may use "testlets" defined by aggregates of individual items. A testlet is a block of test items that are structurally related, as in the reading comprehension example (Douglas, Kim, & Stout, 1996; Wainer, Bradlow, & Wang, 2007; Wainer & Kiely, 1987; Wainer, Sireci, & Thissen, 1991). We can define the testlet score as some function of the item scores for items belonging to the testlet, such as the unweighted sum. The testlet now becomes the measured variable of interest. Conditional independence may be more plausible at the testlet level than at the individual item level (Rosenbaum, 1988).

Linear Independence

Conditional independence is a strong condition, and we can formulate weaker conditions that are analogous but permit varying degrees of dependence. For example, we can stipulate *conditional linear independence* among the measured variables, given the latent variables (McDonald, 1981). To illustrate, let $\Sigma_{(X|W)}$ be the conditional covariance matrix for X given W. Conditional linear independence stipulates that $\Sigma_{(X|W)}$ is a diagonal matrix, with all conditional covariances among the measured variables equal to zero. Conditional linear independence also implies that the conditional correlation matrix

$$R_{(X|W)} = D_{\Sigma_{(X|W)}}^{-1/2} \Sigma_{(X|W)} D_{\Sigma_{(X|W)}}^{-1/2} \tag{2.4}$$

is diagonal: There are no correlations among the measured variables within the homogeneous group of examinees described above. When conditional linear independence is combined with the assumption of conditional multivariate normality for X, the stronger restriction of conditional independence must also hold for X. Normality assumptions of this sort are frequently invoked in multivariate statistical analyses, eliminating the need to distinguish between conditional independence and linear independence. In measurement applications in which the elements of X represent test item scores, normality assumptions for X are unrealistic in most cases. Conditional linear independence does not rule out nonlinear relations among the measured variables and is therefore a weaker condition than conditional independence. Some latent variable models only require this weaker condition, with the linear common factor model being the most familiar example.

Essential Independence

A different approach toward weakening the conditional independence restriction can be developed by viewing the p measured variables in X as a sample from an infinite (or very large) pool of similar variables, all of which are related to the same latent variables W. This "infinite domain" perspective appears in several areas of psychometric theory, such as generalizability theory (Brennan, 2001; Cronbach, Gleser, Nanda, & Rajaratnam, 1972), factor analysis (Guttman & Levy, 1991; Mulaik & McDonald, 1977), and domain-sampling theory (Nunnally, 1978; Tryon, 1957). To illustrate, begin with the typical case in which the elements of X represent test item score variables. In most areas of psychological testing, it is possible to generate alternative sets of items that arguably measure the same attributes. For example, alternative sets of items are routinely generated for large-scale aptitude tests such as the SAT. Under this viewpoint, our interest shifts from the particular set of p items in **X** to the larger domain of possible items and the conditional associations in this domain. This shift has important consequences because the statistical characteristics of the domain as a whole need not strictly apply to samples taken from the domain. The average level of conditional association among items in the entire domain may be low, for example, although a given sample of items may have substantial nonzero conditional associations.

Starting from this infinite domain perspective, Stout (1987, 1990) developed the notion of *essential independence* as a weaker alternative to conditional independence. Under essential independence, nonzero conditional pairwise associations are permitted among the measured variables in the domain and in any finite sample of items from the domain. The average pairwise association must be small in large samples from the domain, however. To be specific, consider the case in which a single latent variable dominates the item domain, in a sense to be defined below. Denote this latent variable as W_1. Essential independence then holds if

$$\frac{\sum_{j=1}^{p}\sum_{i>j}^{p}|\text{Cov}(X_j, X_i\,|\,W_1)|}{\binom{p}{2}} \to 0 \qquad (2.5)$$

as $p \to \infty$, for all values of W_1. Here $\binom{p}{2}$ is the number of unique pairs of variables from among p variables or $p(p-1)/2$. The ratio in Equation 2.5 is the average absolute conditional covariance between pairs of items, given the latent variable. Essential independence holds if on average, this covariance tends to zero as p gets large. The rationale for this condition is that in large item samples, the average inter-item association should be "small" once we condition on the latent variable. This latent variable is dominant in this sense, but we do not rule out the possibility of additional minor latent variables that account for the associations that remain.

Conditional Dependence

Conditional independence is not a required condition for specification of a measurement model. It is possible to formulate measurement models that imply certain forms of conditional dependence among the elements of **X** (Andrich, 1985; Jannerone, 1986, 1997). These models are useful when such dependencies are expected, either due to the nature of the variables in **X** or to the method of measurement. The most common applications are for cases in which the elements of **X** are test item score variables. These items may have content that exhibits a testlet structure, as discussed earlier. Alternatively, response dependencies may arise through learning during real-time sequential administration of the test items via computer. In this case, the purpose of measurement may be to study individual differences in learning behavior. In any of these cases, the latent variable model will assume a parametric form for the MRF that implies conditional dependence among the item responses. Conditional independence is supplanted by other stringent assumptions about the form of the MRF.

Testing Conditional Independence

Given a latent variable model, is conditional independence testable empirically? If conditional independence is to be tested in isolation, apart from any other assumptions, the answer to this question is "no." Given that **X** assumes a finite number of possible values, we can always define a single latent variable W in relation to **X** so that the elements of **X** satisfy conditional independence (Holland & Rosenbaum, 1986; Suppes & Zanotti, 1981). Here the limitation to finite values for **X** is trivial in practice, given that psychological measurements are typically based on items, rating scales, or subtests whose scoring is effectively discrete and bounded. Hence, conditional independence by itself places no testable restrictions on **X**. For a given **X**, however, the latent variable W that satisfies conditional independence may violate other assumptions that we wish to make about the relationship between W and **X**. These other assumptions concern the form of the relationship between **X** and **W**.

Functional Form

The third set of restrictions that are commonly adopted in latent variable models concerns the mathematical form of the MRF in Equation 2.1. The form to be adopted will depend partly on the measurement scales of **X** and **W**. The values for the measured variables **X** are typically discrete and ordered. If the possible number of values for **X** is sufficiently large, **X** is usually regarded as continuous. Continuity here is adopted as an approximation. When the variables in **X** may assume only a few distinct ordered values, the measured variables are regarded as ordered categorical. The scales for the latent variables **W** are less clearly defined. Most latent variable models regard **W** as either continuous or purely categorical with no ordinality (e.g., latent class models). Intermediate cases in which **W** is discrete and ordered are less often used, although models for this situation are available (e.g., Croon, 1990). When both **X** and **W** are purely categorical with no order, issues of form for the MRF are irrelevant.

When both **X** and **W** are taken to be ordered, a natural restriction to be considered for the MRF is monotonicity. This restriction is most simply illustrated for a single measured variable X and a unidimensional latent variable W ($r = 1$). Intuitively, a monotonically increasing MRF means that examinees with higher latent variable scores tend to have higher scores on the measured variable X. This requirement is reasonable for cognitive tests, for example, where the latent variable is understood to represent an ability or level of knowledge relevant to performance on X. We can formally express monotonicity as follows. Let w_1 and w_2 be two distinct values of W with $w_1 < w_2$, and let x be a particular value of X. Then, we will say that the MRF $P(X = x|W)$ is *monotonically increasing* if

$$P(X \geq x|W = w_1) \leq P(X \geq x|W = w_2) \tag{2.6}$$

for all x, w_1, and w_2. Strict monotonicity implies strict inequality in the above. A monotonically increasing MRF means that the probability that an examinee's score on X exceeds any given value will never decrease as we move higher on the latent variable scale. The definition in Equation 2.6 is easily extended to a multivariate latent **W** by requiring that the definition hold for every element of **W**. In attitude or personality testing, items may be scored so that higher measured scores tend to correspond to lower values on the hypothesized latent variable. We can either reverse the scale of the items in such cases to conform to the monotonicity condition in Equation 2.6, or consider MRFs that represent monotonically decreasing functions.

The monotonicity property in Equation 2.6 can be extended to an entire set of measured variables **X** by requiring that the property hold separately for each element of **X**. Weaker extensions are possible however. For the case in which **X** consists of dichotomous item scores, Stout (1987) considered *weak monotonicity* in which the average of the item response functions over the p items meets the monotonicity requirement in Equation 2.6. Under weak monotonicity, individual items may have response functions that violate Equation 2.6 as long as monotonicity holds on average across items.

Some measurement models do not require a monotonic MRF. These models are most often applied to the measurement of attitudes or in personality measurement (Andrich & Luo, 1993; Hoijtink, 1991a, 1991b; Post, 1992; Roberts & Laughlin, 1996). Many of these models are probabilistic extensions of Coomb's unfolding theory (Coombs, 1964), which attempts to scale persons and items on a common scale. A typical item response function for a dichotomous item under one of these models will be a single-peaked function, with the peak corresponding to the item's location on the latent variable scale. Examinees that are too far above or below the item's location will have low probabilities of endorsing the item.

In attitude measurement for example, an attitude item that represents a moderate opinion may be unacceptable to individuals at either end of the attitude continuum.

Monotonicity conditions on the MRF may lead to useful measurement models when combined with assumptions of conditional independence and unidimensionality. No further assumptions about the MRF are needed. To illustrate, suppose that **X** consists of a set of p dichotomous item score variables. If, for this set of items, we have (a) conditional independence for the item response functions, (b) unidimensionality ($r = 1$), and (c) monotonicity in Equation 2.6, the resulting model is known as a *monotone homogeneity model* (MHM) (Mokken, 1971). Some important properties hold for any MHM regardless of the parametric form of the item response functions (Lord & Novick, 1968; Mokken). First, the unweighted sum of the measured variables $T = \Sigma_{j=1}^{p} X_j$ provides a rank ordering of the examinees with respect to the conditional expected value of W, the latent variable. In other words, $E(W|T)$, which is the conditional expectation of W given T, is an increasing function of T. This property provides a rationale for rank-ordering persons by their total scores across a set of test items that fit an MHM. Second, all item pairs (X_i, X_j) must have nonnegative correlations in the population Π. This property of nonnegative association can be extended in various ways, leading to some nonparametric methods for evaluating whether *any* MHM can fit the measured variables **X** (Holland & Rosenbaum, 1986; Junker, 1993; Mokken, 1997; Rosenbaum, 1984). To a great extent, the above consequences also hold for measured variables that are ordered polytomous, although further restrictions are needed in some cases (Hemker, Sijtsma, Molenaar, & Junker, 1997; Molenaar, 1997).

In addition to the monotonicity of the MRF with respect to W, a second form of monotonicity may hold for a pair of dichotomous measured variables (X_i, X_j). Suppose that these variables are scored (0, 1) and that the MRFs for these variables are monotonic as in Equation 2.6, with $r = 1$ (e.g., W is a scalar). If it is also true that

$$P(X_j = 1|W) \le P(X_i = 1|W) \qquad (2.7)$$

for all W, we say that the MRFs for (X_i, X_j) are *doubly monotonic* (Mokken, 1971). If the two measured variables represent dichotomous cognitive test items, for example, double monotonicity implies that X_j is uniformly more difficult than X_i (Rosenbaum, 1984). Double monotonicity can be extended from a pair of measured variables to a larger set, with each pair of MRFs in the set being ordered as in Equation 2.7.

If the property of double monotonicity is combined with the three properties of an MHM, the resulting model is known as a *double monotonicity model*

(DMM) (Mokken, 1971). A set of items **X** that can be ordered by the pairwise relations in Equation 2.7 so that

$$P(X_1 = 1|W) \leq P(X_2 = 1|W) \leq \cdots \leq P(X_p = 1|W) \qquad (2.8)$$

for all W are said to exhibit an *invariant item ordering* (Sijtsma & Junker, 1996). An MHM in which the items show an invariant item ordering is a DMM. Within a DMM, the ordering of the item response functions will match the ordering of the proportions of the population for which $X_j = 1$, $j = 1, \ldots, p$. In cognitive test items, these proportions are known as the "item difficulties." The Rasch model for dichotomous items is an example of a DMM. Models in which items may vary in their discrimination parameters, such as the two-parameter logistic (2PL), need not adhere to a DMM.

The MHM and DMM are examples of a growing trend in latent variable modeling toward "nonparametric" models (Molenaar, 1997; Sijtsma, 1998; Sijtsma & Molenaar, 2002). These models are nonparametric in placing only weak restrictions on the form of the MRF. As in the case of the MHM and DMM, the models may still lead to testable restrictions on the measured variables **X** (Holland, 1981; Holland & Rosenbaum, 1986; Junker, 1993; Mokken, 1971; Rosenbaum, 1984). Given that well-known parametric models for the MRF are special cases of the nonparametric models, tests of the latter have implications for the former. Procedures for nonparametric estimation of the MRF are also now available (Ramsey, 1991, 1997; Ramsey & Silverman, 1997; Ramsey & Winsberg, 1991). Clearly, adoption of an explicit parametric form for the MRF is not a prerequisite for latent variable modeling.

In spite of the above trends, most applications of latent variable models use explicit parametric forms for the MRF. Given that bias investigations based on latent variable models will generally adopt such forms, it is useful to briefly review the more common forms here. Most of these models will be considered in more detail in later chapters.

Classical Test Theory

Classical test theory (Gulliksen, 1950; Lord & Novick, 1968; Spearman, 1904, 1907, 1913) represents the traditional, and most broadly applied, formal theory of measurement in psychology. In its essential form, the theory cannot truly be considered a latent variable theory because the definition of the true score, the central entity in the classical theory, leaves many issues unresolved. It is unclear how true scores should be related across different observed measures that purport to measure the same thing, for example. The definition of the true score makes the score dependent on the scale of the observed measure, and so observed measures on different scales pose a potential problem. The dimensionality of the true score is also left unresolved in the classical theory. These issues can be resolved in various ways within the classical theory but only by adding new assumptions. With additional assumptions, the classical true score can be viewed as a latent variable, and the classical theory can be viewed as a type of latent variable theory (Mellenbergh, 1994). In this section, we will use a separate notation for the true score to emphasize the fact that this score is not necessarily a latent variable as originally conceived.

At the center of classical test theory is the notion of a hypothetical series of independent repeated measurements using the same measure on a single individual, generating a distribution of measurements for that individual. The measurements are "hypothetical" and "independent" in the sense that any actual series of such measurements would be influenced by memory, fatigue, or other cumulative influences that would alter the properties of the measurements across time. These effects are ruled out in the classical thought experiment that leads to the definition of the true score. Let X_{ijl} be the score for the ith individual on the jth measured variable in the lth repeated measurement occasion. Although we are focusing on a single measured variable here, we include the j subscript to permit later generalization to multiple measured variables. Repeated measurement on the jth variable for the ith individual will generate a distribution of values for X_{ijl}. The distribution of values for X_{ijl} that is generated in this series is the "propensity distribution" for the ith individual on the jth variable (Lord & Novick, 1968). This propensity distribution is a good example of the stochastic examinee viewpoint mentioned earlier. The true score for the ith individual on the jth variable is then defined as the expected value

$$E_{ij}(X_{ijl}) = T_{ij}, \tag{2.9}$$

where the expectation is taken with respect to the propensity distribution. The observed scores X_{ijl} vary randomly over repeated measurements, with the true score being fixed for a given person and variable.

Having defined the true score, an "error of measurement" is defined by the deviation between the observed score X_{ijl} and the true score T_{ij}

$$E_{ijl} = X_{ijl} - T_{ij}. \tag{2.10}$$

As a consequence, we must have the expected value $E_{ij}(E_{ijl}) = 0$ with respect to the propensity distribution. The variance of the error scores becomes the variance of the propensity distribution itself

$$\text{Var}(E_{ijl}) = \text{Var}(X_{ijl}) = \sigma_{E_{ij}}^2. \tag{2.11}$$

As a simplifying assumption, this error variance is often taken to be independent of the individual, so that $\sigma_{E_{ij}}^2 = \sigma_{E_j}^2$. The square root of this error variance is the "standard error of measurement."

We can extend the above developments to a population Π of individuals. The true score T_{ij} is regarded as a random variable with respect to selection from this population. Let the variance of T_{ij} in this population be $\sigma_{T_j}^2$. We assume independence between individuals in the population on T_{ij}, X_{ijl}, and E_{ijl}. For any given occasion, we can partition the variance in the observed scores X_{ijl} as

$$\sigma_{X_j}^2 = \sigma_{T_j}^2 + \sigma_{E_j}^2. \tag{2.12}$$

No subscript for "occasion" is needed, as the foregoing assumptions lead to the same partitioning at every occasion. The *reliability* of the jth measured variable is then defined as the ratio of the true score variance $\sigma_{T_j}^2$ to the observed variance $\sigma_{X_j}^2$ in Equation 2.12. As defined, the reliability is a property not simply of the jth variable, but rather of the jth variable in combination with the population Π. For example, if a population shows little variation in true scores T_{ij}, the reliability may be small in comparison to that found in another population with greater true score variation.

In latent variable theory, the MRF gives the conditional probability distribution for the observed scores given the latent variable. In classical test theory, the MRF can be defined by substituting the true score T_{ij} for the latent variable, but this MRF is only weakly defined because the classical theory only specifies the conditional mean and variance of the probability distribution. Strong true score theories do exist that stipulate probability distributions for the MRF (Lord & Novick, 1968).

The definition of the true score in Equation 2.9 implies that the true score depends both on the individual and on the nature of the measured variable. As noted above, the dependence on the nature of the measured variable creates some difficulty because it is unclear how one should relate true scores on X_{i1} to true scores on a second observed variable X_{i2} that is designed to measure the "same thing." For example, if X_{i1} and X_{i2} are two tests of trait anxiety that employ different item sets and response scales, the true scores for the ith individual on the two tests will likely differ. The difference exists because of the different choices for the response scales and item content for the two tests, rather than because of any fundamental difference in what the tests are measuring. This situation is unwieldy if one believes that it is possible to model both tests as measures of a common latent variable that represents trait anxiety.

To resolve this problem, classical test theory introduces the idea of "parallel" measures, along with some generalizations of parallelism. Two measures X_{i1} and X_{i2} are parallel if the true scores on the two measures are identical for any individual, and the standard error of measurement is the same for the two measures. Strictly parallel measures are often difficult to construct in practice. Generalizations of the conditions for parallelism could apply more broadly. For example, within a set of p observed measures X that purport to measure the same attribute, suppose that the true scores for any individual on these measures are linearly related: For any pair of measures, the true scores on one measure are a linear function of the true scores on the other measure. Note that here the true scores are functionally related, rather than simply being associated statistically. Furthermore, suppose that these linear functions are identical across individuals in a given population. No assumptions are made about the standard error of measurements for the p measures. These linearity assumptions form the basis for the "congeneric" model (Jöreskog, 1971a; Meredith, 1965) in classical test theory. Instead of considering a set of pairwise linear relations among the true scores, the model can be reformulated to express the p true scores as linear functions of a common unidimensional latent variable W. Specifically, we assume that

$$E(X|W) = \mu_{(X|W)} = T = \alpha + \Gamma W \qquad \mathrm{Cov}(X|W) = \Sigma_{(X|W)} = \Psi, \qquad (2.13)$$

where

α is a $p \times 1$ vector of additive constants
T is a $p \times 1$ vector of true score random variables
Γ is a $p \times 1$ vector of scaling weights
Ψ is a $p \times p$ diagonal matrix whose diagonal elements are the measurement error variances corresponding to the p measures in X

Note that the model incorporates conditional linear independence for the elements of X. Special cases of the model can be defined from the matrix formulation in Equation 2.13. The model for "essential tau-equivalence" adds the further restriction $\Gamma = 1$, where 1 is a $p \times 1$ unit vector. In this model, the true scores differ only by additive constants. The model for "strictly parallel" measures adds the further requirements $\alpha = 0$ and $\Psi = \sigma_E^2 I$, where I is a $p \times p$ identity matrix and σ_E^2 is a scalar that is the common value of the measurement error variance across the p measures. These special cases lead to several useful methods of reliability estimation (Lord & Novick, 1968).

One failing of classical test theory is that it makes no attempt to model different sources of variation in observed scores apart from variation in true scores and generic error variance. In many practical applications, however, recognizable sources of "error" variance can be distinguished. For example, if the scores on X are provided by a set of raters, we may wish to model variation among raters along with other sources of variance. Generalizability theory (Brennan, 2001; Cronbach et al., 1972) extends classical test theory by providing additive linear models for multiple sources of error in measurements.

For comprehensive treatments of classical test theory, see Lord and Novick (1968), Gulliksen (1950), Allen and Yen (1979), Algina and Penfield (2009), or Novick (1966). A useful discussion of the differences and similarities between classical test theory and general latent variable theory can be found in Borsboom (2005).

The Linear Common Factor Model

The linear common factor model is closely related to the multivariate models generated by classical test theory but is based on a somewhat different conception of the latent variable W. Rather than being defined as simply a linear transformation of the expected value of X_{ijl} as implied by Equation 2.13, the *common factor* W is defined as a common dimension among the measured variables that accounts for their covariances without necessarily accounting for all of the reliable variance in each measured variable. Once the common factor is removed from the measured variables, the variables are mutually uncorrelated but may retain some reliable variance that is unique to each measured variable. The common factor model is indistinguishable from the congeneric true-score model in classical test theory under the assumption that the common factor subsumes all reliable variance in the measured variables. In this special case, the unique factor variance is simply the measurement error variance from classical test theory. Beyond this special case, the common factor W differs from the classical true score and need not even be a linear function of that true score. Furthermore, the common factor model permits multiple common factors to underlie the measured variables **X**.

To make these ideas concrete, consider a set of r common factor variables $(W_1, W_2, \ldots, W_r)$ that assume values for each member of a population Π. For convenience, we will omit the person and occasion subscripts in the following developments. The MRF gives the conditional probability density function for scores on the measured variables **X**, given a value for **W**, the $r \times 1$ vector of common factor scores. The key assumptions of the common factor model concern the structure for the first and second moments of this MRF

$$E(\mathbf{X}|\mathbf{W}) = \mu_{(X|W)} = \tau + \Lambda\mathbf{W} \qquad \text{Cov}(\mathbf{X}|\mathbf{W}) = \Sigma_{(X|W)} = \Theta, \qquad (2.14)$$

Here
  τ is a $p \times 1$ vector of latent factor intercepts
  Λ is a $p \times r$ matrix of factor "loadings"
  Θ is a $p \times p$ diagonal matrix with nonnegative diagonal elements denoted the "unique factor variances"

These unique factor variances are generated by *p unique factors*, with one factor per measured variable. The covariance matrix Θ is usually taken to be diagonal, but generalizations that permit nonzero covariances among the unique factors are sometimes adopted. Apart from these cases, the common factors account for the covariances among the measured variables, and the unique factors account for variation in the measured variables that is unrelated to the common factors **W**. The unique factors are not identical to the measurement errors of classical test theory, although they have some of the same formal properties. The relationship between these two models is explored further in Chapter 4.

Factor analysis begins with a preliminary value for *r*, the number of common factors. The analysis can proceed in various ways depending on the state of knowledge about the factor structure for **X**. Restrictions on this structure can be incorporated into the analysis (e.g., specified values for factor loadings in Λ), leading to a restricted or confirmatory factor analysis. Alternatively, the parameters (Λ, Θ) may be estimated under minimal restrictions in an exploratory factor analysis. Further assumptions about the MRF are often adopted in either type of analysis, such as conditional multivariate normality

$$P(\mathbf{X}|\mathbf{W}) = MVN(\mu_{(\mathbf{X}|\mathbf{W})}, \Sigma_{(\mathbf{X}|\mathbf{W})}). \qquad (2.15)$$

The common factors **W** may also be assumed to have a distribution $g(\mathbf{W}) = MVN(\kappa, \Phi)$, where κ is an $r \times 1$ common factor mean vector and Φ is an $r \times r$ common factor covariance matrix. This choice leads to $P(\mathbf{X}) = MVN(\mu_{\mathbf{X}}, \Sigma_{\mathbf{X}})$, where

$$\mu_{\mathbf{X}} = \tau + \Lambda\kappa \qquad \Sigma_{\mathbf{X}} = \Lambda\Phi\Lambda' + \Theta. \qquad (2.16)$$

Many applications of factor analysis ignore the mean structure, taking both τ and κ to be null vectors. The factor covariance matrix Φ may also be restricted to an identity matrix (i.e., orthogonal factors), especially in exploratory factor analysis. The multiple-group applications to be considered later must include the mean structures and will ordinarily permit the common factors to correlate.

The results of the factor analysis will include estimates of the parameters (Λ, Φ, Θ), possibly including standard errors, and information about the fit of the model under the chosen value for *r* and any parameter restrictions. An estimate of the *communality* for each measured variable is also available, defined as the proportion of variance in the measured variable that is attributable to the common factors. The communality can also be defined as the squared multiple correlation in the linear regression of the measured variable on the common factors.

It is related to the reliability in classical test theory, but the two are not identical in general (Lord & Novick, 1968).

From Equation 2.14, the common factor model incorporates linear conditional independence for $\mathbf{X}$. If additional assumptions of multivariate normality in Equation 2.15 are adopted, the measured variables $\mathbf{X}$ are conditionally independent under the model. The monotonicity of the MRF for the linear factor model depends on the distributional assumptions and on the signs of the factor loadings in $\mathbf{\Lambda}$. In the MVN case of Equation 2.15 with nonnegative elements in $\mathbf{\Lambda}$, the MRF is monotonically increasing in $\mathbf{W}$.

General treatments of the linear common factor model can be found in Gorsuch (1983), MacCallum (2009), Mulaik (2009), McDonald (1985), Basilevsky (1994), and Bartholomew (1987). Extensions of the linear factor model for dichotomous or ordered-categorical measured variables $\mathbf{X}$ are now available (Bartholomew, 1980; Bock & Aitkin, 1981; Bock, Gibbons, & Muraki, 1988; Browne & Arminger, 1995; Christoffersson, 1975; Jöreskog, 1990, 1993; Jöreskog & Moustaki, 2001; Mislevy, 1986; Muthén, 1978, 1984). These extensions permit the use of the linear factor model in the analysis of test item data, which are usually discrete. Factor models for ordered-categorical variables will be described in Chapter 5. The use of the linear factor model in evaluating measurement invariance in continuous measures is covered in Chapter 4.

Latent Class Models

Latent class models differ from classical test theory and linear factor models in that the latent variable W is regarded as a scalar that is discrete and categorical (Lazersfeld, 1950a, 1950b; Lazersfeld & Henry, 1968). Suppose that W can assume R different values, and that these values partition the population $\mathbf{\Pi}$ into R subpopulations. Each of these subpopulations is denoted as a *latent class*. In educational achievement applications, for example, the classes may represent distinct levels of mastery of a content domain. In the simplest case, we might have $R = 2$ classes consisting of "masters" and "non-masters." In clinical psychology, the latent classes could correspond to clinical diagnostic categories. In all cases, the classes are viewed as mutually exclusive and exhaustive subpopulations within the parent population $\mathbf{\Pi}$. In latent class analysis, $g(W)$ represents the prior probability that a randomly selected individual is a member of a given latent class. The actual class membership for any given individual, along with the number R of latent classes, will be unknown in actual practice.

The form of $P(\mathbf{X}|W)$ depends on the scaling of the measured variables in $\mathbf{X}$. Many applications consider discrete measures $\mathbf{X}$ whose values may be purely categorical, as in a set of binary questionnaire items. In these cases, no particular functional form is needed for the MRF, as the MRF simply consists of a set of conditional probabilities. To formally represent this idea, suppose that X_j can assume Q_j distinct values x_{jq}, $q = 1, \ldots, Q_j$. We define the indicator function $I_{jq}(X_j) = 1$ if $X_j = x_{jq}$, and $I_{jq}(X_j) = 0$ otherwise. Then, we can write an expression for the MRF of X_j as

$$P(X_j|W) = \prod_{q=1}^{Q_j} P(X_j = x_{jq}|W)^{I_{jq}(X_j)}. \tag{2.17}$$

Traditional latent class models adopt the restriction of conditional independence, leading to an expression for the MRF of the entire vector **X** as

$$P(\mathbf{X}|W) = \prod_{j=1}^{p} P(X_j|W). \tag{2.18}$$

Combining this expression with the prior probabilities $g(W)$, an expression for the unconditional probabilities $P(\mathbf{X})$ is

$$P(\mathbf{X}) = \sum_{r=1}^{R} g(W = w_r) \prod_{j=1}^{p} P(X_j|W = w_r). \tag{2.19}$$

Expressions for the posterior probability that an individual is a member of a specific latent class, given scores on the measured variables **X**, are derived using Bayes' theorem from the above expressions (Lazersfeld & Henry, 1968).

An important question in any latent class application is the value of R, the number of latent classes. The problem of determining the number of latent classes is analogous to the issue of dimensionality in latent variable models with continuous latent variables, such as the linear factor model. Equation 2.19 leads to an expression for the likelihood in a sample of size N, conditional on a particular choice for R. Maximizing this likelihood results in estimates for the prior probabilities and the MRF, as well as large-sample tests of fit. Typically, different solutions will be evaluated at different values of R, with the final solution being one that fits well for a plausible value of R. Fit evaluation becomes difficult, however, for moderate to large p and/or Q_j. In such cases, the number of possible response patterns on **X** becomes very large (the number is $\prod_{j=1}^{p} Q_j$), and the multiway contingency table formed by the factorial combination of the p measured variables is sparse in all but the largest samples.

The above description of the latent class model is very general, and special cases of this general model will be of interest in particular applications. For example, if the latent classes and the measured variables have ordinal properties, these can be built into the above structure by the use of inequality restrictions on the MRF (Croon, 1990). When the latent classes are discrete and possibly ordered, but the measured variables are continuous in scale, the resulting model is sometimes denoted the latent profile model (Lazersfeld & Henry, 1968). This model resembles the linear factor model in its implications for the moment structure for X and may be difficult to distinguish from the factor model empirically (Bartholomew, 1987; Gibson, 1959; Molenaar & Von Eye, 1994; Waller & Meehl, 1998). Latent mixture modeling, which combines the latent class model with various parametric (often latent variable) models for continuous measured variables, is an active area of research (see Dolan, 2009 or Hancock & Samuelsen, 2008, for recent reviews), General treatments of latent class models can be found in Collins and Lanza (2009), Everitt (1984), Heinen (1996), Langeheine and Rost (1988), and Rindskopf (2009).

Item Response Theory

IRT represents a collection of measurement models for performance on test items. Scores on test items are typically either dichotomous or ordered categorical, and so IRT models are largely designed for discretely measured variables, unlike the linear common factor model. IRT models impose stronger assumptions on the MRF than do models formulated within classical test theory. As a result, IRT models have some practical advantages in comparison to classical test theory, provided that the data meet the stronger assumptions.

IRT models vary in form, but there are some common themes in their design. First, the item response function (or MRF for a set of test items) usually stipulates that the item scores are conditionally independent. Exceptions to this rule have been noted earlier. Second, most current applications of IRT use models in which the latent variable is unidimensional. Multidimensional models are available (Reckase, 1997, 2009; Samejima, 1974; Sympson, 1978), but these models are only just beginning to have a major role in real testing applications. Third, the item response functions in IRT are typically monotonic for dichotomous test items, with conditional expectations that are nonlinear in the latent variable W. Finally, the parameters of the item response function in IRT are separated in two categories: parameters that depend on the item and are invariant over examinees and parameters that are unique to the examinee but are invariant over items. This parameter separation confers some important advantages to IRT models in comparison to classical test theory.

To illustrate these features, we first consider some IRT models for dichotomously scored items. Although item response functions using a normal ogive are available, logistic functions are simpler mathematically and can be scaled to resemble the ogive if desired. The simplest logistic function of interest is that of the Rasch or one-parameter logistic model

(Rasch, 1960). For the score of the ith individual on the jth test item X_{ij}, the Rasch item response function is

$$P(X_{ij} = 1|W) = \frac{1}{1 + \exp[-(W_i - b_j)]}.$$ (2.20)

Here

b_j is the item location or difficulty parameter for the jth item

X_{ij} can assume values of 0 or 1

Conceptually, this location parameter corresponds to the value of W_i that yields a probability of .5 for passing the item (i.e., achieving a score of "1" on the item). For a cognitive test item, high values of the location parameter indicate a difficult item. The Rasch model stipulates that the test items differ only in location, with graphs of the item response functions all having the same shape. For this reason, the item response functions under the Rasch model exhibit double monotonicity, as defined earlier. Another useful property of the model is that the sum of the item scores across items that fit the Rasch model provides a sufficient statistic for W. All of the information about W that is provided by the item responses is contained in this sum. This statistical feature simplifies estimation and fit evaluation in the Rasch model. A large literature exists on the Rasch model and its theoretical advantages (see Fischer & Molenaar, 1995, for a comprehensive treatment).

A more general logistic model is the 2PL, whose item response function is

$$P(X_{ij} = 1|W_i) = \frac{1}{1 + \exp[-a_j(W_i - b_j)]}.$$ (2.21)

Here a_j is the item discrimination parameter. This parameter influences the shape of the item response function. It is proportional to the slope of the tangent line to the item response function, evaluated at $W_i = b_j$. In practice, high values of a_j correspond to items that discriminate well among examinees whose W values are near b_j. A set of test items that fit the 2PL model may have item response functions that have different shapes or that intersect, violating the double monotonicity property found in the Rasch model. As a result, the sum of the item scores across p items is not a sufficient statistic for W: A simple count of the number of items passed does not carry all of the relevant information about W that can be gleaned from the response sequence. The 2PL model is similar in form to the normal ogive model, an older two-parameter model that uses the normal ogive function as the item response function. The two models can be rendered nearly identical in shape by applying a scaling constant in the 2PL item response function

$$P(X_{ij} = 1|W_i) = \frac{1}{1+\exp[-Da_j(W_i - b_j)]},$$ (2.22)

where $D = 1.7$. Most applications of the 2PL model use the item response function as scaled in this "normal" form.

Lord and Novick (1968) provide a theorem that gives sufficient conditions for a normal ogive item response function to hold for a set of p dichotomous items. By implication, this theorem also justifies the use of the 2PL model as scaled in Equation 2.22. The theorem is based on the assumption of an underlying single-factor model for p continuous latent response variates, whose values relative to a set of p thresholds determine the probabilities of passing the items. This threshold formulation is a common way of extending the linear common factor model to discrete observed measurement scales (Bartholomew, 1987; Browne & Arminger, 1995). An important feature of the theorem is that unless the factor loadings of the latent response variates in the single-factor model are identical across variables, the resulting item response functions will not correspond to a Rasch model. The theorem thus provides one explanation for why we might expect the 2PL model to be more realistic in practice. We will return to this theorem in Chapter 6.

A further modification of the 2PL model is introduced to account for items in which the correct answer could be selected through guessing, as in multiple-choice items. The resulting three-parameter logistic (3PL) model has the item response function

$$P(X_{ij} = 1|W_i) = c_j + \frac{1-c_j}{1+\exp[-Da_j(W_i - b_j)]}.$$ (2.23)

Here c_j is denoted the pseudo-guessing parameter. This parameter is the probability of passing the item for examinees whose W values are very low. Although the term "guessing" has traditionally been attached to this parameter, there is nothing in the model to ensure that the parameter actually indexes the chances of passing the item via guessing. The addition of this third parameter will often improve the fit of the model to items in which guessing might play a role (e.g., multiple-choice items). On the other hand, the 3PL usually requires larger samples for adequate estimation in comparison to the 2PL model. In addition, larger values for the guessing parameter c_j will lead to a loss of information about persons who are low on the latent variable W_i because the item response function will be essentially flat in that region.

These logistic models account for the majority of the current applications of IRT in dichotomous item data. Models for ordered-polytomous items are more varied in form (see van der Linden & Hambleton, 1997 or Nering & Ostini, 2010, for reviews). Some of these models represent natural generalizations of the Rasch model to the ordered-polytomous case (Andersen, 1977; Andrich, 1978a, 1978b; Masters, 1982; Rasch, 1960, 1961). These models retain many of the useful properties of the dichotomous Rasch model, such as the sufficiency of the total score across items in relation to the latent variable. Other models for ordered-polytomous items are more complex in form but may have greater generality (Bock, 1972; Muraki, 1992; Samejima, 1969, 1972). Models for ordered-polytomous items are especially useful for personality or attitude questionnaire items, whose response formats are often not dichotomous. General treatments of IRT can be found in De Ayala (2009), Embretson and Reise (2000), Hambleton and Swaminathan (1985), Lord (1980), Nering and Ostini, Thissen and Steinberg (2009), van der Linden and Hambleton (1997), and Fischer and Molenaar (1995). A more detailed discussion of IRT models and their use in the investigation of measurement invariance can be found in Chapters 6 and 7.

Problems in Latent Variable Models

The foregoing discussion has provided an overview of the assumptions adopted in commonly used measurement models. At the center of each of these models is the concept of a latent variable. Although latent variables are now widely used as a basis for psychological measurement, the use of these variables raises some difficult questions. One set of questions concern the claim that a measurement scale is established for the latent variable that defines the measurement model. How do we know, for example, that a fixed unit of measurement is established for the latent variable? Is there a true origin for the latent variable? A second set of questions concern the possibility of locating a given individual's score on the latent variable. Given that the latent variable is unobservable by definition, we cannot know a given person's score on the latent variable with certainty. What then is the meaning of a score "estimate"? How should such estimates be calculated? To what extent are such estimates unique?

Both of these sets of questions have relevance for the issue of bias. Scaling questions are relevant because we wish to establish a scale for the latent variable that provides comparable results across populations.

The questions about score estimates are relevant because ambiguities in the meaning of these estimates have led some researchers to reject latent variable models such as factor analysis as useful bases for measurement (Guttman, 1955, 1992; Maraun, 1996; Steiger & Schönemann, 1978). In this section, we briefly examine the issues of scaling and score estimation, and some attempts to resolve these problems.

Measurement Scales and Latent Variables

The measurement models reviewed earlier, such as the common factor model or models from IRT, presume that there exists a continuous latent variable W on which it is possible to order examinees. Given that W is supposed to provide a basis for measuring examinees, we can ask whether any unit of measurement can be established for W, permitting not only statements about the ordering of examinees but also statements about differences between examinees on W. The establishment of a unit in conjunction with ordinal properties renders the latent scale to be an interval scale (Stevens, 1946). Is it possible to establish a unit for our latent variable? This question refers to the *existence* of an interval scale. Assuming that an interval scale exists, how do we define the unit of measurement? This question refers to the *identification* of an interval scale.

The minimal framework provided by the developments leading to Equation 2.2 does not require the existence of a unit for $\mathbf{W}$. In Equation 2.2, we can replace $\mathbf{W}$ with any monotonically increasing transformation $\mathbf{W}^* = \mathbf{H}(\mathbf{W})$ and adjust $P(\mathbf{X}|\mathbf{W})$ and $g(\mathbf{W})$ accordingly, without affecting $P(\mathbf{X})$. Given that this monotonic transformation need not be linear, no unit for $\mathbf{W}$ exists without further assumptions or restrictions. Any "unit" that will be established for $\mathbf{W}$ is wholly dependent on the type of restrictions adopted. The adoption of a particular distributional form for $g(\mathbf{W})$ has implications for the scaling of $\mathbf{W}$, because transformations of the scale of $\mathbf{W}$ will alter the form of $g(\mathbf{W})$. Similarly, the adoption of a fixed form for $P(\mathbf{X}|\mathbf{W})$ also limits the scaling of $\mathbf{W}$. To what extent do the three classes of restrictions described earlier establish an interval scale for $\mathbf{W}$?

With a few notable exceptions, the measurement model literature is silent on the existence question in latent variable theory. Some exceptions concern the theory underlying the Rasch model and related models (Pfanzagl, 1971). Under the restrictions imposed by the Rasch model, it can be shown that the latent variable scale satisfies the requirements for additive conjoint measurement (see Fischer, 1995b). In doing so, the model establishes the existence of a unit of measurement on the latent scale. Rasch (1960) went further in claiming the existence of both a unit and an origin for the latent scale, leading to statements about ratios of scale scores, but this ratio claim does not appear justified (Fischer). The important point is that under the restrictions leading to the Rasch model, empirical evidence for the fit of the model is often taken as evidence also for the existence of an interval scale for the latent variable. This viewpoint is not universally shared however (Kyngdon, 2008).

An alternative resolution of the existence question is to abandon the requirement of an interval scale for **W** and instead define **W** as an ordinally scaled variable (Cliff, 1979, 1989; Guttman, 1950; Schulman & Haden, 1975). Within this type of model, the measured variables **X** only provide a rank ordering for the examinees on **W**. In many domains of psychological measurement, the existence of a rank ordering among examinees on **W** is plausible even when no clear unit of measurement is established. Ordinal models should therefore have potentially wide application, yet these models are not often used in practice.

The scaling properties of the Rasch model do not extend to other widely used measurement models. For example, no unit of measurement is guaranteed for the common factor scale in factor analysis. The factor model assumes a linear relationship between the factors and the measured variables **X**, along with conditional linear independence for **X** and a fixed dimension for **W**. The question of the existence of a unit for the scale of **W** is circumvented by further assuming distributional forms for the MRF and for the prior distribution $g(\mathbf{W})$. None of these assumptions compel us to regard **W** as having an interval scale, however. The common factor model is not unique in this respect. Measurement models that are based on continuous latent variables typically avoid the existence question by invoking distributional assumptions for the MRF and $g(\mathbf{W})$. Given that these distributional assumptions limit the range of permissible transformations of **W**, the distributional assumptions establish a "unit" by fiat.

The implication of the foregoing is that the fit of these measurement models to data cannot be regarded as evidence for the existence of a latent interval scale. This point does not appear to be widely discussed in the measurement model literature (but see Borsboom, 2005; Cliff, 1993; Michell, 1990, 1999). To the extent that lawful relations are found between the latent variables **W** and other variables that are theoretically relevant, it is argued that the scaling assumptions for **W** are vindicated (Lord & Novick, 1968). This type of justification seems implicit in many applications of measurement models and is part of the construct validity argument.

Even if the existence of a unit on the latent scale is established, there remains a need to choose a particular unit in any given application. Units are not unique. The identification of a unit therefore consists in imposing some model constraints that represent a subset of a wider pool of potential alternative constraints. Which subset is chosen may be arbitrary in theory, but the choice may have practical consequences that are difficult to foresee, especially when multiple populations are involved. To illustrate the choice of constraints, we describe models in two model classes: common factor analysis and IRT.

Common Factor Analysis

The common factor model imposes linearity on $E(\mathbf{X}|\mathbf{W})$ for a fixed value of r, with $\Sigma_{(\mathbf{X}|\mathbf{W})} = \Theta$, a diagonal matrix. Any linear transformation of the form

$$\mathbf{W}^* = \mathbf{AW} + \mathbf{f} \qquad (2.24)$$

with $\mathbf{A}$ an $r \times r$ nonsingular matrix and $\mathbf{f}$ an $r \times 1$ vector, will leave the linearity intact. Hence, the usual assumptions do not fully establish a unit for $\mathbf{W}$. Two sets of additional constraints are adopted for this purpose. First, a location for the $\mathbf{W}$ scale is typically fixed by assuming $\kappa = \mathbf{0}$ (or any other fixed constant). This restriction eliminates $\mathbf{f}$ in Equation 2.24. Second, we must impose r^2 constraints on Λ and/or Φ to eliminate $\mathbf{A}$ in Equation 2.24. For $r > 1$, there are a variety of ways of accomplishing this goal (Anderson & Rubin, 1956). The problem of choosing these constraints is known as the rotational uniqueness problem (Bollen & Jöreskog, 1985). In confirmatory factor analysis, one possibility is to fix an $r \times r$ submatrix of Λ to a known nonsingular matrix Λ^*. Given that the loading matrix for $\mathbf{W}^*$ must be $\Lambda \mathbf{A}^{-1}$, the only value for $\mathbf{A}$ that is consistent with these constraints is $\mathbf{A} = \mathbf{I}$. An alternative approach is to set $\mathrm{Diag}(\Phi) = \mathbf{I}$, with r rows of Λ forming an $r \times r$ diagonal matrix. It should be noted that resolution of the scaling problem for $\mathbf{W}$ does not resolve the problem of how an individual examinee's score on $\mathbf{W}$ might be estimated or predicted.

Item Response Theory

The typical case here is one in which a parametric form is adopted for $P(X|W)$ with $r = 1$, and conditional independence is assumed. As an example, consider the Rasch model represented in Equation 2.20. We can replace W with any additive transformation $W^* = W + f$ and redefine $b_j^* = b_j + f$, leaving the $P(X|W)$ unchanged. This scale indeterminacy is usually resolved by fixing the mean of W, or by requiring $\Sigma\, b_j = 0$. The Rasch model itself can be derived from a number of more fundamental assumptions (Fischer, 1995b). The adoption of the Rasch model can be viewed as a particular resolution of the scaling problem.

The 2PL model introduces an additional scaling uncertainty in that we may now replace $W^* = hW + f$, $b^* = hb + f$, and $a^* = ah^{-1}$. We can resolve these uncertainties by requiring $E(W) = 0$ and $\mathrm{Var}(W) = 1$. An additional possibility is $E(W) = 0$ and $a_j = 1$ for a fixed item j. Identical scaling issues arise in the 3PL. Models for polytomous X variables raise some additional scaling problems.

In both the factor analysis and IRT examples, the use of constraints to fix the latent scale is generally trivial as long as only a single population

Π is considered. Once multiple populations are considered however, the use of scaling constraints becomes more complex. If the distributions of the latent variables are believed to vary across populations, scaling constraints that impose invariance on features of the distributions may lead to distortions in the MRFs across populations. Fixing the latent variable variances to unit values in all populations, for example, may distort the MRFs if population differences in the latent variable variances are present. Studies of measurement bias must consider these complexities when the measurement model is developed.

Score Indeterminacy

Given that a scale is established for **W**, it is natural to ask whether values or scores on **W** can be assigned to individuals once **X** is observed. A central feature of all latent variable models is that the measured variables **X** provide incomplete information about the latent variables **W**: There exists uncertainty about an individual's score on **W** even after **X** is measured. In factor analysis, this uncertainty is known as the problem of *factor score indeterminacy*. The problem has a long, rancorous history (Bartholomew, 1981; Guttman, 1955; Maraun, 1996; McDonald, 1974; Mulaik, 2009; Mulaik & McDonald, 1977; Rozeboom, 1996; Schönemann, 1971; Steiger & Schönemann, 1978; Wilson, 1928). In stark contrast, the same indeterminacy problem in IRT has never evoked comparable levels of controversy, although divergent views exist on the source of randomness in latent variable scores in IRT (Holland, 1990). IRT theorists have largely focused on the statistical properties of various score estimation or prediction methods, rather than dwelling on broader implications of indeterminacy.

Within the factor analytic debate, critics of the factor model have correctly noted that the structure of the model permits an infinite number of potential sets of factor scores. Furthermore, two sets of scores can both satisfy the model yet correlate zero, or even negatively, depending on the strength of relation between the common factor and the measured variables (Guttman, 1955). In view of this fact, what scientific meaning should be given to the statement that a set of measured variables "share a common factor"? For critics of the model, indeterminacy implies that a "common factor" has no coherent meaning beyond the model itself (Maraun, 1996). And while one can build a statistical theory of estimation or prediction for factor scores, doing so simply ignores the fundamental incoherency of the common factor.

The responses to these criticisms have proceeded along various lines historically, but two arguments seem to have received the most attention in recent years. First, a number of theorists have argued that while indeterminacy does indeed exist for finite sets of measured variables, one can resolve the problem by considering the measured set as a sample from an infinite domain of variables, with the factor model holding for the domain (Mulaik & McDonald, 1977; Williams, 1978). The idea of an infinite domain of potential measured variables, all with some common properties that define the domain, is an old one in psychological measurement (Guttman, 1953, 1954; Roff, 1936). It is relatively easy to show that within such a domain, any indeterminacy in the factor scores dissolves under weak conditions on the factor model. In a second line of argument, Bartholomew (1996) asserts that concerns about indeterminacy stem from misunderstandings about the nature of random variables and their realizations as represented in probability theory. On this view, once one has adopted the notion of the factor score as a random variable whose distribution is specified either unconditionally or conditionally on the measured variables, "indeterminacy" is simply a reflection of the randomness in the factor scores. Given that this randomness is irreducible, any attempt to quantify the factor scores should be regarded as a problem in statistical prediction. One addresses this problem by adopting any one of several optimality criteria for prediction. This statistical viewpoint on indeterminacy in factor analysis appears to be the dominant viewpoint among IRT theorists in relation to the "indeterminacy" problem in IRT.

No resolution of the various conflicting viewpoints on indeterminacy seems likely in the near future. Arguments about indeterminacy have potentially important consequences for the topic of this book. If the elimination of indeterminacy is required for a coherent formulation of a "common factor," or more generally of a "latent variable," definitions of measurement bias that rely on latent variable formulations lose coherence under indeterminacy as well. As will be discussed in Chapter 3, a fundamental principle in defining measurement bias is that in investigating bias, we should compare scores on measured variables for individuals from different demographic groups only if the individuals are matched on the latent variable of interest. The indeterminacy argument may undercut the rationale for such "matching" because the latent variable itself is viewed as ill defined due to indeterminacy. This potential consequence of the indeterminacy argument seems to have gone unnoticed in literature on indeterminacy. Guttman (1992) argues for the rejection of factor analysis as a basis for studying group differences, but his arguments do not rest on issues of indeterminacy per se. Presumably, researchers who reject latent variable definitions of measurement bias due to concerns about indeterminacy will wish to adopt other approaches to defining bias, such as those that rely on strict observed-score formulations as described in Chapters 3 and 8. As noted in those chapters, these observed-score approaches have their own limitations.

3

Measurement Bias

This chapter defines the concept of measurement bias, and then explores some of the implications of this definition and its variations. Broadly speaking, measurement bias concerns systematic inaccuracy in measurement. It is "systematic" in the sense of being replicable, and not simply attributable to the randomness or uncertainty inherent in any measurement process. Given that the measurement models in Chapter 2 represent the systematic components in measurement, we will define measurement bias within the measurement model itself. Our definition of bias will be model-based but will be general enough to apply to all of the models reviewed in Chapter 2 and others as well.

The measurement bias that will be of interest in this book is bias that is related to the examinee's membership in an examinee population. These populations can be defined in various ways, but in many applications, the populations of interest are demographic. Other ways of defining the populations of interest are discussed below. The key question in defining measurement bias is whether knowledge of the examinee's population membership tells us anything new statistically about the examinee's score on the measured variable, given the examinee's standing on the target latent variable. To the extent that knowledge of population membership *does* add something new apart from the examinee's standing on the latent variable, we will say that the measured variable is biased relative to the populations and target latent variable under study.

Some forms of measurement bias may not be related to the examinee's membership in a known population. For example, a given measurement model may fail to fit some individuals, even if the model provides a good fit for most individuals. The individuals who are not fit well by the model may share few characteristics, and hence are not readily identifiable as a separate "population." Arguably, however, the measure X is biased for these individuals in relation to the target latent variable. Methods for identifying such individuals have been intensively studied as methods for "appropriateness measurement" or for the assessment of "person-fit" (Drasgow, Levine, & Williams, 1985; Meijer & Sijtsma, 2001; Reise & Flannery, 1996; Tatsuoka, 1996). Studies of person-fit do not typically contrast known populations of examinees, although explanations for misfit may be sought by trying to identify common features among individuals who are fit poorly. Person-fit methods are not treated in any detail in this book.

Multiple Populations

In Chapter 2, we assumed that there exists a single population Π of potential individuals for which measures on X are taken. We now extend this idea to K multiple populations $\Pi = (\Pi_1, \Pi_2, \dots, \Pi_K)$ of individuals. We assume that these populations are distinct: any given individual is a member of at most one population. In many cases, we will confine discussion to the case of two populations: a *reference* population and a *focal* population (Holland & Thayer, 1988). The reference population is typically the "majority" group or the population in which measurement bias is of less concern a priori. In an investigation of a measure that is suspected of being biased against females, for example, the reference group would be males. The focal population is typically the "minority" or protected group, as in females in the above example. The choice of reference and focal groups depends on the context and need not correspond to actual numerical majority versus minority populations. In some applications, there may be no firm basis for designating one group as the reference group.

Any statements about measurement bias must be made with respect to a specified set of populations. An observed measure may be free of bias with respect to one set of populations, while biased in relation to a different set of populations. For example, a test may show no bias with respect to gender within an English-speaking population, yet may show bias when comparing native English speakers to persons for whom English is a second language. Global characterizations of tests as "biased" or "unbiased" are rarely meaningful for this reason. We must therefore devote some discussion to how populations are to be defined for purposes of investigation of bias.

We begin by supposing that there is some vector of discrete random variables $V = (V_1, V_2, \dots, V_s)$ that form the basis for the populations of interest. We denote the variables V as *selection variables*, to represent the idea that the populations of interest can be created using these variables. The selection variables typically include demographic variables such as sex, race, ethnicity, or language group. We may wish to also include variables such as age, which are continuous but are often discretized for purposes of bias investigation (e.g., under 40 years of age versus 40 and over). We assume that it is always possible to specify the desired selection variables V and that we can accurately determine values for all examinees on V. These assumptions are not trivial in practice. Examinees may refuse to supply information on V, or it may simply be difficult to determine the examinee's value on V (Allen & Holland, 1993). For example, racial classifications ordinarily rely on the examinee's self-reported race as chosen from a short list of categories. Persons of mixed race may not be adequately classified by this practice. If V is intended to distinguish levels of language proficiency, it may be difficult to determine an individual's level of proficiency without extensive testing. Inaccuracy in the definition of the selection variables **V** jeopardizes any subsequent conclusions about the bias in the measured variables in relation to **V**.

Once the relevant selection variables are identified, the actual groups to be compared can usually be defined in an obvious way by considering all possible combinations of the values of the variables. For example, suppose that V_1 is gender and V_2 is a binary variable designating whether English is one's primary language or not. The factorial combination of these two binary variables yields four distinct groups: male/English, male/not English, female/English, and female/not English. In some applications, a full factorial representation may not be possible. If V_1 is gender and V_2 is ethnicity, it may be the case that only a subset of the larger set of ethnic groups are available. A different application would involve groups that are created via random assignment from a population defined by **V**. For example, in a true experiment, we might create treatment and control groups through random assignment, with **V** either defining the relevant population from which participants are drawn or defining a set of blocking factors for the experiment. The goal here might be to study the effect of a treatment on the measurement properties of a variable **X**. The literature on alpha, beta, and gamma change in organizational research (Golembiewski, Billingsley, & Yeager, 1976; Millsap & Hartog, 1988; Schmitt, 1982) describes one example of this type of application, where the "treatment effect" is actually revealed through a change in the measurement model structure.

One type of selection variable **V** that is explicitly excluded from consideration is one that includes elements of the studied measure **X** itself. Examples of this type of situation arise when interest lies in studying how explicit selection on **X** affects the measurement properties of **X** in the groups thus created. For example, suppose that $p = 2$ and that $\mathbf{X} = (X_1, X_2)$. We might consider letting $V = X_2$, defining one group as those individuals with $X_2 > X^*$, and the other group as those individuals with $X_2 \leq X^*$. We then may ask whether X_2 is invariant in the measurement sense across the two groups just defined. This problem has been addressed in the literature extensively (Yang Hsu, 1995; Lawley, 1943; Meredith, 1964; Muthén, 1989; Muthén & Yang Hsu, 1993). Under fairly broad conditions, invariance does not hold for X_2 across such groups. We will not pursue these types of group definitions here, and instead we will assume that no explicit dependence of **V** on **X** exists. Under this assumption, we would still be able to consider invariance in X_1, given the above V because V was not defined explicitly by X_1.

Another approach to motivating the idea of multiple populations would consider a "parent population," with the multiple populations to be studied being defined as subpopulations within this parent population. Much of the literature on factorial invariance has adopted this approach (Meredith, 1964; Thurstone, 1947). To the extent that the subpopulations to be considered are defined by a set of specific selection variables **V**, the idea of a "parent population" adds little that is new to the developments already considered here. The parent population is then simply the union of the populations Π_k selected using $\mathbf{V}$. More generally, however, one could consider *all possible* subpopulations that could be defined within a given parent population. An equivalent problem would be to consider subpopulations defined by *all possible* selection variables $\mathbf{V}$, applied within a given parent population. As we will see, formulations of this sort lead to stringent conditions for invariance. A practical difficulty with this extension is that in real investigations, some specific set of selection variables $\mathbf{V}$ must be considered, and it will be impossible to investigate all such variables. For this reason, formulations that apply to all possible selection variables are generally of greater theoretical than practical interest.

Measurement Invariance

Measurement invariance is a property whose definition will lead us to the definition of measurement bias, and so we begin with the definition of invariance. Conceptually, measurement invariance expresses the idea that the measurement properties of $\mathbf{X}$ in relation to the target latent trait $\mathbf{W}_t$ are the same across populations. Alternatively, we can say that under measurement invariance, knowledge of an individual's population membership tells us nothing about $\mathbf{X}$ over and above knowledge of $\mathbf{W}_t$. This idea is expressed formally as follows. Suppose that we have K populations $\Pi_k, k=1,2,\ldots,K$ whose members provide measures on $\mathbf{X}$, and further suppose that $\mathbf{W}_t$ represents one or more target latent traits that $\mathbf{X}$ is designed to measure. Let $P_k(\mathbf{X}|\mathbf{W}_t)$ be the measured response function (MRF) for $\mathbf{X}$ in the kth population. Then we will say that measurement invariance holds for $\mathbf{X}$ in relation to $\mathbf{W}_t$ and $\Pi_k, k=1,2,\ldots,K$ if and only if

$$P_k(\mathbf{X} \mid \mathbf{W}_t) = P(\mathbf{X} \mid \mathbf{W}_t) \tag{3.1}$$

for $k = 1,\ldots,K$ and for all $\mathbf{W}_t$. The measurement response functions for $\mathbf{X}$ in relation to $\mathbf{W}_t$ are identical across populations under measurement invariance. To establish measurement invariance, we must first identify the target latent variable $\mathbf{W}_t$, and we must clearly define the populations to be studied. Some issues in the definition of the relevant populations were discussed earlier. The definition of the target latent variable requires further comment.

The distinction between the target latent variable $\mathbf{W}_t$ and any further nuisance latent variables in $\mathbf{W}$ that might influence $\mathbf{X}$ is important for the definition of measurement invariance. Suppose that r_n nuisance latent variables $\mathbf{W}_n$ are relevant to performance on $\mathbf{X}$, in addition to the target latent variables. We can further suppose that $W = (W_t, W_n)$ represents the "complete latent space" in the sense of Lord and Novick (1968): the MRF for X given W is the same in all populations of interest. By definition, X satisfies measurement invariance in Equation 3.1 in relation to W for all populations of interest. Assuming that it is always possible to supplement W_t with additional nuisance latent variables W_n to complete the latent space, we can always claim that X is measurement invariant in relation to *some* definition of $W = (W_t, W_n)$. For this reason, investigations of measurement invariance are meaningful only if we restrict W to include the target latent variable W_t. The target latent variable is the attribute, or set of attributes, that the variable X was designed to measure. We investigate measurement invariance in X because we suspect that X is a function not only of W_t but also of other influences that are related to population membership. As discussed in Chapter 2, one way of conceptualizing these "other influences" is as additional nuisance latent variables (Ackerman, 1992; Camilli, 1992; Mellenbergh, 1989; Shealy & Stout, 1993b). This viewpoint identifies violations of measurement invariance with the operation of nuisance latent variables. While this viewpoint provides a useful framework for studying bias, it is unclear whether *all* violations of measurement invariance are best understood as due to nuisance latent variables. We will return to the relationship between measurement invariance and latent dimensionality below.

The above definition of measurement invariance permits us to define *measurement bias* as a violation of measurement invariance. We will say that X is biased as a measure of W_t in relation to $\Pi_k, k = 1, 2, \ldots, K$ if for some value of k,

$$P_k(X \mid W_t) \neq P(X \mid W_t) \tag{3.2}$$

for at least one value of W_t. Within at least one population Π_k, the measurement response function is different from the function that holds in the remaining $K - 1$ populations. The presence of measurement bias implies that for individuals from this kth population, the conditional distribution of observed scores on X at some value of W_t will be different than the conditional distribution of X for individuals from the other populations.

As discussed in Chapter 1, we use the term "bias" here in preference to "DIF" to emphasize the importance of the target variable concept in the definition of invariance or lack of invariance. In defining invariance, it is important to be clear about what the variable X is designed to measure: the target latent variable. This target latent variable is often univariate, but multivariate target latent variables are conceivable. A given measure X may or may not be viewed as showing measurement bias, depending on the conception of the target latent variable. For example, a reading comprehension item may yield systematically lower scores for females than males, even within examinee groups that are "matched" on the target latent variable. Scrutiny of the item content may reveal that the males found the content to be of greater interest than did the females. We might conceptualize this "content interest" dimension as an additional latent variable, and we could plausibly argue that it is a nuisance dimension because interest in the content of the Σ comprehension items is not itself a target latent variable. Under this view, the gender difference in performance on the item within groups of examinees that are matched on the target comprehension variable is evidence of measurement bias. On the other hand, suppose that the reading comprehension item is part of a test designed to measure comprehension within a given topic area, with the item content being relevant to this topic. For example, the purpose of the test may be to evaluate whether the examinee can read and understand technical instructions within a given job area (e.g., lab technician). Now the status of the additional content interest latent variable is less clear; we may no longer view this as a nuisance variable. We may decide that the gender difference in performance on the item must be reevaluated using possibly two target latent variables: comprehension and content interest. The point of this example is that any investigation of measurement bias must first consider the definition of the target latent variable, and particularly the number of such variables. The use of the "bias" terminology to describe violations of measurement invariance is based on the assumption that target latent variables can be defined conceptually.

To illustrate the measurement invariance concept as applied to specific measurement models, consider the case in which $\mathbf{X}$ is a vector of dichotomous item score random variables, each scored $(0, 1)$, and $\mathbf{W}_t$ is a scalar target latent variable (i.e., $r_t = 1$). Here measurement invariance states that the item response functions for the items in $\mathbf{X}$ are invariant across the K populations. This condition is the traditional definition of "lack of item bias" in item response theory (Lord, 1980; Mellenbergh, 1989). The definition can be extended to the polytomous item case, where the MRF is more complex. Item bias is then defined by violations of measurement invariance as in Equation 3.2.

As a different illustration, suppose that $\mathbf{X}$ represents p continuous variables that fit a common factor model in each of the K populations, with $\mathbf{W}_t$ being a vector of r_t common factor score variables. When $\mathbf{X}$ has a conditionally multivariate normal (MVN) distribution in each population, measurement invariance holds if

$$\boldsymbol{\mu}_{k(\mathbf{X}|\mathbf{W}_t)} = \boldsymbol{\mu}_{(\mathbf{X}|\mathbf{W}_t)} = \boldsymbol{\tau} + \boldsymbol{\Lambda}\mathbf{W}_t, \tag{3.3}$$

$$\boldsymbol{\Sigma}_{k(\mathbf{X}|\mathbf{W}_t)} = \boldsymbol{\Sigma}_{(\mathbf{X}|\mathbf{W}_t)} = \boldsymbol{\Theta}. \tag{3.4}$$

The conditional mean and covariance matrix for $\mathbf{X}$ given $\mathbf{W}_t$ are identical across populations when the parameters $\{\boldsymbol{\tau}, \boldsymbol{\Lambda}, \boldsymbol{\Theta}\}$ are invariant. Note that the common factor covariance matrix $\mathbf{\Phi}_k$ and common factor mean $\mathbf{\kappa}_k$ need not be invariant under measurement invariance in Equation 3.1, as these parameters govern the distribution of $\mathbf{W}_t$. In the general case in which $\mathbf{X}$ has an arbitrary distribution, establishing invariance of the parameters in Equations 3.3 and 3.4 may not be sufficient for measurement invariance in Equation 3.1. The additional requirement is that the distributional form for the conditional distribution of $\mathbf{X}$ given $\mathbf{W}_t$ must be invariant across $\Pi_k, k = 1, 2, \ldots, K$. This fact has led factor analysts to define weaker forms of invariance (factorial invariance) that focus on the conditional means and covariance structure, as discussed below.

Measurement invariance as defined in Equation 3.1 may hold even though the score distributions on the measured variables $\mathbf{X}$ differ across populations, as noted in Chapter 1. Population differences in average scores on $\mathbf{X}$ do not necessarily violate measurement invariance, for example. Measurement invariance refers to comparisons of groups who are *matched* on the target latent variable $\mathbf{W}_t$. Under measurement invariance, we should find no population differences in score distributions on the measured variables $\mathbf{X}$ within a group of examinees who are matched on the target latent variable $\mathbf{W}_t$. This matching principle underlies all present statistical methods of bias detection, although the matching will assume different forms under the different detection methods. In contrast, comparisons between unmatched individuals from different populations may reveal population differences on $\mathbf{X}$. In studies of item bias, these population differences in score distributions on $\mathbf{X}$ are sometimes denoted *impact*, to distinguish such differences from measurement bias in Equation 3.2 (Dorans & Holland, 1993; Holland & Thayer, 1988). Population differences in score distributions among unmatched individuals may have important social consequences for the use of the measured variables (e.g., employment selection), but these differences do not clearly establish measurement bias. A rival explanation in such cases is that the score distributions on $\mathbf{X}$ arise from population differences in target latent variable distributions. The matching strategy is designed to challenge this rival explanation.

Weaker Forms of Invariance

The definition of invariance in Equation 3.1 is stringent, and it is natural to consider weaker forms of invariance that would be useful in practice, either because they closely approximate full invariance in Equation 3.1 or because the weaker conditions are enough to satisfy practical requirements.

To begin, consider *first-order measurement invariance*, defined as

$$E_k(\mathbf{X}\,|\,\mathbf{W}_t) = E(\mathbf{X}\,|\,\mathbf{W}_t) \tag{3.5}$$

for $k = 1,\ldots, K$ and for all $\mathbf{W}_t$. Under this form of invariance, the conditional mean for $\mathbf{X}$ is invariant across populations, but other features of the conditional distribution (e.g., variance) may vary. In other words, the regression functions for the regression of $\mathbf{X}$ on $\mathbf{W}_t$ are identical across populations. For dichotomous $\mathbf{X}$ variables, first-order invariance is the same as measurement invariance in Equation 3.1. For polytomous or continuous $\mathbf{X}$ variables, however, the two forms of invariance may diverge. If $\mathbf{X}$ represents polytomous item scores, for example, first-order invariance need not imply measurement invariance in Equation 3.1, although the two forms of invariance are equivalent under the most commonly used item response functions (Chang & Mazzeo, 1994). If $\mathbf{X}$ fits a common factor model with the same number of factors in each studied population, first-order measurement invariance implies that the latent intercepts and loadings $\{\boldsymbol{\tau}, \boldsymbol{\Lambda}\}$ in Equation 3.3 are invariant across the studied populations. First-order measurement invariance does not require invariance in the unique factor variances. In this common factor case, Meredith (1993) denotes first-order measurement invariance as "strong factorial invariance." It has also been denoted "scalar invariance" (Steenkamp & Baumgartner, 1998). This form of factorial invariance can be further weakened by requiring that only the factor pattern matrices $\boldsymbol{\Lambda}$ be invariant across groups, permitting group differences in latent intercepts. This weaker invariance condition has been described in a variety of ways in the literature, as metric invariance (Horn & McArdle, 1992; Steenkamp & Baumgartner), pattern invariance (Millsap, 1995), or weak factorial invariance (Widaman & Reise, 1997).

First-order measurement invariance is sufficient for some practical purposes because it implies that *on average*, individuals from different populations who are identical on $\mathbf{W}_t$ will have identical observed scores on $\mathbf{X}$. This condition would seem to be the minimum requirement needed in order to regard $\mathbf{X}$ as unbiased in the measurement sense. Violations of first-order invariance imply that for the individuals mentioned above, the expected observed score will differ depending on the individual's population membership. As a result, group comparisons on $\mathbf{X}$ do not have any clear interpretation in terms of differences on the target latent variable $\mathbf{W}_t$.

A stronger form of invariance can be defined by supplementing first-order invariance with the requirement that

$$\boldsymbol{\Sigma}_{k(\mathbf{X}|\mathbf{W}_t)} = \boldsymbol{\Sigma}_{(\mathbf{X}|\mathbf{W}_t)} \tag{3.6}$$

for $k = 1,\ldots, K$ and for all $\mathbf{W}_t$. When Equations 3.5 and 3.6 hold, we will say that $\mathbf{X}$ satisfies *second-order measurement invariance*. Meredith (1993) denotes this form of invariance as "weak measurement invariance." Now, in addition to invariance in the regression of $\mathbf{X}$ on $\mathbf{W}_t$, we require that the variability in $\mathbf{X}$ for a fixed value of $\mathbf{W}_t$ be the same in all populations.

Second-order invariance is still less stringent than full measurement invariance in Equation 3.1, as higher-order moments of the conditional distribution of **X** given **W**ₜ may still vary across populations under second-order invariance. To the extent that the higher order moments are negligible, however, second-order invariance will closely approximate full measurement invariance. As applied to the common factor case, second-order measurement invariance is equivalent to "strict factorial invariance" as described by Meredith. The invariance literature has tended to emphasize the greater importance of first-order invariance, but second-order invariance can be equally important in some cases (DeShon, 2004; Lubke & Dolan, 2003).

The foregoing definitions of invariance in Equations 3.1, 3.5, and 3.6 have considered all measured variables simultaneously, applying invariance constraints to the entire set of p measures in **X**. In actual practice, we may find that some of the p measured variables adhere to the invariance constraints, and other measured variables do not. For example, under a common factor model for **X**, we may find that the latent intercept parameters τ for some of the p measures are invariant, while the parameters for other measures are not. This condition is denoted "partial measurement invariance" in the literature (Byrne, Shavelson, & Muthén, 1989), with the full description depending on the measurement model. In the latent intercept example, we would say that "partial scalar invariance" holds for **X**. The possibility of partial invariance leads to questions about how one should determine which parameters and which variables are responsible for any lack of invariance. We will return to this question in the context of specific models in Chapters 4 through 7.

Stronger Forms of Invariance

The definition of measurement invariance in Equation 3.1 is a statement about conditions that hold in K fixed populations. Formally, these fixed populations are defined using a vector of selection variables **V**, but the resulting set of K populations may not include all *possible* subpopulations that might be defined using **V**. For example, if **V** contains the demographic variables of sex and ethnicity, the K populations may exclude some combinations of these two variables. As another example, suppose that **V** consists of a list of countries from which a cross-cultural researcher might sample in conducting a cross-cultural study. The actual study might only involve a subset of the larger list represented in **V**, but there may ultimately be an interest in generalizing to the larger set of countries. This fact suggests that we can strengthen the definition of measurement invariance to denote all possible subpopulations that could be defined based on **V**. This number of such populations may be quite large, depending on **V**.

To make the above concrete, let $\Pi_k, k=1,2,\ldots,M$ represent the set of *all possible* subpopulations that can be created on the basis of **V**, with $K \leq M$. We will say that *complete measurement invariance* holds for **X** in relation to $\mathbf{W_t}$ and **V** if and only if Equation 3.1 holds for $k = 1, 2, \ldots, M$, where M defines the number of possible subpopulations that can be defined from **V**. Meredith and Millsap (1992) showed that complete measurement invariance may hold if and only if

$$P(\mathbf{X}|\mathbf{W_t}, \mathbf{V}) = P(\mathbf{X}|\mathbf{W_t}) \tag{3.7}$$

for all $\mathbf{W_t}$ and **V**. Here **X** and **V** are conditionally independent given the target latent variable. This conditional independence characterizes complete measurement invariance.

In simple cases, there will be no distinction between measurement invariance in Equation 3.1 and complete measurement invariance. For example, if V is a scalar that defines the individual's sex, and Π consists of two populations, males and females, there can be no distinction between the two forms of invariance. In other cases, however, the set of populations studied empirically may not include all possible subpopulations that could be created from **V**. Suppose, for example, that **V** contains the variables sex and age. We may create populations Π_k, $k = 1, 2, \ldots, K$ by selecting only certain age groups, with both sexes being represented. Complete measurement invariance would require consideration of *all* combinations of age and sex. In these cases, it is possible that measurement invariance holds for the populations studied, but complete measurement invariance fails to hold.

Local Homogeneity

The notion of complete measurement invariance has some important theoretical implications if the definition of **V** is expanded sufficiently to permit isolation of specific individuals. In this case, "all possible subpopulations" would include all possible subsets of some parent population defined by the union of $\Pi_k, k=1,2,\ldots,M$. A subset here could consist of a single individual. This situation has been studied by Ellis and van den Wollenberg (1993) in defining "local homogeneity" of a latent variable model in item response theory. The question of local homogeneity only makes sense within the stochastic subject view of the MRF because the MRF is undefined for a fixed examinee in the random sampling view.

For present purposes, we can describe local homogeneity as follows. Let **V** include information needed to identify all possible subsets of a parent population. The parent population itself could be defined in any number of ways. The definition is not crucial to what follows. In the extreme case, **V** will simply include the labels for all individuals in the parent population.

For this case, we could let **Π** represent "subpopulations" defined by individuals in the parent population, and so $\Pi_k, k = 1, 2, \ldots, M$ would represent the individuals in the parent population of size M. Here **Π** and **V** are identical. We can then define complete measurement invariance as

$$P(\mathbf{X} \mid \mathbf{W_t}, \Pi_k) = P(\mathbf{X} \mid \mathbf{W_t}) \tag{3.8}$$

for all $\mathbf{W_t}$ and Π_k. Complete measurement invariance says that individuals with identical values of the latent variable $\mathbf{W_t}$ are indistinguishable in their MRFs. In the context of **X** as a set of dichotomous item score variables, Ellis and van den Wollenberg (1993) define the latent variable model as meeting local homogeneity if Equation 3.8 holds. Under local homogeneity, the only information about the individual that is of relevance to the item scores **X** is the individual's score on the target latent variable.

Once local homogeneity is granted for a given parent population, it must be true that for *any* set of subpopulations that could be defined within that parent population, measurement invariance will hold. Another way of expressing this condition is to say that for a parent population in which local homogeneity holds, complete measurement invariance in Equation 3.7 must hold for *any* set of selection variables **V** that can be specified for that parent population. Local homogeneity represents what is perhaps the strongest possible formulation of measurement invariance. Ellis and van den Wollenberg (1993) show that for a set of items with monotone, unidimensional item response functions under local independence, local homogeneity implies nonnegative covariances between every pair of items in *every* subpopulation. This characterization provides a way of empirically testing local homogeneity, but investigations of every possible subpopulation will not be possible in practice. Furthermore, violations of local homogeneity need not imply violations of invariance in the context of Equation 3.1 for a fixed set of K populations. In practice, investigations of measurement invariance will focus on populations defined by specific combinations of variables **V**.

Dimensionality and Invariance

We have considered the measurement invariance of **X** in relation to the target latent variable $\mathbf{W_t}$. Suppose, however, that additional nuisance latent variables $\mathbf{W_n}$ are present and are related to performance on **X**. For example, if **X** is a set of reading comprehension items, $\mathbf{W_n}$ might be a set of testwiseness variables that emerge from prior familiarity with the format of the test items. Examinees who are higher on the testwiseness dimensions tend to score higher on **X**, apart from their status on the target latent variable. Scenarios of this type are often used to motivate concern for measurement bias. Under these scenarios, any bias that is present in **X** in relation to the target latent variable is attributed to the operation of additional nuisance latent variables (Ackerman, 1992; Camilli, 1992; Kok, 1988; Linn, Levine, Hastings, & Wardrup, 1981; Shealy & Stout, 1993). These nuisance variables represent unanticipated, and generally unwanted, sources of individual differences in scores on **X**.

Although it is tempting to attribute all manifestations of measurement bias to the presence of such nuisance variables, nuisance variables may not always provide a useful explanation for the source of bias. A simple thought experiment should make this clear. Consider an experiment in which examinees are randomly assigned to two conditions of administration of the measure **X**: A standard condition, and a distraction condition in which distracting environmental stimuli are introduced during the administration of **X**. We can assume that there exists some level of distractor stimulus intensity that would affect score levels on **X**. Given that between-group score differences can be produced in this experiment, and given that random assignment eliminates expected group differences on any target latent variable, it is clear that the observed score differences are a product of bias as defined in Equation 3.2, with **V** defined by the experimental populations. Here the bias is experimentally induced, and no nuisance latent variables need to be considered as explanations for the bias. One could define a nuisance "latent" variable to account for the bias by incorporating **V** itself as a latent variable. The grouping variable **V** is not really latent, however, and it is simpler to regard **V** as a measurable feature of the testing situation. We need not consider any latent sources of individual differences that would explain the bias in this example.

An objection to this thought experiment is that the "conditions of administration" are responsible for the bias in this case, rather than any intrinsic feature of the measure **X**. It is often difficult, however, to separate the "measure **X**" from the "conditions of administration for measure **X**" in practice. An important goal in standardized testing is to control unwanted influences on test performance by standardizing the conditions of administration. Not all situational influences can be eliminated in this manner, however. The central question is whether the situational influences are confounded with the populations to be compared as defined by **V**. The above experimental scenario is an extreme example of such confounding, but less extreme examples may be relevant in real situations. For example, in attitude measurement, the examinee's perception of a lack of anonymity may affect those responses, and these effects may differ by population. An example would be a measure of racial prejudice in which the race of the examiner differentially affects the responses of examinees from different races. A further example in cognitive measurement is the phenomenon of stereotype threat (Steele & Aronson, 1995), in which group differences in cognitive test scores are produced through experimental manipulation of situational stimuli. This phenomenon can be approached as a problem of measurement invariance (Wicherts, Dolan, & Hessen, 2005).

The key point is that the sources of measurement bias may be difficult to anticipate in practice. Nuisance latent variables represent an important class of explanations for bias. These explanations are reasonable when the bias is thought to be due to individual differences in secondary attitudes, abilities, or personality influences relevant to the measure under study. An exclusive focus on individual differences in such attributes as sources of bias may blind investigators to other explanations, such as those that are environmental, situational, or social in origin.

It is important to note that the mere presence of nuisance latent variables is not sufficient to create bias. Let $\mathbf{W} = (\mathbf{W}_t, \mathbf{W}_n)$ be the total set of latent variables relevant to performance on $\mathbf{X}$, and let $P(\mathbf{X}|\mathbf{W})$ be the resulting measurement response function. Suppose that with reference to $\mathbf{W}$, we have complete measurement invariance with respect to the selection variables $\mathbf{V}$. In other words, suppose it is true that

$$P(\mathbf{X}|\mathbf{W}, \mathbf{V}) = P(\mathbf{X}|\mathbf{W}). \tag{3.9}$$

Bias could arise if $\mathbf{W}$ is replaced with the target latent variable $\mathbf{W}_t$. Bias of this sort would require an additional condition, as represented in the following theorem. Let $g_k(\mathbf{W}_t, \mathbf{W}_n)$ be the joint distribution of $\mathbf{W}_t$ and $\mathbf{W}_n$ in the kth population defined from $\mathbf{V}$. We assume that the latent variables $\mathbf{W}$ are continuous.

Theorem 3.1

Suppose that Equation 3.9 holds for $\mathbf{W}$ and the selection variables $\mathbf{V}$. Then the measurement response functions $P_k(\mathbf{X}|\mathbf{W}_t)$ will vary over k only if

$$g_k(\mathbf{W}_n|\mathbf{W}_t) \neq g(\mathbf{W}_n|\mathbf{W}_t) \tag{3.10}$$

for some value of k, $k = 1,\ldots,K$ and of $\mathbf{W}_t$.

Proof of this theorem is given in the Appendix to this chapter. Results similar to Theorem 3.1 can be found in Kok (1988), Camilli (1992), and Shealy and Stout (1993). The theorem shows that given the presence of nuisance variables, a necessary requirement for bias is that the populations must differ in their conditional distributions of the nuisance variables, given the target latent variable. Shealy and Stout label this condition as the "potential" for bias. As an example, population differences in the regression of $\mathbf{W}_n$ on $\mathbf{W}_t$ would create the potential for bias. Note that the potential for bias depends on the populations being compared. This fact may appear to violate the earlier distinction between "bias" and "impact," but recall that impact was created by group differences in target latent variable distributions. In contrast, Theorem 3.1 concerns the conditional distribution of the nuisance latent variable given the target latent variable. Target latent variable distributions may vary over groups without inducing group differences in these conditional distributions.

To illustrate the role of nuisance latent variables and the potential for bias, consider the special case in which $(\mathbf{W}_t, \mathbf{W}_n)$ are MVN with

$$E_k(\mathbf{W}_t, \mathbf{W}_n) = (\boldsymbol{\mu}_{kt}, \boldsymbol{\mu}_{kn}) = \boldsymbol{\mu}_{Wk} \tag{3.11}$$

and

$$\mathrm{Cov}_k(\mathbf{W}_t, \mathbf{W}_n) = \boldsymbol{\Sigma}_{Wk} = \begin{vmatrix} \boldsymbol{\Sigma}_{ktt} & \boldsymbol{\Sigma}_{ktn} \\ \boldsymbol{\Sigma}_{knt} & \boldsymbol{\Sigma}_{knn} \end{vmatrix}. \tag{3.12}$$

Then by standard theory,

$$g_k(\mathbf{W}_n \mid \mathbf{W}_t) = \mathrm{MVN}(\boldsymbol{\mu}_{kn.t}, \boldsymbol{\Sigma}_{kn.t}), \tag{3.13}$$

with

$$\boldsymbol{\mu}_{kn.t} = \boldsymbol{\mu}_{kn} + \boldsymbol{\Sigma}_{knt} \boldsymbol{\Sigma}_{ktt}^{-1}(\mathbf{W}_t - \boldsymbol{\mu}_{kt}), \tag{3.14}$$

$$\boldsymbol{\Sigma}_{kn.t} = \boldsymbol{\Sigma}_{knn} - \boldsymbol{\Sigma}_{knt} \boldsymbol{\Sigma}_{ktt}^{-1} \boldsymbol{\Sigma}'_{knt}. \tag{3.15}$$

In general, population differences in the joint distribution of $\mathbf{W}_t$ and $\mathbf{W}_n$ lead to population differences in $g_k(\mathbf{W}_n|\mathbf{W}_t)$ and to the potential for bias. For example, suppose that $\boldsymbol{\Sigma}_{Wk} = \boldsymbol{\Sigma}_W$ and $\boldsymbol{\mu}_{kt} = \boldsymbol{\mu}_t$ for all k, but $\boldsymbol{\mu}_{kn} \neq \boldsymbol{\mu}_n$. Then the population differences in the conditional means $\boldsymbol{\mu}_{kn.t}$ are determined entirely by the differences in the unconditional means $\boldsymbol{\mu}_{kn}$. The population with the highest average score on the nuisance variables $\mathbf{W}_n$ will have the highest conditional average as well. The potential for bias exists in this case.

From the above, it is clear that population differences in the target latent variable distributions can contribute to the potential for bias. In other words, these group differences in target latent variable distributions can help bring about the conditions that are necessary for bias to exist in Theorem 3.1. The source of the problem is that features of the target latent variable distributions are part of the conditional distributions $g_k(\mathbf{W}_n|\mathbf{W}_t)$

in Theorem 3.1. Consider the MVN example just described. Population differences in either $\mathbf{\mu}_{kt}$ or $\mathbf{\Sigma}_{ktt}$ will generally contribute to differences in the conditional moments in Equations 3.13 and 3.14. For example, suppose that $\mathbf{\mu}_{wk} = \mathbf{\mu}_w$, $\mathbf{\Sigma}_{knn} = \mathbf{\Sigma}_{nn}$, and $\mathbf{\Sigma}_{ktn} = \mathbf{\Sigma}_{tn}$, for all k, but $\mathbf{\Sigma}_{ktt} \neq \mathbf{\Sigma}_{tt}$ for at least some value of k. Then it must be true that $\mathbf{\mu}_{kn.t} \neq \mathbf{\mu}_{n.t}$ for some k, and so measurement invariance may be violated. The source of the potential bias in this example is the population difference in the covariance structure for the target latent variables. If only a single target latent variable is present, the population difference lies in the variance of this latent variable. A variety of hypothetical scenarios of this sort can be developed (Ackerman, 1992; Camilli, 1992; Oshima & Miller, 1990).

When no nuisance latent variables are present, the presence of multiple target latent variables can lead to erroneous conclusions of bias if a bias detection procedure that assumes a single target latent variable is used. As will be described in subsequent chapters, many statistical methods for bias detection are based on an explicit, or implicit, assumption that the measured variables fit a unidimensional latent variable model. If such methods are applied to measured variables that are influenced by multiple target latent variables, the additional target latent variables will serve as "nuisance" latent variables in the context of the unidimensional analysis. When the conditions of Theorem 3.1 are fulfilled in relation to these "nuisance" latent variables, false conclusions of bias in some measured variables may result. Camilli (1992) illustrates this problem with several hypothetical examples.

The foregoing developments illustrate that when performance on $\mathbf{X}$ is influenced by multiple latent variables, careful consideration of the number and nature of these latent variables is needed if bias is to be investigated. Bias investigations are closely linked with methods for assessing the number of latent variables that underlie the measured variables. Many current methods for investigating bias rely on unidimensional latent variable models, either explicitly or implicitly. If the target latent variable is unidimensional and any nuisance latent variables influence only a small number of items, the unidimensionality assumption that is central to most bias detection procedures will not cause problems. In this case, the presence of the nuisance influences in some items may lead to those items being flagged as biased under typical bias detection procedures. If multiple target latent variables are present, however, group differences in the joint distributions on these target latent variables can lead to erroneous conclusions of bias from detection methods that rely on unidimensionality. This problem exists even if no nuisance latent variables are present. The solution to this problem requires that the separate target latent variables be recognized explicitly in some way. One approach is to formally model the multiple latent variables, as done in factor analysis. Another approach would first separate the measured variables into sets according to which target latent variable is influential for that set. Separate unidimensional analyses would then be applied to each set. This approach assumes that any single measured variable is influenced by only a single latent target latent variable.

Conditioning on Observed Scores

Measurement invariance as defined in Equation 3.1 is difficult to investigate empirically because the target latent variable $\mathbf{W_t}$ is not directly measurable. In the absence of any perfect measure of $\mathbf{W_t}$, we cannot directly match examinees on $\mathbf{W_t}$ to investigate bias. Solutions to this problem are typically classified in two categories (Meredith & Millsap, 1992; Millsap & Meredith, 1992; Thissen, Steinberg, & Wainer, 1993). *Latent variable methods* attempt to model the MRF in each population, followed by tests of invariance for the MRF. These methods are further classified by the type of model chosen for the MRF. *Observed variable methods* use one or more measured variables as proxies for $\mathbf{W_t}$. Population differences in $\mathbf{X}$ are then studied within blocks of examinees who are matched on the observed proxy variables. A variety of observed-score methods are used in bias investigations, including the Mantel–Haenszel method (Holland & Thayer, 1988; Mantel & Haenszel, 1959), logistic regression (Rogers & Swaminathan, 1993), standardization methods (Dorans & Kulick, 1986), and log-linear methods (Kelderman, 1989). In this section, we describe some general properties of these observed variable methods, with emphasis on the forms of invariance being tested by the methods.

Let $\mathbf{Z} = (Z_1, Z_2, ..., Z_q)$ be a $q \times 1$ vector of observable random variables that are intended to serve as proxy variables for $\mathbf{W_t}$ in the bias investigation. In the common case in which $\mathbf{W_t}$ is a scalar ($r = 1$), the variable $\mathbf{Z}$ will also typically be a scalar. In most applications, $\mathbf{Z}$ is some function of $\mathbf{X}$. For example, we might choose $Z = \sum_{j=1}^{p} X_j$ as the unweighted total score among the items when $\mathbf{X}$ is a vector of item score variables. The matching variable $\mathbf{Z}$ could also be chosen as a vector of external variables (i.e., different from $\mathbf{X}$) that presumably measure $\mathbf{W_t}$, but this option is not commonly pursued in practice. In most applications, $\mathbf{Z}$ is chosen as a scalar ($q = 1$) without any explicit consideration of the dimensionality of $\mathbf{W_t}$.

Observed variable methods typically evaluate whether the conditional distribution of $\mathbf{X}$ given $\mathbf{Z}$ is the same across populations. We can represent this form of invariance as

$$P_k(\mathbf{X}|\mathbf{Z}) = P(\mathbf{X}|\mathbf{Z}) \tag{3.16}$$

for $k = 1,...,K$. We will denote the conditional distribution $P_k(\mathbf{X}|\mathbf{Z})$ as the *observed response function* (ORF) within the kth population. Equation 3.16 stipulates that the ORFs are identical across the K populations. We will denote this invariance condition as *observed conditional invariance* (OCI), to distinguish it from measurement invariance in Equation 3.1 (Millsap & Meredith, 1992). Observed variable methods seek to test OCI or a weaker version of OCI. For example, we could limit invariance of the ORF to just the conditional expected value

$$E_k(\mathbf{X}|\mathbf{Z}) = E(\mathbf{X}|\mathbf{Z}) \qquad (3.17)$$

for $k = 1,...,K$. By analogy with earlier definitions, we can denote the condition in Equation 3.17 as *first-order* OCI. If the measured variables $\mathbf{X}$ are dichotomous, OCI and first-order OCI are equivalent. More generally, first-order OCI is a weaker form of invariance in comparison to OCI in Equation 3.15. We can also define *second-order* OCI as holding when first-order OCI holds and

$$\text{Cov}_k(\mathbf{X}|\mathbf{Z}) = \mathbf{\Sigma}_{k\mathbf{X}|\mathbf{Z}} = \mathbf{\Sigma}_{\mathbf{X}|\mathbf{Z}} \qquad (3.18)$$

for $k = 1,...,K$. Under second-order OCI, both the conditional expected values and the conditional covariance structure of $\mathbf{X}$ given $\mathbf{Z}$ are invariant.

Measurement invariance in Equation 3.1 and OCI in Equation 3.16 are not equivalent conditions in general (Meredith & Millsap, 1992; Millsap, 1995, 1997; Zwick, 1990). Tests of OCI do not necessarily provide clear evidence for or against measurement invariance in general. For this reason, it is important to understand some theoretical conditions under which the two forms of invariance will be equivalent or will diverge. The next several sections describe some general conditions that affect the equivalence between the two forms of invariance. Results tailored to individual observed variable methods can be found in later chapters.

Bayes Sufficiency of Z

An important condition under which the use of $\mathbf{Z}$ as a matching variable should lead to equivalent tests of OCI and measurement invariance occurs when $\mathbf{Z}$ contains all of the information in the data that is relevant for $\mathbf{W}_t$ in its relation to $\mathbf{X}$. Formally, this condition is described by saying that $\mathbf{Z}$ is sufficient (or Bayes sufficient, as in Lehmann, 1986) for $\mathbf{W}_t$ in relation to $\mathbf{X}$. The property of sufficiency is well known in statistical estimation theory, where the sufficiency of a statistic for a parameter means that all of the information in the data that is relevant to the estimation of the parameter is contained in the statistic. In the measurement bias context, $\mathbf{W}_t$ is not viewed as a fixed parameter but as a latent random variable, and so the phrase "Bayes sufficient" is perhaps more appropriate for describing the condition of interest. We can define Bayes sufficiency of $\mathbf{Z}$ in relation to $\mathbf{W}_t$ as holding if and only if

$$P_k(\mathbf{X}|\mathbf{Z}, \mathbf{W}_t) = P_k(\mathbf{X}|\mathbf{Z}) \tag{3.19}$$

for $k = 1, \ldots, K$. Here $\mathbf{X}$ and $\mathbf{W}_t$ are conditionally independent given $\mathbf{Z}$ within each population. In this sense, all of the information in $\mathbf{X}$ that is relevant to $\mathbf{W}_t$ is contained in $\mathbf{Z}$. Meredith and Millsap (1992; Millsap & Meredith, 1992) present general theorems demonstrating that when $\mathbf{Z}$ is Bayes sufficient for $\mathbf{W}_t$, measurement invariance in both $\mathbf{X}$ and $\mathbf{Z}$ implies that OCI also holds for $\mathbf{X}$ in relation to $\mathbf{Z}$. Hence, under Bayes sufficiency, observed variable methods that employ $\mathbf{Z}$ should support OCI when measurement invariance in fact holds for $\mathbf{X}$ and $\mathbf{Z}$. On the other hand, the theorems do not necessarily apply if $\mathbf{Z}$ fails to be measurement invariant but $\mathbf{X}$ is invariant. For example, suppose that Z is the sum of all item scores but $\mathbf{X}$ consists of a subset of the items. In addition, suppose that the items in $\mathbf{X}$ are measurement invariant but some of the additional items included in Z are not invariant. In this case, the use of Z could lead to a violation of OCI for $\mathbf{X}$ although $\mathbf{X}$ is invariant. The question to be addressed is how serious the violations of invariance in Z must be before spurious conclusions of bias in $\mathbf{X}$ occur. This question is a topic of active research, as described in Chapter 8.

Some latent variable models for $\mathbf{X}$ imply that there exists an observed variable $\mathbf{Z}$ for which Bayes sufficiency holds. Under these models, it may be possible to create $\mathbf{Z}$, so that invariance can be investigated using observed variable methods. As an example, suppose that $\mathbf{X}$ consists of p dichotomous items that fit a Rasch model, with $\mathbf{W}_t$ a scalar. If $Z = \sum_{j=1}^{p} X_j$ is an unweighted total score, it is well known that Z meets the sufficiency property in Equation 3.19. Hence, in the Rasch case, the use of Z as the matching variable in an observed variable method (e.g., the Mantel–Haenszel method) should provide a test of both OCI and measurement invariance (Fischer, 1993; Holland & Thayer, 1988; Zwick, 1990). The same condition holds when the items are polytomous and fit one of the polytomous Rasch models. In more general latent variable models for dichotomous items, we can define a weighted composite $Z = \sum_{j=1}^{p} h_j X_j$ with weights $(h_1, h_2, \ldots, h_p)$, yielding a measure Z that meets the sufficiency requirement (Fischer; Meredith & Millsap, 1992). For example, any latent variable model in which the MRF is a member of the exponential family will yield some sufficient measure $\mathbf{Z}$ that is a function of $\mathbf{X}$. Unfortunately, the function will generally require weights whose values can only be estimated. The two-parameter logistic model, for example, can be shown to lead to $Z = \sum_{j=1}^{p} a_j X_j$, where the a_j, $j = 1,...,p$, are the item discrimination parameters. Substitution of estimated parameter values in the composite that defines Z may or may not produce an adequate matching variable.

The above arguments relating to sufficiency can be applied to the common factor model for continuous $\mathbf{X}$ by using results given by Bartholomew (1987). Bartholomew notes that in the case of a continuous $\mathbf{X}$ with the MRF meeting local independence and with $\mathbf{W_t}$ of dimension r, there will exist an r-dimensional sufficient statistic $\mathbf{Z}$ for $\mathbf{W_t}$ if the MRF for each element of $\mathbf{X}$ is a member of the exponential family. In other words, a condition leading to sufficiency in this case is that the MRF can be expressed as

$$P_k(X_j \mid \mathbf{W_t}) = \exp\left[\sum_{i=1}^{r} c_i(\mathbf{W_t}) Z_{ij}(X_j) + d(\mathbf{W_t}) + h(X_j)\right] \qquad (3.20)$$

for real-valued functions $(c_1, c_2, ..., c_r)$, d, h, and Z_{ij}, and for $j = 1,...,p$. The joint MRF can be written, under local independence, as

$$P(\mathbf{X} \mid \mathbf{W_t}) = D(\mathbf{W_t}) H(\mathbf{X}) \exp\left[\sum_{i=1}^{r} Z_i c_i(\mathbf{W_t})\right]. \qquad (3.21)$$

Here $Z_i = \sum_{j=1}^{p} Z_{ij}(X_j)$, $H(\mathbf{X}) = \exp\left[\sum_{j=1}^{p} h(X_j)\right]$, and $D(\mathbf{W_t}) = \exp[pd(\mathbf{W_t})]$. By the factorization theorem for sufficiency (Bickel & Doksum, 1977), it is clear from the above that the elements of $\mathbf{Z}$ are sufficient statistics for $\mathbf{W_t}$.

To illustrate, suppose that the MRF for $\mathbf{X}$ in the common factor case follows the MVN distribution, which is a member of the exponential family. Let $\mathbf{W_t} = \mathbf{W}$ for simplicity, and suppose

$$P(\mathbf{X} \mid \mathbf{W}) = MVN(\mathbf{\mu}_{(x \mid w)}, \mathbf{\Sigma}_{(x \mid w)}), \qquad (3.22)$$

with $\mathbf{\mu}_{(x \mid w)} = \mathbf{\tau} + \mathbf{\Lambda W}$ and $\mathbf{\Sigma}_{(x \mid w)} = \mathbf{\Theta}$, a $p \times p$ diagonal matrix. We will ignore the multiple populations for the moment and simply describe a model for a single population. Using the above along with the definition of the MVN distribution and Equation 3.21, it is found that

$$\exp\left[\sum_{i=1}^{r} Z_i c_i(\mathbf{W})\right] = \exp\left[\sum_{i=1}^{r} Z_i(\mathbf{X}) W_i\right], \qquad (3.23)$$

where

$$Z_i(\mathbf{X}) = \sum_{j=1}^{p} \frac{\lambda_{ji} X_j}{\theta_j}. \qquad (3.24)$$

The sufficient statistics in this factor analytic case are weighted linear functions of the scores on the p measured variables, with the weights depending on the unknown factor loadings and unique factor variances. As a result, it will ordinarily be impossible to use these sufficient statistics in order to stratify the sample in studies of measurement bias. In the special case in which $r = 1$ (only one factor), $\lambda_{ji} = \lambda$, and $\theta_j = \theta$ for $j = 1, \ldots, p$, the model parameters become a constant multiplier that can be dropped, and we have $Z(\mathbf{X}) = \sum_{j=1}^{p} X_j$. This case corresponds to the situation in which the measured variables are "parallel" measures of W_j, as noted in Chapter 2. This hypothesis of parallelism is testable (Millsap & Everson, 1991). This case provides a simple unweighted sum statistic that is sufficient for W_j and would permit stratification using Z.

An interesting empirical question would be whether "near sufficiency" can be achieved when the factor loadings and unique factor variances are approximately identical across variables.

A different route to sufficiency can be developed by considering what happens when the number of measured variables p becomes very large, holding constant the dimension of $\mathbf{W_t}$. This case would arise, for example, if $\mathbf{X}$ represented a set of test item scores, and we lengthen the test by adding more items that measure $\mathbf{W_t}$. We can define $\bar{Z}_p = 1/p \sum_{j=1}^{p} X_p$ as the average score across the p measured variables for a given value of p. Given the MRFs for the observed measures $\mathbf{X}$, a composite MRF can be defined for $\bar{Z}_p$ as $P(\bar{Z}_p | \mathbf{W_t})$. Our interest lies in the behavior of this composite MRF as p, the number of items, grows large.

We begin with the case in which $r = 1$, with a single target latent trait. Suppose that conditional independence holds for the MRFs of the measured variables given $\mathbf{W_t}$, and suppose that the composite MRF is monotonic in $\mathbf{W_t}$. We do not require that the measured variables be dichotomous, but it is assumed that all of the measured variables are bounded in value. We also assume that $\sigma^2(X_j | \mathbf{W_t}) < \varepsilon$ for all j, for some positive number ε, where $\sigma^2(X_j | \mathbf{W_t})$ is the conditional variance of X_j. This condition would be easily met for psychological test items. Then we have the following theorem for the single population case:

Theorem 3.2

If $E(\overline{Z}_p|\mathbf{W}_t)$ is the conditional expectation for $\overline{Z}_p$ given $\mathbf{W}_t$, then

$$\overline{Z}_p - E(\overline{Z}_p|\mathbf{W}_t) \to 0 \tag{3.25}$$

almost surely as $p \to \infty$.

Proof
Follows from the Kolmogorov strong law of large numbers (Rao, 1973), because the sufficient condition for almost sure convergence is that the series

$$\sum_{j=1}^{\infty} \frac{\sigma^2(X_j|\mathbf{W}_t)}{j^2} \tag{3.26}$$

must itself converge. The convergence of this series is certain because of the bound on the conditional variance for each X_j. Note that "almost sure" convergence is somewhat stronger than the ordinary concept of weak convergence or convergence in probability (see Rao). ∎

The implication of this theorem is that for a sufficiently large value of p, the difference between $\overline{Z}_p$ and $E(\overline{Z}_p|\mathbf{W}_t)$ is negligible. Coupled with the assumed monotonicity of the composite MRF, the theorem implies a degeneracy in the joint distribution of $\overline{Z}_p$ and $\mathbf{W}_t$. The expected value $E(\overline{Z}_p|\mathbf{W}_t)$ is a strictly monotonic function of $\mathbf{W}_t$, and hence each value of $\mathbf{W}_t$ maps onto a different value of $\overline{Z}_p$. As a result, $\overline{Z}_p$ becomes (nearly) Bayes sufficient for $\mathbf{W}_t$, and we can condition on $\overline{Z}_p$ in order to control $\mathbf{W}_t$.

Theorem 3.2 assumes conditional independence for $\mathbf{X}$ given $\mathbf{W}_t$. This independence assumption can be weakened by replacing it with the essential independence condition of Stout (1990; Junker, 1991). Junker applies the essential independence concept to consistency in estimation for the polytomous case. Suppose that the sequence of measured variables $(X_1, X_2, ..., X_p)$ satisfies the condition of essential independence with respect to a unidimensional $\mathbf{W}_t$. Then $\overline{Z}_p$ converges in probability to $E(\overline{Z}_p|\mathbf{W}_t)$ as $p \to \infty$ (see Theorem 3.1 in Junker). Stout gives the same result for the dichotomous case. It is clear that conditional independence is not a strict requirement for near sufficiency of $\overline{Z}_p$ for $\mathbf{W}_t$.

Theorem 3.2 also restricted consideration to a unidimensional target latent variable. What if $r > 1$, or the target latent variable is multidimensional? Alternatively, what if $r_t = 1$, but nuisance latent variables are also present? The effects of multidimensionality depend on the dominance of the additional latent variables. In the case of $r_t = 1$ with some additional minor nuisance dimensions, the results of Stout and Junker indicate that as long as essential independence holds for the measured variables in relation to $\mathbf{W}_t$, the convergence of $\bar{Z}_p$ to $E(\bar{Z}_p|\mathbf{W}_t)$ in probability will hold. On the other hand, suppose that there are multiple target latent variables underlying the measured variables. In this situation, scores on the vector $\mathbf{W}_t$ will not be uniquely associated with values of $E(\bar{Z}_p|\mathbf{W}_t)$ in general. For example, in the case of the common factor model with r common factors, we have for any value of p,

$$E(\bar{Z}_p|\mathbf{W}_t) = \tau^{*\prime} + \lambda^{*\prime}\mathbf{W}_t, \tag{3.27}$$

where $\tau^* = 1/p\,\mathbf{1}'\tau$ and $\lambda^* = 1/p\,\mathbf{1}'\Lambda$, with $\mathbf{1}$ a $p \times 1$ unit vector. In Equation 3.27, different values of $\mathbf{W}_t$ may result in the same value for $E(\bar{Z}_p|\mathbf{W}_t)$. The convergence of $\bar{Z}_p$ to $E(\bar{Z}_p|\mathbf{W}_t)$ does not lead to Bayes sufficiency in this situation. When $r_t > 1$, it will generally be necessary to use more than one statistic $\bar{Z}_p$ in order to achieve Bayes sufficiency, even with very long tests. Unless discrete sets of measured variables are known to be associated with individual target latent variables, it will be difficult to construct multiple statistics $\bar{Z}_p$ for this purpose.

The above results on Bayes sufficiency in large sets of measured variables have ignored the question of multiple populations and the possible existence of measurement bias in the measured variables $\mathbf{X}$ in relation to $\mathbf{W}_t$. Suppose that multiple populations exist and that some portion of the measured variables $\mathbf{X}$ are biased in relation to $\mathbf{W}_t$. Consider the aggregate population created by combining the separate examinee populations. What can be said about the convergence of $\bar{Z}_p$ to $E(\bar{Z}_p|\mathbf{W}_t)$ in the case of $r_t = 1$? Here the expected value $E(\bar{Z}_p|\mathbf{W}_t)$ may differ as a function of examinee population membership due to measurement bias in $\mathbf{X}$. Under the conditions of Theorem 3.2, or in the essentially independent case considered by Junker (1991), it is clear that $\bar{Z}_p$ still provides near Bayes sufficiency for large p. In other words, as long as the required conditions for convergence hold within each population, Bayes sufficiency is achieved. Measurement bias could in some cases preclude Bayes sufficiency, however. The key issue is whether the bias is substantial enough to violate essential independence in relation to $\mathbf{W}_t$. If within one or more populations, a dominant nuisance latent variable operates to destroy essential independence of $\mathbf{X}$ in relation to $\mathbf{W}_t$, we may not achieve Bayes sufficiency for $\bar{Z}_p$ in those populations. The results on convergence of $\bar{Z}_p$ cannot be fully relied upon if measurement bias is present in $\mathbf{X}$ unless the bias is confined to a negligible subset of the measured variables. For a discussion of the interpretation to be given to such subsets in the context of multidimensionality, see Stout (1990). The question of how large the subset of affected variables could be or how "dominant" the nuisance latent variable could be without destroying essential independence is a problem that requires further research. We return to this topic in Chapter 8.

We can summarize the results of this section on Bayes sufficiency as follows. First, Bayes sufficiency of $\mathbf{Z}$ in relation to $\mathbf{W_t}$ holds when $\mathbf{Z}$ contains all of the relevant information in the measured variables $\mathbf{X}$ in relation to $\mathbf{W_t}$. Under some relatively simple latent variable models for $\mathbf{X}$, the simple unweighted sum $Z = \sum_{j=1}^{p} X_j$ of the measured variables will be Bayes sufficient in relation to a unidimensional $\mathbf{W_t}$. For example, this holds for the Rasch model and for the common factor model under restrictions of parallelism. Approximate or "near" Bayes sufficiency may hold for sufficiently long tests under very general conditions. For example, we can achieve Bayes sufficiency of Z for dichotomous item data even if the Rasch model does not hold, if p is sufficiently large. If Bayes sufficiency holds for Z, and $\mathbf{X}$ is measurement invariant in relation to $\mathbf{W_t}$, we will have OCI also for $\mathbf{X}$ in relation to Z and $\mathbf{W_t}$. The practical value of this idea of Bayes sufficiency is undercut to some degree by two considerations, however. First, if $r_t > 1$ (more than one target latent variable), it will generally not be possible to achieve Bayes sufficiency with a univariate matching variable Z. Multiple matching variables $\mathbf{Z}$ would generally be required, and this option is seldom pursued in actual practice (see Chapter 8). Second, the presence of measurement bias in some of the measured variables $\mathbf{X}$ can destroy the correspondence between OCI and measurement invariance, depending on which variables are affected and whether the affected variables are the focus of study or are simply part of the matching variable Z. For example, under the Rasch model for $\mathbf{X}$, if only one measured variable X_j violates measurement invariance, OCI will not hold for X_j in relation to Z, and so the evaluation of OCI as a substitute for directly examining measurement invariance will work properly. On the other hand, the presence of additional variables in $\mathbf{X}$ that violate measurement invariance may invalidate the use of OCI with Z as the matching variable as a method for testing measurement invariance. More details on this problem will be found in Chapter 8.

Conditional Independence of X and Z

An interesting special case of observed variable conditioning arises when $\mathbf{X}$ and $\mathbf{Z}$ are conditionally independent given $\mathbf{W_t}$ within each population, or when

$$P_k(\mathbf{X}|\mathbf{Z}, \mathbf{W_t}) = P_k(\mathbf{X}|\mathbf{W_t}) \tag{3.28}$$

for $k = 1,...,K$. Conditional independence cannot generally occur when $\mathbf{Z}$ itself is created as a function of $\mathbf{X}$, as in $\bar{Z}_p$ defined above. Other situations might lead to conditional independence, however. If $\mathbf{Z}$ is created from an item set that does not overlap with the items in $\mathbf{X}$ in a study of item bias, then conditional independence of $\mathbf{X}$ and $\mathbf{Z}$ may hold if both sets of items fit a common latent variable model with the target latent variable. Another situation that might lead to independence would arise if $\mathbf{Z}$ is chosen as a set of external measures, such as scores on one or more tests that purport to measure $\mathbf{W}_t$. Conditional independence will then hold to the extent that the variables $(\mathbf{X}, \mathbf{Z})$ meet the traditional conditional independence assumption, given $\mathbf{W}_t$.

Given conditional independence in Equation 3.28, Meredith and Millsap (1992, Theorem 4) showed that for the case of a discrete $\mathbf{W}_t$, if both $\mathbf{X}$ and $\mathbf{Z}$ are measurement invariant with respect to $\mathbf{W}_t$ for the populations under study, then we must have

$$P_k(\mathbf{X}|\mathbf{Z}) \neq P(\mathbf{X}|\mathbf{Z}) \tag{3.29}$$

for some values of k. In other words, OCI will fail to hold even though no bias is present in either $\mathbf{X}$ or $\mathbf{Z}$. This situation is an example of a case in which the investigation of measurement bias via OCI may lead to spurious findings of bias. The proof in Meredith and Millsap (1992) was limited to the discrete latent variable case. If $\mathbf{W}_t$ is continuous, a similar theorem can be proved. The theorem (Theorem 3.3) and its proof are given in the Appendix.

Theorem 3.3 says that if both $\mathbf{X}$ and $\mathbf{Z}$ are measurement invariant, and if these variables are conditionally independent given $\mathbf{W}_t$ and $\mathbf{V}$, we cannot have OCI for $\mathbf{X}$ and $\mathbf{Z}$. Tests of OCI will tend to indicate failure of invariance when in fact no bias is present in either $\mathbf{X}$ or $\mathbf{Z}$. The theorem is quite general and does not depend on any particular form for the MRF of $\mathbf{X}$ or $\mathbf{Z}$. The theorem does require that neither $\mathbf{Z}$ nor $\mathbf{W}_t$ be independent of $\mathbf{V}$. This requirement is trivial in most bias investigations, as population differences in both the distributions of the matching variable $\mathbf{Z}$ and the target latent variable $\mathbf{W}_t$ are typically hypothesized to exist. Population differences on $\mathbf{Z}$ are testable directly, and population differences on $\mathbf{W}_t$ are usually assumed to exist.

One immediate application of Theorem 3.3 lies in the practical question of whether to include the studied item in the total score $\mathbf{Z}$ in studies of item bias (Holland & Thayer, 1988; Zwick, 1990). If the set of items are conditionally independent given $\mathbf{W}_t$, with $\mathbf{Z}$ defined as the total score omitting the jth studied item X_j, then it must be true that $\mathbf{Z}$ and X_j are conditionally independent. If in addition we have measurement invariance for all items, Theorem 3.3 establishes that OCI cannot hold for X_j in relation to $\mathbf{Z}$. Observed-score methods such as the Mantel–Haenszel will tend to indicate bias in X_j where none exists. An easy solution to this problem is to include the studied item in the total score $\mathbf{Z}$, as is standard practice.

A further application of Theorem 3.3 would lie in the use of external variables in $\mathbf{Z}$, or variables that are not functions of the measures $\mathbf{X}$ that are under study. For example, $\mathbf{Z}$ could consist of a battery of test scores that are thought to measure $\mathbf{W}_t$, yet are different from $\mathbf{X}$. The variables in $\mathbf{Z}$ might be chosen because previous research has found them to be relatively free of bias, and hence these variables are logical candidates for use as proxies for $\mathbf{W}_t$. To the extent that the combined set of variables $(\mathbf{X}, \mathbf{Z})$ are truly measures of $\mathbf{W}_t$ and also fulfill conditional independence given $\mathbf{W}_t$, Theorem 3.3 suggests that OCI will fail for $\mathbf{X}$ in relation to $\mathbf{Z}$ even when no measurement bias is present. Relatively few bias investigations use external measures in this way at present, and so this phenomenon has not been frequently encountered.

The conditional independence between $\mathbf{X}$ and $\mathbf{Z}$ in Equation 3.28 generally precludes Bayes sufficiency of $\mathbf{Z}$ for $\mathbf{W}_t$ (Meredith & Millsap, 1992). To see this intuitively, consider the case in which $\mathbf{X}$ and $\mathbf{Z}$ represent disjoint subsets of items, all of which measure $\mathbf{W}_t$. In general, $\mathbf{Z}$ will not include all of the information in $\mathbf{X}$ that is relevant to $\mathbf{W}_t$ in this situation, and so Bayes sufficiency of $\mathbf{Z}$ will not hold. An exception to this rule would arise if the number of items in $\mathbf{Z}$ increases, as noted earlier. In the limit, the joint distribution of $(\mathbf{Z}, \mathbf{W}_t)$ becomes nearly degenerate, and $\mathbf{Z}$ approaches Bayes sufficiency in relation to $\mathbf{W}_t$. The number of items in $\mathbf{Z}$ needed to achieve Bayes sufficiency will depend on the nature of the latent variable model.

The conditional independence required by Theorem 3.3 is implied by many latent variable models when $\mathbf{X}$ and $\mathbf{Z}$ represent disjoint measures or sets of measures. Most IRT models imply conditional independence, for example, as noted in Chapter 2. Results similar to that given by Theorem 3.3 are obtainable under weaker assumptions, however, depending on the model. Suppose that $p = 1$, so that X is a single measured variable, and let $\mathbf{Z}$ represent a set of measures different from X. Suppose also that $(X, \mathbf{Z})$ jointly fit a common factor model with common factors $\mathbf{W}_t$ in K populations. Under this model, X and $\mathbf{Z}$ are conditionally uncorrelated given $\mathbf{W}_t$, but need not be independent. Finally, assume that second-order measurement invariance holds for $(X, \mathbf{Z})$, or that

$$E_k(X, \mathbf{Z} | \mathbf{W}_t) = E(X, \mathbf{Z} | \mathbf{W}_t), \tag{3.30}$$

$$\mathrm{Cov}_k(X, \mathbf{Z} | \mathbf{W}_t) = \mathrm{Cov}(X, \mathbf{Z} | \mathbf{W}_t) \tag{3.31}$$

for $k = 1, \ldots, K$. Then if $\mathrm{Cov}_k(\mathbf{W}_t)$ varies over k, it will generally be true that

$$E_k(X | \mathbf{Z}) \neq E(X | \mathbf{Z}) \tag{3.32}$$

for some k (Millsap, 1997, 1998). OCI fails to hold in this situation even though both X and Z fulfill second-order measurement invariance. Parallel results hold when X and Z satisfy only first-order measurement invariance. The implication of these results is that when X and Z fit a common factor model, observed variable methods for studying bias that use Z as a proxy for W_t may lead to erroneous conclusions of bias.

To summarize, conditional independence between X and Z, given W_t, places limits on the use of OCI as an approach to investigating measurement invariance. As a practical matter, many applications of OCI strategies will employ a proxy variable Z that includes X, as when Z is the sum of the item scores including items in X. In this case of inclusion, conditional independence will not hold, and the results of this section will not apply. On the other hand, when X and Z are disjoint measures, as when X consists of item scores and Z contains external measures, conditional independence may hold. For example, if (X, Z) fit a common factor model with common factors W_t under the usual multivariate normality assumptions, conditional independence will hold. As shown in Chapter 9, the conditional independence results also have implications for the use of tests in prediction, and for group differences in prediction equations given measurement invariance.

Appendix

Proof of Theorem 3.1

For the kth population, we can express the measurement response function $P_k(X|W_t)$ as

$$P_k(X|W_t) = \frac{\int P(X|W_t, W_n) g_k(W_t, W_n) dW_n}{\int g_k(W_t, W_n) dW_n}, \qquad (3.A.1)$$

where the integration is understood to be multiple. Given that we can factor the joint density $g_k(W_t, W_n) = g_k(W_n|W_t) g_k(W_t)$, we can reduce the above expression to

$$P_k(X|W_t) = \frac{\int P(X|W_t, W_n) g_k(W_n|W_t) dW_n}{\int g_k(W_n|W_t) dW_n} \qquad (3.A.2)$$

and so unless the condition of the theorem holds (i.e., that $g_k(W_n|W_t)$ varies over k), the measurement response function must be invariant, and no measurement bias exists for X in that case. ∎

Theorem 3.3

Here we state and prove a theorem that establishes violations of OCI under measurement invariance for $\mathbf{Z}$ and $\mathbf{X}$ when $\mathbf{Z}$ and $\mathbf{X}$ are conditionally independent given the target latent variable $\mathbf{W_t}$. We begin with the following Lemma, which is useful for the proof of the theorem to follow.

Lemma 3.1

Let $\mathbf{Z}$, $\mathbf{W}$, and $\mathbf{V}$ be possibly multivariate random variables, with $\mathbf{Z}$ and $\mathbf{V}$ being discrete and $\mathbf{W}$ being continuous, and let the conditional probabilities $P(\mathbf{Z}|\mathbf{W}, \mathbf{V})$ and $P(\mathbf{W}|\mathbf{Z}, \mathbf{V})$ be well defined. Then if both

$$P(\mathbf{Z}|\mathbf{W},\mathbf{V})=P(\mathbf{Z}|\mathbf{W}), \quad P(\mathbf{W}|\mathbf{Z},\mathbf{V})=P(\mathbf{W}|\mathbf{Z}), \tag{3.A.3}$$

it must be true that $\mathbf{Z}$ and $\mathbf{W}$ are each marginally independent from $\mathbf{V}$, or that

$$P(\mathbf{V})=P(\mathbf{V}|\mathbf{Z})=P(\mathbf{V}|\mathbf{W}). \tag{3.A.4}$$

Proof
From Equation 3.A.3, we must have both

$$P(\mathbf{V}|\mathbf{W},\mathbf{Z})=P(\mathbf{V}|\mathbf{W}), \quad P(\mathbf{V}|\mathbf{Z},\mathbf{W})=P(\mathbf{V}|\mathbf{Z}), \tag{3.A.5}$$

implying that $P(\mathbf{V}|\mathbf{W}) = P(\mathbf{V}|\mathbf{Z})$ for all $\mathbf{Z}$, $\mathbf{W}$, and $\mathbf{V}$. But the latter equality implies that

$$P(\mathbf{V})=\int P(\mathbf{V},\mathbf{W})d\mathbf{W}=\int P(\mathbf{V}|\mathbf{Z})P(\mathbf{W})d\mathbf{W}=P(\mathbf{V}|\mathbf{Z}), \tag{3.A.6}$$

where the integration is multiple. Note that the expression after the second equality follows from Equation 3.A.5. We also have

$$P(\mathbf{V})=\sum_{Z} P(\mathbf{V},\mathbf{Z})=\sum_{Z} P(\mathbf{V}|\mathbf{W})P(\mathbf{Z})=P(\mathbf{V}|\mathbf{W}), \tag{3.A.7}$$

where the summation is across all values of $\mathbf{Z}$. ∎

Versions of Lemma 3.1 for completely continuous or completely discrete random variables can be proven, but the particular mixture of discrete and continuous variables was chosen to match the variables used in the following theorem.

Theorem 3.3

Let the following conditions hold for the measured variables $(\mathbf{X}, \mathbf{Z})$ and the target latent variables $\mathbf{W}_t$:

$$P(\mathbf{X}|\mathbf{Z}, \mathbf{W}_t, \mathbf{V}) = P(\mathbf{X}|\mathbf{W}_t, \mathbf{V}), \qquad (3.A.8)$$

$$P(\mathbf{Z}|\mathbf{W}_t, \mathbf{V}) = P(\mathbf{Z}|\mathbf{W}_t), \qquad (3.A.9)$$

$$P(\mathbf{X}|\mathbf{W}_t, \mathbf{V}) = P(\mathbf{X}|\mathbf{W}_t). \qquad (3.A.10)$$

Also, suppose that neither $\mathbf{W}_t$ nor $\mathbf{Z}$ are independent of $\mathbf{V}$. Then $P(\mathbf{X}|\mathbf{Z}, \mathbf{V}) \neq P(\mathbf{X}|\mathbf{Z})$.

Proof
Equations 3.A.8 through 3.A.10 imply that

$$P(\mathbf{X}, \mathbf{Z}|\mathbf{V}) = \int P(\mathbf{X}|\mathbf{W}_t)P(\mathbf{W}_t|\mathbf{Z}, \mathbf{V})d\mathbf{W}_t, \qquad (3.A.11)$$

where the integral is understood to be multiple. Dividing the above by $P(\mathbf{Z}|\mathbf{V})$, where this probability is nonzero, leads to

$$P(\mathbf{X}|\mathbf{Z}, \mathbf{V}) = \int P(\mathbf{X}|\mathbf{W}_t)P(\mathbf{W}_t|\mathbf{Z}, \mathbf{V})d\mathbf{W}_t. \qquad (3.A.12)$$

Note that given Lemma 3.1 and the conditions of the theorem, we cannot have $P(\mathbf{W}_t|\mathbf{Z}, \mathbf{V}) = P(\mathbf{W}_t|\mathbf{Z})$.

Now suppose that the conclusion of the theorem is not true or that $P(\mathbf{X}|\mathbf{Z}, \mathbf{V}) = P(\mathbf{X}|\mathbf{Z})$. Then

$$P(\mathbf{X}|\mathbf{Z}, \mathbf{V}) = P(\mathbf{X}|\mathbf{Z}) = \int P(\mathbf{X}, \mathbf{W}_t|\mathbf{Z}, \mathbf{V})d\mathbf{W}_t. \qquad (3.A.13)$$

Because $P(\mathbf{X}, \mathbf{W}_t|\mathbf{Z}, \mathbf{V}) = P(\mathbf{X}|\mathbf{W}_t)P(\mathbf{W}_t|\mathbf{Z}, \mathbf{V})$ under the conditions of the theorem, and because we know that $P(\mathbf{W}_t|\mathbf{Z}, \mathbf{V}) \neq P(\mathbf{W}_t|\mathbf{Z})$, we cannot have $P(\mathbf{X}, \mathbf{W}_t|\mathbf{Z}, \mathbf{V}) = P(\mathbf{X}, \mathbf{W}_t|\mathbf{Z})$. Also, we know that

$$P(\mathbf{X}|\mathbf{Z}) = \int P(\mathbf{X}, \mathbf{W}_t|\mathbf{Z})d\mathbf{W}_t. \qquad (3.A.14)$$

Hence, it must be true that

$$\int P(\mathbf{X}, \mathbf{W_t} \mid \mathbf{Z}) d\mathbf{W_t} = \int P(\mathbf{X}, \mathbf{W_t} \mid \mathbf{Z}, \mathbf{V}) d\mathbf{W_t} \tag{3.A.15}$$

or

$$\int [P(\mathbf{X}, \mathbf{W_t} \mid \mathbf{Z}) - P(\mathbf{X}, \mathbf{W_t} \mid \mathbf{Z}, \mathbf{V})] d\mathbf{W_t} = 0 \tag{3.A.16}$$

for all $\mathbf{X}$, $\mathbf{Z}$, and $\mathbf{V}$. Letting $P(\mathbf{X}, \mathbf{W_t}|\mathbf{Z}) = P(\mathbf{X}, \mathbf{W_t}|\mathbf{Z}, \mathbf{V})$ for the value of $\mathbf{V}$ that defines the kth population, Equation 3.A.16 implies that $P_j(\mathbf{X}, \mathbf{W_t}|\mathbf{Z}) = P_k(\mathbf{X}, \mathbf{W_t}|\mathbf{Z})$ for all j, k. But this is a contradiction because we know that $P(\mathbf{X}, \mathbf{W_t}|\mathbf{Z}, \mathbf{V}) \neq P(\mathbf{X}, \mathbf{W_t}|\mathbf{Z})$ for at least one value of $\mathbf{V}$. ∎

4

The Factor Model and Factorial Invariance

Current latent variable methods for investigating measurement bias have their roots in early work on *factorial invariance*. The question of factorial invariance concerns the extent to which the factor structure underlying the measured variables is the same across multiple populations. The invariance question can also be posed with respect to multiple occasions of measurement in longitudinal research, or even multiple sets of measures from a common domain, but these extensions will not concern us here. Early studies of factorial invariance employed exploratory factor analysis (EFA), combined with rotational procedures designed to bring the factor pattern matrices into congruence (Ahmavaara, 1954; Meredith, 1964; Thomson & Lederman, 1939; Thurstone, 1947). The development of restricted or confirmatory factor analysis (CFA) now permits a wider range of invariance hypotheses to be tested, including restrictions on unique factor variances and on mean structures. More recently, procedures for handling discrete measured variables have been extended to multiple populations, enabling the testing of invariance hypotheses in such data (Browne & Arminger, 1995; Christoffersson, 1975; Muthén, 1978, 1984). This extension permits the CFA to more properly address invariance at the level of individual test items.

This chapter and the next chapter describe the use of the common factor model in the investigation of measurement bias. This chapter focuses on the traditional case of a continuously measured variable **X**. Although few psychological measures are truly continuous in practice, factor models for continuous measures are often used as approximations. Chapter 5 considers the use of the factor model in discrete data, such as responses to individual test items. Both chapters emphasize the use of CFA because of its versatility as a tool for testing hypotheses about factorial invariance.

The emphasis placed on CFA requires the investigator to have some understanding of the factor structure for **X** before investigating factorial invariance. If the intended factor structure of the measured variables in the reference population is not understood, tests of hypotheses about factorial invariance are probably premature. For example, the number of target latent variables or factors that underlie **X** in the reference population should be specified. The investigator should have some sense of the measured variables that are most closely related to each of these factors. These preliminary ideas about the intended factor structure may later be found to be incorrect for some populations. We may find that unanticipated factors arise in certain populations or that the measured variables do not array themselves in the same pattern of loadings across populations.

We begin this chapter with a description of the common factor model in multiple populations. Issues of model identification and estimation are discussed with reference to this multiple-population case. The multiple-population case raises some new issues with respect to identification, and the relationship between identification and tests of invariance. The evaluation of model fit is discussed next. A nested series of model fit evaluations is described for testing invariance hypotheses. The series of models represent a series of increasingly stringent invariance restrictions. These fit evaluations are illustrated using data on the Wechsler adult intelligence scale-revised (WAIS-R). An Appendix to the chapter discusses the topic of selection into subpopulations and the effects of selection on factorial invariance. This topic is advanced, but selection theorems motivated much of the early work on factorial invariance, and so the topic is important from a historical perspective.

The Common Factor Model in Multiple Populations

A brief outline of the common factor model was given in Chapter 2. Here we consider the model in greater depth, extending it to multiple populations $\Pi_k, k = 1, 2, \ldots, K$. Model parameters will be subscripted to denote values specific to a given population. Initially, random variables such as the measured variables in X will not be subscripted by population. It is to be understood that all random variables are defined for multiple populations and may have distributions that depend on these populations.

The common factor model expresses the scores on the jth continuously measured variable X_j as a linear function of r common factor scores and a single unique factor score

$$X_j = \tau_{jk} + \sum_{m=1}^{r} \lambda_{jmk} W_m + U_j, \qquad (4.1)$$

where
   τ_{jk} is a latent intercept parameter for the jth measured variable in the kth population
   $\lambda_{jmk}, m = 1, \ldots, r$ are the factor pattern parameters for the jth measured variable corresponding to the r common factors in the kth population
   W_m are the common factor score variables for the r factors
   U_j is the unique factor score variable for the jth measured variable

Letting $\mathbf{W}' = (W_1, W_2, \ldots, W_r)$ and $\mathbf{U}' = (U_1, U_2, \ldots, U_p)$, we can define the following moments with respect to the kth population

$$E_k(\mathbf{W})=\boldsymbol{\kappa}_k, \quad \mathrm{Cov}_k(\mathbf{W})=\boldsymbol{\Phi}_k, \quad E_k(\mathbf{U})=\mathbf{0}, \quad \mathrm{Cov}_k(\mathbf{U})=\boldsymbol{\Theta}_k \qquad (4.2)$$

with $\boldsymbol{\Theta}_k$ ordinarily taken as a $p \times p$ diagonal matrix. It is also typically assumed that $\mathrm{Cov}_k(\mathbf{W}, \mathbf{U}) = \mathbf{0}$, an $r \times p$ null matrix. This assumption, together with the uncorrelated nature of the unique factors, reflects the idea that only the common factors account for the associations among the measured variable $\mathbf{X}$.

From the above assumptions, we can express the conditional mean and covariance structure for $\mathbf{X}$ given $\mathbf{W}$ in the kth population as

$$E_k(\mathbf{X}\,|\,\mathbf{W})=\boldsymbol{\tau}_k +\boldsymbol{\Lambda}_k\mathbf{W}, \quad \mathrm{Cov}_k(\mathbf{X}\,|\,\mathbf{W})=\boldsymbol{\Theta}_k, \qquad (4.3)$$

where $\boldsymbol{\tau}'_k =(\tau_{1k}, \tau_{2k}, \ldots, \tau_{pk})$ and $\boldsymbol{\Lambda}_k$ is the complete $p \times r$ factor pattern matrix whose element in the jth row and mth column is λ_{jmk}. The conditional moments in Equation 4.3 play a central role in the MRF for the factor model. Studies of factorial invariance focus on the parameters $\boldsymbol{\tau}_k$, $\boldsymbol{\Lambda}_k$, and $\boldsymbol{\Theta}_k$ to investigate their invariance across populations. The unconditional moments for the measured variables $\mathbf{X}$ are expressed as

$$E_k(\mathbf{X})=\boldsymbol{\mu}_{Xk}=\boldsymbol{\tau}_k + \boldsymbol{\Lambda}_k\boldsymbol{\kappa}_k, \quad \mathrm{Cov}_k(\mathbf{X})=\boldsymbol{\Sigma}_{Xk}=\boldsymbol{\Lambda}_k\boldsymbol{\Phi}\boldsymbol{\Lambda}'_k + \boldsymbol{\Theta}_k. \qquad (4.4)$$

Note that the common factor mean vector $\boldsymbol{\kappa}_k$ and covariance matrix $\boldsymbol{\Phi}_k$ do not appear in the expressions for the conditional moments but do appear unconditionally.

Before proceeding, it is worth noting that investigations of factorial invariance in the continuous case should be based on analyses of the covariance and mean structures, rather than correlation matrices. Single-population EFA in psychology is often conducted using the correlation matrix for $\mathbf{X}$ because the scales of the measured variables are arbitrary in many cases. Most CFA software is designed for the analysis of the covariance matrix however, and so analyses based on the correlation matrix can raise some difficulties (Cudeck, 1989). In the multiple-population case, the use of correlation matrices creates additional problems because the implicit population-specific standardizations implied by the correlation metric may obscure any invariant factor structure. For example, population differences in factor covariance matrices $\boldsymbol{\Phi}_k$ will create population differences in the diagonal elements of $\boldsymbol{\Sigma}_{Xk}$ even if the factor structure is invariant in other respects. As a result, the rescaling used to create correlation matrices in each population will be population-specific, and the resulting correlation matrices may not be well approximated by an invariant factor model. This entire problem is avoided by basing the analyses on the covariance matrices.

The factor model provides a structure for the conditional moments of **X**, but further distributional assumptions are frequently adopted once parameter estimation and fit evaluation are considered. The most common approach is to assume that (**W**, **U**) are multivariate normal (MVN) with moments given in Equation 4.2, leading to an MVN distribution for **X** with moments given in Equation 4.4. In the multiple-population case, these assumptions can be extended to all populations. As noted earlier, these assumptions imply that **W** and **U** are statistically independent, as are the elements of **U**. Weaker distributional assumptions for (**W**, **U**) and **X** are considered when the MVN distribution is implausible, and fit evaluation procedures under these weaker assumptions are available, as discussed later.

The Role of Unique Factors

The unique factor score variable U_j in Equation 4.1 can be further divided as

$$U_j = U_{ej} + U_{sj},$$
(4.5)

where

    U_{ej} is an error score that represents classical measurement error
    U_{sj} is a specific factor score that represents a reliable but unique source of variance (Lord & Novick, 1968)

As this partitioning reveals, the unique factors are not necessarily solely a function of measurement error, but rather a composite of different sources of variance unique to the measured variable. Across multiple populations, these different sources of variance may also have different invariance properties.

Consider first some assumptions typically made about U_{ej} and U_{sj} in a single population. First, the error scores are assumed to be mutually uncorrelated and also uncorrelated with the specific factors:

$$\text{Cov}(U_{ej}, U_{sj}) = \text{Cov}(U_{ej}, U_{ej'}) = 0$$
(4.6)

for all j, j'. Second, the specific factors are also assumed to be mutually uncorrelated:

$$\text{Cov}(U_{sj}, U_{sj'}) = 0$$
(4.7)

leading to

$$\text{Var}(U_j) = \theta_j = \theta_{ej} + \theta_{sj}.$$
(4.8)

Here θ_{ej}, θ_{sj} are the variances of U_{ej}, U_{sj}. Letting $\boldsymbol{\Theta}_{ek}$ and $\boldsymbol{\Theta}_{sk}$ be the diagonal matrices whose diagonal elements are θ_{ej} and θ_{sj}, respectively, we have

$$\boldsymbol{\Theta} = \boldsymbol{\Theta}_{ek} + \boldsymbol{\Theta}_{sk}, \tag{4.9}$$

under the above assumptions. With regard to mean structure, it is typically assumed that $E(U_{ej}) = 0$, implying from Equation 4.2 that $E(U_{sj}) = 0$. Beyond checking for the diagonal structure for $\boldsymbol{\Theta}_{k}$, it is difficult to verify any of these assumptions in measurements taken on a single occasion.

In the multiple-population case, the above assumptions about the behavior of the specific factors may be less tenable. Consider first the mean structure. We might plausibly permit

$$E_k(U_{sj}) = \tau_{sjk} \neq 0. \tag{4.10}$$

We can then rewrite Equation 4.3 as

$$E_k(\mathbf{X} \mid \mathbf{W}) = \boldsymbol{\tau}_k + \boldsymbol{\Lambda}_k \mathbf{W} + \boldsymbol{\tau}_{sk} = \boldsymbol{\tau}_k^* + \boldsymbol{\Lambda}_k \mathbf{W}. \tag{4.11}$$

Here we have $\boldsymbol{\tau}'_{sk} = [\tau_{s1k}, \tau_{s2k}, \dots, \tau_{spk}]$. The mean of the unique factor is absorbed into the intercept. Even if the original intercept is invariant (i.e., $\boldsymbol{\tau}_k = \boldsymbol{\tau}$ for all k), the specific factor means will lead to apparent violations of intercept invariance whenever these means vary across populations. This phenomenon is one explanation for group differences in intercepts. For example, suppose that $\mathbf{X}$ is a vector of WAIS subtest scores and that the specific factors are method effects due to the particular item types used in each subtest. For example, the Digit Symbol subtest is a coding test that is given under timed conditions. Here the combination of unusual item content (i.e., coding symbols) and strict timing may produce specific variance. These method effects might not be identical across populations. The impact of the strict timing may vary across cultures or across age groups, for example. In this case, we might expect the specific factor means to differ across populations. This difference would be manifested as a group difference in intercepts. In practice, it will usually not be possible to separately identify the intercept $\boldsymbol{\tau}_k$ and the specific mean $\boldsymbol{\tau}_{sk}$.

Another plausible feature of the multiple-population case is that the specific factor covariance matrix $\boldsymbol{\Theta}_{sk}$ may vary over populations. Given that the specific factors are reliable sources of variance, there is no reason why these factors must have variances that remain the same in all populations. Population differences in the specific factor covariance matrices $\boldsymbol{\Theta}_{sk}$ will in turn lead to population differences in the unique factor covariance matrices $\boldsymbol{\Theta}_{k}$. A further generalization is possible if nonzero covariances in $\boldsymbol{\Theta}_{sk}$ are permitted in some or all populations. Depending on the configuration of these nonzero covariances, the covariances may form the basis for additional "common factors" in some populations. Returning to the WAIS example, suppose that a subset of the measured variables involves a common method of measurement. The Digit Span, Digit Symbol, and Arithmetic subtests each involve simple numerical stimulus material, along with some demands on short-term memory in completing the items. In some populations, these common features may be relatively unimportant in determining examinee performance, and in other populations, the features may confer an advantage, or a disadvantage, to the examinees. In this case, we might find that in the first set of populations, Θ_{sk} is a diagonal matrix. In the second set of populations, the specific factors have nonzero covariances for Digit Span, Digit Symbol, and Arithmetic that reflect the shared influence of the common features of measurement. If we fit the traditional factor model with uncorrelated unique factors in all populations, the nonzero covariances in Θ_{sk} may alternatively be represented by an additional common factor in some populations. For the WAIS example, an additional common factor would simply require that the 3×3 submatrix of Θ_{sk} for the variables Digit Span, Digit Symbol, and Arithmetic be reproduced via a single factor model. This hypothetical example illustrates how the emergence of new common factors in some populations might arise.

More generally, when the separate populations under study can be considered to be selected from some parent population in which the traditional common factor model holds, specific factors may lead to misfit of the same common factor model in the selected subpopulations. For example, suppose that in the parent population, the common and specific factors are uncorrelated. In the selected subpopulations, the correlations between the common and specific factors may be nonzero, leading to misfit of the factor model (Bloxom, 1972; Muthén, 1989). We will return to this topic when we discuss selection below.

Identification

The common factor model is not identified without further restrictions because there are an infinite number of matrices and vectors $(\tau_k, \kappa_k, \Lambda_k, \Phi_k, \Theta_k)$ that will reproduce the structure in Equation 4.4. The global identification problem in factor analysis is to find constraints on $(\tau_k, \kappa_k, \Lambda_k, \Phi_k, \Theta_k)$ that are sufficient to uniquely define these parameters given (Σ_{Xk}, μ_{Xk}) and that are minimal in some sense. The latter provision is necessary, as it will always be possible to uniquely define the parameters given sufficient constraints, but the constraints may also imply a reproduced moment structure that is ill-fitted to the data. The global identification problem is not fully solved, although results are available in special cases (Algina, 1980; Anderson & Rubin, 1956; Bekker, 1986; Bekker & ten Berge, 1997; Dunn, 1973; Howe, 1955; Jennrich, 1978; Jöreskog, 1979; McDonald & Krane, 1977, 1979; Shapiro, 1985), and general algorithmic methods are available (Bekker, Merckens, & Wansbeek, 1994). When multiple populations are considered, new possibilities for identification arise because constraints that operate across populations can be introduced. A full treatment of the identification problem in factor analysis will not be attempted here, and instead we will focus on issues that are especially relevant for bias applications.

Part of the global identification problem lies in the nonuniqueness of the factor pattern and covariance matrices Λ_k and Φ_k. Assuming that Θ_k is known, let $\mathbf{T}$ be an $r \times r$ nonsingular matrix, and define $\Lambda_k^* = \Lambda_k \mathbf{T}$ and $\Phi_k^* = \mathbf{T}^{-1} \Phi_k \mathbf{T}^{-1'}$. Then we have

$$\Sigma_{Xk} - \Theta_k = \Lambda_k \Phi_k \Lambda'_k = \Lambda_k^* \Phi_k^* \Lambda_k^{*'} \tag{4.12}$$

and it is clear that even if Θ_k is known, Λ_k and Φ_k are not uniquely defined. This problem has been labelled the "rotational uniqueness" problem, to distinguish it from the wider global identification problem of which it is a part (Bollen & Jöreskog, 1985). The "rotation" problem in EFA is essentially the rotational uniqueness problem. We will discuss the available results on rotational uniqueness and their use in multiple-population models and then return to the global identification problem.

Rotational Uniqueness

Within the kth population, the rotational uniqueness problem can be solved by imposing r^2 constraints on the elements of Λ_k and/or Φ_k. Approaches for the placement of these constraints have been discussed by Jöreskog (1979), Algina (1980), Bekker (1986), and Howe (1955). EFA software solves this problem by automatically adopting constraints that are hidden from the user. For example, principal factor analysis typically sets $\Phi_k = \mathbf{I}_r$, an $r \times r$ identity matrix, and $\Lambda'_k \Lambda_k = \mathbf{D}_{rk}$, an $r \times r$ diagonal matrix. Maximum likelihood factor analysis often adopts $\Phi_k = \mathbf{I}_r$ and $\Lambda'_k \Theta_k^{-1} \Lambda_k = \mathbf{D}_{rk}$. The constraints in EFA are adopted to obtain an initial solution, after which further rotations may be applied. As discussed below, the unwitting use of EFA software in separate analyses within multiple populations can interfere with investigations of factorial invariance due to the above constraints.

In CFA, the constraints needed to resolve the rotational uniqueness problem can be chosen by the investigator, although some software programs have default constraints that are in force if the investigator fails to choose. For multiple-population studies, one can apply the constraints needed for a single population repeatedly within each additional population. Although one could vary the placement of these constraints across populations, there will rarely be a compelling need to do so (one such case will be reviewed below). Furthermore, variations in the placements of the constraints across populations may interfere with later attempts to fit models under invariance constraints.

To illustrate, one approach to constraining Λ_k and Φ_k to achieve uniqueness would be to select r rows of Λ_k to fix as rows of an $r \times r$ identity matrix I_r. The r rows are selected so that the placement of the fixed unit value corresponds to the desired marker or reference variable for each of the r factors. No constraints are introduced for Φ_k. Extending this to multiple populations, one would select the *same* r rows to constrain for $k = 1,\ldots,K$. Note that the result of this choice is to create r^2 constraints in each of the K populations. It is assumed here that the model of interest specifies r common factors in each population. Modifications would be required if the number of factors is permitted to vary across populations. The above approach to achieving uniqueness will be denoted the "oblique factor" approach because these constraints permit the r factors to covary. An alternative version of this approach would proceed as described, except that the fixed unit elements would be placed along the diagonal of Φ_k, instead of appearing in Λ_k. The elements that would have been fixed to unit values in Λ_k are simply freed, but all elements that were fixed to zero values are retained. This option standardizes the factors. The option is of less interest in multiple group invariance studies because as described earlier, the standardization of the factors within each group can interfere with the goal of finding invariant structure.

A second general specification that would achieve uniqueness, while yielding fit statistics that are ordinarily identical to the oblique factor approach, employs constraints on Φ_k to create orthogonal factors. There are at least two variants of this specification. The first variant would fix $\Phi_k = I_r$ for $k = 1,\ldots,K$, and then would also fix $r(r-1)/2$ elements of each Λ_k to values of zero. The placement of these constraints should be such that each Λ_k can be represented (possibly after appropriate permutations of rows and columns) as

$$\Lambda_k = \begin{bmatrix} \Lambda_k^1 \\ \Lambda_k^2 \end{bmatrix} \tag{4.13}$$

with Λ_k^1 being an $r \times r$ submatrix whose upper triangular elements are all zeroes. The placement of these zeroes can be identical across populations. The second variant would restrict $\Phi_k = D_r$, an $r \times r$ diagonal matrix, for $k = 1,\ldots,K$. Within each Λ_k, $r(r + 1)/2$ additional constraints would be needed, including one nonzero fixed element in each column of Λ_k. From Equation 4.6, these constraints could be implemented by fixing the diagonal elements of Λ_k^1 to unit values, while fixing the upper triangular elements to zeroes. These two methods will both be denoted "orthogonal factor" methods of achieving uniqueness, given the uncorrelated factors produced by the methods.

A distinct disadvantage of the orthogonal factor methods when applied in multiple populations is that the requirement of orthogonality may conflict with later attempts to fit models that specify invariant pattern matrices. The nature of the problem is revealed by counting the number of additional constraints needed to achieve invariant pattern matrices. Assume that the same placement of constraints is adopted in all populations. In the first variant of the orthogonal factor method, the number of additional constraints needed to achieve invariant pattern matrices (i.e., $\Lambda_k = \Lambda$ for $k = 1,...,K$) is $(K-1)(pr - (r(r-1)/2))$. By contrast, if the oblique factor method is adopted, the number of additional constraints needed for pattern invariance is only $(K-1)(pr - r^2)$. The difference is that the oblique factor method requires $(K-1)(r(r+1)/2)$ fewer constraints to achieve pattern invariance. The implication is that it will be more difficult to fit an invariant pattern model if simultaneous orthogonality is also required for all populations. Note that this result extends to the usual situation in EFA in which separate analyses within each population are done under requirements of orthogonality. Given that the factor covariance matrices are not part of the MRF for the factor model (see Equation 4.3), requirements of orthogonality across populations should be avoided if pattern invariance is sought.

All of the above constraints for uniqueness require that some elements of Λ_k be fixed to zero values. A natural question to ask is whether varying placements of these fixed elements will alter the fit of the model or estimates of the model parameters. Model parameter estimates will be affected by the placement of the constraints because changes in placement produce different rescalings of the remaining nonzero elements of Λ_k. In most cases, the fit of the model will be unaltered by the placement of the constraints, but exceptions do occur. Millsap (2001) presents several examples in which changing constraint placements led to very different fit results. Further problems can arise if the number of factors is misspecified.

In addition to the oblique and orthogonal factor methods above, a third approach to achieving rotational uniqueness makes explicit use of invariance constraints. In this approach, invariance of the pattern matrices is first required: $\Lambda_k = \Lambda$ for $k = 1,...,K$. Second, it is assumed that a sufficient number of fixed zero elements in Λ have been imposed to render Λ unique. This number is $r(r - 1)$. No fixed nonzero constraints are required for Λ. Finally, for some chosen value of k, it is required that $\text{diag}(\Phi_k) = \mathbf{I}$. The factor variances in a single group are fixed to unit values. Taken together, these three sets of constraints are sufficient for rotational uniqueness in all populations. The constraints are more stringent than those required by the oblique factor method described earlier, due to the invariance requirements. The constraints do provide a useful starting point for specification searches that seek to identify which loadings are invariant, as described below.

A fundamentally different approach to attaining uniqueness, and one that exceeds the constraint levels of some of the foregoing alternatives, is based on the notion of "parallel proportional profiles," or the "confactor" model, as developed by Cattell (1944, 1966a, 1972; Cattell & Cattell, 1955). A more recent treatment of this model can be found in McArdle and Cattell (1994). The concept underlying this approach is that to the extent that the factor pattern is invariant across populations, a unique orientation for the factors can be achieved by imposing proportionality among the factors across at least a subset of the populations. Invariance constraints on the pattern matrices are combined with orthogonality restrictions within a subset of the populations to achieve uniqueness.

The confactor approach can be simply illustrated for the $K = 2$ case. Assume here that the pattern matrices are constrained to invariance: $\Lambda_1 = \Lambda_2 = \Lambda$. The confactor approach then sets $\Phi_1 = I_r$ and $\Phi_2 = D_r$, constraining both matrices to orthogonality but permitting the factor variances to vary. No constraints are placed on Λ, apart from invariance. The invariance constraints, combined with the orthogonality constraints, are sufficient to resolve the rotational uniqueness problem. The approach does not require the investigator to identify any marker or reference variables in Λ.

A difficulty with the confactor approach is that in assuming invariance, the approach exceeds the number of constraints necessary to attain rotational uniqueness. In the $K = 2$ case, the confactor method imposes $r(p - r)$ additional constraints beyond those imposed by the oblique factor method. For the case in which the pattern matrices are truly invariant, the additional constraints should not degrade the fit of the model. This fact can be understood by considering that any two positive definite factor covariance matrices Φ_1 and Φ_2 can be simultaneously diagonalized by pre- and post-multiplication by a nonsingular matrix and its transpose (Rao, 1973), as done in the confactor method. The transformations will in turn not alter the invariance of the pattern matrices, even though the invariant pattern itself is altered. If pattern invariance does not hold, however, the confactor constraints will generally be more restrictive than the constraints considered earlier.

The confactor approach can be extended to the $K > 2$ case by selecting two populations in which to impose the above orthogonality, leaving the remaining factor covariance matrices unconstrained. The pattern matrices are constrained to invariance in all K populations. McArdle and Cattell (1994) describe this extension in detail.

Global Identification

Sufficient constraints to achieve global identification in the factor model are known for special cases in the single-population case, and these can be simply extended to the multiple-population case. We will first consider the constraints used to identify parameters in the covariance structure, and then will turn to the mean structure.

Suppose that Λ_k has the following two characteristics: (a) each measured variable has only one nonzero loading and (b) each factor has at least three measured variables with nonzero loadings. Under these conditions, it is easy to show that global identification can be achieved by fixing one loading for each factor to a nonzero value or by fixing the diagonal elements of Φ_k to nonzero values (Bollen, 1989). We will refer to the condition (a) as "independent cluster structure" for Λ_k. This structure is also known as "congeneric" structure in the literature (Jöreskog, 1971a). Independent cluster structure, combined with a sufficient number of measured variables per factor, will lead to global identification once the scales for the factors have been set by fixing loadings or factor variances as above. When $r > 1$, the constraints needed to achieve independent cluster structure exceed those needed for rotational uniqueness, and this structure may not fit well in some cases even if the number of factors is adequate. We can weaken the requirement (b) by requiring only two measured variables per factor, but an additional requirement is then needed: (c) each row of Φ_k must have at least one nonzero off-diagonal element. This requirement rules out the orthogonal factor case in which all factors are mutually uncorrelated. The scale of each factor must be fixed as above.

Although these constraints are sufficient to achieve global identification, they are not necessary constraints for identification, nor are they trivial in any sense. For example, different placements of the fixed zeroes in Λ_k will generally lead to different values for fit statistics. Careful consideration must be given to the nature of the measured variables in deciding on a potential independent cluster structure. Independent cluster structure reflects the notion that each measured variable should be related to one, and only one, common factor. This structure represents an ideal that may be only poorly approximated in real data.

The foregoing sufficient conditions for achieving identification of the covariance structure can be extended to the multiple-population case simply by requiring that the conditions hold in each of the K separate populations. In this extension, we will generally wish to locate the fixed zero elements in Λ_k identically for all $k = 1,\ldots,K$. In doing so, we are invoking an invariance restriction on the pattern matrices known as "configural invariance" (Horn, McArdle, & Mason, 1983; Thurstone, 1947). Configural invariance permits the nonzero elements of the pattern matrices Λ_k to vary over groups (apart from those used to fix the scales for the factors), while forcing the zero elements to have the same locations across populations. Note that we can require configural invariance even if the number of fixed zero elements in each pattern matrix is less than that required by independent cluster structure. In such cases, some or all of the measured variables may have nonzero loadings on multiple factors. The zero loadings would have the same locations in all populations, however. The requirement that these zero elements be placed in identical locations across groups is not necessary for global identification and represents a falsifiable hypothesis. One could substitute a different set of constraints that would permit some variation across groups in the locations of the zero elements, while still achieving global identification. In the context of investigations of factorial invariance, however, configural invariance represents a model worth pursuing. We will return to this possibility below in discussing sequences of model evaluations.

The constraints that are sufficient for global identification of the parameters τ_k and κ_k are easily implemented. To see the need for these constraints, note that within any given population, if we define new parameters $\kappa_k^* = \kappa_k + c$ and $\tau_k^* = \tau_k - \Lambda_k c$, we then have from Equation 4.4

$$E_k(X) = \tau_k + \Lambda_k \kappa_k = \tau_k^* + \Lambda_k \kappa_k^* \qquad (4.14)$$

and so the intercept and latent mean parameters are not identified even if Λ_k is known. We require a minimum of r constraints on τ_k and κ_k to achieve identification. One option is to fix $\kappa_k = 0$ for all k. An alternative approach is to fix r elements of τ_k to zero values, selecting those elements to correspond to measured variables chosen as marker variables for purposes of fixing the scale of each common factor (Bollen, 1989; Millsap & Everson, 1993). In the absence of any invariance constraints on the nonzero elements of Λ_k across groups, this choice sets each factor mean equal to the mean of the marker variable for that factor. The constraints will produce values for τ_k and κ_k that exactly reproduce the mean structure for X and will identify the parameters τ_k and κ_k regardless of whether the factor pattern matrices have independent cluster structure.

A third possibility is to (a) require $\tau_k = \tau$ for all k and (b) $\kappa_k = 0$ for some chosen value of k. The first constraint imposes invariance on all intercepts without fixing the values of any of them. This invariance condition is generally only useful if the pattern matrices are also invariant. The second constraint fixed the factor means to zero in one group only. Collectively, (a) and (b) involve more constraints than are needed to identify τ_k and κ_k for all k, but they do provide a useful starting point for investigating partial invariance in τ_k, as discussed next.

In multiple-population studies, the constraints needed for identification play a dual role in that while their explicit purpose is to permit a unique solution for the remaining parameters, the constraints also imply invariance for the constrained model parameters. For example, if the same factor loading is fixed to one in each population, this constraint also implies that the loading has the same value across the populations. We can freely choose a different nonzero value for this parameter, but as long as the same value is used for each population, the implication of invariance is maintained. Similarly, if the same elements of τ_k are fixed to zero across populations, the constraints imply invariance in those elements of τ_k. Unfortunately, we rarely are certain in practice that the parameters chosen for identification constraints are truly invariant. If invariance does not hold for one or more of the constrained parameters, the constraints may produce distortions in the estimates of the unconstrained parameters. These distortions may affect tests of invariance for the unconstrained parameters.

To illustrate these points, consider the two covariance matrices $\mathbf{A}$ and $\mathbf{B}$ in Table 4.1. Covariance matrix $\mathbf{A}$ was generated as $\Sigma_A = \Lambda_A \Phi_A \Lambda'_A + \Theta$ with

$$\Lambda_A = \begin{bmatrix} .4 \\ .6 \\ .5 \\ .3 \end{bmatrix}, \quad \Phi_A = 1.0, \quad \mathrm{diag}(\Theta) = \begin{bmatrix} .1 \\ .1 \\ .1 \\ .1 \end{bmatrix}. \tag{4.15}$$

Covariance matrix $\mathbf{B}$ was generated as $\Sigma_B = \Lambda_B \Phi_B \Lambda'_B + \Theta$ with

$$\Lambda_B = \begin{bmatrix} .4 \\ .4 \\ .5 \\ .6 \end{bmatrix}, \quad \Phi_B = 2.0 \tag{4.16}$$

TABLE 4.1

Reference Variable Example Covariance Matrices

Covariance matrix $\mathbf{A}$			
.26			
.24	.46		
.20	.30	.35	
.12	.18	.15	.19
Covariance matrix $\mathbf{B}$			
.26			
.16	.26		
.20	.20	.35	
.24	.24	.30	.46

and with Θ as in Equation 4.15. Among the four elements of Λ_A and Λ_B, two have invariant values in A and B, while the remaining two differ across groups. If one chooses an invariant loading such as Λ_{31} to fix to one in each group, the resulting parameter estimates are

$$\widehat{\Lambda}_A = \begin{bmatrix} .8 \\ 1.2 \\ 1.0 \\ .6 \end{bmatrix}, \quad \widehat{\Phi}_A = .25, \quad \widehat{\Lambda}_B = \begin{bmatrix} .8 \\ .8 \\ 1.0 \\ 1.2 \end{bmatrix}, \quad \widehat{\Phi}_B = .5 \qquad (4.17)$$

with Θ estimated as in Equation 4.15. Note that Λ_{11} is invariant. From this baseline model, one can proceed to test invariance hypotheses on other model parameters without difficulty. On the other hand, suppose that the loading chosen as the reference variable is Λ_{21}. The resulting parameter estimates are

$$\widehat{\Lambda}_A = \begin{bmatrix} .667 \\ 1.0 \\ .833 \\ .5 \end{bmatrix}, \quad \widehat{\Phi}_A = .36, \quad \widehat{\Lambda}_B = \begin{bmatrix} 1.0 \\ 1.0 \\ 1.25 \\ 1.5 \end{bmatrix}, \quad \widehat{\Phi}_B = .32. \qquad (4.18)$$

In this solution, Λ_{11} is given different values in the two groups even though the loading should be invariant. Conversely, Λ_{21} in A is given the same value as Λ_{11} in B, even though these loadings should have different values. The use of a reference variable whose loading is not invariant has led to distortions in the estimates, producing inaccuracy in subsequent tests of invariance. Hypothetical examples involving identification constraints on τ_k can be created to show that poor choices for which elements of τ_k are fixed to zero in all groups can have distorting influences on subsequent tests of invariance on the intercept parameters. Again, it is difficult in practice to know which subset of r variables among the p measured variables should serve as markers for the mean structure in all groups.

Rensvold and Cheung (2001) have developed an iterative scheme for addressing the reference variable problem in studies of invariance. The scheme begins by assuming that metric invariance has been rejected in the data, but configural invariance holds. In the test for metric invariance, one measured variable is chosen as a reference variable in all groups, with the loading for that variable being fixed to one in all groups. After rejection of metric invariance, the next steps require repeated tests of partial metric invariance, with each test focusing on a different pair of measured variables. One member of the pair is designated as a reference variable (the "referent" variable) whose loading is fixed to one in all groups. The second member of the pair (the "argument" variable) has its loading constrained to invariance across groups. All other loadings are free to vary across groups. All possible unique pairs are tested for invariance in this fashion. With p measured variables, there are $p(p-1)/2$ pairs of variables to be tested. At the end of this process, the fit statistics are systematically examined to identify subsets of measured variables that can be considered to have invariant loadings. The fit statistics in question may be chi-square differences or changes in other statistics between the congeneric and partially invariant models. Rensvold and Cheung present an example using chi-square difference statistics and the corresponding significance probabilities. The final outcome of the procedure is a list of measured variables whose loadings are regarded as invariant, unconfounded with the choice of reference variable. This iterative procedure appears to give reasonable results in real data and is potentially useful. Two potential problems with the procedure are the large number of tests required when p is large and the inflation of the Type 1 error rate due to multiple significance tests. The second problem can be addressed via the use of Bonferroni adjustments, as shown in Rensvold and Cheung.

An alternative "backward elimination" approach (Yoon & Millsap, 2007) to the reference variable problem that requires fewer tests would proceed as follows, again assuming that configural invariance holds. First, metric invariance is tested without selecting a reference variable. This invariance test forces all loadings to be invariant, fixing the factor variances to have unit values in one group only, as described earlier. Rejection of this model suggests that one or more loadings have different values in different groups. The next step releases the invariance constraint on the loading for the variable with the largest Lagrange multiplier (LM) statistic (i.e., modification index) in the full metric invariance model, while retaining invariance constraints on all other loadings. This partially invariant model is fit to the data. If the fit statistics suggest rejection, the invariance constraints on another loading are released using the loading that shows the highest LM statistic in the first partially invariant model. This second partially invariant model is fit. The process continues sequentially, releasing constraints on loadings to maximize the expected improvement in fit, until one of two events occur. Either only r invariant loadings remain or a partially invariant model with more than r invariant loadings is found to fit. In the former case, the procedure leads to uncertainty about which of the loadings are invariant, while recognizing that at least some loadings are not invariant. In contrast, if a partially invariant model fits, the procedure has located a subset of measured variables whose loadings appear to be invariant.

Given p measured variables, the above backward elimination procedure requires no more than $p-1$ model evaluations. The procedure is exploratory in that no theory is used to choose which loadings are constrained or released from constraints at a given step. The data determine the order in which the loadings are tested for invariance, and when tests are halted. As in the Rensvold and Cheung (2001) procedure, the researcher must choose a rule for deciding when to reject models at any given step. Which statistic will be used, and what value of the statistic will be the threshold for halting testing? We return to this fit issue below. The advantage of the backward elimination procedure is that no a priori choice of reference variable is needed.

An analogous backward elimination procedure can be used for the intercept parameter, starting with the full invariance for the intercepts and $\kappa_k = 0$ for a single chosen group. Invariance constraints are then removed sequentially, guided by local fit information as in the case of the loading constraints. The process continues until either r invariance constraints remain on the intercepts or fit is achieved with more than r invariance constraints. Systematic studies are needed to determine whether this backward elimination approach can successfully locate violations of invariance in either loadings or intercepts under realistic conditions.

In an absolute sense, no perfect solution exists for the problem illustrated above because we are always uncertain about the invariance of the measures under study. The chosen reference variable may fail to be invariant, leading to the above distortions. The problem can be minimized, however, by including some measured variables that are believed to be invariant, or nearly so. Confidence on this point must be based on both prior empirical work and theory.

Estimation

Given that sufficient constraints are imposed to identify the model parameters, estimation proceeds in the multiple-population case by extending the theory for the single-population case. All of the estimation procedures to be discussed here are large-sample procedures in that their optimal properties are based on large samples. The method of estimation to be adopted will depend on the distributional assumptions for X. As a general rule, stronger assumptions will lead to more efficient estimation provided that the assumptions are met. Estimation methods under weak distributional assumptions are available, but these methods typically require very large samples for adequate performance.

To begin, let x_{ik}, $i = 1,...,N_k$, be the $p \times 1$ vector of observed random variables for the ith individual in the kth population Π_k in a sample of size N_k. The vectors x_{ik} are assumed to be independently distributed, both within and between populations. Let $\bar{\mathbf{X}}_k$ be the usual sample estimator of $\boldsymbol{\mu}_{Xk}$, with

$$\bar{\mathbf{X}}_k = N_k^{-1} \sum_{i=1}^{N_k} \mathbf{x}_{ik}, \tag{4.19}$$

and let

$$\mathbf{S}_{Xk} = N_k^{-1} \sum_{i=1}^{N_k} (\mathbf{x}_{ik} - \bar{\mathbf{X}}_k)(\mathbf{x}_{ik} - \bar{\mathbf{X}}_k)', \tag{4.20}$$

be the sample estimator of $\boldsymbol{\Sigma}_{Xk}$. With some exceptions, estimation in CFA can be treated in a unified way by viewing the different estimation methods as seeking parameter values to minimize different discrepancy functions $F(\bar{\mathbf{X}}_k, \mathbf{S}_{Xk}, \boldsymbol{\mu}_{Xk}, \boldsymbol{\Sigma}_{Xk})$ (Browne, 1982). Expressions for $\boldsymbol{\mu}_{Xk}$ and $\boldsymbol{\Sigma}_{Xk}$ under the factor model are given in Equation 4.4, and we seek values for the parameters $(\boldsymbol{\tau}_k, \boldsymbol{\Lambda}_k, \boldsymbol{\kappa}_k, \boldsymbol{\Phi}_k, \boldsymbol{\Theta}_k)$ to minimize the discrepancy function. Once such estimates are obtained, we can reproduce the mean and covariance structures in the sample by substituting the parameter estimates in Equation 4.4. These reproduced structures under the model are sometimes denoted the "fitted" mean and covariance structures. While the form of the discrepancy function varies depending on the method, all discrepancy functions meet three conditions: (a) the function is nonnegative, (b) the function is twice continuously differentiable with respect to the parameters, and (c) the function is zero if and only if $\bar{\mathbf{X}}_k = \boldsymbol{\mu}_{Xk}$ and $\mathbf{S}_{Xk} = \boldsymbol{\Sigma}_{Xk}$. The third point means that the discrepancy function is zero if and only if the fitted factor fully reproduces the sample mean and covariance structures. The discrepancy function thus provides a measure of the "closeness" of the fitted covariance and mean structures under the specified factor model to the structure found in the data.

Under MVN assumptions for $\mathbf{X}$ in each population, Jöreskog (1971b) presented a maximum likelihood estimation procedure that was extended by Sörbom (1974) to permit estimation of both mean and covariance structures. It is assumed that $\mathbf{x}_{ik}$ has an MVN($\boldsymbol{\mu}_{Xk}, \boldsymbol{\Sigma}_{Xk}$) distribution in the kth population, with $\boldsymbol{\mu}_{Xk}$ and $\boldsymbol{\Sigma}_{Xk}$ having the structure given in Equation 4.4. The normal maximum likelihood discrepancy function for the multiple-population case is

$$F_{ML} = \sum_{k=1}^{k} \left(\frac{N_k}{N} \right) \mathbf{F}_{MLk}. \tag{4.21}$$

We define F_{MLk} here as

$$F_{MLk} = (\bar{X}_k - \mu_{Xk})' \Sigma_{Xk}^{-1} (\bar{X}_k - \mu_{Xk}) + \ln \frac{|\Sigma_{Xk}|}{|S_{Xk}|} + \text{tr}[\Sigma_{Xk}^{-1} S_{Xk}] - p, \qquad (4.22)$$

with N the total sample size across groups. The discrepancy function has been modified to include both mean and covariance structures. This discrepancy function will be minimized after introducing constraints used for both identification and for specification of the desired model. If no invariance constraints or other cross-population constraints are imposed, minimization of F_{ML} could be achieved by separate minimizations within each of the K populations. If invariance constraints are imposed, however, estimation must be done using software that can support multiple-group analyses, such as LISREL (Jöreskog & Sörbom, 2002), EQS (Bentler, 1995), AMOS (Arbuckle & Wothke, 1999), or Mplus (Muthén & Muthén, 1998–2006).

If the distributional assumptions are met and the specified model is correct, the parameter estimates found through minimization of F_{ML} will have the optimal properties found in large samples in the single-population case. Estimates will be consistent, will have standard errors that are themselves estimable, and will have normal sampling distributions. The discrepancy function value at the minimum of F_{ML} can be used to calculate a chi-square test statistic for the null hypothesis that the specified model fits exactly in the K populations. The discrepancy function value also leads to estimates for the noncentrality parameter that are useful for fit evaluation when the null hypothesis fails. Fit evaluation is discussed below.

An alternative discrepancy function that produces results similar to F_{ML} in the MVN case, but is applicable more broadly, is the generalized least squares (GLS) discrepancy function (Browne, 1974). To describe this function, let $s_k = \text{vec}(S_{Xk})$ and $\sigma_k = \text{vec}(\Sigma_{Xk})$ where the vec operator concatenates the nonredundant elements of successive columns of the specified matrix. Hence, both s_k and σ_k are vectors of length $p(p + 1)/2$. Furthermore, define

$$a_k' = [\bar{X}_k' \quad s_k'] \qquad \omega_k' = [\mu_{Xk}' \quad \sigma_{Xk}'], \qquad (4.23)$$

as vectors of length $p + (p[p + 1]/2)$. Then the multiple-population GLS discrepancy function is

$$F_{GLS} = \sum_{k=1}^{K} F_{GLSk}, \qquad (4.24)$$

where

$$F_{GLSk} = (a_k - \omega_k)' C_k^{-1}(a_k - \omega_k), \tag{4.25}$$

with C_k a positive definite weight matrix. Different choices for C_k lead to different estimates once F_{GLS} is minimized. The general strategy is to pick C_k as a consistent estimator for the covariance matrix Ω_k of $N_k^{1/2}(a_k - \omega_k)$. When X_k has an MVN(μ_{Xk}, Σ_{Xk}) distribution, this covariance matrix has the form

$$\Omega_k = \begin{vmatrix} \Sigma_{Xk} & 0 \\ 0 & 2H_p'(\Sigma_{Xk} \otimes \Sigma_{Xk})H_p \end{vmatrix}, \tag{4.26}$$

where
  $\otimes$ is the Kronecker product operator
  H_p is the $p^2(p(p+1)/2)$ transition matrix described by Browne (see also Magnus & Neudecker, 1988)

After substitution of S_{Xk} for Σ_{Xk} to yield C_k, the resulting expression for F_{GLSk} is

$$F_{GLSk} = (\bar{X}_k - \mu_{Xk})' S_{Xk}^{-1}(\bar{X}_k - \mu_{Xk}) + \left(\frac{1}{2}\right) tr[S_{Xk}^{-1}(S_{Xk} - \Sigma_{Sk})]. \tag{4.27}$$

This GLS function is sometimes denoted the normal theory GLS function. Under the conditions that justify normal theory ML estimation, the use of F_{GLSk} in Equation 4.27 will lead to estimates that are generally similar to ML estimates.

When X_k is not MVN, a variety of choices for C_k are possible depending on the distribution assumed for X_k. The most general case simply requires X_k to have finite fourth-order moments, with no specific distributional form assumed for X_k. The matrix Ω_k in this case is a full matrix whose elements are expressions involving the second-, third-, and fourth-order central moments of X_k (see Browne & Arminger, 1995, or Muthén, 1989, for exact expressions). The matrix C_k is then chosen as a matrix of the corresponding sample moments. The resulting discrepancy function F_{GLS} is denoted as the "asymptotically distribution-free" (ADF) function, or sometimes as the "weighted least squares" (WLS) function, leading to ADF or WLS estimators. These estimators are efficient in large samples under very general conditions. While ideal in theory, simulations have found that the estimators perform poorly in small to moderate sample sizes, especially in large models (Boomsma & Hoogland, 2001; Muthén & Kaplan, 1992).

For example, Boomsma and Hoogland recommend that to avoid bias in standard error estimates and fit statistics in a single-population study, a minimum sample size of 50 times the number of variables be used. A CFA of $p = 10$ variables would require $N = 500$. The multiple-population extension of this advice is unclear at present. In general, the problems with ADF stem from the need to use estimates of fourth-order moments, which themselves require large samples for stable estimation.

To reduce the sample size demands of ADF estimation, an alternative method is to define $\mathbf{\Omega}_k$ to be a diagonal matrix whose diagonal elements are the variances of $N_k^{1/2}(a_k - \mathbf{\omega}_k)$. The sample estimates of these variances are then used to define a diagonal matrix $\mathbf{C}_k$ in F_{GLSk}. The use of this form of the discrepancy function is known as "diagonally weighted least squares" (DWLS) estimation. Only $p + (p[p + 1]/2)$ elements of $\mathbf{C}_k$ must be estimated in DWLS, and no matrix inversion is needed in Equation 4.25 because the reciprocals of the diagonal elements of $\mathbf{C}_k$ become the weights.

The ML, GLS, ADF, WLS, and DWLS estimators are not the only estimators that have been considered for CFA, although these methods account for the bulk of multiple-population applications. A potentially interesting alternative estimator is the two-stage least squares (2SLS) estimator (Bollen, 1996), which is often used to generate start values for the aforementioned estimation methods. The 2SLS estimator requires no assumptions about the distributional forms of the variables $\mathbf{X}_k$, an advantage when the data do not meet traditional assumptions. Furthermore, the 2SLS estimator is not iterative and is relatively easy to calculate. Under some conditions, the 2SLS estimator is robust to modest misspecification in the model. Bollen (2001) presents a simultaneous 2SLS estimator whose robustness properties are enhanced in comparison to previous 2SLS estimators (see Kaplan, 1988, for some results on robustness for these previous estimators). Studies examining how the 2SLS estimator performs in finite samples in the multiple-population case have not yet appeared in the literature.

Bayesian methods of estimation provide another alternative, one that is becoming more widely used in CFA (Cai, in press; Edwards, 2010; Lee, 1981, 2007; Lee & Song, 2002; Scheines, Hoijtink, & Boomsma, 1999; Shi & Lee, 1998; Song & Lee, 2001). Bayesian estimation in factor analysis is not new (e.g., Martin & McDonald, 1975), but it has been made more practical through the use of Markov chain Monte Carlo (MCMC) simulation methods (Bolstad, 2010 provides a recent introduction to MCMC methods). Multiple group extensions of Bayesian estimation in CFA are available (Song & Lee) but are not yet used widely for invariance investigations. One potential application of Bayesian methods that is especially useful is in item-level analyses, where the number of measured variables is often large and the model itself is complex due to the discrete scale of measurement (Edwards). We will return to the topic of Bayesian estimation in Chapter 6 in describing the use of item response theory.

Fit Evaluation

Hypotheses about factorial invariance require that we evaluate the fit of the factor model to the data. Methods for fit evaluation in covariance structure modeling have been intensively studied in recent years, leading to a variety of approaches. We will not attempt to review all of these methods here. The methods to be discussed below are the most commonly used methods at present. We can expect that ongoing research on fit evaluation will produce additional methods in the future.

Most methods of fit evaluation are based, in some way, on the discrepancy between the actual covariance and mean structure, and the covariance and mean structure implied by the hypothesized model. In the sample, the actual covariance and mean structure in the kth group are represented by the sample covariance matrix $\mathbf{S}_{Xk}$ and mean vector $\bar{\mathbf{X}}_k$. The sample estimates of the factor model parameters lead to the "fitted" sample covariance matrix $\mathbf{S}_{0Xk}$ and mean vector $\bar{\mathbf{X}}_{0k}$. Similarly, in the kth population, there exists an actual covariance matrix $\boldsymbol{\Sigma}_{Xk}$ and mean vector $\boldsymbol{\mu}_{Xk}$. If we could fit the hypothesized model within the entire kth population, we would generate a "fitted" population covariance matrix $\boldsymbol{\Sigma}_{0Xk}$ and mean vector $\boldsymbol{\mu}_{0Xk}$. If the hypothesized model is correct, we know that $\boldsymbol{\Sigma}_{Xk} = \boldsymbol{\Sigma}_{0Xk}$ and $\boldsymbol{\mu}_{Xk} = \boldsymbol{\mu}_{0Xk}$, but we will likely find that $\mathbf{S}_{Xk} \neq \mathbf{S}_{0Xk}$ and $\boldsymbol{\mu}_{Xk} \neq \boldsymbol{\mu}_{0Xk}$ due to sampling error. Fit evaluation procedures use these sample discrepancies to decide whether the hypothesized model fits in the population. If the model is found not to fit in the population, interest then centers on quantifying the extent of the lack of fit and on identifying the sources of any lack of fit.

We can distinguish tests and measures of "global" fit from tests and measures of "local" fit. Global measures of fit summarize the fit of the entire model in a single index, and global tests of fit evaluate the fit of the entire model using statistical hypothesis tests. In the multiple-population case, global tests and measures can be extended to consider simultaneous fit in several populations. When p is large or there are multiple populations, a global fit measure may fail to be sensitive to departures from adequate fit that are concentrated in a small portion of the model. Local measures of fit that focus on specific parameters or particular measured variables are of interest for this reason. A local measure of fit may assess, for example, whether the relaxation of a constraint on a specific parameter will improve the fit. Hence, local measures can be of considerable value, but their use must be tempered by recognizing that many such measures can be calculated, and some may be large due to chance fluctuations.

Global Fit

The chi-square goodness-of-fit statistic is the most well-known global fit statistic. The chi-square statistic can be used in a test of exact global fit. The null hypothesis in this case is H_0: $\Sigma_{Xk} = \Sigma_{0Xk}$, $\mu_{Xk} = \mu_{0Xk}$ for $k = 1,...,K$. If $\hat{F}$ is the sample discrepancy function value, the chi-square statistic is $\chi^2 = (N - 1)\hat{F}$, with the degrees of freedom equal to the difference between the number of unique variance, covariance, and mean elements to be modeled, and the number of independent parameters to be estimated. In large samples, the chi-square statistic is available for either the F_{ML} or F_{GLS} discrepancy functions. It is assumed that the chosen discrepancy function is appropriate for the data.

Suppose that we are working with a pair of factor models A and B in which model B is logically nested within model A as a restricted case. Here "logically nested" means that it is possible to arrive at B by placing constraints on the parameters of model A. It is possible to use a difference-in-chi-square test to determine if the parameter constraints that have led to model B are plausible. Specifically, if $\chi_A^2(df_A)$ and $\chi_B^2(df_B)$ are the chi-square and degrees of freedom for A and B, respectively, then $\chi_D^2 = \chi_B^2 - \chi_A^2$ with $df_D = df_B - df_A$ are the difference chi-square and difference df. Under the usual assumptions for the chi-square statistic, along with an assumption that model A fits, the difference chi-square can be used to test whether the constraints leading to B are producing lack of fit in comparison to model A. A statistically significant difference in chi-square suggests that model B fits less well than model A. In practice, the requirement that model A fit the data is often ignored, and the chi-square difference test is used even when $\chi_A^2(df_A)$ is statistically significant. Yuan and Bentler (2004) shows that this practice can produce misleading results.

A weakness of the traditional chi-square statistic associated with maximum likelihood or normal-theory GLS estimation is that it requires normality assumptions that may fail to hold in real data. This weakness has led investigators to seek alternative global fit statistics that are robust to non-normality. One approach that is easy to implement uses some transformations to the global chi-square statistic. The scaled chi-square statistic (Satorra & Bentler, 1994) in the single-population case is

$$\hat{T} = \frac{\chi^2}{c}, \tag{4.28}$$

where
   χ^2 is the global chi-square statistic associated with a particular estimation method (e.g., ML)
   c is a scaling factor

$$c = d^{-1}\,\text{tr}[\mathbf{U}\boldsymbol{\Omega}], \qquad (4.29)$$

where
d is the degrees of freedom
$\boldsymbol{\Omega}$ is the asymptotic covariance matrix for the unique elements of $\mathbf{S}_x$

$$\mathbf{U} = \mathbf{M} - \mathbf{M}\boldsymbol{\Delta}(\boldsymbol{\Delta}'\mathbf{M}\boldsymbol{\Delta})^{-1}\boldsymbol{\Delta}'\mathbf{M} \qquad (4.30)$$

with $\boldsymbol{\Delta}$ the Jacobian matrix, and $\mathbf{M}$ is a weight matrix chosen to match the chi-square statistic in use. When $\mathbf{M}$ is chosen as a diagonal matrix, the resulting test statistic in Equation 4.28 is called the WLSM chi-square in Mplus (Muthén & Muthén, 1998–2006). In the general ML case with a full weight matrix, we have

$$\mathbf{M} = 2\mathbf{H}_p'(\boldsymbol{\Sigma}_X \otimes \boldsymbol{\Sigma}_X)\mathbf{H}_p \qquad (4.31)$$

with $\mathbf{H}_p$ defined earlier. This scaled chi-square statistic has been found to perform well in simulations in comparison to the unscaled chi-square under non-normality (Chou, Bentler, & Satorra, 1991; Curran, West, & Finch, 1997; Hu, Bentler, & Kano, 1992). A sample estimator for c is obtained by replacing the population quantities in Equation 4.29 with their sample counterparts. The multiple-population extension of the scaled chi-square statistic is given in Satorra (2000). The effect of the scaling is to shift the mean of the sampling distribution for T to be appropriate for non-normal data. In the normal case, the scaling has little effect on the chi-square.

An adjusted chi-square statistic provides a second robust alternative to the traditional chi-square statistic for the non-normal case (Bentler, 1995; Satorra & Bentler, 1988). The adjusted statistic is

$$\widehat{T} = \frac{a\chi^2}{\text{tr}[\mathbf{U}\boldsymbol{\Omega}]} \qquad (4.32)$$

with χ^2, $\mathbf{U}$, and $\boldsymbol{\Omega}$, as defined earlier, and with α the closest integer to

$$\frac{[\text{tr}(\mathbf{U}\boldsymbol{\Omega})]^2}{\text{tr}(\mathbf{U}\boldsymbol{\Omega})^2}. \qquad (4.33)$$

This adjustment alters both the mean and the variance of the distribution of χ^2. Multiple-population extensions of this adjusted chi-square statistic exist (Satorra, 2000). The chi-square statistic in Equation 4.32 using a diagonal weight matrix $\mathbf{M}$ is known as the WLSMV chi-square in Mplus (Muthén & Muthén, 1998–2006).

From a scientific standpoint, a difficulty with the global chi-square statistic is that rejection of the null hypothesis of exact fit is not informative when considered in isolation. We often have less interest in knowing that the model fails to fit perfectly than in knowing the extent and location of the misfit. Even the smallest misfit will lead to rejection given a sufficiently large sample. In bias investigations, rejection of an invariance hypothesis raises additional questions. How large are the group differences in the parameters? Which parameters differ across groups? Answers to these questions require that we consider additional information that may help quantify the size of the misfit.

One approach to quantifying the extent of the misfit in the hypothesized model is to create a summary index for the residuals between the sample covariances and means, and the implied or fitted covariances and means under the model. These residuals are calculated as

$$\mathbf{E}_{Ck} = \mathbf{S}_{Xk} - \mathbf{S}_{0Xk} \qquad \mathbf{E}_{Mk} = \bar{\mathbf{X}}_k - \bar{\mathbf{X}}_{0k}. \tag{4.34}$$

Most software programs will report these residuals. A global index for the residuals in the covariance matrix is the root mean square residual (RMSR). Letting $\mathbf{e}_{Ck} = \text{vec}(\mathbf{E}_{Ck})$, the RMSR for the kth group is

$$\text{RMSR}_k = \left[\frac{\mathbf{e}'_{Ck}\mathbf{e}_{Ck}}{p(p+1)/2} \right]^{1/2}. \tag{4.35}$$

The resulting index gives some sense of the absolute residual size. The RMSR may be difficult to interpret due to the varying metrics among the covariance matrix elements. A standardized RMSR is created by placing $\mathbf{S}_{Xk}$ and $\mathbf{S}_{0Xk}$ in correlation metric prior to the calculation of $\mathbf{E}_{Ck}$. Under this transformation, the standardized RMSR ranges between zero and one. Values near zero (e.g., <.05) are considered to be consistent with a good fit.

As a global index, the RMSR has several drawbacks. First, the RMSR includes no direct information on the misfit in the means as given by $\mathbf{E}_{Mk}$. The fit of the model to the means is important in studies of factorial invariance. Second, the RMSR confounds two sources of potential misfit:

sampling error and error in the approximation of Σ_{Xk} by Σ_{0Xk}. Sampling error creates inaccuracy in the estimation of Σ_{Xk} by S_{Xk} and in the estimation of Σ_{0Xk} by S_{0Xk}. In sufficiently large samples, we expect to reduce or eliminate these inaccuracies. The error in the approximation of Σ_{Xk} by Σ_{0Xk} will not be reduced, however. This error reflects inaccuracy in the hypothesized model. Unfortunately, it is unclear which of these sources of misfit is dominant in a given application of the RMSR.

A third global fit index, the root mean square error of approximation (RMSEA) (Browne & Cudeck, 1993; Steiger, 1990; Steiger & Lind, 1980), focuses specifically on the error in Σ_{0Xk} as an approximation to Σ_{Xk}. Unlike the RMSR, the RMSEA simultaneously considers both covariance and mean structures as long as the discrepancy function used in estimation also includes mean structures. The RMSEA uses the information provided by the discrepancy function F to estimate a measure of closeness between (Σ_{0Xk}, μ_{0Xk}) and (Σ_{Xk}, μ_{Xk}). The RMSEA assumes that the discrepancy function F is appropriate for the data and that the errors of approximation for (Σ_{Xk}, μ_{Xk}) in relation to (Σ_{0Xk}, μ_{0Xk}) are not too large (see Steiger, Shapiro, & Browne, 1985, for a discussion of the latter point). If $\hat{F}$ is the sample value of the discrepancy function in a single group, the estimate of the RMSEA is

$$\text{RMSEA}_1 = \left[\max\left\{ \frac{\hat{F}}{d} - \frac{1}{n}, 0 \right\} \right]^{1/2}, \tag{4.36}$$

where
$n = N - 1$
N is the sample size
d is the degrees of freedom for the specified model

Note that the RMSEA evaluates $\hat{F}$ relative to the degrees of freedom, in effect penalizing models that achieve fit by including unnecessary parameters. In multiple-population studies, a modification to the formula in Equation 4.36 is recommended. The sample size N in this case is the combined sample size across groups. If the study includes K populations, the modified RMSEA is $\text{RMSEA}_k = (K)^{1/2}\text{RMSEA}_1$. Steiger (1998) discusses this multiple-population extension.

What values for the RMSEA (in either single or multiple populations) are considered indicative of an acceptable fit? Browne and Cudeck (1993) suggest that values below .05 are consistent with a "good" fit, and values between .05 and .08 indicate a "fair" fit. These authors also recommend that confidence intervals accompany any point estimate of the RMSEA. A 90% confidence interval for the RMSEA can be written as

$$(\hat{\varepsilon}_{.05}, \hat{\varepsilon}_{.95}) = \left(\left[\frac{\hat{\lambda}_{.05}}{nd} \right]^{1/2}, \left[\frac{\hat{\lambda}_{.95}}{nd} \right]^{1/2} \right), \qquad (4.37)$$

where
$\hat{\varepsilon}_c$ is the estimated bound for the RMSEA at the $(100 \times c)$ percentile
$\hat{\lambda}_c$ is the estimated bound for the noncentrality parameter of the non-central chi-square distribution with $df = d$ and $n = N - 1$

The bounds on the noncentrality parameter can be found using numerical approximation as discussed in Steiger and Lind (1980) and Steiger and Fouladi (1997). Tests of hypotheses about the RMSEA are also feasible. For example, a test of "close fit" would evaluate H_0: RMSEA $\leq$ .05 versus H_1: RMSEA $>$ .05. Failure to reject this hypothesis suggests that although the fit may not be perfect, the data do not support rejection of a "close" fit. Given access to software for computing quantiles of the distribution of the noncentral chi-square distribution, other hypotheses about the RMSEA can be tested. Procedures for calculating the power of hypothesis tests involving the RMSEA are also available (MacCallum, Browne, & Sugawara, 1996). These procedures evaluate power for tests of exact fit (e.g., H_0: RMSEA $= 0$) or close fit (H_0: RMSEA $\leq$ .05). Power calculation procedures for the RMSEA are presently designed for the single-population case. Modifications needed for the multiple-population case do not yet appear to have been studied.

The RMSEA index provides a useful and versatile index of approximate fit. It is unaffected by the scaling adopted for the measured variables **X** as long as the discrepancy function used in the parameter estimation is also "scale-free" (Browne & Cudeck, 1993). The F_{MLN} and F_{GLS} discrepancy functions have this property. Four points should be kept in mind, however, when using the RMSEA and its associated confidence intervals and test statistics. First, the theory underlying the RMSEA assumes that the discrepancy function used is proper for the data at hand. If the data are not MVN for example, the F_{MLN} discrepancy function should not be used as a basis for the RMSEA. Second, the error of approximation is assumed to not be too large. When the errors are large, the RMSEA becomes inaccurate as an index of the lack of fit. Finally, the RMSEA is a large sample index. Investigations of its behavior in small samples are ongoing (Curran, Bollen, Chen, Paxton, & Kirby, 2003; Curran, Bollen, Paxton, Kirby, & Chen, 2002). Finally, the use of specific cutpoints for what is considered a "close fit" has been criticized as lacking generality across models and data conditions (Barrett, 2007; Beuducel & Wittmann, 2005; Fan & Sivo, 2005; Marsh, Hau, & Wen, 2004; Yuan, 2005).

An entirely different approach to global fit evaluation uses comparative fit indices (CFIs) that evaluate the fit of the specified model relative to a more restricted baseline model. The baseline model is typically chosen as the most restrictive model one would consider for the data at hand. For example, a common choice for a model that specifies a structure for the covariance matrix alone is to use the baseline model $\Sigma_{Xk} = D_{Xk}$, where D_{Xk} is a diagonal matrix. This baseline model says that the measured variables are mutually uncorrelated or that there are no common factors underlying the measured variables. This choice is now implemented in some software programs as the default (e.g., LISREL). Clearly, other baseline models are plausible and may have advantages in comparison to the above choice. We return to this question below.

Although there are a variety of CFIs (see Tanaka, 1993, for a review), one index that has received some support in simulation studies is the CFI (Bentler, 1990). This index is calculated as CFI $= 1 - (\alpha_m/\alpha_0)$, where $\alpha_m = \max(d_m, 0)$ and $\alpha_0 = \max(d_0, d_m, 0)$, with

$$d_0 = \chi_0^2 - df_0, \quad d_m = \chi_m^2 - df_m, \tag{4.38}$$

and (χ_0^2, df_0) being the chi-square and degrees of freedom for the baseline model, and (χ_m^2, df_m) being the corresponding quantities for the model of interest. The CFI modifies the Relative Noncentrality Index (McDonald, 1989; McDonald & Marsh, 1990) to ensure that $0 \le$ CFI ≤ 1. Values of the CFI above .90 were considered to be indicative of a "good fit" (Bentler), but more recent simulations suggest that a higher threshold is needed. Hu and Bentler (1995) suggest CFI values greater than .95 as indicative of good fit.

The fit of a model as indicated by the CFI will depend heavily on the choice of the baseline model, but it is not always clear which baseline model should be used (Marsh, 1998; Rigdon, 1998a, 1998b). For example, how should mean structures be represented in the baseline model in multiple-population applications? One option is to leave the mean structures unconstrained, yet tests of factorial invariance will ultimately constrain these structures. Given that the baseline model is generally chosen to be at least as restrictive as any model of interest, some constraints on the means seem necessary. At the other extreme, one can use a baseline that specifies complete invariance of means for the measured variables. This highly restrictive baseline will often produce high CFI values but will exceed the degree of restriction that is plausible for many applications. For example, group differences in common factor means will generally produce group differences in the means of the measured variables even if loadings and intercepts are invariant. At present, there is no consensus on the proper baseline model to use for mean structures.

A further consideration in the interpretation of the CFI is the general strength of association among the measured variables in Σ_{Xk}. When the measured variables are weakly correlated, the approximation of Σ_{Xk} by $\mathbf{D}_{Xk}$ will be relatively good, and so χ_0^2 will not be high. In this case, the improvement in fit afforded by the model of interest may be relatively small even if the fitted covariance matrix Σ_{0Xk} is very close to $\mathbf{S}_{0Xk}$. The CFI will not be large in such cases. An example of this situation might be when the measured variables are item scores, which tend to be weakly correlated. At the other extreme, if the measured variables are highly intercorrelated, the approximation of Σ_{Xk} by $\mathbf{D}_{Xk}$ will be very poor, and χ_0^2 will be very high. The model of interest may generate a high CFI value in this case even if the fitted matrix Σ_{0Xk} is not that close to $\mathbf{S}_{0Xk}$, due to the large improvement in fit in comparison to the baseline model.

Another distinctive set of global fit indices are based on Akaike's information criterion (AIC) (Akaike, 1973). Technically, this index estimates the expected Kullback–Liebler distance between the proposed model and the "true model." This distance can be defined as the information lost in approximating the probability distribution implied by the "true model" by the probability distribution implied by the proposed model. Because the true model is unknown, the AIC only provides a relative measure of distance in practice. When a set of alternative models is proposed, the AIC can be used to select which model minimizes this relative distance. The AIC is not intended as an absolute measure of fit for a single model in isolation; no AIC cutpoints for adequate fit exist. Instead, AIC values are calculated for all models in the set under consideration, and the model with the minimum AIC value is chosen. The formula for the AIC is

$$\mathrm{AIC} = \chi^2 + 2q, \tag{4.39}$$

where

χ^2 is the global chi-square fit statistic
q is the number of parameters that are estimated under the model

AIC was developed in conjunction with maximum likelihood theory, and, hence, AIC is most appropriate when χ^2 is based on likelihood estimation. When the number of free parameters q is large relative to the sample size, a modified AIC index is recommended, known as the "consistent Akaike information criterion" (CAIC):

$$\mathrm{CAIC} = \chi^2 + 2q \left[\frac{N}{N - q - 1} \right], \tag{4.40}$$

where N is the sample size (Hurvich & Tsai, 1989; Sugiura, 1978). Burnham and Anderson (1998) recommend the use of the CAIC in preference to AIC when $N/q < 40$. Finally, an important consideration in using either index is that the models being compared need not be nested.

Local Fit Indices

The most direct measures of local fit are the errors $\mathbf{E}_{Ck}$ and $\mathbf{E}_{Mk}$ in Equation 4.34. Scrutiny of these errors can reveal which variables appear to be most poorly approximated by the hypothesized model. The differing metrics among elements of $\mathbf{S}_{Xk}$ and $\bar{\mathbf{X}}_k$ preclude any fixed rules for judging which errors are large. Some software programs provide "standardized" residuals that are ratios of the elements of $\mathbf{E}_{Ck}$ and $\mathbf{E}_{Mk}$ to estimates of their asymptotic standard errors. Under normality assumptions, these ratios can be regarded as standard normal deviates in large samples. Large residuals are then identified by considering appropriate cutoffs for the tail probabilities associated with these deviates. Interpretation is clouded, however, by the large number of residuals being considered when p is large. In large samples, many of the standardized residuals may exceed conventional cutpoints for significance even if the raw residuals are not large in an absolute sense.

An alternative set of local fit indices focuses on the individual parameter constraints implied by the model. The univariate language multiplier (LM) test evaluates the improvement in fit that would accrue from the removal of the constraint on a single parameter, while keeping all other constraints in place. For example, a factor model may restrict a particular factor pattern element to zero. An LM test would evaluate the improvement in fit that would result if this element were permitted to assume any value. The LM test can be extended to multiple parameter tests in which the constraints on an entire set of parameters are evaluated for fit. In large samples, the LM statistic will have a chi-square distribution under the null hypothesis that the constraints hold, with *df* equal to the number of parameters being evaluated. The LM statistic for evaluating constraints on a $c \times 1$ vector of parameters $\boldsymbol{\omega}$ is calculated as

$$LM = \hat{\boldsymbol{\Delta}}' (\hat{\mathbf{I}}(\boldsymbol{\omega}))^{-1} \hat{\boldsymbol{\Delta}}, \qquad (4.41)$$

where $\hat{\boldsymbol{\Delta}} = \partial L / \partial \boldsymbol{\omega}$ is a $c \times 1$ vector of partial derivatives evaluated at the parameter estimates obtained under the model being evaluated, with L being the log likelihood function for the data and $\hat{\mathbf{I}}(\boldsymbol{\omega})$ being the $c \times c$ Fisher information matrix, also evaluated at the estimated parameter values. The LM statistic was developed under MVN assumptions, and it may provide misleading results in non-normal data. Many software programs compute LM statistics for all individual constrained parameters. The univariate LM statistics are denoted as "modification indices" in LISREL. Some programs (e.g., EQS) offer multivariate LM statistics in addition to univariate statistics.

A difficulty associated with the interpretation of LM statistics is that in large samples, trivial violations of the constraints can lead to rejection of the constraints. Kaplan (1989) recommends that researchers consider the "expected parameter change" (EPC) statistics in this situation along with the LM statistic. The EPC statistic gives the expected change in the value of the parameter estimate once the constraint on the parameter is removed. For example, if the constrained value for the parameter is zero, the EPC for that parameter is the expected value of the parameter estimate once the constraint is removed. In large samples, if the LM statistic is large for a given constrained parameter but the EPC for that parameter is small, we may decide that the lack of fit resulting from the constraint is not important practically. It should be noted, however, that the EPC for an individual parameter may not be accurate if entire sets of parameters are simultaneously freed.

The array of available global and local fit indices makes it tempting to use such indices as a sole basis for introducing modifications to an initially misspecified model. Local fit indices in particular can be used to introduce a series of model modifications that improve the fit. Numerous authors have criticized the use of extensive data-based modifications (MacCallum, 1986; MacCallum, Roznowski, & Necowitz, 1992). In bias investigations, a sequence of models is evaluated, each model representing a particular hypothesis about the source of bias in **X**. At any stage in this sequence, rejection of a model will naturally lead to the potential for data-based modifications to improve the fit. Investigators must be aware that data-based modifications may improve the fit to the data at hand but may also fail to cross-validate in subsequent studies, especially when many modifications are made.

Invariance Constraints

We now consider a sequence of models that can be evaluated for fit in studies of factorial invariance. Jöreskog (1971b) may have been the first to propose a general sequence for this purpose in the context of CFA, although earlier work had distinguished different forms of invariance (Meredith, 1964; Thurstone, 1947). Jöreskog excluded mean structures from consideration. Sörbom (1974) extended Jöreskog's approach to models in multiple groups with hypothesized structures on means. More recently, a number of authors have considered nested sequences of models in this context (Byrne, Shavelson, & Muthén, 1989; Reise, Widaman, & Pugh, 1993; Steenkamp & Baumgartner, 1998; Vandenberg & Lance, 2000).

We begin with the question of whether *any* differences exist in the mean and covariance structures across populations. Jöreskog (1971b) described a test of invariance for the covariance matrices Σ_{xk}, but this test can be expanded to include tests for invariance in the mean vectors μ_{Xk}. Specifically, the model being tested is represented as

$$H_{01}: \Sigma_{Xk} = \Sigma_X, \quad \mu_{Xk} = \mu_X \tag{4.42}$$

for $k = 1,\ldots,K$. This hypothesis can be tested in a variety of ways without the use of structural equation modeling software (e.g., Anderson, 1984), but it is easily tested using such software by proper specification of the parameters in Equation 4.4. A simple approach is to set $r = p$, $\Lambda_k = I_r$, $\Theta_k = 0$, $\kappa_k = 0$ for $k = 1,\ldots,K$. The invariance constraints $\Phi_k = \Phi$, $\tau_k = \tau$ are then imposed for $k = 1,\ldots,K$. These constraints lead to H_{01} in the context of the other restrictions. Rejection of the model will imply that the populations differ in either covariance structure, mean structure, or both. It should be noted that failure to reject the model does not confirm the fit of the common factor model in Equations 4.3 and 4.4 for $r < p$. Failure to reject the model could be used to justify pooling data from the K populations for purposes of testing hypotheses about factor structure, as noted by Jöreskog. Traditional hypotheses about the factor structure could then be tested in the pooled sample. We will not pursue these options here, as such models are essentially single group factor models.

Assuming that H_{01} is rejected, the next question of interest would be to decide whether the linear factor model that specifies $r < p$ factors in each population provides an adequate representation for the data, apart from any invariance restrictions. The researcher must decide between two possible approaches to this question. One approach is to simply ask whether *any* set of r common factors will suffice. Alternatively, one can directly test whether a set of r factors that have a particular structure will fit the data. Both approaches stipulate r common factors, but the latter approach adds further restrictions on the factor pattern matrix in each population.

We first consider the weaker model that simply requires r common factors, including sufficient constraints for rotational uniqueness but no invariance constraints. The specification of this factor model in the single-population case was discussed by Jöreskog (1979) and more recently by Mulaik and Millsap (2000). The value of r must be chosen based on knowledge of the variables in X and on prior research. The number of common factors should correspond to the number of target latent variables that X was designed to measure. If great uncertainty exists regarding the proper choice of r, the variables in X are probably not ready for the confirmatory approach adopted here, as discussed earlier. Assuming that r can be specified, the model to be tested is

$$H_{02}: \Sigma_{Xk} = \Lambda_k \Phi_k \Lambda_k' + \Theta_k, \quad \mu_{Xk} = \tau_k + \Lambda_k \kappa_k \tag{4.43}$$

for $k = 1,\ldots,K$, with minimal constraints on Λ_k and/or Φ_k needed for uniqueness. The constraints on the parameters in the mean structure equation would be those sufficient to identify the parameters. No invariance constraints are considered here. As a result, the equation for the mean structure places no testable restrictions on the observed means and will reproduce them perfectly. The covariance structure equation will impose testable restrictions, however. Rejection of H_{02} suggests that the common factor model with r factors is untenable for at least one or more populations. In this case, it is clear that factorial invariance with r common factors is unrealistic for the data at hand. Naturally, one could repeat the test, now specifying $r + 1$ common factors in each group. This type of testing approach is essentially an EFA, however, and as noted above, the need for this type of analysis may simply indicate that not enough is known about the variables in X to justify studies of factorial invariance. On the other hand, the researcher may have a focused hypothesis that certain populations require $r + 1$ factors while others require only r common factors. Hypotheses of this sort can be tested by repeating H_{02} but permitting $r + 1$ factors where appropriate. We will return to this possibility below.

A drawback of the above test of minimally restricted structure with r factors is that many parameters are needed for large p and r. An alternative approach is to require an independent cluster structure (i.e., each measured variable loads on one and only one factor) for each Λ_k, with configural invariance of this structure as defined earlier. We can represent this hypothesis as

$$H_{03}: \Sigma_{Xk} = \Lambda_{kc}\Phi_k\Lambda'_{kc} + \Theta_k, \quad \mu_{Xk} = \tau_k + \Lambda_{kc}\kappa_k \qquad (4.44)$$

for $k = 1,\ldots,K$, where Λ_{kc} denotes that the pattern matrices have the cluster structure, with configural invariance. If elements of the pattern matrices are used to fix the scales of the factors, each pattern matrix will have a maximum of $p - r$ nonzero free elements. The model in H_{03} implies that there are the same number of factors in each population and that these factors are associated with the same subsets of variables in each population. Note that H_{02} and H_{03} imply different factor structures only if $r > 1$. The model in H_{03} places no restrictions on the observed means, assuming again that minimal identification constraints are placed on the parameters in the mean equations.

Assuming that H_{02} (or, alternatively, H_{03}) cannot be rejected, the next model to consider would be one in which the pattern matrices are constrained to be fully invariant:

$$H_{04}: \Sigma_{Xk} = \Lambda\Phi_k\Lambda' + \Theta_k, \quad \mu_{Xk} = \tau_k + \Lambda\kappa_k \qquad (4.45)$$

for $k = 1,\ldots,K$. We will denote this condition as one of *pattern invariance*. Pattern invariance has been denoted alternatively as *metric invariance* (Horn & McArdle, 1992; Thurstone, 1947) or as weak factorial invariance

(Widaman & Reise, 1997). Pattern invariance can be considered in several distinct forms, depending on what additional restrictions in Λ are introduced. One possibility is to introduce only minimal restrictions needed for uniqueness, as in H_{02}. In this case, H_{04} might be evaluated following H_{02}, with H_{04} being simply a restricted version of H_{02}. A second possibility is to incorporate the confactor restriction in H_{04}, as reviewed earlier. A third possibility is to reach H_{04} by adding invariance restrictions to H_{03}, with the invariant pattern now meeting the requirements of independent cluster structure. This third possibility is common enough to have its own designation as

$$H_{05}: \Sigma_{Xk} = \Lambda_c \Phi_k \Lambda_c' + \Theta_k, \quad \mu_{Xk} = \tau_k + \Lambda_c \kappa_k \qquad (4.46)$$

for $k = 1,\dots,K$. The model specified in H_{05} is the most restricted form of pattern invariance that would be considered in practice. Note that H_{05} still places no testable restrictions on the observed means, assuming that only minimal identification constraints are placed on the parameters τ_k and κ_k.

Assuming that some form of pattern invariance cannot be rejected, the sequence of further models that might be tested will depend on the needs of the investigation. In most cases, interest will center on invariance restrictions in the latent intercepts τ_k and the unique factor covariance matrices Θ_k. Together with the factor pattern matrices Λ_k, it is these parameters that determine factorial invariance. We will begin with a model that adds restrictions to H_{04} to have invariance in the intercepts

$$H_{06}: \Sigma_{Xk} = \Lambda \Phi_k \Lambda' + \Theta_k, \quad \mu_{Xk} = \tau + \Lambda \kappa_k \qquad (4.47)$$

for $k = 1,\dots,K$. This model is consistent with the *strong factorial invariance* condition defined by Meredith (1993). The model has also been known as the *scalar invariance* model (Steenkamp & Baumgartner, 1998). Note that we could also impose constraints in H_{06} using the model from H_{05}, if the cluster structure is desired. The model in H_{06} specifies that population differences in means μ_{Xk} for the observed variables X are attributable solely to population differences in common factor means. The model in H_{06} also meets the condition of first-order measurement invariance, as defined in Chapter 3. Unlike the previous models considered, this model places testable restrictions on the means of the measured variables.

A different model that could be tested would restrict H_{04} by imposing invariance on the unique factor covariance matrices

$$H_{07}: \Sigma_{Xk} = \Lambda \Phi_k \Lambda' + \Theta, \quad \mu_{Xk} = \tau_k + \Lambda \kappa_k \qquad (4.48)$$

for $k = 1,\dots,K$. This model implies that population differences in the covariance structure of the measured variables are due solely to population differences in the common factor covariance structure. No restrictions are placed on the means of the observed variables here, assuming the usual identification constraints on the parameters of the mean equations.

The models represented by H_{06} and H_{07} are not nested and could be evaluated in any order. Alternatively, we can combine H_{06} and H_{07} into a single model that incorporates both sets of invariance restrictions

$$H_{08}: \mathbf{\Sigma}_{Xk} = \mathbf{\Lambda}\mathbf{\Phi}_k\mathbf{\Lambda}' + \mathbf{\Theta}, \qquad \mathbf{\mu}_{Xk} = \mathbf{\tau} + \mathbf{\Lambda}\mathbf{\kappa}_k \qquad (4.49)$$

for $k = 1,\ldots,K$. This model represents second-order measurement invariance, as defined in Chapter 3. It is also consistent with the condition of *strict factorial invariance* of Meredith (1993). Under strict factorial invariance, population differences in the means and covariance structure for the measured variables are attributable to differences in common factor distributions, rather than to measurement bias. Hence, failure to reject H_{08} is equivalent to failure to detect measurement bias as revealed through the means and covariance structure for **X**. Technically, strict factorial invariance is not equivalent to measurement invariance unless additional distributional assumptions are introduced, as noted earlier.

The above sequence of tests has omitted consideration of invariance restrictions on the factor covariance matrices $\mathbf{\Phi}_k$ or the factor mean vectors $\mathbf{\kappa}_k$. This omission is intentional: invariance restrictions on either $\mathbf{\Phi}_k$ or $\mathbf{\kappa}_k$ are not part of factorial invariance as usually defined. As defined earlier, factorial invariance concerns the conditional distribution of the measured variables $\mathbf{X}_k$ given the factor scores $\mathbf{W}_k$. After conditioning on the factor score, the parameters governing the distribution of the factor scores are no longer relevant. Hence, group differences in either $\mathbf{\Phi}_k$ or $\mathbf{\kappa}_k$ have no implications for the issue of factorial invariance. We may of course wish to test invariance restrictions on these parameters for other reasons.

The foregoing set of models represented in H_{01} to H_{08} are summarized in Table 4.2. Note that the model order listed in Table 4.2 does not reflect a strictly nested sequence, although selected models do have nested relations. For example, the model in H_{03} is nested within the model in H_{02} because H_{03} can be reached via simple restrictions on the model in H_{02}. On the other hand, H_{07} is not nested within H_{06}. Also, any given investigation of factorial invariance may or may not evaluate all of these models. The constraints to be adopted for the factor loadings may influence the choice of which models will be tested. It is common practice to adopt an independent cluster pattern for multiple factors, with each measured variable loading on only a single factor. This cluster pattern may be inappropriate for the data at hand, however, and could complicate the evaluation of invariance. In such cases, it may be more useful to evaluate invariance without imposing a full cluster structure on the loadings.

TABLE 4.2

Models of Factorial Invariance

Model	Description
H_{01}: $\Sigma_{Xk} = \Sigma_X$, $\mu_{Xk} = \mu_X$	Complete homogeneity of mean and covariance structures across populations
H_{02}: $\Sigma_{Xk} = \Lambda_k \Phi_k \Lambda'_k + \Theta_k$, $\mu_{Xk} = \tau_k + \Lambda_k \kappa_k$	Factor model with r common factors holds in each population
	Only identification restrictions on loadings
H_{03}: $\Sigma_{Xk} = \Lambda_{kc} \Phi_k \Lambda'_{kc} + \Theta_k$, $\mu_{Xk} = \tau_k + \Lambda_{kc} \kappa_k$,	Factor model with r common factors holds in each population
	Independent cluster loading structure. Configural invariance
H_{04}: $\Sigma_{Xk} = \Lambda \Phi_k \Lambda' + \Theta_k$, $\mu_{Xk} = \tau_k + \Lambda \kappa_k$,	Invariant factor loadings across populations for r factors: pattern invariance
	Only identification restrictions on loadings
H_{05}: $\Sigma_{Xk} = \Lambda_c \Phi_k \Lambda'_c + \Theta_k$, $\mu_{Xk} = \tau_k + \Lambda_c \kappa_k$,	Invariant factor loadings with independent cluster structure
H_{06}: $\Sigma_{Xk} = \Lambda \Phi_k \Lambda' + \Theta_k$, $\mu_{Xk} = \tau + \Lambda \kappa_k$,	Invariant loadings and invariant factor intercepts: strong factorial invariance. Loading structure may or may not be independent cluster
H_{07}: $\Sigma_{Xk} = \Lambda \Phi_k \Lambda' + \Theta$, $\mu_{Xk} = \tau_k + \Lambda \kappa_k$,	Invariant loadings and invariant unique factor variances. Could combine with to H_{06} achieve strict factorial invariance
H_{08}: $\Sigma_{Xk} = \Lambda \Phi_k \Lambda' + \Theta$, $\mu_{Xk} = \tau + \Lambda \kappa_k$	Invariant loadings, intercepts, and unique variances: strict factorial invariance

Partial Invariance

All of the models specified by H_{04} to H_{08} have included invariance constraints on the nonzero elements of one or more of the parameter matrices $\{\tau_k, \Lambda_k, \Theta_k\}$. These invariance constraints are introduced as a block of constraints involving an entire matrix in each case. Yet it is clearly possible in every case to selectively introduce invariance constraints on isolated elements or sets of elements in any of the parameter matrices $\{\tau_k, \Lambda_k, \Theta_k\}$. Byrne et al. (1989) denote the conditions induced by such limited constraints as *partial invariance*. Partial invariance exists with respect to a given parameter matrix when some, but not all, of the matrix elements are invariant. Partial invariance could arise by design if one purposefully introduces limited invariance constraints. Examples of this case are given below. Alternatively, partial invariance may arise after rejection of one of the hypotheses H_{04} to H_{08}, followed by a search for misspecification.

An example of purposeful partial invariance could exist when Λ_k is assumed to have an independent cluster structure and $r > 1$, as in H_{05}. Instead of imposing pattern invariance for all common factors as in H_{05}, one could pick a subset of the r common factors and impose invariance constraints on the columns of the pattern matrix corresponding to those factors. Partial invariance in this form would be useful if one suspected that only a subset of the measured variables (i.e., those loading on a particular factor or set of factors) should be regarded as unbiased. Corresponding partial invariance constraints could then be adopted for the intercepts τ_k and the unique factor variances in Θ_k. The requirement of cluster structure in this case permits one to locate the source of the violation of H_{05} in particular common factors and corresponding variable subsets. Of course, it is possible that the violations of H_{05} are not neatly confined to particular factors, but rather involve selected variables from different factors. From a purely statistical viewpoint, this more complex possibility presents no difficulty, but the interpretation of the resulting mixture of invariance and bias may be unclear.

If a cluster structure is not assumed for Λ_k, partial invariance constraints could still be introduced, but their interpretation may be difficult in some cases. For example, one could impose invariance constraints on selected columns of Λ_k, letting other columns assume varying values across populations. The resulting model would include, for any given measured variable, a mixture of invariant and population-specific factor loadings. The choice of which columns to designate as invariant may be difficult, however.

Another form of partial invariance might be introduced after rejection of H_{02}. Suppose that the number of common factors is found to vary across populations. In the simplest case of $K = 2$ populations, we can let r_1 and r_2 be the number of common factors in the two populations, with $r_1 < r_2$. We might hypothesize that there are r_1 factors that are common to the two populations, with the additional $r_2 - r_1$ factors being specific to population two. It would then be possible to test a sequence of invariance hypotheses regarding just the r_1 factors that are believed to operate similarly in the two groups. For example, the r_1 columns of Λ_2 that are believed to correspond to these r_1 factors could be constrained to equal Λ_1. This type of investigation would be worthwhile if one wished to establish that the bias in X is due to the presence of additional factors in one or more populations.

A third possibility for partial invariance by design might occur if one has prior hypotheses about which measured variables violate invariance. These hypotheses could be based on prior research or on considerations of the content of the measured variables. The hypotheses would need to not only identify which variables are problematic but also which parameters in the set $\{\tau_k, \Lambda_k, \Theta_k\}$ are affected. Here tests of partial invariance become tests of the bias hypothesis. This approach to invariance testing is underutilized.

A common situation leading to partial invariance arises when rejection of one of the hypotheses H_{04} to H_{08} is followed by a search for which parameters are the source of the rejection. The end result is that some parameters can be constrained to invariance while others cannot. This type of search is an example of a specification search (MacCallum, 1986; MacCallum et al., 1992).

The search is guided by a mixture of theory and data-generated fit information. When p and/or r is large, the search can require many implicit hypothesis tests and is vulnerable to capitalization on chance. Controls for type I error rate inflation may be needed if formal statistical tests are used. A further problem is that constraints used for identification can interfere with the search for misspecification, as noted earlier. All of these influences work against the chances of a successful search. Researchers have begun to study this type of specification search (Oort, 1998; Yoon & Millsap, 2007). The same problem has been intensively studied for methods of bias detection using IRT and for observed score methods. For example, what sample sizes are needed to have adequate power for detecting which variables are violating invariance? How does the performance of the search vary depending on the proportion of items that violate invariance?

An Example

The data to be used in this example consist of scores on the 11 subtests of the WAIS-R for $N = 1880$ individuals in the United States, obtained from a nationwide cross-sectional sample in 1979. The data formed the standardization sample for the 1980 standardization of the WAIS-R. The demographic variable of interest in the analyses reported here is sex. The sample contains 940 females and 940 males. Table 4.3 presents the means, standard deviations, and correlations for the male and female subsamples on the seven subtests to be analyzed here.

One difficulty facing factor analytic studies of the WAIS-R is that the subtests were never originally created to follow any particular factor theory (Flanagan, McGrew, & Ortiz, 2000). Previous analyses of the WAIS-R have led to varying conclusions about the factor structure of the 11 subtests, but a three-factor structure has received some support (for a review, see Leckliter, Matarazzo, & Silverstein, 1986). The three factors have been labelled Verbal Comprehension, Perceptual Organization, and Working Memory/Freedom from Distractibility. The analyses reported here are confined to 7 of the original 11 subtests, dropping Digit Span, Arithmetic, Digit Symbol, and Object Assembly. Digit Span, Arithmetic, and Digit Symbol form the Working Memory/Freedom from Distractibility factor found in many studies of the WAIS-R. Digit Span and Digit Symbol have higher means in the female group, unlike the other nine subtests. Dropping Digit Span, Arithmetic, and Digit Symbol, the remaining eight subtests typically divide into two factors: Verbal Comprehension (Information, Vocabulary, Comprehension, Similarities) and Perceptual Organization (Picture Completion, Picture Arrangement, Block Design,

TABLE 4.3

WAIS-R Correlations, Standard Deviations, and Means
for Male and Female Groups

	Info	Voca	Comp	Simi	Pcmp	Parr	Bdes
Males							
Info	1.000						
Voca	.822	1.000					
Comp	.670	.738	1.000				
Simi	.637	.680	.630	1.000			
Pcmp	.472	.489	.447	.569	1.000		
Parr	.455	.454	.427	.524	.583	1.000	
Bdes	.450	.455	.413	.554	.590	.577	1.000
SDs	3.104	3.058	3.094	3.220	2.998	3.100	3.095
Means	9.822	9.412	9.606	9.007	9.151	8.967	9.159
Females							
Info	1.000						
Voca	.822	1.000					
Comp	.716	.768	1.000				
Simi	.695	.722	.709	1.000			
Pcmp	.521	.536	.549	.577	1.000		
Parr	.480	.493	.504	.539	.591	1.000	
Bdes	.463	.479	.477	.532	.612	.518	1.000
SDs	2.803	2.968	3.055	3.181	3.240	3.092	2.864
Means	8.978	9.252	9.329	8.973	8.659	8.537	8.421

Object Assembly). In the current data, a preliminary examination of a
two-factor model for the eight subtests in the male and female subsamples
showed that Object Assembly does not conform to this two-factor structure. The problem lies in the large correlation between Object Assembly
and Block Design, particularly among males (males = .711, females = .662).
Object Assembly was dropped from the model for the analyses reported
here, but inclusion of Object Assembly in the same sequence of analyses
does not lead to any suggestion of bias in this subtest in relation to sex.

The first model fit to the data omitted any invariance constraints and
simply examined whether a two-factor model could be used as a basis for
further modeling. The factor pattern matrices in each group incorporated
minimal constraints needed for rotational uniqueness, with the Vocabulary
subtest having a fixed unit loading on the first factor and the Block Design
subtest having a fixed unit loading on the second factor. The latent intercepts are indentified by fixing two intercepts to zero in each group, corresponding to the two subtests used in the identification of the pattern
matrices. Fit statistics for this model and all subsequent models are given

TABLE 4.4

Fit Statistics for WAIS-R Factor Analytic Models in Male
and Female Groups

Model	Chi-square	df	RMSEA (90% Confidence Interval)	SRMR Males	SRMR Females	CFI
1	32.818	16	.0333 (.0165, .0496)	.0088	.0078	.999
2	88.744	26	.0409 (.0289, .0531)	.0313	.0306	.997
3	277.635	31	.0943 (.0846, .1040)	.0511	.0478	.981
4	169.379	31	.0683 (.0583, .0786)	.0292	.0336	.990
5	88.225	30	.0450 (.0341, .0561)	.0307	.0315	.996
6	121.428	37	.0488 (.0392, .0587)	.0341	.0373	.994

Notes: Model 1, no invariance constraints; Model 2, invariant loadings; Model 3, invariant clustered loadings; Model 4, invariant nonclustered loadings, invariant intercepts; Model 5, same as Model 4 with group differences in information intercept; Model 6, same as Model 5 with invariant unique factor variances.

in Table 4.4. All analyses were performed using LISREL 8.52 (Jöreskog & Sörbom, 2002) with maximum likelihood estimation. As shown in Table 4.4, the two-factor model does not provide an exact fit but is acceptable by conventional standards of approximate fit. Table 4.5 presents the factor loading estimates for each group. Note that Similarities shows fairly large loadings on both factors in each group, while the other subtests array themselves into the expected factors described earlier. The correlations between the two factors were .62 for males and .69 for females.

The next model imposes invariance on the factor pattern matrices. Here the constraints needed for identification are shifted to require the factor variances to equal one in the male group. The factor variances in the female group are unconstrained. The factor pattern elements that were constrained to zero in the first model are still constrained in this second model. No fixed nonzero elements in the factor pattern matrices are needed. The identification constraints for the intercepts are identical to those used in the first model. The fit of this second model is worse than that of the first model, but the degree of approximate fit remains acceptable. Both the RMSEA and the SRMSR values are within conventional bounds. The results do not provide any strong evidence for group differences in the factor pattern matrices.

TABLE 4.5

Factor Loading Estimates from Model 1

	Males		Females	
Subtest	F1	F2	F1	F2
Information	.876	.095	.867	.046
Vocabulary[a]	1.0	0	1.0	0
Comprehension	.755	.152	.772	.266
Similarities	.504	.584	.641	.498
Picture completion	.055	.932	.007	1.256
Picture arrangement	.027	.952	.079	.977
Block design[a]	0	1.0	0	1.0

[a] Loadings fixed for identification.

A third model is attempted next that forces the invariant factor pattern matrix to have an independent cluster structure. Each subtest is required to load on only one factor. The Information, Vocabulary, Comprehension, and Similarities subtests are allocated to factor one. The Picture Completion, Picture Arrangement, and Block Design subtests are allocated to factor two. All identification constraints are the same as those used in the second model. This third model provides a poor fit, as indicated by the RMSEA statistic. The SRMSR values also increase but are arguably still within the acceptable range. Given that the strict cluster structure is not required for purposes of investigating factorial invariance, we reject this third model while retaining the invariant pattern constraints from the second model.

The fourth model adds invariance constraints on the latent intercepts to the second model. The identification constraints for the factor pattern matrix remain the same as in the second model. The identification constraints for the latent intercepts are changed, now fixing the latent means in the male group to zero. The latent means in the female group are unconstrained. None of the latent intercepts are fixed in either group. This fourth model shows some loss of fit in relation to the second model. The RMSEA value, while still smaller than the .08 cutpoint for a fair fit, is larger than .05. The 90% confidence interval around the RMSEA lies wholly above the .05 value. The fit statistics suggest that we should examine the local fit indices for the source of the lack of fit. In Table 4.2, the largest group difference in means across the studied subtests is in the Information subtest, suggesting that this subtest may be partially responsible for the lack of fit. This view is supported by the modification indices, with the largest modification index among the intercepts corresponding to the Information intercept. A fifth model is specified that relaxes the invariance constraint on the Information intercept, while retaining all other constraints as in the fourth model. The fit of this fifth model is improved considerably in

TABLE 4.6

Factor Model Parameter Estimates from Model Six[a]

Subtest	Factor Loadings		Unique Variances	Latent Intercepts
	F1	F2		
Factor loadings				
Information	.839	.050	.239	9.822 (9.121)
Vocabulary	.939	0[b]	.118	9.395
Comprehension	.704	.150	.344	9.567
Similarities	.506	.377	.352	9.159
Picture completion	.046	.762	.371	9.170
Picture arrangement	.050	.699	.464	8.993
Block design	0[b]	.755	.430	9.039

[a] Common metric completely standardized scaling used for factor loading and unique variance estimates.

[b] Parameter fixed to zero for identification.

comparison to the fourth model. The RMSEA estimate is now below .05, with a 90% confidence interval that includes .05. Further removal of constraints on the latent intercepts might improve the fit, but the modification indices do not indicate that dramatic improvement is likely. A final model is tested that adds invariance constraints on the unique factor variances to the fifth model. This sixth model shows some loss of fit relative to the fifth model, but the loss is small. We retain this sixth model as the final model for these data. Parameter estimates from Model 6 are given in Table 4.6.

To summarize, all relevant model parameters are invariant in relation to sex, with one exception. The exception is the latent intercept for the Information subtest. The sample means for this subtest were 9.82 for males and 8.98 for females. The intercept estimates for Information were 9.822 for males and 9.121 for females. The group difference in the observed means was thus .84, of which about .70 is due to the intercept difference. In other words, while a mean difference favoring males appears on the Information subtest, most of this difference is accounted for by influences apart from the two common factors modeled here.

Appendix: Factorial Invariance and Selection

Suppose that **X** fits a common factor model in a single population. Suppose also that K subpopulations are created from the single parent population through selection. What is the factor structure for **X** in these subpopulations? What aspects of that structure are invariant across the subpopulations? This selection problem has a long history in the factor analytic literature (Ahmavaara, 1954; Bloxom, 1972; Cattell, 1944; Meredith, 1964; Thomson & Lederman, 1939; Thurstone, 1947). Depending on the basis for the selection, general theorems on the consequences of selection for multivariate observations can be applied to the problem (Aitken, 1934; Lawley, 1943; Pearson, 1902). The selection problem has clear relevance for the topic of this chapter, given our interest in invariance over multiple populations.

The typical approach to the selection problem begins with the assumption that a common factor structure holds for X in the parent population. Suppose that X meets the assumptions of the common factor model with r common factors for all members of the parent population:

$$X_j = \tau_j + \sum_{m=1}^{r} \lambda_{jm} W_m + U_j \qquad (4.A.1)$$

for $j = 1,\ldots,p$. Note that the above model is identical to Equation 4.1 without the group subscripts. Letting W and U be vectors containing W_m and U_j, respectively, we also assume

$$\mathrm{Cov}(W,U) = 0, \quad \mathrm{Cov}(W) = \Phi, \quad \mathrm{Cov}(U) = \Theta, \qquad (4.A.2)$$

with Θ being a $p \times p$ diagonal matrix. We can also specify $E(W) = 0$ and $E(U) = 0$ without any loss of generality. Meredith (1993) denotes the above conditions on X, W, and U as defining what is meant by saying that X is "factorial" in the parent population.

Now consider K disjoint subpopulations Π_k, $k=1,\ldots,K$, selected from the parent population by any method of selection. Given that Equation 4.A.1 holds for every member of the parent population, it must also hold in any subpopulation. However, the further conditions on the moments of (W, U) need not hold in all subpopulations. Specifically, within the kth subpopulation, we have

$$\mathrm{Cov}_k(W,U) = \gamma_k, \quad \mathrm{Cov}_k(W) = \Phi_k, \quad \mathrm{Cov}_k(U) = \Theta_k, \qquad (4.A.3)$$

with Θ_k being possibly a non-diagonal matrix. Also, we have for the means

$$E_k(W) = \kappa_k, \quad E_k(U) = \upsilon_k. \qquad (4.A.4)$$

These means may have nonzero values in the subpopulations. Combining Equations 4.A.3 and 4.A.4, the covariance structure in the kth subpopulation is

$$\mathrm{Cov}_k(X) = \Sigma_{Xk} = \Lambda \Phi_k \Lambda' + \Lambda \gamma_k' + \gamma_k \Lambda' + \Theta_k, \qquad (4.A.5)$$

and the mean structure is

$$E_k(\mathbf{X}) = \boldsymbol{\mu}_{Xk} = \boldsymbol{\tau} + \boldsymbol{\Lambda}\boldsymbol{\kappa}_k + \mathbf{v}_k. \tag{4.A.6}$$

These results can be found in Bloxom (1972) and in Meredith (1993). The most important implication of Equation 4.A.5 is that $\mathbf{X}$ need not be factorial in the kth subpopulation. The matrix $\boldsymbol{\Sigma}_{Xk} - \boldsymbol{\Lambda}\boldsymbol{\Phi}_k\boldsymbol{\Lambda}'$ need not be diagonal and is not solely a function of the unique factor variables. Also, in Equation 4.A.6, the unique factor subpopulation means contribute to the means on the measured variables. Hence, subpopulation differences in the means on the measured variables are not solely due to the common factors.

On the basis of the above results, we have no reason to expect that the factor analysis of $\mathbf{X}$ in separate subpopulations will find that $\mathbf{X}$ fits a common factor model with r factors in each case, nor should we expect any structure that is found to meet the conditions for factorial invariance. These results were derived for the completely general case in which no assumptions are made regarding the selection mechanism leading to the subpopulations. Stronger results are available if some assumptions about this mechanism are tenable. We turn now to considering assumptions of this type.

Linear Relations

A multivariate selection theorem given by Lawley (1943), based on earlier work by Pearson (1902) and Aitken (1934), provides a useful starting point for considering selection models. We begin with a general statement of the theorem and then show its application to the factor analytic case.

Lawley's Theorem

Let $\mathbf{f}$ and $\mathbf{g}$ be $m \times 1$ and $t \times 1$ vectors of random variables, respectively. Suppose that the regression of $\mathbf{f}$ on $\mathbf{g}$ is linear and homoscedastic or that (a) $E(\mathbf{f}|\mathbf{g})$ is a linear function of $\mathbf{g}$ and (b) $\mathrm{Cov}(\mathbf{f}|\mathbf{g})$ does not depend on $\mathbf{g}$. Also, suppose that a subpopulation is created based solely on $\mathbf{g}$. The precise method of selection need not be defined, but the selection must be based on $\mathbf{g}$. Lawley's theorem gives the covariance and mean structure for $(\mathbf{g}, \mathbf{f})$ in the selected subpopulation in relation to the structure in the parent population.

To describe these results, define the following notation for the parent population:

$$E(\mathbf{f}) = \boldsymbol{\mu}_f, \quad E(\mathbf{g}) = \boldsymbol{\mu}_g, \quad \mathrm{Cov}(\mathbf{f}) = \boldsymbol{\Sigma}_{ff}, \quad \mathrm{Cov}(\mathbf{g}) = \boldsymbol{\Sigma}_{gg}, \tag{4.A.7}$$

$$\mathrm{Cov}(\mathbf{f}, \mathbf{g}) = \boldsymbol{\Sigma}_{fg}. \tag{4.A.8}$$

We will denote the subpopulation counterparts of the above by an asterisk superscript. For example, Σ_{ff}^* is the covariance matrix for f in the subpopulation. Finally, suppose that the regression of f on g in the parent population is given as

$$E(f|g) = \alpha + Bg, \tag{4.A.9}$$

where
  α is an $m \times 1$ vector of intercepts
  B is the $m \times t$ matrix of regression weights, with $B = \Sigma_{fg}\Sigma_{gg}^{-1}$ by standard theory

We can now state the central result of Lawley's theorem. If Σ_{gg}^* and μ_g^* represent the covariance matrix and mean vector, respectively, for g in the selected subpopulation, Lawley's theorem says that

$$\Sigma_{fg}^* = \Sigma_{fg}\Sigma_{gg}^{-1}\Sigma_{gg}^* = B\Sigma_{gg}^*, \tag{4.A.10}$$

$$\Sigma_{ff}^* = \Sigma_{ff} + B(\Sigma_{gg}^* - \Sigma_{gg})B', \tag{4.A.11}$$

$$\mu_f^* = \mu_f + B(\mu_g^* - \mu_g). \tag{4.A.12}$$

Note that Equation 4.A.10 implies that

$$\Sigma_{fg}^*\Sigma_{gg}^{*-1} = \Sigma_{fg}\Sigma_{gg}^{-1} = B \tag{4.A.13}$$

and so the regression weights in the regression of f on g are unchanged in the subpopulation. The regression intercepts are also unchanged in the subpopulation because Equation 4.A.12 implies that

$$\mu_f^* = \alpha + B\mu_g^*. \tag{4.A.14}$$

The theorem requires no distributional assumptions about f and g, other than the linearity and homoscedasticity assumptions.

Factor Analytic Applications

Lawley's theorem is applied to the factor model by first assuming that Equation 4.A.1 holds for X in the parent population, along with the conditions in Equation 4.A.2. We now replace f with W, the $r \times 1$ vector of common factor variables and require that (a) $E(\mathbf{W}|\mathbf{g})$ is linear, (b) $Cov(\mathbf{W}|\mathbf{g})$ does not depend on $\mathbf{g}$, and (c) $\mathbf{g}$ and $\mathbf{U}$ are independent in the parent population. The linear regression of $\mathbf{W}$ on $\mathbf{g}$ implies that

$$\mathbf{W} = E(\mathbf{W}|\mathbf{g}) + \mathbf{e} = \boldsymbol{\alpha} + \mathbf{B}\mathbf{g} + \mathbf{e} \tag{4.A.15}$$

with $Cov(\mathbf{g}, \mathbf{e}) = 0$ and $E(\mathbf{e}|\mathbf{g}) = 0$. Then from Equation 4.A.1, we have

$$\mathbf{X} = \boldsymbol{\tau} + \boldsymbol{\Lambda}\boldsymbol{\alpha} + \boldsymbol{\Lambda}\mathbf{B}\mathbf{g} + \boldsymbol{\Lambda}\mathbf{e} + \mathbf{U} \tag{4.A.16}$$

or

$$\mathbf{X} = \boldsymbol{\upsilon} + \boldsymbol{\beta}\mathbf{g} + \mathbf{h}, \tag{4.A.17}$$

with $\boldsymbol{\upsilon} = \boldsymbol{\tau} + \boldsymbol{\Lambda}\boldsymbol{\alpha}$, $\boldsymbol{\beta} = \boldsymbol{\Lambda}\mathbf{B}$, and $\mathbf{h} = \boldsymbol{\Lambda}\mathbf{e} + \mathbf{U}$. Note that $Cov(\mathbf{g}, \mathbf{h}) = 0$.

From Equation 4.A.17, it is clear that the regression of $\mathbf{X}$ on $\mathbf{g}$ is linear, meeting the first condition of Lawley's theorem. The homoscedasticity condition is not clearly met, however, because while $\mathbf{U}$ is homoscedastic in relation to $\mathbf{g}$, the composite $\mathbf{h}$ may not be. To use Lawley's theorem, we must fulfill an additional requirement (d) $Cov(\mathbf{h}|\mathbf{g})$ does not depend on $\mathbf{g}$. Combining this fourth assumption with the three earlier assumptions, we can now apply Lawley's theorem to yield

$$\boldsymbol{\Sigma}^*_{Xg} = \boldsymbol{\beta}\boldsymbol{\Sigma}^*_{gg} = \boldsymbol{\Lambda}\mathbf{B}\boldsymbol{\Sigma}^*_{gg}, \tag{4.A.18}$$

$$\boldsymbol{\Sigma}^*_{XX} = \boldsymbol{\Sigma}_{XX} + \boldsymbol{\beta}(\boldsymbol{\Sigma}^*_{gg} - \boldsymbol{\Sigma}_{gg})\boldsymbol{\beta}' = \boldsymbol{\Lambda}\boldsymbol{\Phi}^*\boldsymbol{\Lambda}' + \boldsymbol{\Theta}. \tag{4.A.19}$$

Here $\boldsymbol{\Phi}^* = \boldsymbol{\Phi} + \mathbf{B}(\boldsymbol{\Sigma}^*_{gg} - \boldsymbol{\Sigma}_{gg})\mathbf{B}'$. This result says that in the selected subpopulation, the factor structure for $\mathbf{X}$ will differ from the structure in the parent population only in the common factor covariance matrix $\boldsymbol{\Phi}^*$.

Turning to the mean structure for $\mathbf{X}$, the theorem implies that

$$\boldsymbol{\mu}^*_X = \boldsymbol{\mu}_X + \boldsymbol{\beta}(\boldsymbol{\mu}^*_g - \boldsymbol{\mu}_g). \tag{4.A.20}$$

We know that $\boldsymbol{\mu}_X = \boldsymbol{\tau} + \boldsymbol{\Lambda}\boldsymbol{\kappa}$, and so

$$\boldsymbol{\mu}^*_X = \boldsymbol{\tau} + \boldsymbol{\Lambda}\boldsymbol{\kappa} + \boldsymbol{\Lambda}\mathbf{B}\boldsymbol{\mu}^*_g - \boldsymbol{\Lambda}\mathbf{B}\boldsymbol{\mu}_g, \tag{4.A.21}$$

or

$$\boldsymbol{\mu}^*_X = \boldsymbol{\tau} + \boldsymbol{\Lambda}\boldsymbol{\kappa}^*, \tag{4.A.22}$$

with $\boldsymbol{\kappa}^* = \boldsymbol{\kappa} + \mathbf{B}(\boldsymbol{\mu}^*_g - \boldsymbol{\mu}_g)$. This result says that the latent intercepts in the subpopulation will have the same values as in the parent population.

The general implication of Equations 4.A.19 and 4.A.22 is that factorial invariance should hold in *any* subpopulation selected on the basis of **g**. The implication does not require that **g** be measured or known. All that is required is that *some* vector of random variables in **g** exist for which assumptions (a)–(d) of the theorem hold in relation to **W**. Lawley's theorem provides a rationale for expecting that factorial invariance will be found in subpopulations selected from a parent population.

The application of Lawley's theorem to the factor analytic model encounters at least three problems, however. These problems undercut its value for actual bias investigations to varying degrees. First, the relation of **g** to **V**, the measured vector of actual selection variables that define the populations **Π**, must be clarified. To the extent that **V** contains information relevant to **W** that is not found in **g**, the assumptions of Lawley's theorem are violated. In this case, selection is not based solely on **g** but rather on additional information. We can express this formally by saying that the following condition must also hold for Lawley's theorem to apply to **Π**:

$$E(\mathbf{W}|\mathbf{g},\mathbf{V}) = E(\mathbf{W}|\mathbf{g}). \qquad (4.A.23)$$

Here **V** contributes nothing to the regression of **W** on **g**. Given that **g** is unmeasured, this condition will be difficult to verify empirically.

We can of course satisfy Equation 4.A.23 by simply declaring that **V** = **g**. This step has the advantage of permitting the assumptions of the theorem to be studied empirically. A different problem arises here however. Suppose that the mapping from values of **V** to the subpopulations is such that within any subpopulation, $\mathbf{\Sigma}_{VV}^{*} = \mathbf{0}$. As an example, if **V** consists of the single variable "sex" and the subpopulations are "males" and "females," we have $\sigma_V^2 = 0$ within each subpopulation. Under this condition, we must have **B** = **0** from Equation 4.A.13, implying that $\mathbf{\mu}_x^{*}$ does not vary over **V** from Equation 4.A.19. Also, because we require that Cov(**W**|**g**) does not vary over **g** by assumption, we must have $\mathbf{\Phi}^{*} = \mathbf{\Phi}$. This in turn implies that $\mathbf{\Sigma}_{xx}^{*}$ does not vary over **V**. Hence, by choosing **V** = **g**, we find that the assumptions of the theorem preclude any meaningful implications of the theorem. The case of **V** = **g** is only useful to the extent that $\mathbf{\Sigma}_{VV}^{*} \neq \mathbf{0}$ in the subpopulations.

A second difficulty concerns the assumptions made about the relationship of **g** to **U**, the unique factor variables. It is assumed that **U** and **g** are independent in the parent population. Independence need not hold and may be especially implausible in relation to the specific portion of **U**. An alternative approach to this problem would be to stipulate that **U** also has a linear, homoscedastic regression on **g**. We can develop this argument by defining **f** = (**W**, **U**), with

$$\mathbf{X} = \mathbf{\tau} + \mathbf{\Xi}\mathbf{f}, \quad \mathbf{\Xi} = [\mathbf{\Lambda} \; \mathbf{I}_p], \quad E(\mathbf{f}) = \begin{bmatrix} \mathbf{\kappa} \\ \mathbf{0} \end{bmatrix}, \qquad (4.A.24)$$

$$\text{Cov}(\mathbf{f}) = \mathbf{P} = \begin{bmatrix} \mathbf{\Phi} & \mathbf{0} \\ \mathbf{0} & \mathbf{\Theta} \end{bmatrix}. \tag{4.A.25}$$

Then the regression of $\mathbf{f}$ on $\mathbf{g}$ is

$$E(\mathbf{f}|\mathbf{g}) = \boldsymbol{\alpha} + \mathbf{B}\mathbf{g}. \tag{4.A.26}$$

Expanding this into an equation for $E(\mathbf{X}|\mathbf{g})$,

$$E(\mathbf{X}|\mathbf{g}) = \boldsymbol{\tau} + \boldsymbol{\Xi}\boldsymbol{\alpha} + \boldsymbol{\Xi}\mathbf{B}\mathbf{g} + \boldsymbol{\Xi}\mathbf{e} \tag{4.A.27}$$

or

$$E(\mathbf{X}|\mathbf{g}) = \boldsymbol{\upsilon} + \boldsymbol{\beta}\mathbf{g} + \mathbf{h}, \tag{4.A.28}$$

with $\boldsymbol{\upsilon} = \boldsymbol{\tau} + \boldsymbol{\Xi}\boldsymbol{\alpha}$, $\boldsymbol{\beta} = \boldsymbol{\Xi}\mathbf{B}$, and $\mathbf{h} = \boldsymbol{\Xi}\mathbf{e}$. The regression now satisfies Lawley's theorem, and so

$$\boldsymbol{\Sigma}_{XX}^* = \boldsymbol{\Sigma}_{XX} + \boldsymbol{\beta}(\boldsymbol{\Sigma}_{gg}^* - \boldsymbol{\Sigma}_{gg})\boldsymbol{\beta}' = \boldsymbol{\Xi}\mathbf{P}\boldsymbol{\Xi}' + \boldsymbol{\Xi}\mathbf{B}(\boldsymbol{\Sigma}_{gg}^* - \boldsymbol{\Sigma}_{gg})\mathbf{B}'\boldsymbol{\Xi}' \tag{4.A.29}$$

or

$$\boldsymbol{\Sigma}_{XX}^* = \boldsymbol{\Xi}\mathbf{P}^*\boldsymbol{\Xi}', \tag{4.A.30}$$

with $\mathbf{P}^* = \mathbf{P} + \mathbf{B}(\boldsymbol{\Sigma}_{gg}^* - \boldsymbol{\Sigma}_{gg})\mathbf{B}'$. Unfortunately, the resulting factor structure will not be that of a common factor model because $\mathbf{P}^*$ need not be block-diagonal as is $\mathbf{P}$. We are back into a structure that resembles that of Equation 4.A.5. The results found here are equivalent to those found by selecting subpopulations under the assumption that the observed measures $\mathbf{X}$ are related to $\mathbf{g}$ as in Lawley's theorem (i.e., setting $\mathbf{X} = \mathbf{f}$). We can conclude that in general, the application of Lawley's theorem to selection for *both* $\mathbf{W}$ and $\mathbf{U}$ leads to no useful simplification.

A third difficulty with Lawley's theorem as applied to the factor model is that it rests on an assumption of Equation 4.A.1 for every member of the parent population. A consequence is that Equation 4.A.1 must also hold for *any* subpopulation selected from the parent population, whether the selection depends on $\mathbf{g}$ or on any other set of variables. Hence, the assumption represented in Equation 4.A.1 effectively eliminates competing hypotheses about the factor structure. For example, it may be the case that no single set of parameters $(\boldsymbol{\tau}, \boldsymbol{\Lambda})$ are appropriate for all subpopulations and that the model that specifies subpopulation-specific models is more realistic. This problem is not unique to Lawley's theorem, but rather applies to all theories of invariance that begin with a single model for the parent population.

5

Factor Analysis in Discrete Data

In this chapter, we consider the use of factor analytic models in the investigation of bias in ordered-categorical observed measures. Here a measured variable X_j can assume $C + 1$ discrete values that form an ordinal scale. A typical example of such a variable is a Likert-scaled attitude questionnaire item, with response categories ranging from "strongly disagree" to "strongly agree." A dichotomous test item that is scored pass versus fail is another example with $C = 1$. Although the value of C may vary across different measured variables, we will simplify discussion in this chapter by assuming that the p measured variables X each entail $C + 1$ ordered-categorical responses. Extensions to cases in which the value of C varies are straightforward. Ordered-categorical measures need not be confined to test items. Most test scores could be regarded as ordered-categorical because their metric properties are not firmly established (Cliff & Keats, 2003).

When the ordered-categorical measures X range over a small number of values, the linear factor model in Chapter 4 is no longer an adequate model in general. The failings of the linear factor model in such data have long been studied (Carroll, 1945, 1983; McDonald & Ahlawat, 1974). The problem is most starkly illustrated in the case of a set of dichotomous measures X. For this case, under the linear single-factor model, we have

$$E(X_j \mid W) = P(X_j = 1 \mid W) = \tau_j + \lambda_j W. \tag{5.1}$$

Unless bounds are placed on W, the linear regression of X_j on W is not bounded and may yield values outside of the $(0, 1)$ range needed for the probability in Equation 5.1. The model is therefore structurally improper. Also, it is easily shown that $\text{Var}(X_j \mid W)$ is generally a function of W, unlike the continuous factor model case. As the number of scale points $C + 1$ increases, the continuous factor model more closely approximates the ordered-categorical model (Babakus, Ferguson, & Jöreskog, 1987; Bernstein & Teng, 1989; Olsson, 1979; Rigdon & Ferguson, 1991). With $C > 6$, the methods of Chapter 4 could be adopted as good approximations (but see Lubke & Muthén, 2004, for a contrary view).

In this chapter, we consider alternatives to the linear factor model that are more useful in ordered-categorical data but can still be classified as common factor models. Alternative approaches based on item response theory will be discussed in Chapters 6 and 7. The most common modeling approach for ordered-categorical data within the common factor model relies on the use of latent response variates in a threshold formulation. This threshold formulation will be described in detail, first in the context of a single population and then in the multiple-population case. Special attention is given to the identification problem in both contexts. Estimation is reviewed, and tests of factorial invariance in the ordered-categorical case are described.

The Factor Model

We first describe the factor model for ordered-categorical measures in the case of a single population. This case has been widely discussed in the literature (Bartholomew, 1983, 1984, 1987; Bock & Aitkin, 1981; Browne & Arminger, 1995; Christofferson, 1975; Jöreskog, 1993; Maydeu-Olivares, 2005; Mislevy, 1986; Muthén, 1978, 1984; Wirth & Edwards, 2007). The multiple-population extension will permit the use of parameters, such as factor means, that are not an essential part of the single-population model. For ease of transition with the models of Chapter 4, we first describe the factor model with a parameterization that includes the full range of parameters found in the continuous variable case. As will be described, identification problems arise in the use of all of these parameters in ordered-categorical data.

The Single-Population Case

We begin by assuming that the measured variables X_j can take discrete, ordered values $0, 1, 2, ..., C$, for $j = 1, ..., p$. The numbering of these values could be altered; only their ordinal properties are of interest. The factor model for these variables supposes that for the jth measured variable, there exists a continuous, metric, latent response variate X_j^* whose value determines the category in which X_j will fall. This category is determined by the value of X_j^* in relation to a set of threshold parameters $\nu_j = (\nu_{j0}, \nu_{j1}, ..., \nu_{jC+1})$, with $\nu_{j0} = -\infty$ and $\nu_{jC+1} = \infty$. With the latter restrictions, there are C threshold parameters that may vary, given $C + 1$ ordered categories for the measured variable. We have then

$$P(X_j = c) = P(\nu_{jc} \leq X_j^* \leq \nu_{jc+1}) \qquad (5.2)$$

for $c = 0, 1, \ldots, C$. Note here that the threshold values may be different for different measured variables. The factor model is then introduced for the latent response variables $\mathbf{X}^{*\prime} = (X_1^*, X_2^*, \ldots, X_p^*)$ as

$$E(\mathbf{X}^* \mid \mathbf{W}) = \tau + \Lambda \mathbf{W}, \quad \text{Cov}(\mathbf{X}^* \mid \mathbf{W}) = \Theta, \tag{5.3}$$

where
  $\mathbf{W}$ is the $r \times 1$ vector of common factor scores
  Θ is the $p \times p$ diagonal matrix of unique factor variances
  τ is the $p \times 1$ vector of latent intercept parameters
  Λ is the $p \times r$ factor pattern matrix

The expressions for the conditional mean and covariance structure in Equation 5.3 arise from the score-level representation

$$\mathbf{X}^* = \tau + \Lambda \mathbf{W} + \mathbf{u}, \tag{5.4}$$

with $\mathbf{u}$ a $p \times 1$ vector of unique factor scores such that $E(\mathbf{u}) = 0$ and $\text{Cov}(\mathbf{u}) = \Theta$. For the common factor scores $\mathbf{W}$, we have $E(\mathbf{W}) = \kappa$ and $\text{Cov}(\mathbf{W}) = \Phi$. Also, we assume $\text{Cov}(\mathbf{u}, \mathbf{W}) = 0$. Under this parameterization, we have

$$E(\mathbf{X}^*) = \mu^* = \tau + \Lambda \kappa, \quad \text{Cov}(\mathbf{X}^*) = \Sigma^* = \Lambda \Phi \Lambda' + \Theta. \tag{5.5}$$

The common factor representation for the latent response variates thus parallels the usual linear factor representation for observed variables described in Chapter 4.

In addition to the moment structure for $\mathbf{X}^*$ as just described, the traditional factor analytic model for ordered-categorical data includes the assumption that $\mathbf{X}^*$ has an MVN distribution. This distributional assumption can either be made directly or be derived via similar assumptions for the joint distribution of $(\mathbf{W}, \mathbf{u})$. A great advantage of the MVN distribution in this context is that no moment structures for $\mathbf{X}^*$ beyond the second-order need be considered, and only pairwise associations among the elements of $\mathbf{X}^*$ need be specified in order to study the associations among the measured variables $\mathbf{X}$. Alternatives to the MVN distribution have been considered for use in this context (Bartholomew, 1987; Quiroga, 1992), but these alternatives do not appear to have been used widely in real applications. Under the MVN assumption for the latent response variates, the joint probability for any pair of measured variables X_j and X_h can be written as

$$P(X_j = c, X_h = b) = \int_{v_{jc}}^{v_{jc+1}} \int_{v_{hb}}^{v_{hb+1}} \phi(X_j^*, X_h^*) dX_j^* \, dX_h^*, \tag{5.6}$$

where $\phi()$ is the bivariate normal density function. An important parameter of this density function is the covariance or correlation between the latent response variates. The scales of these variates are not uniquely defined, and so we may regard them as having unit variances in this case. As a result, the correlation between the latent response variates becomes the parameter of interest. This correlation can be estimated from the $(C + 1) \times (C + 1)$ contingency table of response frequencies for X_j and X_h (Olsson, 1979; Olsson, Drasgow, & Dorans, 1982). If $C = 1$, the correlation is a tetrachoric correlation. For $C > 1$, the correlation is a polychoric correlation.

Identification

From the expressions for the marginal and joint probabilities in Equations 5.2 and 5.6 under the MVN assumptions, it can be shown that the parameters of the model in Equation 5.5 are not identified. For example, we can replace X^* with the standard scores

$$Z^* = D_{\Sigma^*}^{-1/2}(X^* - \mu^*) \tag{5.7}$$

given that the response variates cannot be directly measured and have no natural location or scale. Under this standardization, we have

$$P(v_{jc} \leq X_j^* < v_{jc+1}) = P(v_{zjc} \leq Z_j^* < v_{zjc+1}), \tag{5.8}$$

for $j = 1,\ldots,p$ and $c = 0, 1,\ldots, C$, where

$$v_{zjc} = \sigma_j^{*-1}(v_{jc} - \mu_j^*) \tag{5.9}$$

is the transformed threshold under the standardization, σ_j^* is the standard deviation of X_j^*, and μ_j^* is the mean. Both variates X^* and Z^* could be used to represent the measured variable X, and so they are indistinguishable empirically. The factor representations for X^* and Z^* are different, however, creating the identification problem. More generally, any linear transformation

$$Y^* = D(X^* - b) \tag{5.10}$$

with D a $p \times p$ diagonal matrix with nonnegative elements and b a $p \times 1$ vector of constants will create a new set of variates Y^* that are indistinguishable from X^* in reproducing X. The factor models for X^* and Y^* will differ.

In the single-population case, one way to resolve this identification problem is as follows. First, we set the common factor mean and latent intercepts to zero:

$$\kappa = 0, \quad \tau = 0. \tag{5.11}$$

As a result, we must have $\mu^* = 0$ from Equation 5.5. Second, we constrain the latent response variates to unit variance

$$D_{\Sigma^*} = I. \tag{5.12}$$

The combined restrictions in Equations 5.11 and 5.12 put the latent response variates in standard score metric. As a result, the probabilities of various outcomes for X_j in Equation 5.2 can be calculated using the standard normal distribution. Also, the threshold parameters are identified and can be estimated once the empirical response frequencies for X_j are known.

Under the restrictions in Equations 5.11 and 5.12, the remaining parameters of the factor model are the factor loadings Λ and the factor covariance matrix Φ, with

$$\Sigma^* = R^* = \Lambda\Phi\Lambda' + \Theta. \tag{5.13}$$

The diagonal covariance matrix for the unique factors Θ is not independent due to the restrictions in Equation 5.12. The matrix R^* is directly estimable as a polychoric (or tetrachoric) correlation matrix. Once the rotational indeterminacy problem is solved for (Λ, Φ), we can identify these parameters. This rotational problem can be resolved as in the continuous factor case of Chapter 4. One method is to specify r rows of Λ as rows of an $r \times r$ identity matrix. Other approaches are described in Chapter 4. The essential requirement is that r^2 restrictions be imposed on (Λ, Φ).

The location restrictions in Equation 5.11 leave the threshold parameters to be estimated while restricting the means of the latent response variates to zero. An alternative set of restrictions that is equally appropriate in the single-population case would fix one threshold to zero for each of the p response variates. For example, we could fix the threshold corresponding to $c = 1$

$$v_{j1} = 0, \tag{5.14}$$

for $j = 1,\ldots,p$. In addition, we would need to fix r elements of (τ, κ) to ensure identification. This could be done by either fixing $\kappa = 0$ or by fixing r

elements of τ to zero. If the latter option is adopted, some coordination between the restrictions on τ and those later adopted for Λ would be needed, as described in Chapter 4. See Browne and Arminger (1995) for a discussion and illustration of the use of constraints as in Equation 5.14.

From the above discussion of identification, it is clear that in the single-population case, the intercept parameters τ are not really needed in the model and could be omitted without loss. In fact, these parameters have often been ignored in descriptions of the factor model for ordered categorical data in single populations (Mislevy, 1986; Muthén & Christoffersson, 1981). The intercept parameters were included here to ease the transition from models presented in Chapter 4.

The Multiple-Population Case

We now extend the model by assuming that $\mathbf{X}$ is measured in multiple populations $\mathbf{\Pi}$. The multiple-population extension is less widely discussed than the single-population case, but some literature exists (Browne & Arminger, 1995; Lee, Poon, & Bentler, 1989; Millsap & Yun-Tein, 2004; Muthén & Christoffersson, 1981; Poon, Lee, Afifi, & Bentler, 1990). As in the single-population case, scores on X_j are assumed to be determined by the value of the latent response variate X_j^* in relation to a set of threshold parameters ($v_{jk0}, v_{jk1}, \ldots, v_{jkC+1}$) whose values may now depend on both the variable and the population, for $k = 1,\ldots,K$ populations. It is assumed throughout that $v_{jk0} = -\infty$ and $v_{jk0} = \infty$ for $j = 1,\ldots,p$ and all populations, leaving C finite threshold parameters $\boldsymbol{v}_{jk} = (v_{jk1}, v_{jk2}, \ldots, v_{jkC})$. Analogous to Equation 5.2, we have

$$P_k(X_j = c) = P_k(v_{jkc} \leq X_j^* < v_{jkc+1}). \tag{5.15}$$

We will let $\mathbf{T}_K$ represent the $p \times C$ matrix of finite threshold parameters in the kth population, with jth row equal to $\boldsymbol{v}_{jk}$. A given column of this matrix represents the thresholds for a particular response to each of the p measured variables in the kth population. Columns will be denoted as $\boldsymbol{v}_{kc}$. The latent response variates in the kth population are in turn given a common factor representation whose parameters may vary over populations. Specifically, we assume that in the kth population

$$\mathbf{X}^* = \boldsymbol{\tau}_k + \boldsymbol{\Lambda}_k \mathbf{W} + \mathbf{u}. \tag{5.16}$$

We also have

$$E_k(\mathbf{X}^* | \mathbf{W}) = \boldsymbol{\tau}_k + \boldsymbol{\Lambda}_k \mathbf{W}, \quad \mathrm{Cov}_k(\mathbf{X}^* | \mathbf{W}) = \boldsymbol{\Theta}_k. \tag{5.17}$$

Combining these expressions with $E_k(\mathbf{W}) = \boldsymbol{\kappa}_k$ and $\mathrm{Cov}_k(\mathbf{W}) = \boldsymbol{\Phi}_k$, we have

$$\boldsymbol{\mu}_k^* = \boldsymbol{\tau}_k + \boldsymbol{\Lambda}_k \boldsymbol{\kappa}_k, \quad \boldsymbol{\Sigma}_k^* = \boldsymbol{\Lambda}_k \boldsymbol{\Phi}_k \boldsymbol{\Lambda}_k' + \boldsymbol{\Theta}_k, \tag{5.18}$$

assuming that $E_k(\mathbf{u}) = 0$ and $\mathrm{Cov}_k(\mathbf{W}, \mathbf{u}) = 0$. The factor representation here is identical in form to the multiple-population model for continuous observed variables in Chapter 4.

As in the single-population case, some distributional assumptions must be made for the latent response variates. The MVN assumption is typically adopted for the variates in each population. This assumption leads to expressions for the joint probabilities of scores on pairs of observed variables in $\mathbf{X}$ that are identical to the expression in Equation 5.6, with the exception that now the probabilities may depend on the population.

Identification

As will become clear, four separate cases must be considered in deciding which identification constraints are sufficient to identify the factor model for ordered-categorical data in the multiple-population case. The four cases are created by the cross-classification of two dimensions. The first dimension is whether $C = 1$ (dichotomous measures) or $C > 1$. Special consideration must be given to the $C = 1$ case. The second dimension is whether the factor pattern $\boldsymbol{\Lambda}_k$ has an independent cluster structure, with each response variate loading on a single factor and with multiple factors possible across variates. The identification problem is greatly simplified in the independent cluster case. We first consider the $C > 1$ cases.

C > 1, With Cluster Structure

Here the measured variables are polytomous with $C > 1$. The factor pattern matrices $\boldsymbol{\Lambda}_k$ have an independent cluster structure. A given row of $\boldsymbol{\Lambda}_k$ will have only one nonzero element. Any single-factor model fulfills this condition. In a multiple-factor model, each latent response variate is related to a single factor, with different sets of variables related to different factors. We assume that at least three indicators per factor are present. Single indicators, or factors determined by only two indicators, require additional conditions. In the continuous linear factor model, the independent cluster structure in $\boldsymbol{\Lambda}_k$ leads to an identified model under fairly weak conditions (Bollen, 1989). In the factor model for ordered-categorical measures, some additional constraints are needed to achieve identification. Millsap and Yun-Tein (2004) show that the following constraints are sufficient to identify the factor model for ordered-categorical data:

1. In one group to be designated the "reference group," fix $\mu_k^* = 0$ and $\text{diag}(\Sigma_k^*) = I$.
2. Fix $\kappa_k = 0$ in the reference group.
3. In all groups, fix $\tau_\kappa = 0$ and also pick one nonzero loading in each column of Λ_k to fix to one. Each variate chosen for this purpose is denoted the "reference variate" for the corresponding factor.
4. Require that for a given single column of T_k, $\nu_{km} = \nu_m$ for the chosen mth column and for $k = 1,\dots,K$. Additionally, require that for each of the r reference variates, a second threshold parameter must be invariant. A total of $p + r$ thresholds are thus invariant.

The above constraint system begins with the constraints $\text{diag}(\Sigma_k^*) = I$ in (1) for the reference group. An alternative set of constraints would fix $\Theta_k = I$ for the reference group, without fixing $\text{diag}(\Sigma_k^*) = I$. Millsap and Yun-Tien (2004) show that this alternative set of constraints also leads to identification of model parameters when combined with the other constraints in (1)–(4).

Condition (1) places the latent response variates in standard score metric within the reference group. As noted earlier, the thresholds are directly estimable in this case using the observed response frequencies for X_k. Conditions (2) and (3) lead to identification of Λ_k, Φ_k, and Θ_k in the reference group by taking advantage of the independent cluster structure. Condition (4) leads to identification of the thresholds in all groups, as shown in Millsap and Yun-Tein (2004). To illustrate the restrictions in (4), consider six 4-category measures ($C = 3$) in two groups. The matrices T_1 and T_2 might have the following structure under condition (4) for $r = 2$:

$$
T_1 = \begin{bmatrix} v_{11} & v_{12} & v_{113} \\ v_{21} & v_{212} & v_{213} \\ v_{31} & v_{312} & v_{313} \\ v_{41} & v_{42} & v_{413} \\ v_{51} & v_{512} & v_{513} \\ v_{61} & v_{612} & v_{613} \end{bmatrix} \quad
T_2 = \begin{bmatrix} v_{11} & v_{12} & v_{123} \\ v_{21} & v_{222} & v_{223} \\ v_{31} & v_{322} & v_{323} \\ v_{41} & v_{42} & v_{423} \\ v_{51} & v_{522} & v_{523} \\ v_{61} & v_{622} & v_{623} \end{bmatrix}. \tag{5.19}
$$

In the above, the first columns in T_1 and T_2 are invariant, along with the elements in the second column in rows 1 and 4. The remaining four elements in the second column are free, as are the third columns in T_1 and T_2. Complete invariance of thresholds is not required for identification.

The above constraints are sufficient for identification, but other sets of constraints exist that will also lead to identification. For example, it is possible to impose invariance on additional threshold parameters beyond those in condition (4), while permitting nonzero latent intercepts τ_k to vary across groups. The choice of constraints must be based on the researcher's understanding about which model parameters can be taken as invariant without distortion in the remaining portions of the model. Little research exists at present on the consequences of various constraints under violations of invariance in the ordered-categorical case.

C = 1, With Cluster Structure

In this case, the measured variables are dichotomous and the factor pattern matrices Λ_k have an independent cluster structure. Each latent response variate X_j^* is associated with a single threshold parameter, making T_k a $p \times 1$ vector. The identification constraints used for the polytomous case must be modified. Millsap and Yun-Tein (2004) establish that the following set of constraints is sufficient to identify the model:

1. In one group to be designated the "reference group," fix $\mu_k^* = 0$ and $\text{diag}(\Sigma_k^*) = I$.

2. Fix $\kappa_k = 0$ in the reference group.

3. In all groups, fix $\tau_k = 0$ and also pick one nonzero loading in each column of Λ_k to fix to one. Each variate chosen for this purpose is denoted the "reference variate" for the corresponding factor.

4. Require that $T_k = T$ for all $k = 1, \ldots, K$. All thresholds are invariant.

5. Require r diagonal elements of Σ_k^* to be invariant, for $k = 1, \ldots, K$. The chosen elements should correspond to the reference variates in (3).

These constraints are identical to those found in the polytomous independent cluster case, with the exception that r variances of the latent response variates are made invariant. Invariance implies that the selected variances are equal to one due to (1). The locations of the selected variances should be coordinated with the choice of reference variates in (3).

As in the $C > 1$ case, an alternative set of constraints would replace $\text{diag}(\Sigma_k^*) = I$ in (1) with $\Theta_k = I$ for the reference group. In the dichotomous $C = 1$ case, however, additional constraints are needed. These additional constraints replace the r invariance constraints on $\text{diag}(\Sigma_k^*)$ in (5) with r invariance constraints on Θ_k for $k = 1, \ldots, K$. Paired with the reference group restrictions in (1), these additional constraints imply that r elements of Θ_k should be coordinated with the choice of reference variables in (3). Millsap and Yun-Tein (2004) show that these alternative constraints, when combined with the other constraints in (1)–(5), are sufficient to identify the model parameters. The use of Θ_k for the constraints, in place of diag(Σ_k^*), means that r elements of Θ_k must be assumed invariant rather than tested. On the other hand, the use of r invariance constraints in diag(Σ_k^*) means that r elements of diag(Σ_k^*) are fixed to unit values. Given that Θ_k is likely to vary across groups, the constraints on diag(Σ_k^*) mean that for at least r elements of Θ_k, no tests of invariance are possible. The implication here is that in the dichotomous indicator case, it will not be possible to test invariance for all elements of Θ_k. This is the price of using dichotomous indicators.

C > 1, General Structure

Here we consider polytomous measured variables whose factor pattern matrix Λ_k does not meet the requirements for independent cluster structure. These models include multiple common factors ($r > 1$) with at least one variable that loads on more than one factor. As noted in Chapter 4 for the continuous linear factor model, full identification conditions for this general structure are unknown, although results are available in special cases (e.g., Anderson & Rubin, 1956). This problem extends to the factor model for ordered-categorical measures. Millsap and Yun-Tein (2004) show that the following constraints will identify the threshold parameters and will render the factor model to be rotationally unique:

1. In one group to be designated the "reference group," fix $\mu_k^* = 0$ and diag(Σ_k^*) = I.

2. Fix $\kappa_k = 0$ in the reference group.

3. In all groups, fix $\tau_k = 0$ and place constraints on (Λ_k, Φ_k) to achieve rotational uniqueness in each group. Choices for the constraints were described in Chapter 4. A common choice would fix r rows of Λ_k to be rows of an $r \times r$ identity matrix.

4. For two chosen values of m (i.e., two columns in T_k) and for $j = 1,\ldots,p$, fix $v_{jkm} = v_{jm}$ for all k. Two thresholds are constrained to invariance for each latent response variate.

Conditions (4) and (1) lead to identification of the two chosen thresholds for each latent response variate. As shown in Millsap and Yun-Tein (2004), these thresholds permit identification of (μ_k^*, Σ_k^*) for all k. Condition (3) provides rotational uniqueness for (Λ_k, Φ_k) for all k. In many cases, this uniqueness is sufficient for identification of all remaining parameters. Exceptions exist, however, as noted in Chapter 4.

As in the independent cluster case, we can replace the constraint diag(Σ_k^*) = I in (1) with Θ_k = I in the reference group. This alternative constraint set can be shown to yield identification of the threshold parameters and rotational uniqueness for the factor model (Millsap & Yun-Tein, 2004).

C = 1, General Structure

Here the measured variables are dichotomous and the factor pattern matrix does not meet the requirements for independent cluster structure. Again the more complex structure leads to identification problems. The constraints used for the $C > 2$ case cannot be adopted in the dichotomous case because only one threshold parameter is needed for each latent response variate. The following set of constraints can be used in the dichotomous case:

1. In one group to be designated the "reference group," fix $\mu_k^* = 0$ and $\text{diag}(\Sigma_k^*) = I$.
2. Fix $\kappa_k = 0$ in the reference group.
3. In all groups, fix $\tau_k = 0$ and place constraints on (Λ_k, Φ_k) to achieve rotational uniqueness in each group. Choices for the constraints were described in Chapter 4. A common choice would fix r rows of Λ_k to be rows of an $r \times r$ identity matrix.
4. Require that $T_k = T$ for all $k = 1,\ldots,K$. All thresholds are invariant.
5. Require $\text{diag}(\Sigma_k^*) = D$ for all $k = 1,\ldots,K$, where D is a fixed $p \times p$ diagonal matrix that is invariant.

The combination of conditions (1) and (5) leads to $D = I$. As a result, all latent response variates are forced to have unit variance in all groups. The response variate means μ_k^* may vary across groups. In Millsap and Yun-Tein (2004), it is shown that the constraints identify $(T_k, \mu_k^*, \Sigma_k^*)$ for all k, with rotational uniqueness for (Λ_k, Φ_k). As in the independent cluster case, we can replace $\text{diag}(\Sigma_k^*) = I$ in (1) with $\Theta_k = I$ for the reference group. We must also replace $\text{diag}(\Sigma_k^*) = D$ in (5) with $\Theta_k = \Theta$ (i.e., full invariance for Θ_k) for $k = 1,\ldots,K$. This invariance constraint, combined with (1), implies $\Theta_k = I$ for $k = 1,\ldots,K$. The net effect of either the original constraints on $\text{diag}(\Sigma_k^*)$ or the alternative constraints on Θ_k is to render invariance of Θ_k untestable in the general, dichotomous case.

Estimation

Parameter estimation for the factor model in ordered-categorical data has been widely discussed in the single-population case (Bartholomew, 1980, 1983, 1984, 1987; Bock, Gibbons, & Muraki, 1988; Christoffersson, 1975; Jöreskog, 1993; Muthén, 1978). Some of these single-population methods do not yet have extensions to the multiple-population case that would permit tests of invariance across groups. The multiple-population methods that are available are all based on MVN assumptions for the latent response variates $\mathbf{X}^*$ in each population. Alternative distributional assumptions for the multiple-population case do not seem to have been considered, although some attention has been given to such alternatives in the single-population case (Bartholomew, 1987; Quiroga, 1992). In this section, we will describe the major estimation approaches available for the factor analysis of ordered-categorical data in multiple populations.

A variety of methods are now available for the estimation of the threshold parameters $\mathbf{T}_k$, and the means $\boldsymbol{\mu}_k^*$ and covariance matrices $\boldsymbol{\Sigma}_k^*$ of the latent response variates $\mathbf{X}_k^*$ (Lee et al., 1989; Poon et al., 1990). These methods do not proceed with estimation of the factor model parameters that underlie $\boldsymbol{\mu}_k^*$ and $\boldsymbol{\Sigma}_k^*$, but the methods are useful in providing initial tests of distributional assumptions and of general invariance hypotheses. The methods may also be useful for providing estimates that can later be used in invariance testing. It is assumed initially that the observed variables arise through the threshold formulation in Equation 5.15 and that realizations of the latent response variates $\mathbf{X}_k^*$ are independently and identically distributed within each population, with

$$\mathbf{X}_k^* \sim MVN(\boldsymbol{\mu}_k^*, \boldsymbol{\Sigma}_k^*), \tag{5.20}$$

for $k = 1,\ldots,K$. Frequencies of scores on the p observed variables $\mathbf{X}_k$ in the kth population are distributed across a contingency table of dimension $(C + 1)^p$, the distribution being determined by the MVN distribution of the response variates in Equation 5.20 in conjunction with the threshold parameters $\mathbf{T}_k$. Some identification restrictions are needed in order to generate unique estimates of the parameters $(\mathbf{T}_k, \boldsymbol{\mu}_k^*, \boldsymbol{\Sigma}_k^*)$. Poon et al. and Lee et al. adopt the reference group restrictions $\boldsymbol{\mu}_k^* = \mathbf{0}$ and $\mathrm{diag}(\boldsymbol{\Sigma}_k^*) = \mathbf{I}$ for a fixed value of k (e.g., $k = 1$). In addition, the threshold parameters are restricted as $\boldsymbol{\nu}_{jk} = a_j \boldsymbol{\nu}_{j1}$ for $k = 2,\ldots,K$, where population one is chosen as the reference group and $a_j, j = 1,\ldots,p$ are fixed constants. Ordinarily, $a_j = 1$ for $j = 1,\ldots,p$ and so the restrictions create full invariance of the thresholds. These restrictions are somewhat stronger than those discussed in Millsap and Yun-Tein (2004), but the estimation cannot take advantage of the constraints given by the factor model in this case.

With the above assumptions and restrictions, estimates of $(\mathbf{T}, \boldsymbol{\mu}_k^*, \boldsymbol{\Sigma}_k^*)$ can be obtained via maximum likelihood. The full maximum likelihood approach of Lee et al. (1989) is computationally demanding. Poon et al. (1990) present an alternative maximum likelihood approach in which instead of working with full p-variate likelihood, the $p(p - 1)/2$ bivariate likelihoods are separately maximized to obtain parameter estimates. Standard errors for all estimates are available. Large-sample tests of hypotheses on the parameters (μ_k^*, Σ_k^*), such as invariance hypotheses, can be constructed. Any of these can be preceded by an omnibus chi-square test of fit for the model under the identification constraints. This omnibus test would appear to be a useful first step in any bias investigation as a way of evaluating the MVN model. Preliminary tests of MVN assumptions underlying the threshold formulation have been proposed elsewhere (Muthén & Hofacker, 1988).

The above methods do not provide estimates of the factor model parameters $(\Lambda_k, \kappa_k, \Phi_k, \Theta_k)$ in multiple populations under invariance constraints. Methods for estimating such parameters were first developed for the dichotomous case (Christoffersson, 1975; Muthén & Christoffersson, 1981) and are now available for general ordered-categorical data (Browne & Arminger, 1995; Muthén, 1984). A number of efficient likelihood estimation approaches have been developed for the single-population case (Lee, Poon, & Bentler, 1992), and Bayesian approaches are also available (see Edwards [2010] for a recent review), but we will not review these here as they have not yet been extended to multiple populations.

The general approach taken in the available methods for estimation in multiple populations is to use the MVN threshold formulation described earlier, with multiple stages of estimation culminating in the use of generalized (or weighted) least squares in the final stage. Descriptions of this approach can be found in Browne and Arminger (1995), Muthén (1984), Muthén and Christoffersson (1981), and Muthén, du Toit, and Spisac (in press).

The first stage of estimation provides maximum likelihood estimates of the standardized threshold parameters, using separate maximizations in each group. The likelihoods used here are based on the univariate marginal frequencies for each of the p measured variables. Let L_{jk}, $j = 1,...,p$, $k = 1,...,K$, be the univariate log-likelihood for the jth variable in the kth group. Then

$$L_{jk} = \sum_{c=0}^{C+1} n_{jck} \log[P_k(X_j = c \mid \mathbf{W})], \qquad (5.21)$$

where
   n_{jck} is the frequency of responses in the cth category of the jth variable in the kth group
   $P_k(X_j = c \mid \mathbf{W})$ is given in Equation 5.15

The latter probability is solely a function of the standardized threshold parameters, and the maximization of L_{jk} leads to estimates of these thresholds. The results of this maximization will be C standardized threshold estimates for each measured variable in each group. A large-sample estimate of the covariance matrix for these estimates can be obtained (Jöreskog, 1993; Muthén, 1984). Strategically, it may be necessary to collapse or combine some categories within some observed variables prior to beginning estimation due to low frequencies of response.

The second estimation stage provides estimates of the polychoric correlations between each pair of measured variables using the bivariate frequencies of response. Again, separate estimations can be performed within each group because no parameter restrictions are imposed at this stage. The threshold estimates from the first stage of estimation will be used in the second stage. Maximum likelihood using the joint bivariate probabilities will be the method of estimation. Modifying Equation 5.21, we have for $j \neq h$

$$L_{jhk} = \sum_{c=0}^{C+1} \sum_{b=0}^{C+1} n_{cb} \, P_k(X_j = c, X_h = b \mid \mathbf{W}), \qquad (5.22)$$

where

L_{jhk} is the bivariate log-likelihood for the jth and hth variables in the kth group

n_{cb} is the frequency of response in category c of the jth variable and category b of the hth variable

$P()$ is given in Equation 5.6

The latter probability uses the threshold estimates produced in the first stage. An estimate of the large-sample covariance matrix for the polychoric correlation matrix is needed. Estimates for this matrix are described in Muthén and Satorra (1995) and Browne and Arminger (1995).

The third and final estimation stage uses the estimated standardized thresholds and polychoric correlations from the earlier stages, along with their estimated large-sample covariance matrix, to obtain generalized least squares (GLS) estimates of the remaining model parameters $\omega_k = (\mathbf{T}_k, \Lambda_k \kappa_k \Phi_k, \Theta_k)$, where the parameters have been arrayed in a supervector ω_k. Note that the unstandardized threshold parameters appear in this set. Identification constraints and any other desired constraints are introduced during this stage. The number of standardized thresholds in the kth group is $p(C)$, and the number of polychoric correlations (including unit diagonal elements) is $p(p + 1)/2$. Let $\hat{\sigma}_k$ be the $b \times 1$ vector, with $b = pC + p(p + 1)/2$, that contains the estimated thresholds and polychoric correlations for the kth group. Let $\hat{\Omega}_k$ be the $b \times b$ covariance matrix containing the estimated variances and covariances of the elements of $\hat{\sigma}_k$. Let $\sigma_k(\omega)$ be the standardized thresholds and polychoric correlations as functions of the unknown model parameters, subject to any desired restrictions, in the kth group.

Then GLS estimates for ω_k, $k = 1,...,K$, are found by minimizing the discrepancy function

$$F_{CGLS} = \sum_{k=1}^{K} (\hat{\sigma}_k - \sigma_k(\omega))' \hat{\Omega}_k^{-1} (\hat{\sigma}_k - \sigma_k(\omega)). \quad (5.23)$$

Here "CGLS" is used to denote the GLS estimator in the categorical measure case, as distinct from the more general GLS case. The choice for the matrix $\hat{\Omega}_k$ should be a consistent estimator of Ω_k.

Let $\hat{\omega}_k$ be the GLS estimator for the parameters in the kth group, found by minimizing F_{CGLS}. In large samples, $\hat{\omega}_k$ will be distributed as MVN with an expected value of ω_k and a covariance matrix that is

$$\psi_k = (\Delta_k \Omega_k^{-1} \Delta_k)^{-1}, \quad (5.24)$$

where

$$\Delta_k = \frac{\partial \sigma_k(\omega)}{\partial \omega_k} \quad (5.25)$$

is an $a \times b$ matrix of partial derivatives of $\sigma_k(\omega)$ with respect to ω_k, with a being the number of elements in ω_k. The total number of independent parameters to be estimated is $q = \sum_{k=1}^{K} a_k$, with $a_k \leq a$, since identification constraints and other restrictions will reduce the number below the maximum possible value of Ka. Estimates of ψ_k can be obtained by substituting values for $\hat{\omega}_k$ and $\hat{\Omega}_k$ into the expression for ψ_k in Equation 5.24. In large samples, the minimum value of F_{CGLS} has a central chi-square distribution under the specified model with degrees of freedom of $Kb - q$. This chi-square statistic can be used to test the fit of the proposed model, either directly or through the calculation of other fit indices such as the RMSEA.

In practice, with even a moderate number of variables, the matrix $\hat{\Omega}_k$ will be very large and the estimates in the matrix may be unstable in all but the largest samples. An alternative estimation approach that was mentioned in Chapter 4 is available: restrict Ω_k to be a diagonal matrix whose diagonal elements are the variances of the elements in $\hat{\sigma}_k$. This option greatly reduces the number of elements in Ω_k to be estimated and also facilitates inversion of the matrix. The statistical package programs for performing multiple-group CFA in discrete data address this option in different ways. In LISREL (Jöreskog & Sörbom, 2003), this option is known as "diagonally weighted least squares" (DWLS) estimation (Christoffersson, 1975).

In Mplus (Muthén & Muthén, 1998–2006), the option is included in the WLSM and WLSMV options. Each of these options is in turn associated with its own chi-square fit statistic, as described in Chapter 4. Simulation studies have so far supported the use of these alternative chi-square statistics in modest samples (Flora & Curran, 2004).

Aside from the chi-square test of exact fit, some of the global and local fit indices reviewed in Chapter 4 for the continuous case will also be available for the discrete case. The RMSEA statistic is again available, now based on whatever chi-square statistic is being used for exact fit. The rules of thumb for interpretation of the RMSEA are unclear, however; further investigation is needed on this point, although there is no specific reason to expect that the behavior of the statistic will differ greatly from the continuous case. Similarly, a CFI value can be computed with reference to Σ_k^*, rather than Σ_k as in the continuous case. The rules for interpreting the CFI in the discrete case are again unclear. The root mean square residual (RMSR) and its standardized version will be based on the discrepancies $E_k^* = S_k^* - \Sigma_{0k}^*$, where S_k^* is the estimate of Σ_k^* based on the data and Σ_{0k}^* is the fitted matrix based on the model parameter estimates. The resulting RMSR should be interpretable in the usual way. Local fit indices for the discrete case will also be of interest. The residuals E_k^* can be studied for clues to the sources of any misfit. Lagrange multiplier and expected parameter change statistics are also available and should be interpretable.

Tests of Invariance

As in the continuous case of Chapter 4, tests of factorial invariance for ordered-categorical variables can be done as a sequence of nested hypothesis tests. Muthén and Christoffersson (1981) may have been the first to describe the explicit use of such tests in ordered-categorical data under the common factor model. The sequence of tests parallels the sequence pursued for the continuous case by Jöreskog (1971b) and Sörbom (1974). Some limitations on this sequence are imposed by the identification restrictions needed for the ordered-categorical case, however. Also, the use of "latent response variates" as intermediate variables operating between the ordered-categorical indicators and the factors raises additional complexities.

Measurement invariance for **X** in the context of the ordered-categorical factor model holds if

$$P_k(\mathbf{X} \mid \mathbf{W}) = P(\mathbf{X} \mid \mathbf{W}), \tag{5.26}$$

for all values of **X** and **W**, and all populations $k = 1,...,K$. The conditional distribution of **X** given **W** is determined by (a) the thresholds $\mathbf{T}_k$, and (b) the conditional distribution of the latent response variates **X*** given **W**. Let $P_k(\mathbf{X}^*|\mathbf{W})$ be the conditional distribution of **X*** given **W** within the kth population, $k = 1,...,K$. A sufficient set of conditions for measurement invariance of **X** is that both of the following hold

$$\mathbf{T}_1 = \mathbf{T}_2 = \cdots = \mathbf{T}_k, \tag{5.27}$$

$$P_k(\mathbf{X}^*|\mathbf{W}) = P(\mathbf{X}^*|\mathbf{W}), \tag{5.28}$$

for all **X*** and **W**. The second condition in Equation 5.28 requires some distributional assumptions, with the assumption of multivariate normality being the most common choice. These normality assumptions provide a motivation for studying factorial invariance in ordered-categorical data, which focuses on second-order moments and mean structure. Given multivariate normality for $P_k(\mathbf{X}^*|\mathbf{W})$, invariance in the factor model parameters $(\boldsymbol{\tau}_k, \boldsymbol{\Lambda}_k, \boldsymbol{\Theta}_k)$ leads to Equation 5.28. In this multinormal case, we can test for measurement invariance by examining the invariance in the factor model parameters. If multivariate normality does not hold for $P_k(\mathbf{X}^*|\mathbf{W})$, invariance in the factor model parameters need not lead to Equation 5.28 because groups may differ in their higher order moment structure. In this case, the motivation for studying factorial invariance is less clear. Unlike the continuous case in Chapter 4, invariance in the factor model parameters need not imply strong or strict factorial invariance. Note that for the jth measured variable,

$$E_k(X_j \mid \mathbf{W}) = \sum_{c=1}^{C} cP_k(X_j = c \mid \mathbf{W}) = \sum_{c=1}^{C} cP_k(v_{jkc-1} < X_j^* < v_{jkc} \mid \mathbf{W}). \tag{5.29}$$

Strong factorial invariance requires that the above expected value be independent of k. Clearly, independence of k requires that $P_k(\mathbf{X}^*|\mathbf{W})$ also be independent of k, but this need not follow from invariance in the factor model parameters in the non-normal case. Investigators who wish to study measurement invariance in the ordered-categorical case must either believe in multivariate normality assumptions or develop a rationale for studying factorial invariance that does not depend on normality assumptions.

We begin the sequence of tests with a hypothesis of invariance in thresholds, covariance matrices, and mean vectors for the latent response variates.

$$H_{c01}: \boldsymbol{\Sigma}_k^* = \boldsymbol{\Sigma}^*, \quad \boldsymbol{\mu}_k^* = \boldsymbol{\mu}^*, \quad \mathbf{T}_k = \mathbf{T}. \tag{5.30}$$

This hypothesis can be tested independently of any factor model for the data (Lee et al., 1989). Alternatively, one can create the structure in H_{c01} using the factor model under the restrictions $r = p$, $\Lambda_k = \mathbf{I}$, $\Phi_k = \Phi$, $\Theta_k = 0$, $\kappa_k = \kappa$, and $\mathbf{T}_k = \mathbf{T}$. Failure to reject H_{c01} does not confirm any particular structure in the factor model. Failure to reject H_{c01} would suggest that the data could be pooled across populations for exploration of the factor structure. We will assume that H_{c01} has been rejected in what follows.

The next stage in testing will evaluate the fit of a factor model for $r < p$ factors in all populations. Here the number of common factors is chosen to be the hypothesized number of target latent variables. The investigator must decide whether to impose further structure on the factor model at this stage. One option is to use a minimally constrained factor pattern matrix, permitting most variables to load on multiple factors if $r > 1$. A second choice is to adopt an independent cluster structure for the pattern matrices Λ_k. A third choice would use the confactor structure discussed in Chapter 4. Other choices are possible, depending on the needs of the investigation. In all cases, the identification constraints on the threshold parameters $\mathbf{T}_k$ could permit some thresholds to vary across populations unless the measured variables are dichotomous.

In most applications, the two hypotheses of interest are the minimally constrained structure

$$H_{c02}: \Sigma_k^* = \Lambda_k \Phi_k \Lambda_k' + \Theta_k, \quad \mu_k^* = \Lambda_k \kappa_k, \tag{5.31}$$

and the independent cluster case represented by

$$H_{c03}: \Sigma_k^* = \Lambda_{ck} \Phi_k \Lambda_{ck}' + \Theta_k, \quad \mu_k^* = \Lambda_{ck} \kappa_k, \tag{5.32}$$

where Λ_{ck} is the factor pattern matrix under independent cluster constraints, for $k = 1, \ldots, K$. The distinction between the two hypotheses is relevant only if $r > 1$. Both hypotheses require constraints for identification, as described earlier. Ordinarily, both hypotheses also represent configural invariance: The locations of nonzero and zero factor pattern elements are the same across populations. The hypothesis H_{c03} is more parsimonious, requiring fewer parameters.

A poor fit for H_{c02} raises several possibilities. One source of lack of fit may be that the number of factors varies among the K populations. This possibility could be explored by varying the number of factors across groups to evaluate the improvement in fit. Unless some theory can be used to guide the choice of the number of factors, these further analyses will be exploratory factor analyses. A simpler possibility is that the original value of r is uniformly too low and that a larger value of r is needed while maintaining the same number of factors in each group. Assuming that a new and larger value of r is found to produce an adequate fit, invariance hypotheses could again be investigated under this new choice for the number of factors. The problem here, however, is that the original factor structure has been rejected, and the additional factors may not be well motivated theoretically or may be poorly understood. Any results found in further tests of invariance hypothesis will be difficult to interpret. A third possibility is that the factor model itself is inappropriate for the data. An alternative approach in this case might use models from item response theory as described in Chapters 6 and 7.

A poor fit for H_{c03} could be due to any of the above possibilities, but a simpler explanation is that the cluster structure in Λ_{ck} is too restrictive. For example, some latent response variates may load on more than one factor, or a variate may be incorrectly grouped with other variates that all load on a particular factor. Investigators should anticipate these possibilities and should consider which variates are vulnerable to these problems as suggested by any relevant theory. One could use such theory to selectively alter constraints on subsets of variates, changing the same constraints across groups to maintain configural invariance. If extensive modifications of this type are needed to achieve fit, a clear understanding of the factor structure is probably lacking. Investigations of invariance may be premature in this case.

If the factor model with r factors provides an adequate fit under either H_{c02} or H_{c03}, the next hypothesis to be tested imposes invariance on the factor pattern matrix Λ_k. Two cases are distinguished here, paralleling H_{c02} and H_{c03}. Under the minimally constrained structure in H_{c02}, we proceed with

$$H_{c04}: \Sigma_k^* = \Lambda \Phi_k \Lambda' + \Theta_k, \quad \mu_k^* = \Lambda \kappa_k, \tag{5.33}$$

for $k = 1,\ldots,K$. Here the factor loadings are restricted to invariance without imposing the independent cluster structure on the loadings. This approach has the advantage of preventing small departures from the cluster structure from leading to rejection of invariance hypotheses when such departures occur in all populations. A disadvantage is that the model may include many unnecessary parameters. Investigators who wish to maintain the independent cluster structure from H_{c03} can proceed with

$$H_{c05}: \Sigma_k^* = \Lambda_c \Phi_k \Lambda_c' + \Theta_k, \quad \mu_k^* = \Lambda_c \kappa_k, \tag{5.34}$$

for $k = 1,\ldots,K$. This hypothesis imposes both the independent cluster structure and invariance on the factor pattern matrix. Both H_{c04} and H_{c05} represent "metric invariance" in the ordered-categorical context (Horn & McArdle, 1992; Thurstone, 1947). Rejection of either H_{c04} or H_{c05}

could be followed by tests of weaker versions of either hypothesis that permit some nonzero loadings to vary in value across groups. Muthén and Christoffersson (1981) provide an illustration of a partial invariance hypothesis of this type in the ordered-categorical case. A general problem in testing for partial invariance is that inappropriate choices for which variates will serve as reference variates for identification can disrupt tests of partial invariance. This problem exists in the continuous factor case as well, as noted in Chapter 4. One can adopt the constraint configuration used in Chapter 4 here as well. Within the group chosen as the reference group, restrict the diagonal elements of $\mathbf{\Phi}_k$ to have unit values. Do not fix any nonzero elements in the factor pattern matrix $\mathbf{\Lambda}$, but require enough zero elements in $\mathbf{\Lambda}$ to render the pattern to be rotationally unique. Constrain the pattern matrices to be invariant as in H_{c04} or H_{c05}. This parameterization frees the investigator from choosing which factor loadings to fix to common nonzero values across groups. If either H_{c04} or H_{c05} is rejected, however, one must still decide which loadings will be permitted to vary across groups. At present, no respecification procedure exists that can be relied on to locate which loadings should vary across groups in all cases. General principles suggest that the search is more likely to be successful when (a) relatively few loadings lack invariance, (b) samples are large, and (c) relevant theory can point to which loadings vary.

One final case in which either H_{c04} or H_{c05} might fail to hold arises when the variables in $\mathbf{X}$ are dichotomous. In this $C = 1$ case, the model was identified by requiring all thresholds to be invariant ($\mathbf{T}_k = \mathbf{T}$ for $k = 1,\ldots,K$). In practice, this choice of identification may produce problems if the proportions endorsing a given item or a set of items are widely discrepant across groups. Once the factor loadings have been constrained to invariance, the discrepant proportions may create lack of fit. To resolve this problem, one must first identify which variables have the discrepant proportions. Suppose that the jth variable is one such case. Then one can relax the invariance constraint on the threshold for the jth variable ($v_{jlk} = v_{jl}$ for all k). This choice still achieves identification but permits the thresholds to vary for the jth variable, which in turn allows better representation of the discrepant proportions across groups. Identification is maintained due to the invariance constraints on the factor loadings.

If the invariance hypotheses in H_{c04} or H_{c05} can be retained, or if few loadings are found to vary across groups under either hypothesis, the next step will be to restrict the threshold parameters to invariance:

$$H_{c06}: \mathbf{T}_1 = \mathbf{T}_2 = \cdots = \mathbf{T}_k. \tag{5.35}$$

This hypothesis is only of interest in the polytomous case in which $C > 1$. In the dichotomous case, the thresholds are already constrained to invariance for identification. Rejection of H_{c06} suggests that at least one threshold parameter varies across groups and that the conditions for measurement invariance in Equation 5.27 are not fully met. Following rejection, one could investigate which threshold parameters are varying across groups by selectively freeing invariance constraints. The same problems occur here as in tests of partial invariance on factor loadings: many potential alternative structures exist, and the invariance constraints needed for identification may introduce distortions if violations of invariance are present. Purely exploratory searches for varying thresholds that cycle through many combinations of invariance constraints are unlikely to produce replicable results unless samples are quite large.

A final step in the sequence of invariance hypotheses would test for invariance in the unique factor variances

$$H_{c07}: \mathbf{\Sigma}_k^* = \mathbf{\Lambda}\mathbf{\Phi}_k\mathbf{\Lambda}' + \mathbf{\Theta}, \quad \mathbf{\mu}_k^* = \mathbf{\Lambda}\mathbf{\kappa}_k, \quad (5.36)$$

for $k = 1,\ldots,K$. This hypothesis is only fully testable in the polytomous case in which $C > 1$. Unique factor variances in the dichotomous case may or may not be evaluated for invariance, depending on the structure in the factor loadings. Even under the independent cluster loading structure, at least r of the p unique variances in each group are constrained to invariance for identification purposes. Hence, it will not be possible to test all of the unique variances for invariance when the measured variables are dichotomous. If H_{c07} is retained and either H_{c04} or H_{c05} is fully retained as well, the only source of group differences in $\mathbf{\Sigma}_k^*$ is the variation in common factor covariance matrices $\mathbf{\Phi}_k$. If the parameters $(\mathbf{\Lambda}_k, \mathbf{\Theta}_k, \mathbf{T}_k)$ are fully invariant, any further violations of measurement invariance for $\mathbf{X}_k$ must be due to group differences in the higher order moment structure for $\mathbf{X}_k^*$ after conditioning on $\mathbf{W}_k$. As noted earlier, this situation would imply non-normality in $P_k(\mathbf{X}^*|\mathbf{W})$.

Table 5.1 presents the seven invariance hypotheses just discussed in compact form. The seven hypotheses form an approximate sequence, the exceptions being that one will generally either choose to leave the factor pattern matrix in a general form (H_{c02}, H_{c04}) or will constrain the loadings to an independent cluster structure (H_{c03}, H_{c05}). Naturally, the sequence will also be modified if partial invariance is introduced.

An Example

The Minnesota Multiphasic Personality Inventory (MMPI) (Hathaway & McKinley, 1940, 1983; MMPI-2: Butcher, Dahlstrom, Graham, Tellegen, & Kaemmer, 1989) is a general measure of psychopathology that is used widely

TABLE 5.1

Models of Factorial Invariance in Ordered-Categorical Measures

Model	Description
H_{c01}: $\Sigma_k^* = \Sigma^*$, $\mu_k^* = \mu^*$, $T_k = T$	Complete homogeneity of covariance structures, means, and thresholds across populations
H_{c02}: $\Sigma_k^* = \Lambda_k \Phi_k \Lambda_k' + \Theta_k$, $\mu_k^* = \Lambda_k \kappa_k$	Factor model with r common factors holds in each population Only identification restrictions on loadings
H_{c03}: $\Sigma_k^* = \Lambda_{kc} \Phi_k \Lambda_{kc}' + \Theta_k$, $\mu_k^* = \Lambda_{kc} \kappa_k$	Factor model with r common factors holds in each population Independent cluster loading structure. Configural invariance
H_{c04}: $\Sigma_k^* = \Lambda \Phi_k \Lambda' + \Theta_k$, $\mu_k^* = \Lambda \kappa_k$	Invariant factor loadings across populations for r factors: Pattern invariance.
H_{c05}: $\Sigma_k^* = \Lambda_c \Phi_k \Lambda_c' + \Theta_k$, $\mu_k^* = \Lambda_c \kappa_k$	Invariant factor loadings with independent cluster structure
H_{c06}: $\Sigma_k^* = \Lambda_c \Phi_k \Lambda_c' + \Theta_k$, $\mu_k^* = \Lambda_c \kappa_k$, $T_k = T$	Invariant thresholds and loadings
H_{c07}: $\Sigma_k^* = \Lambda \Phi_k \Lambda' + \Theta$, $\mu_k^* = \Lambda \kappa_k$, $T_k = T$	Invariant loadings, thresholds, and invariant unique factor variances

in clinical applications and in some employment settings. The MMPI contains 550 items, with each item presenting the examinee with a descriptive statement to which the examinee responds either "true" or "false," depending on the perceived accuracy of the statement. The MMPI produces scores on 10 clinical scales that are each associated empirically with diagnostic categories in use when the original items were developed. While these diagnostic categories are no longer used, the MMPI clinical scales are still used as descriptions of personality, with an emphasis on pathological features. The MMPI also produces scores on three validity scales used to help judge the accuracy of the clinical scales as descriptors.

The original scales of the MMPI were not constructed to follow any particular dimensional conception of human personality but rather were intended to discriminate empirically among different clinical categories. Perhaps as a result, simultaneous item-level factor analyses of the entire MMPI item pool have led to varying conclusions regarding the nature of the factors that underlie the MMPI (Archer & Klinefelter, 1991; Costa, Zonderman, McCrae, & Williams, 1985; Johnson, Butcher, Null, & Johnson, 1984; Reddon, Marceau, & Jackson, 1982; Stewart, 1974; Waller, 1999). It is generally agreed that the 10 clinical scales are not individually unidimensional. Waller constructed a set of 16 alternative scales from an item-level factor analysis of the entire MMPI item pool. Each scale was constructed to measure primarily a single factor, with no item overlap across factors. One of these factor scales will be used in the example described here.

Ethnic differences in MMPI/MMPI-2 scores have been intensively studied (for a meta-analytic review, see Nagayama-Hall, Bansal, & Lopez, 1999). The MMPI excluded ethnic minorities from its standardization sample; minority group members were included in the standardization sample of the MMPI-2. Based on a meta-analysis of 25 comparative studies of ethnic differences on the MMPI or MMPI-2, Nagayama-Hall et al. conclude that the differences on the 10 clinical scales are generally small, with higher scores for ethnic minority group members on some scales and lower scores on others. All of the studies reviewed by Nagayama-Hall et al. were simply descriptive, however. These studies did not examine measurement invariance in the MMPI/MMPI-2 items.

The data to be analyzed here consist of MMPI item responses from 1,277 Caucasian males and 511 African American males. These data are part of a larger set of data used in Wenk (1990) to study the career paths of young offenders in the California Youth Authority (CYA). The data were collected in 1964–1965 from offenders housed under the CYA. Waller, Thompson, and Wenk (2000) selected the 1,788 cases included here after applying stringent selection criteria to the larger set of MMPI protocols. For a list of these criteria, see Waller et al. As reported by Waller et al., the average ages at the time of the data collection in the Caucasian and African American samples were 19.01 and 18.97 years, respectively.

The items to be modeled here belong to one of the 16 factor scales reported in Waller (1999). These factor scales emerged from an item-level factor analysis of more than 28,000 MMPI protocols from the original Hathaway Data Bank. The factor analyses consisted of iterated exploratory factor analyses of tetrachoric correlation coefficients, with Varimax rotation. Waller provides a summary of the results of these analyses. Unlike the traditional clinical scales, these factor scales are each dominated by a single factor as described in Waller. The analyses described below used items from the Assertiveness scale. The scale contains 12 items in its original form, but three items had no variance in the present sample and were excluded from all analyses reported below. Two additional items were excluded based on preliminary analyses within groups that showed the two items to fit poorly to the single factor. The remaining seven items formed the basis for the invariance analyses reported here. All items are scored dichotomously with the more assertive response being

TABLE 5.2

Sample Proportions and Tetrachoric Correlations for African
Americans and Caucasians

Item	AS1	AS2	AS3	AS4	AS6	AS9	AS10
Sample proportions responding "true"							
African Americans	.836	.405	.804	.634	.401	.838	.875
Caucasians	.826	.385	.825	.395	.235	.782	.793
Sample tetrachoric correlations: African American ($N = 511$)							
AS2	.104						
AS3	.098	.139					
AS4	.005	.091	.045				
AS6	−.087	−.027	.076	.216			
AS9	.187	.138	.387	.294	.132		
AS10	.221	.047	.337	.255	.091	.469	
Sample tetrachoric correlations: Caucasian ($N = 1277$)							
AS2	.110						
AS3	.102	.075					
AS4	.046	.113	.133				
AS6	.094	.121	.186	.209			
AS9	.250	.102	.321	.242	.227		
AS10	.297	.144	.351	.162	.199	.510	

given the higher numeric score. Table 5.2 gives the tetrachoric correlations
and sample proportions for the seven items, displayed separately for the
two ethnic groups.

All analyses were performed using Mplus 3.1 (Muthén & Muthén, 1998–
2006) with WLSMV estimation. All of the fit results for the models to be
examined here are given in Table 5.3. The analyses began with a test of H_{c01},
which stipulates invariant thresholds, covariance matrices Σ^* and mean
vectors μ^*. This hypothesis is tested without assuming that a common factor model is appropriate for the data. The hypothesis simply asserts complete invariance of thresholds and latent response variate distributions.
The results in Table 5.3 suggest rejection of the hypothesis. We conclude
that the populations differ either in thresholds or in latent response variate
distributions. The second model assumes that a single factor underlies the
seven variables in each population. Only invariance constraints imposed
for identification purposes are included here. Thresholds are constrained
to invariance due to the dichotomous response format of the items. This
model produced an acceptable fit. A single-factor model seems appropriate for these variables. The third model adds invariance constraints on the
factor loadings to the preceding model. The fit of this model worsened in
comparison to the previous model, as shown by the significant chi-square.

TABLE 5.3

Fit Statistics for Models in MMPI Example

	Model				
Hypothesis	**Chi-square**	***df***	***p*-Value**	**CFI**	**RMSEA**
1. H_{c01}	146.543	24	$p < .0001$	.718	.076
2. H_{c03}: $r = 1$	37.594	26	$p = .066$	.973	.022
3. H_{c05}: $\boldsymbol{\Lambda}_k = \boldsymbol{\Lambda}$	66.372	31	$p = .0002$	.919	.036
4. Same as (3) with one free threshold	34.217	30	$p = .2722$	.990	.013
5. Same as (4) with $\boldsymbol{\Theta}_k = \boldsymbol{\Theta}$	74.962	35	$p < .0001$	.908	.036
6. Same as (5) with one free unique variance	40.920	34	$p = .1927$	.984	.015

TABLE 5.4

Parameter Estimates from Final Model

	African American		**Caucasian**
λ_1		1.0[a]	
λ_2		.624	
λ_3		1.499	
λ_4		1.019	
λ_6		1.139	
λ_9		3.069	
λ_{10}		3.010	
κ	.081		0[a]
ϕ	.105		.115
ν_1		−.979	
ν_2		.297	
ν_3		−.982	
ν_4	−.279		.280
ν_6		.772	
ν_9		−1.126	
ν_{10}		−1.215	
θ_1		1.0[a]	
θ_2		1.0	
θ_3		1.0	
θ_4		1.0	
θ_6	6.628		1.0
θ_9		1.0	
θ_{10}		1.0	

[a] Fixed for identification.

Scrutiny of the residuals suggested that the threshold constraint on item 4 was contributing substantially to the poor fit. This constraint was present at baseline, but its impact was only felt once both thresholds and loadings were constrained. Table 5.2 reveals that the proportions endorsing item 4 vary greatly between the two groups. To address this problem, the threshold for item 4 was permitted to vary across groups. No identification problem is created by freeing this threshold constraint because the loadings are fully invariant. This fourth model fits well. Next, invariance constraints on the unique factor variances are added to the model. This fifth model shows some lack of fit, with the chi-square again becoming significant. Residual information produced under the model points to the unique factor variance for item 6 as the source of poor fit. In the sixth and final model, the unique factor variance for item 6 is permitted to vary across groups. The fit of this model is acceptable. Table 5.4 gives the raw parameter estimates from the final model. As revealed in this table, item 4 has a lower threshold value in the African American group, suggesting that this item will be endorsed with greater probability in that group. Item 6 has a larger unique factor variance in the African American group, indicating a weaker relationship between this item and the common factor. In other words, item 6 appears to be a poorer measure of the latent variable in the African American group. The item has a communality estimate of .02 in the African American group and that of .13 in the Caucasian group.

6

Item Response Theory: Models, Estimation, Fit Evaluation

In this chapter and the next, we discuss methods of bias detection that are based on a large class of latent variable models arising from item response theory (IRT). We focus on models for discrete measures **X**. IRT models for continuous measures are available but are not yet widely used. Both models for dichotomous and polytomous measures are discussed. The theory is similar in these two cases, although developments for the polytomous case have lagged behind those for the dichotomous case. We also draw parallels between IRT methods and the factor analytic methods discussed in Chapter 5. In these brief chapters, we cannot provide a full treatment of model specification, estimation, and fit evaluation in IRT. Readers who wish to obtain more detailed treatments should consult texts such as Lord (1980), Fischer and Molenaar (1995), Baker (1992b), Van der Linden and Hambleton (1997), Hambleton and Swaminathan (1985), Embretson and Reise (2000), Nering and Ostini (2010), and De Ayala (2009).

IRT models are generally designed for item-level analyses of test data. When polytomous IRT models are available and interest lies in bias at the testlet level, the analysis may shift from the item level to the testlet level. A testlet is a block of items that collectively produce a single score for each examinee, usually an unweighted sum of item scores. The items may be scored together because of a common feature, such as a block of multiple-choice questions that refer to a common reading selection in a reading comprehension test. Formally, models for testlets present no new features beyond those encountered in other polytomous models, and hence testlet models do not require separate treatment. In bias investigations, however, issues of interpretation can arise, which are unique to the testlet case. For example, a testlet may include items that are biased, but whose biases are countervailing, resulting in little detectable bias at the testlet level. We will address these issues of interpretation but will provide no separate formal treatment of testlet models. For further information on testlet models, see Wainer, Bradlow, and Wang (2007).

Recent work in IRT has emphasized the value of "nonparametric" models for modeling item responses (Junker, 1993; Ramsay, 1991; Sijtsma, 1998; Sijtsma & Molenaar, 2002). Most research on the question of measurement bias has been undertaken using fully parametric models. A general difficulty with such parametric approaches is that issues of model fit may be confounded with tests of invariance. In other words, lack of fit in the parametric model used to form the basis for any tests of invariance may contribute to an apparent failure of invariance, possibly leading to false conclusions of bias. Nonparametric approaches could provide a useful resolution to this dilemma, but research on this topic is just beginning. We discuss some aspects of this work below.

This chapter is organized as follows. We begin with a description of some of the most commonly used IRT models and their properties. Some attention is given to the relationship between these models and the factor analytic models of Chapter 5. Next, we describe the estimation approaches that are most often used for IRT models, with some discussion of estimation in multiple populations. This is followed by a description of model fit evaluation for IRT models in general, apart from specific applications to the investigation of measurement bias. These fit evaluation methods would be used to evaluate a baseline model as a starting point for any bias investigation. Chapter 7 presents IRT-based methods for bias investigation.

Models

Nearly all present applications of IRT in the investigation of measurement bias use models that specify a single latent variable W. Multidimensional IRT models are under active development (Ackerman, 1992; McDonald, 1997; Reckase, 1997, 2009), but their use in bias investigations is uncommon at present. We focus on the unidimensional case here. In addition, although models exist that depart from the monotonicity and conditional independence assumptions as noted in Chapter 2, these models are not yet used in bias investigations to any great extent. We will therefore focus primarily on the large class of unidimensional, monotonic, and conditionally independent models that form the basis for most present applications of IRT. These models can be partitioned into those designed for dichotomously scored items and those developed for polytomous items. The next section describes the most common models used for dichotomous item data, followed by a description of models for polytomous items.

Dichotomous Measures

Suppose that $\mathbf{X}$ represents a vector of p item score variables $(X_1, X_2, ..., X_p)$ that are dichotomous. We can arbitrarily designate the values taken by X_j as (0, 1) for $j = 1, ..., p$. Each individual provides a vector of responses on the p items, and we can represent the individual's response vector as an observation from one of the 2^p cells in a contingency table formed by considering all possible score vectors on the p items. The IRT model specifies an item response function for each item. This function expresses the conditional probability of responding positively to the item, given the individual's status on the latent variable W. For now, we ignore the possible dependence of this probability on the individual's population membership. The item response function is then $P(X_j = 1|W)$, with $P(X_j = 0|W) = 1 - P(X_j = 1|W)$, and so we need only to consider $P(X_j = 1|W)$. Under conditional independence, the joint conditional probability for $\mathbf{X}$ is written as

$$P(\mathbf{X} = \mathbf{x} \,|\, W) = \prod_{j=1}^{p} P(X_j = 1\,|\,W)^{x_j}\, p(X_j = 0\,|\,W)^{1-x_j},\qquad (6.1)$$

where $\mathbf{x}$ represents a realization of $\mathbf{X}$. Equation 6.1 gives the conditional probability associated with any cell of the complete contingency table formed by the 2^p possible response vectors. Different IRT models are distinguished by the forms adopted for the item response functions in Equation 6.1, especially with respect to the roles of the item-specific parameters.

The Rasch Model

The simplest IRT model that is of realistic interest is the Rasch model (Rasch, 1960, 1961). This model assumes that the items are distinguishable on only a single property and that the item's status on this property is represented by a single item parameter. In cognitive applications, this parameter is denoted the "item difficulty" because of its direct interpretation as the item's location on the scale of "ability" defined by the latent variable W. This characterization of the parameter is less appealing in noncognitive applications, and so we will denote this parameter as a *location* parameter in general. The Rasch model specifies the item response function for the jth item as the logistic function

$$P(X_j = 1\,|\,W) = \frac{1}{1+\exp[-(W - b_j)]},\qquad (6.2)$$

where b_j is the location parameter for the jth item. The location parameter effectively locates the item on the latent variable scale in relation to W. If W represents an "ability" dimension, a hard item will correspond to a high value for b_j.

Several things should be noted immediately about this model. First, the probabilities of binary events are often expressed in terms of the "odds" of a given outcome, or the logit (log odds) corresponding to the odds. Under the Rasch model, the logit takes an especially simple form

$$\text{logit}(X_j) = \ln\left[\frac{P(X_j = 1 \mid W)}{P(X_j = 0 \mid W)}\right] = W - b_j. \tag{6.3}$$

As a function of W, this logit is linear with slopes that are identical across items, but with varying intercepts. The logit leads to a useful interpretation of the Rasch model as an instance of general conjoint scaling (Fischer, 1968; Perline, Wright, & Wainer, 1979). Second, it is clear that the item parameters are not uniquely defined in relation to the latent trait scale, since the addition of a constant to W can be offset by subtraction of the constant from b_j. This identification problem can be resolved in several ways, depending on the needs of a particular investigation. One solution is to fix the location parameter for a specific item to be zero. Alternatively, one can fix the mean value of the latent variable W to zero. In bias investigations, constraints on the location parameters are more useful because it is usually unrealistic to fix the mean of W to zero in all groups.

The Rasch model is of fundamental importance for an additional reason: it is the only unidimensional, conditionally independent, monotonic IRT model for dichotomous items in which the unweighted sum of the item scores is a sufficient statistic for W. Sufficiency of the total or sum score for W means that the conditional probability of the item score given the total score does not depend on W. All of the information in $\mathbf{X}$ that is relevant to W is captured by the total score. The sufficiency property facilitates parameter estimation, but it is also helpful in bias investigations that use the total score as a basis for matching examinees, as noted in Chapter 3.

The Rasch model can be derived from simpler assumptions about the form of the item response function, the joint conditional distribution of item responses, and the existence of a simple sufficient statistic for W (see Fischer, 1995b, for an extended discussion of derivations for the Rasch model). An important feature of these derivations is that they form a basis for arguing that the Rasch model provides an interval scale metric for W, the latent variable. This metric property is of great interest, given the use of the model as a basis for scaling individuals on the latent variable. The purported interval property for the latent scale that is produced via Rasch scaling is debatable, however (Kyngdon, 2008; Michell, 1990, 1999). Unlike the Rasch model, other IRT models (and latent variable models generally) simply assume that the latent variable has interval scale properties. See Chapter 2 for a further discussion of this point.

The theoretical properties of the Rasch model involving sufficiency and scaling are advantageous, but their advantages only accrue to the extent that the model is appropriate for the data. This fact provides a motivation for using the Rasch model in test construction, bringing together items that fit the model. Rasch (1960, 1961) developed the model to satisfy the principle of "specific objectivity." Broadly speaking, specific objectivity means that in the measurement of objects on some property, the results of the measurement (e.g., quantitative relations among the objects) should not depend on the choice of measuring device. Applying this principle to psychological measurement, the "device" could be a test item, the "property" is a latent variable, and the result might be the score of a person on the item. A test item that fulfills specific objectivity can be used to scale any pair of individuals on the latent variable, and the result of this scaling does not depend on the item parameter value for the item in question. The specific objectivity principle has relevance for the issue of measurement bias. Bias violates specific objectivity: the comparison between two individuals now may depend on the item parameter because the item parameter varies with the individuals' population membership. The results of the scaling may now depend on whether the individuals belong to different populations. Unfortunately, given multiple populations, one does not necessarily achieve specific objectivity with respect to all populations by verifying specific objectivity within a single population. In other words, we cannot conclude that a set of test items is unbiased in all populations defined by **V** from the fit of the Rasch model in a single population (Millsap, 2008).

The 2PL Model

The next model of interest for dichotomous measures is the two-parameter logistic model (2PL), which generalizes the Rasch model by permitting items to vary not simply in terms of location but also in *discrimination*. The 2PL item response function is

$$P(X_j = 1 \mid W) = \frac{1}{1 + \exp[-a_j(W - b_j)]}, \tag{6.4}$$

where a_j is the discrimination parameter for the jth item. Note that if $a_j = a$, so that discrimination is identical across items, the model becomes equivalent to the Rasch model because the scaling parameter a can now be absorbed by redefining the metrics for W and the b_j parameters. The rationale for labeling the parameter a_j as a discrimination parameter is made clear by the expression for the logit

$$\text{logit}(X_j) = \ln\left[\frac{P(X_j = 1 \mid W)}{P(X_j = 0 \mid W)}\right] = a_j(W - b_j) = a_j W - a_j b_j. \tag{6.5}$$

Here a_j acts as a slope parameter, denoting the difference in the logit per unit difference in the latent variable W. Large values for a_j imply that the logit changes markedly in response to differences in W or that the item is more sensitive to examinee differences on the latent variable. Unlike the Rasch model, the 2PL model permits the items to vary on this property of sensitivity.

For items fitting the 2PL model, the weighted sum of the item scores, with weights determined by the item discrimination parameters, is a sufficient statistic for the latent variable W. This point is easily demonstrated by rewriting the joint item response function as

$$\prod_{j=1}^{p} P(X_j \mid W) = \left[\prod_{j=1}^{p}(1 - P(X_j = 1 \mid W)) \right] \exp\left(W \sum_{j=1}^{p} a_j X_j \right) \exp\left(-\sum_{j=1}^{p} a_j b_j X_j \right).$$

(6.6)

Letting $T_W = \sum_{j=1}^{p} a_j X_j$ be the weighted-sum statistic, Equation 6.6 has the form

$$P(X \mid W) = f(W, T_W) h(X),$$

(6.7)

which implies that T_W is a sufficient statistic for W by the factorization theorem (Lord & Novick, 1968). Note that the sufficiency of the unweighted sum $T = \sum_{j=1}^{p} X_j$ in the Rasch model is implied by assuming $a_j = a$ for $j = 1, \ldots, p$. Allan Birnbaum, in Lord and Novick, establishes that only models equivalent to the 2PL provide weighted-sum statistics that are minimally sufficient. In practice, however, this sufficiency property of the 2PL model is less useful than the sufficiency property of the Rasch model discussed earlier. The weights used to create T_W are unknown, and even if they could be accurately estimated, the weighted sum generally offers no savings in comparison to the response sequence itself. Assuming the common situation in which the discrimination parameters are different for every pair of items, the weighted sum T_W will ordinarily assume 2^p different values, with a unique value for every response sequence.

Verhelst and Glas (1995) describe a one-parameter logistic model in which the Rasch model is extended by permitting unequal discrimination parameters as in the 2PL in Equation 6.4, but requiring that these discrimination "parameters" have known values, possibly specified from theory. Proper choices for the discrimination values lead to workable estimation procedures for the unknown location parameters. In practice, however, it is difficult to justify choices for the discrimination values from theory alone, and some trial and error is required.

An older model that is similar to the 2PL is the normal ogive model, whose item response function is

$$P(X_j = 1 \mid W) = \int_{-\infty}^{G_j} \phi(u)\, du, \tag{6.8}$$

where $G_j = a_j(W - b_j)$ and ϕ is the univariate standard normal density function. The 2PL and normal ogive item response functions can be made to nearly coincide by an appropriate scaling of the 2PL logit. If we multiply the 2PL logit by the factor $D = 1.7$, the two functions are brought to within .01 of each other throughout the range of W. This scaling is commonly adopted in applications of the 2PL model. Because the two models can be transformed to closely resemble one another and the 2PL model is mathematically simpler, the 2PL model is now used more widely than the normal ogive model.

Lord and Novick (1968) demonstrated an interesting connection between the normal ogive model and the common factor model for dichotomous variables as described in Chapter 5. Assume that the common factor model for dichotomous variables fits a set of items with a single factor. Also assume that the latent response variates $\mathbf{X}^*$ described in Chapter 5 have an MVN distribution. Then Lord and Novick show that the item response functions for all of the items can be taken to be normal ogives, with conditional independence for the item scores. Specifically, the item parameters of the normal ogive are related to those of the factor model as

$$a_j = \frac{\lambda_j}{\sqrt{\theta_j}}, \quad b_j = \frac{v_j}{\lambda_j}, \tag{6.9}$$

where
the common factor variance $\phi = 1$
v_j is the threshold parameter for the jth variable
λ_j is the factor loading
θ_j is the unique variance

The same result can be found in Muthén and Christoffersson (1981), extended there to the multiple-population case. The discrimination parameter a_j is a function of both the item's factor loading and its unique variance. In many applications, however, the variances of the latent response variates $\mathbf{X}^*$ are fixed to unit values for identification, leading to $\lambda_j^2 + \theta_j = 1$. Under this restriction, the discrimination parameter can be written as a function of the loadings only. Hence, requiring that all items have identical discrimination parameters implies that all items have identical factor loadings in this formulation. Although Lord and Novick derived the above relations for the normal ogive, the close similarity between the normal ogive and the properly scaled 2PL suggests that similar relations hold for the 2PL parameters and the factor model parameters. The Rasch model can be seen as the special case in which $a_j = a$ for $j = 1, \ldots, p$, or $\lambda_j = \lambda$ and $\theta_j = \theta$ for $j = 1, \ldots, p$. These relationships among the normal ogive, 2PL, and common factor models suggest that in the normal unidimensional case, the three models should be empirically indistinguishable in dichotomous data. Further discussion on this point can be found in Bartholomew (1987) and in Kamata and Bauer (2008).

The 3PL Model

The 2PL model can be further generalized by permitting individuals with low values for W to have a fixed nonzero probability of responding positively to the item. One motivation for this generalization is to account for guessing behavior on items for which such behavior could lead to a correct answer, as in multiple-choice cognitive test items. The resulting three-parameter logistic (3PL) item response function has the form

$$P(X_j = 1 \mid W) = c_j + \frac{1 - c_j}{1 + \exp[-a_j(W - b_j)]}, \tag{6.10}$$

where c_j is the *pseudo-guessing* parameter. From Equation 6.10, it is clear that $P(X_j = 1 \mid W) \to c_j$ as $W \to -\infty$, and so c_j can be interpreted as the probability of a positive response for low values of W. The 3PL can be simplified by requiring that $c_j = c$ for $j = 1, \ldots, p$, a restriction that is often useful for practical reasons. One way of justifying this restriction would be to assume that c_j truly represents the probability of guessing correctly and that guessing is purely random, with all items presenting the examinee with the same number of options. Although the assumption of purely random guessing is probably inaccurate, the inclusion of the parameter c_j as a nonzero lower asymptote for the item response function often leads to some improvement in model fit in comparison to the 2PL or Rasch model. On the other hand, under the 3PL model, there is no longer a simple weighted-sum statistic T_W that is sufficient for W.

Polytomous Measures

We now consider the case in which X_j assumes C possible ordered values $(0, 1, \ldots, C - 1)$ for $j = 1, \ldots, p$, as in Chapter 5. We again simplify the presentation by requiring that all items assume the same set of C possible values. Generalizations to the mixed case in which C varies across items are straightforward. The values assigned to the response categories are generally arbitrary apart from their order. If the order of the response categories is also unimportant, we have a purely nominal or categorical item. IRT models exist for such items, but we will confine discussion to the ordered-categorical case.

Before describing any specific polytomous models, it will be useful to establish some terminology in relation to the polytomous case. The conditional probability of responding in a given response category for the *j*th item, given the latent variable, is here denoted the *category response function* and is written as $P(X_j = c \mid W)$ for $c = 0, 1, \ldots, C - 1$. In the dichotomous case in which $C = 2$, this function was denoted as the item response function. We earlier restricted consideration to monotonic item response functions. In the polytomous case, the category response functions need not be monotonic in W. For all but the highest category of response, we expect the category response function to eventually decrease for large values of W. We can, however, define a response function in the polytomous case that will be monotonic in W for the polytomous models considered here. This function is often described as the *item true-score function* and is expressed as

$$E(X_j \mid W) = \sum_{m=0}^{c-1} mP(X_j = m \mid W). \tag{6.11}$$

The true-score function is simply a weighted sum of the category response functions, with weights corresponding to the numbers $(0, 1, \ldots, C - 1)$ chosen to represent the C response categories. For the dichotomous case, the true-score function in Equation 6.11 and the item response function are identical. It can be shown that for a broad class of polytomous IRT models, the true-score function is monotonic in W (Chang & Mazzeo, 1994). The form of the function will depend on the numbers chosen to represent the item scoring categories. In Equation 6.11, the integers from 0 to $C - 1$ are used, but this choice is arbitrary in that other ordered sequences of integers are equally appropriate in most cases.

Polytomous Rasch Models

The simplest models for the ordered-categorical polytomous case are those that represent generalizations of the Rasch model for dichotomous items. The first model to be considered is the rating-scale model (Andersen, 1977; Andrich, 1978a, 1978b) that was originally proposed by Rasch (1961). Although this model has several versions, a general expression for the category response function is

$$P(X_j = c \mid W) = \frac{\exp[\alpha_c W - b_{jc}]}{\sum_{m=0}^{C-1} \exp[\alpha_m W - b_{jm}]} \tag{6.12}$$

for $c = 0, 1, \ldots, C - 1$, where α_c is a *scoring* parameter whose value is the same across items but unique to category c and b_{jc} is a *location* parameter that varies with both the category and the item. The scoring parameters in Equation 6.12 are restricted by requiring that

$$\alpha_c - \alpha_{c-1} = d, \tag{6.13}$$

where d is a fixed constant, for $c = 1, \ldots, C - 1$. In other words, the scoring parameters are equally spaced. The value of d is not fixed by the model, however, and any linear transformation of the scoring parameters will be equally appropriate. Andrich (1978a) presents arguments in support of choosing $d = 1$ with $\alpha_0 = 0$. The resulting scoring parameters then have an interpretation as the number of boundaries or thresholds passed in responding to the item. This choice for the scoring parameters is commonly adopted.

   The location parameters are typically given a special structure in the rating-scale model, although several choices for this structure are available. Rasch (1961) recommended the multiplicative simplification $b_{jc} = \alpha_c b_j$. This choice, when combined with the scaling of the scoring parameters as suggested by Andrich (1978a), simplifies the category response function in Equation 6.12. A more commonly used choice, however, was presented by Andrich as

$$b_{jc} = \alpha_c b_j - \sum_{m=0}^{c} t_m, \tag{6.14}$$

where the t_m are threshold parameters that are common to all items with $t_0 = 0$, for $m = 0, \ldots, C - 1$. Note that the threshold parameters are common across items. Combining the structure in Equation 6.14 with the earlier scaling for the scoring parameters gives

$$P(X_j = c \mid W) = \frac{\exp[c(W - b_j) + \kappa_c]}{\sum_{m=0}^{C-1} \exp[m(W - b_j) + \kappa_m]}. \tag{6.15}$$

Here $\kappa_c = -\sum_{q=0}^{c} t_q$ for $c = 0, 1, \ldots, C - 1$. The location parameters $b_j, j = 1, \ldots, p$, are not identified without further restrictions. A typical choice here is to set $\sum_{j=1}^{p} b_j = 0$. We also have $\kappa_0 = t_0 = 0$. No other restrictions are imposed on the threshold parameters, and these thresholds need not be equidistant. For example, $t_3 - t_2 \neq t_2 - t_1$ is a possible result.

   Some insight into the combined roles of the location and threshold parameters in the rating-scale model can be gained by asking for what value of W will the probability of response in either of two adjacent categories be equal? In other words, for what value of W will $P(X_j = c|W) = P(X_j = c - 1|W)$? A little algebra shows that this equality holds when $W = b_j + t_c$. For the jth item, the set of latent trait values $\{b_j + t_1, b_j + t_2, \ldots, b_j + t_{c-1}\}$ represent points on the latent continuum in which the adjacent category response functions intersect. The distances between these intersection points are identical for all items, but their absolute locations are shifted up or down depending on the value of b_j, the location parameter.

The partial-credit model (Masters, 1982, 1985) generalizes the rating-scale model, while staying within the Rasch family of models. The partial-credit model specifies the category response function as

$$P(X_j = c|W) = \frac{\exp[\alpha_c W - b_{jc}]}{\displaystyle\sum_{m=0}^{C-1} \exp[\alpha_m W - b_{jm}]}, \tag{6.16}$$

where $\alpha_0 = 0$ and $\alpha_c = c$ for $c > 0$ are the scoring parameters, and the location parameters are given the structure

$$b_{jc} = \sum_{m=0}^{c} \tau_{jm}, \tag{6.17}$$

with $\tau_{jc} = 0$ for $c = 0$. The category location parameters τ_{jc} are not given further structure in the partial-credit model, unlike the rating-scale model. Their interpretation can again be understood by considering the value of the latent variable W at which two adjacent category response functions intersect: $P(X_j = c|W) = P(X_j = c - 1|W)$. This intersection occurs when $W = \tau_{jc}$, and so the entire set of intersection points for the jth item is $(\tau_{j1}, \tau_{j2}, \ldots, \tau_{jC-1})$. The distances between these intersection points may vary from item to item, unlike what was true for the rating-scale model. In fact, there is no guarantee that the ordering of the category location parameters for an item will match the order of the scoring categories. It is possible that $\tau_{j3} < \tau_{j2}$, for example (see Masters & Wright, 1997, for a discussion of this point).

Considering the scores on all p items that fit either the rating-scale or partial-credit model, we can derive a sufficient statistic for the latent variable W as follows. Letting c_j be the score for X_j for $j = 1, \ldots, p$, under conditional independence, it can be shown that for either model, the joint conditional probability for $\mathbf{X}$ is

$$P(\mathbf{X}|W) = \prod_{j=1}^{p} P(X_j = c_j|W) = \frac{W \exp\left[\sum_{j=1}^{p} \alpha_{c_j}\right] \exp\left[\sum_{j=1}^{p} b_{jc_j}\right]}{\prod_{j=1}^{p} \sum_{m=0}^{C-1} \exp[\alpha_m W - b_{jm}]}. \tag{6.18}$$

This joint probability thus takes the form given in Equation 6.7, and it is therefore clear that the total score statistic

$$T = \sum_{j=1}^{p} \alpha_{c_j} \tag{6.19}$$

is sufficient for W. The scoring parameters $(\alpha_0, \alpha_1, \ldots, \alpha_{C-1})$ are known under both the rating-scale and partial-credit models. Under either model, the total score T in Equation 6.19 is simply the accumulated total across items of the number of response categories exceeded by the individual's responses. Hence, either model would justify the use of this simple total score statistic as a summary of the information in the response vector about the latent variable W.

One interesting generalization of both the rating-scale and partial-credit models is the generalized partial-credit model (Muraki, 1992). The category response function for this model can be written

$$P(X_j = c \mid W) = \frac{\exp[a_j(\alpha_c W - b_{jc})]}{\displaystyle\sum_{m=0}^{C-1} \exp[a_j(\alpha_m W - b_{jm})]}. \tag{6.20}$$

Here $\alpha_c = c$ for $c = 0, \ldots, C - 1$, and a_j is a new parameter that serves as a discrimination parameter specific to the item. Commonly, a_j is replaced with a rescaled parameter $a_j^* = Da_j$, with $D = 1.7$ being the logistic scaling constant. The location parameters b_{jc} are given the additive decomposition used in the rating-scale model in Equation 6.15, with $t_0 = 0$ for identification. As in the rating-scale model, the t_m are threshold parameters common to all items. The generalized partial-credit model permits the items to vary in the strength of relationship between the latent variable W and the conditional probability of responding in the higher of two adjacent categories. To see this point, note that for two adjacent categories c and $c - 1$, we can write the conditional probability of responding in category c, given that the response is either in category $c - 1$ or c, as

$$\frac{P(X_j = c \mid W)}{P(X_j = c-1 \mid W) + P(X_j = c \mid W)} = \frac{\exp[g_{jc}(W)]}{1 + \exp[g_{jc}(W)]} \tag{6.21}$$

under the rating-scale, partial-credit, or generalized partial-credit models. The rating-scale model, using the specification in Equation 6.12, corresponds to

$$g_{jc}(W) = W - (b_j + t_c). \tag{6.22}$$

The partial-credit model yields

$$g_{jc}(W) = W - \tau_{jc}. \tag{6.23}$$

In both of these models, for a fixed value of c, the items only differ in their location (or category location) parameters. Apart from these parameters, all items have the same general shape for the conditional probability in Equation 6.21. The generalized partial-credit model departs from this common property, however, giving

$$g_{jc}(W) = a_j[W - (b_j + t_c)]. \tag{6.24}$$

Here the items differ on two parameters, the location parameter b_j and the discrimination parameter a_j. As a result, for a fixed value of c, the items will vary in the steepness as well as the location of the conditional probability function in Equation 6.21. Note that discrimination is constant across all categories, however. The generalized partial-credit model resembles the 2PL model in terms of item discrimination.

A consequence of the additional item parameter available in the generalized partial-credit model is that the total score in Equation 6.19 is no longer a sufficient statistic for W, the latent variable. Instead, it can be shown that the sufficient statistic is

$$T = \sum_{j=1}^{p} a_j \alpha_{c_j}. \tag{6.25}$$

This statistic requires knowledge of the discrimination parameters a_j, and it will not be practically useful in general for reasons already discussed for the 2PL.

The Graded Response Model

All of the models discussed thus far are extensions of the dichotomous Rasch formulation to the ordered-categorical case, with the generalized partial-credit model representing the first departure from the Rasch tradition. A different rationale from that of the Rasch tradition is used to motivate the graded response model (Samejima, 1969, 1972). The graded response model is actually a family of models, each of which can be developed within a common framework. We will not consider all of these models here but will confine our attention to the most commonly used variants. The entire graded response system provides a remarkably flexible approach to modeling polytomous items. For a more general recent treatment, see Samejima (1997).

The graded response model views the response categories $(0, 1, \ldots, C - 1)$ as representing a series of steps. In a cognitive test item, the steps represent an ordered sequence of stages in the complete solution of the problem. Samejima (1997) defines a *processing function* $M_{jc}(W)$ as the conditional probability that an examinee with latent variable score W will pass stage c on the jth item, given that stages $0, 1, \ldots, c - 1$ have been passed. We define $M_{j0}(W) = 1$. Let

$$G_{jc}(W) = \prod_{m \leq c} M_{jm}(W) \qquad (6.26)$$

be the conditional probability that the examinee with latent variable score W passes all stages up to c or higher for the jth item. Then we can represent the category response function as the difference

$$P(X_j = c \mid W) = G_{jc}(W) - G_{jc+1}(W) = \left[\prod_{m \leq c} M_{jm}(W) \right] [1 - M_{jc+1}(W)], \quad (6.27)$$

for $j = 1, \ldots, p, c = 0, 1, \ldots, C - 1$ with $M_{jC}(W) = 0$ by definition. The different versions of the graded response model are then created by different choices for the processing functions. Samejima (1997) discusses some criteria that such choices should fulfill. In the most common case, the conditional probabilities in Equation 6.26 are all given the same form (the homogeneous case). One choice for this form that has useful properties is the general form

$$G_{jc}(W) = \int_{-\infty}^{a_j(W - b_{cj})} \Omega(t)\, dt, \qquad (6.28)$$

where $\Omega(t)$ is a chosen unimodal function that has derivatives at least up to the fourth order. If $\Omega(t)$ is chosen as the standard normal density function, the resulting conditional probability in Equation 6.28 is a normal ogive. This choice leads to the category response function

$$P(X_j = c \mid W) = \int_{a_j(W - b_{cj+1})}^{a_j(W - b_{cj})} \phi(t)\, dt, \qquad (6.29)$$

where $\phi(t)$ is the standard normal density. It can be shown that for the dichotomous case of $C = 2$, Equation 6.29 corresponds to the dichotomous normal ogive model. A logistic version of the graded response model can be developed that has properties that are similar to the model in Equation 6.29.

The graded response model using Equation 6.29 can be shown to have several useful properties. First, the same model will hold if adjacent scoring categories $(0, 1, \ldots, C - 1)$ are collapsed or combined to yield a smaller number of scoring categories (Samejima, 1997). For example, if the item response scale is transformed to be simply dichotomous, the dichotomous normal ogive model results. Given that the number of scoring categories is often arbitrary in psychological measurement, the flexibility of the graded response model in this respect is an advantage. Secondly, the likelihood function for any response pattern in **X** using Equation 6.29 can be shown to have a unique maximum. This uniqueness property means that latent variable scores for all examinees are potentially estimable using maximum likelihood estimation. The graded response model does not provide a sufficient statistic for W that is an unweighted sum of the item scores, unlike the rating-scale and partial-credit models. Hence, estimation methods that condition on this unweighted sum will not be useful for the graded response model.

The foregoing summary of models for polytomous items does not include all such models, and it is likely that new models will become available. Further information on polytomous IRT models is available in Van der Linden and Hambleton (1997), Fischer and Molenaar (1995), Thissen and Steinberg (1984), De Ayala (2009), and Nering and Ostini (2010).

Estimation

Parameter estimation methods used in IRT are varied, ranging from relatively simple conditional maximum likelihood (CML) methods used for Rasch-family models to Bayesian methods that are potentially applicable to any IRT model. Some of the estimation approaches that are theoretically feasible have not been implemented in widely available software. In bias investigations, the primary interest lies in item parameter estimation, followed by comparisons of the resulting estimates between groups. We will therefore restrict attention to the estimation of item parameters here. Most of the widely available software programs for parameter estimation use some form of maximum likelihood, but Bayesian methods are becoming more widely used. No attempt will be made to provide a complete account of estimation theory in relation to IRT models. The intent here will be to focus on the general outline of methods typically used, with special emphasis on issues relevant to multiple-group applications. The multiple-group case presents some difficulties that are unique, yet relatively little has been written about multiple-group estimation in IRT.

At present, the two most widely used maximum likelihood estimation methods are CML and marginal maximum likelihood (MML). CML estimation is confined to the Rasch family of models for either dichotomous or ordered-categorical cases. The key requirement for practical use of this estimation method is that there must exist a sufficient statistic for W, either as an unweighted sum of item scores or a weighted sum with known weights. By conditioning on this statistic, item parameters may be estimated without the need for simultaneous estimation of scores on the latent variable W. Unfortunately, this estimation method cannot be used for models that do not yield a sufficient statistic for W. MML methods are useful in this more general case but are also applicable in cases covered by CML. In the MML approach, the marginal likelihood for $\mathbf{X}$ is made available by integration over W, eliminating the need to estimate scores on W. The central requirement of this method is that some form for the distribution of W be specified, either based on theory or using the data at hand.

A third estimation option, joint maximum likelihood (JML), estimates both item parameters and latent variable scores simultaneously using an alternating estimation scheme. This method is implemented in some software packages (e.g., Winsteps [Linacre, 2001]). We will not pursue this method here for two reasons. First, estimates of scores on W are generally not needed in bias investigations. Second, attempts to estimate both item parameters and latent variable scores encounter theoretical difficulties with regard to the growth of the number of latent variable scores with increasing sample size (Andersen, 1970; Neyman & Scott, 1948). The problem lies in the lack of consistency in the item parameter estimates in this case. Although corrections that essentially resolve the problem are known in some cases, there is now little need to pursue JML in bias investigations given the availability of other viable methods.

Conditional Maximum Likelihood

Let T represent a sufficient statistic for W in the conditional likelihood function for $\mathbf{X}$. Then the conditional likelihood is

$$L(\mathbf{X}_i \mid W) = \prod_{i=1}^{N} P(\mathbf{X}_i \mid W) = \prod_{i=1}^{N} P(\mathbf{X}_i \mid T_i)P(T_i \mid W) \qquad (6.30)$$

for a sample of N examinees responding to the measures $\mathbf{X}$. In this expression, the likelihood is factored into two components, one of which expresses the conditional probability of the response vector $\mathbf{X}$ given the statistic T, and the other gives the conditional probability of the statistic T given the latent variable. The sufficiency of T guarantees that the first component need not incorporate W, the latent variable. The item parameters alone determine the value of this first component. These parameters are estimated in CML estimation by choosing parameter values to maximize

$$L_{\text{CML}} = \prod_{i=1}^{N} P(\mathbf{X}_i | T_i) \tag{6.31}$$

for given values of $\mathbf{X}_i$ and T_i, $i = 1, \ldots, N$. The method assumes that a sufficient statistic T exists that will satisfy Equation 6.30 and that this statistic is directly calculable for all examinees (i.e., T involves no unknown parameters). Models that fulfill this requirement include the dichotomous Rasch model, the rating-scale model, and the partial-credit model. The generalized partial-credit model and the graded response model do not meet the requirement for T.

For the dichotomous Rasch model, it can be shown that

$$P(\mathbf{X}_i | T_i) = \frac{\exp\left(-\sum_{j=1}^{p} X_{ij} b_j\right)}{\Upsilon(T_i, b_1, b_2, \ldots, b_p)}, \tag{6.32}$$

where $\Upsilon(T_i, b_1, b_2, \ldots, b_p)$ is the elementary symmetric function, expressed as

$$\Upsilon(T_i, b_1, b_2, \ldots, b_p) = \sum_{X_{ij}:T_i} \exp\left(-\sum_{j=1}^{p} X_{ij} b_j\right). \tag{6.33}$$

The summation in Equation 6.33 is over all response patterns $\mathbf{X}_i$ such that $T_i = \sum X_{ij}$. The expression for $P(\mathbf{X}_i | T_i)$ does not involve the latent variable W, and so maximization of the conditional likelihood in Equation 6.31 can be done without estimating these scores. CML estimation has become more efficient with the introduction of fast and accurate methods for calculation of the elementary symmetric functions (Verhelst, Glas, & Van der Sluis, 1984). The use of CML requires that some constraints be introduced to identify the item parameters. Commonly, the constraint $\sum b_j = 0$ is adopted, although a single item could also be chosen to fix $b_j = 0$ for some choice of j.

A similar formulation is possible for the partial-credit and rating-scale models. Under either model, the total score T is defined by Equation 6.19. In the partial-credit model, we can write the conditional probability for $\mathbf{X}_i = (c_1, c_2, \ldots, c_p)$ as

$$P(\mathbf{X}_i | T_i) = \frac{\exp\left(-\sum_{j=1}^{p} b_{jc_j}\right)}{\Upsilon(T_i, b_{10}, b_{11}, \ldots, b_{1c-1}, b_{20}, \ldots, b_{pc-1})} \tag{6.34}$$

with b_{jc_j} being the b_{jc} in Equation 6.17 corresponding to the value of c_j. The elementary function in the denominator of Equation 6.34 is expressed as

$$\Upsilon(T_i, b_{10}, b_{11}, \ldots, b_{1c-1}, b_{20}, \ldots, b_{pc-1}) = \sum_{X_{ij}:T_i} \exp\left(-\sum_{j=1}^{p} b_{jc}\right). \qquad (6.35)$$

The summation is over all values of $\mathbf{X}_i$ that would yield a total score of T_i. It is again true that the conditional probability in Equation 6.34 does not involve the latent variable W. For identification, it is usual to require that $b_{j0} = 0$ for $j = 1, \ldots, p$. An additional constraint is needed, and for this, it is common to use

$$\sum_{j=1}^{p}\sum_{m=0}^{c-1} a_m b_{jm} = 0, \qquad (6.36)$$

where the category parameters a_m are known, as described earlier. Note that this constraint is identical to that considered for the dichotomous Rasch model when $C = 2$. The formulation for the rating-scale model is identical to the above for the partial-credit model, with the simpler structure for b_{jc} given in Equation 6.15.

In the multiple-population case, CML estimation is performed separately within each population, yielding item parameter estimates with estimates of their standard errors. As will be discussed below, the standard errors can be used in Wald tests for invariance of the item parameters across groups. It is also possible to construct likelihood ratio (LR) tests of invariance under CML by calculating two likelihoods, one for the two populations considered in isolation, and one calculated for the pooled sample, ignoring population distinctions. In either case, the extension of CML estimation to multiple populations is done by simply performing the procedures described earlier within each population.

One difficulty that will arise in multiple-group CML estimation that is unique to the multiple-population case concerns the choice of identification constraints. A general rule for choosing such constraints in this context is that the same set of constraints should be adopted in all populations. Clearly, the use of different constraints in different groups may lead to item parameter estimates that appear to be different across groups, even when the parameters are truly invariant. But suppose that not all parameters are invariant. Even if the same constraints are adopted in the different populations, the resulting parameter estimates may obscure the nature of the group differences. For example, consider three items whose location parameters are (.2, .2, .6) in the focal group and (.2, .2, −.2) in the reference group. Suppose that for identification, we impose $b_3 = 0$ in both groups. Then we might expect to have estimates of (−.4, −.4, 0) in the focal group and (.4, .4, 0) in the reference group under this constraint. The lack of invariance appears to lie in b_1 and b_2 under this identification. Alternatively, if we impose the identification $\sum b_j = 0$ within each population, we should find that the estimates for the focal group are approximately (−.13, −.13, .26) and are (.13, .13, −.26) for the reference group. Under this identification, none of the location parameters appear to be invariant. This identification problem must be surmounted whenever direct comparisons of parameter values across groups are conducted, as in Wald tests of invariance. We return to this problem below.

Marginal Maximum Likelihood

The conditioning used in CML estimation requires a sufficient statistic for W, but sufficient statistics are lacking for many models. In these cases, we can isolate the item parameters by explicitly modeling the distribution of W, followed by integration over this distribution to yield a marginal likelihood for $\mathbf{X}$. To illustrate, let $g(W)$ be the population density function for W. We will confine discussion to a single population initially. The marginal likelihood for $\mathbf{X}$ under conditional independence for the elements of $\mathbf{X}$ given W is

$$L(\mathbf{X}) = \int P(\mathbf{X} \mid W) g(W) \, dW = \prod_{j=1}^{p} \int P(X_j \mid W) g(W) \, dW. \qquad (6.37)$$

In Equation 6.37, the integration is with respect to the entire domain of W. The density $g(W)$ is specified from theory, or the data are used to generate an estimated distribution. In either case, once the density $g(W)$ is specified, the item parameters can be estimated by maximizing $L(\mathbf{X})$. The resulting estimates are known as MML estimates. The MML estimates are generally found using an expectation-maximization (EM) algorithm (Bock & Aitkin, 1981). This MML-EM approach is adopted in standard IRT software (e.g., BILOG-MG [Zimowski, Muraki, Mislevy, & Bock, 2003]) and has been extended for use with the dichotomous Rasch model, as an alternative to CML methods (Thissen, 1982).

The identification problem is altered by the introduction of a distribution for W, depending on how the parameters of that distribution are handled. If the distribution of W is fully specified, including values for the parameters of that distribution, it will generally be unnecessary to impose constraints on the item parameters for identification purposes. For example, a common choice in the single-population case is to specify that $g(W)$ is $N(0, 1)$. Alternatively, one can specify a distributional form for $g(W)$ (e.g., normal) but estimate the parameters of this distribution from the data.

Under the choice of the normal distribution, one would need to estimate μ_w and σ_w. In this case, identification constraints on the item parameters such as those considered earlier are needed. These constraints are also needed in the case in which the distribution of W is based entirely on the data at hand. In the multiple-population case, full specification of $g(W)$ in all populations will ordinarily not be possible, as population differences in these distributions must be permitted. In this situation, constraints on the item parameters will be needed. The choice of constraints will be important if direct comparisons of parameter values between groups are to be done, as the constraints may distort the item parameter comparisons as described earlier. On the other hand, it is possible to test invariance hypotheses without conducting any direct comparisons, using LR tests as discussed below.

Bayesian Estimation

Historically, estimation methods based on joint, conditional, or marginal likelihoods have dominated in IRT. Alternative approaches based on Bayesian theory have been proposed and are now practical, given computational advances. Detailed descriptions of Bayesian approaches to IRT estimation are available for a number of IRT models and response formats (Beguin & Glas, 2001; Bradlow, Wainer, & Wang, 1999; Fox & Glas, 2001; V. E. Johnson & Albert, 1999; M. S. Johnson & Sinharay, 2005; Patz & Junker, 1999a, 1999b; Sinharay, 2005). Only a general description will be given here. For a concise introduction to Bayesian data analysis, see Hoijtink (2009).

The Bayesian approach to IRT parameter estimation requires a full specification of prior distributions on all model parameters, along with the distribution of the latent variable. The prior distribution for a model parameter, such as an item location parameter b_j, represents our state of knowledge or uncertainty about the values b_j might have. At one extreme, we may have virtually no information about b_j, apart from lower and upper values beyond which the parameter is unlikely to range. In this case, we might specify b_j to have a uniform (b_L, b_H) distribution for lower and upper bounds b_L and b_H, respectively. In other cases, previous experience with the item or other items of this type might lead to a fairly restrictive prior that stipulates b_j to have a normal $(.2, .3)$, which is centered at $b_j = .2$ with fixed variance. Choices for prior distributions must be made in this fashion for all model parameters. Note that the parameter values that govern the prior distributions may or may not be explicitly specified. It is possible to leave these unspecified and specify prior distributions for those parameters as well. Certain choices for prior distributions have become common in IRT applications, such as normal densities for the latent variable or log-normal densities for discrimination parameters a_j.

The latter choice preserves the nonnegative range of the parameter. This process of choosing prior distributions is familiar to IRT researchers who have used software such as BILOG (Zimowski et al., 2003), which gives users the option to specify priors for binary model parameters.

Following specification of the prior, the next step is to consider the joint posterior distribution of the model parameters, given the data. In a Bayesian analysis, the joint posterior distribution contains all of the information that is relevant to inference about the model parameters. For example, if a point estimate of an item location parameter is needed, the expected value of that parameter in the posterior could be used. These point estimates could in turn be used to estimate the item response function. The uncertainty in the point estimate of any parameter is represented using credible regions or intervals of values for the parameter that include a fixed percent of the posterior distribution. A 90% credible region has lower and upper bounds that include the central 90% of the posterior distribution.

The joint posterior distribution for the parameters in many IRT models will be complex and of unknown form. Even in cases for which the form of the distribution is known, the distribution is multivariate and difficult to work with directly. For these reasons, methods of parameter estimation based on simulating observations from the joint posterior distribution have grown in popularity (Gelman, Carlin, Stern, & Rubin, 2003). Markov Chain Monte Carlo (MCMC) methods consist in drawing repeated samples from the joint posterior distribution and estimating the parameters of interest using the simulated data. Two MCMC methods that have been applied to the IRT problem are the Gibbs sampler and the Metropolis–Hastings algorithm (Geman & Geman, 1984; Hastings, 1970; Metropolis, Rosenbluth, Rosenbluth, Teller, & Teller, 1953). The Gibbs sampler divides the parameters into subsets and samples separately for each subset, conditioning on the remaining parameters. This approach can be useful when the conditional distributions are known and relatively simple. Unfortunately, the ordinary Gibbs sampling scheme is often impractical because the conditional posterior distributions for individual parameters do not have simple forms. One alternative in this case is to modify the Gibbs method to include steps from the Metropolis–Hastings algorithm. These steps do not require that the form of the individual conditional posteriors be known. The Metropolis–Hastings algorithm requires some skill in choosing features of the algorithm that determine its performance, such as the nature of the "proposal" distributions that are used as substitutes for the unknown joint posterior distributions. Properly structured, a hybrid Gibbs/Metropolis–Hastings algorithm is practical as the core of an estimation scheme for IRT modeling. The MCMC approach has the advantage of flexibility, as it is able to accommodate a wide range of IRT models and choices for prior distributions. The MCMC approach also requires considerable care to be successful, however. Convergence of the sequence of observation sets to the target distribution must be monitored and is not guaranteed. The initial sets of observations are generally discarded because of serial correlations that are normally present in the sequence. The number of observations to discard is a matter of judgment, although conventions exist. Finally, it is usually best to divide the total number of model parameters to be estimated into subsets, with separate runs being used for the different subsets. For example, separate runs for item and person parameters are typically used, taking advantage of presumed independence between these subsets. Further subsetting of the item parameters is possible as well.

Model Fit Evaluation

Model fit evaluation in IRT ordinarily combines formal hypothesis-testing procedures with informal graphical displays and goodness-of-fit indices. The method of fit evaluation varies depending on the specific model under consideration. For example, the Rasch family of models can be evaluated for fit using a variety of test statistics with known asymptotic properties. Many of these statistics do not generalize to more complex models, however. All of these factors make it difficult to provide a fully comprehensive description of fit evaluation methods in IRT. In lieu of such a description, we here describe some general procedures for fit evaluation that are broadly applicable. The next chapter provides a detailed account of methods for evaluating invariance in item response functions across multiple populations.

A bias investigation usually begins with a general parametric IRT model that provides an adequate fit in all populations. This *baseline model* permits population differences in the item response functions for the set of items being studied. This model becomes the starting point for tests of invariance in the item response functions. The model is typically chosen based on theoretical considerations and on prior experience with items such as those under study. The baseline model must be shown to fit adequately in all of the populations to be studied. If the model fails to fit within some populations while providing an adequate fit within other populations, this result is evidence against measurement invariance for the items under study. For example, in dichotomous item data, it may happen that the Rasch model fits well in the reference group but fits poorly in the focal group. Unless a different model can be found that is theoretically plausible and fits well in both populations, the hypothesis of measurement invariance for the items will be rejected. It is important to carefully evaluate the fit of the baseline model.

Assume that item response data on p items are available for N_k persons in the kth population, $k = 1, \ldots, K$. The number of items p is assumed to be identical in all populations. The initial goal is to find a common parametric model for the p item response functions in all populations without restricting the functions to be invariant across these populations. For example, the items may be found to fit a 2PL model in all populations, but with item parameter values that vary depending on the population. The 2PL model then becomes the baseline model for further investigation of bias. Given that the K populations are independent, the fit of any proposed baseline model can be evaluated separately within each population. In some cases, a global fit index may be created from the population-specific indices to give an overall sense of fit.

Formal statistical tests of fit have a role to play in the fit evaluation of any proposed baseline model, but they cannot be relied upon as the sole basis for deciding which model to retain. In most applications, any proposed baseline model can provide only an approximate fit. The investigator's task is to evaluate whether the approximation can be considered adequate. Given an imperfect fit, proper statistical tests of fit will always lead to rejection of the model if the available sample is large enough. Hence, formal tests of fit must be supplemented by indices of the size of the departure from perfect fit. The investigator must use these indices to arrive at a decision about the adequacy of the fit. Judgment is clearly involved here, and no absolute decision rules are available.

Given p items, each with C response categories, there are C^p different response patterns that could potentially be observed. The examinees are sorted into some or all of the C^p possible subgroups defined by these response patterns. Let $\mathbf{X}_q$ be a specific $p \times 1$ response vector for $q = 1, \ldots, C^p$. Let $P(\mathbf{X}_q)$ be the marginal probability of the qth response vector in a given population, with $\sum_q P(\mathbf{X}_q) = 1$. Without any restrictions on $P(\mathbf{X}_q)$, it is easily shown that for any sample of respondents from the population, the maximum likelihood estimate of $P(\mathbf{X}_q)$ is simply the observed proportion of the sample respondents who have response vectors $\mathbf{X}_q$. An IRT model restricts $P(\mathbf{X}_q)$ by combining a parametric form for the item response function with a distribution for W, the latent variable. For example, the marginal probability of a given response vector $\mathbf{X}_q$ under an IRT model is, from Equation 6.1,

$$P_0(\mathbf{X}_q) = \int P_0(\mathbf{X}_q \mid W) g_0(W) dW, \tag{6.38}$$

with hypothesized item response function $P_0(\mathbf{X}_q|W)$ and with $g_0(W)$ the hypothesized density function for W. Given estimates of the item parameters in $P_0(\mathbf{X}_q|W)$ and the parameters governing $g_0(W)$, the marginal probability in Equation 6.38 can be evaluated. Let p_q be the observed proportion of examinees with response vectors of $\mathbf{X}_q$. Then a general large-sample fit statistic that can be applied to nearly any IRT model is the Pearson chi-square statistic

$$\chi^2 = \sum_{q=1}^{C^p} \frac{[p_q - P_0(\mathbf{X}_q)]^2}{P_0(\mathbf{X}_q)}, \qquad (6.39)$$

where the marginal probabilities are evaluated using the available parameter estimates. If the number of unique parameters estimated in order to evaluate $P_0(\mathbf{X}_q)$ is equal to t, the chi-square statistic in Equation 6.39 will have $C^p - t - 1$ degrees of freedom. The test statistic evaluates the null hypothesis that the data follow $P_0(\mathbf{X}_q)$, the hypothesized IRT model, against a general multinomial alternative hypothesis. The model here includes not only the assumed item response function $P_0(\mathbf{X}_q | W)$ but also the hypothesized distribution $g_0(W)$.

Unfortunately, the chi-square statistic in Equation 6.39 will not be useful in many applications because of low or zero expected frequencies for many of the C^p possible response vectors. In the simple dichotomous case ($C = 2$), a 20-item test will yield $2^{20} = 1,048,576$ different response vectors. Relatively few of these vectors will be observed unless the sample size is truly large. The test statistic in Equation 6.39 will therefore be useful only for small values of p in general. Note also that in cases in which p is small enough to permit use of the statistic, the calculation of $P_0(\mathbf{X}_q)$ will require the evaluation of the integral in Equation 6.38. This integral cannot be evaluated exactly in most cases, but discrete quadrature approximations are available.

The next section describes some fit evaluation methods for models belonging to the Rasch family. Fit procedures for the dichotomous case are presented first, followed by fit procedures for polytomous Rasch models. After discussing fit procedures for the Rasch family of models, we turn to fit evaluation for more complex models, first describing procedures for dichotomous item models and then discussing the polytomous case. Fewer fit procedures are available for these complex models in comparison to the Rasch models.

Rasch Models

Fit evaluation methods that are useful specifically for models belonging to the Rasch family will vary depending on whether dichotomous or ordered-categorical response scales are considered. The methods vary in their sensitivity to violations of model assumptions as well. In the dichotomous case, for example, some procedures are designed to be sensitive to violations of parallelism of the item response functions across items, while others are primarily sensitive to multidimensionality in *W*. Fortunately, we now have fit evaluation procedures for the Rasch model whose large-sample properties are well understood. As will become clear, the sufficiency of the unweighted sum of item scores in relation to *W* that is central to the Rasch family is a crucial feature of many of the fit evaluation methods. For a more thorough survey of methods of fit evaluation for models in the Rasch family, see Glas and Verhelst (1995a, 1995b). The RSP program (Glas & Ellis, 1994) can conduct many of the fit tests discussed by these authors.

Consider first the case of dichotomous items $\mathbf{X} = (X_1, X_2, \ldots, X_p)$, and let $T = \sum_j X_j$ be the total score across items. We will confine discussion to a single population. The first set of tests to be described are designed to be sensitive to violations of the assumption that all item response functions for the *p* items are parallel. This assumption is important for distinguishing the Rasch model from models such as the 2PL or 3PL, which permit varying discrimination parameter values among the items, leading to item response functions whose shapes may be dissimilar across items. The general approach taken in all of these test procedures is to divide the sample into score groups based on the total score *T* and then to compare the actual frequencies of positive response to an item to the expected frequencies based on the fitted Rasch model. Substantial deviations from the expected frequencies are produced if the item discriminates more or less than expected across score groups. Early versions of these tests were proposed by Wright and Panchapakesan (1969) and by Mead (1976). The distributional properties of these early procedures are unclear, although chi-square approximations are used in practice. Currently available procedures have known asymptotic properties in most cases, as discussed below.

To begin, the sample of *N* respondents is initially partitioned according to their scores on *T*. Excluding score groups corresponding to the perfect scores of 0 or *T*, there are $p - 1$ potential score groups. Depending on *N*, these $p - 1$ subgroups may be combined to yield fewer groups that have samples of adequate size. Suppose that the resulting number of score groups is $M \leq p - 1$, and let f_{mj} be the number of respondents who respond positively to the *j*th item in the *m*th score group. Given estimates of the item parameters, the conditional expected value for f_{mj} can be estimated as $E(f_{mf} | \hat{\mathbf{b}}, N_m)$, where $\hat{\mathbf{b}}$ represents the item parameter estimates and N_m is the number of respondents in the *m*th score group. We will assume that $\hat{\mathbf{b}}$ represents estimates derived via CML for now. The deviation score

$$d_{mf} = f_{mj} - E(f_{mf} | \hat{\mathbf{b}}, N_m) \tag{6.40}$$

expresses the discrepancy between the number of examinees that actually respond positively to the item in the *m*th score group and the number that are expected to do so under the model. Note that this expectation is conditional because no attempt is made to model the N_m, $m = 1, \ldots, M$. Instead, these score group frequencies are regarded as fixed for purposes of fit evaluation. This approach is appropriate for CML estimation, where no assumptions are needed regarding the distribution of W.

The deviation scores in Equation 6.40 can be used in several ways to provide a general test of fit. Define $\mathbf{d}_m = (d_{m1}, d_{m2}, \ldots, d_{mp})$ as a $p \times 1$ vector of deviation scores for the mth score group. Then the statistic is

$$R_{1c} = \sum_{m=1}^{M} (N_m^{-1}) \mathbf{d}'_m \mathbf{A}_m^{-} \mathbf{d}_m, \tag{6.41}$$

where $\mathbf{A}_m$ is a $p \times p$ covariance matrix corresponding to $\mathbf{d}_m$, with $\mathbf{A}_m^{-}$ its generalized inverse. Here the "generalized inverse" is invoked because $\mathbf{A}_m$ is singular, thus lacking a regular inverse. In Equation 6.41, R_{1c} can be shown to be distributed as central chi-square in large samples under the Rasch model for $\mathbf{X}$ (Glas, 1988, 1989). The degrees of freedom for R_{1c} are $(p-1)(M-1)$. An expression for $\mathbf{A}_m$ can be found in Glas (1988). In general, this matrix is not diagonal because the elements of $\mathbf{d}_m$ are not independent. The need to find an inverse for $\mathbf{A}_m$ places some practical limits on the number of items that can be considered. Glas notes that R_{1c} has the same asymptotic distribution as the earlier Martin-Löf (1973) T-statistic but is derived from more general assumptions.

Asymptotic standard errors for the elements of $\mathbf{d}_m$ are found as the square roots of the diagonal elements of $\mathbf{A}_m$. Let $a_{jm}^{1/2}$, $j = 1, \ldots, p$, be these standard errors. Then the "standardized" deviations $z_{jm} = d_{jm} a_{jm}^{-1/2}$ can be used to evaluate the relative sizes of the discrepancies represented by the elements of $\mathbf{d}_m$. In large samples, R_{1c} may reach statistical significance even though none of the z_{jm} are particularly large. Trends in the sizes of the z_{jm} for specific items may provide indications about the source of the lack of fit. Van den Wollenberg (1982) proposed the following test statistic that explicitly uses the standardized deviations z_{jm}

$$Q_1 = \frac{p-1}{p} \sum_{j=1}^{p} \sum_{m=1}^{M} z_{jm}^2. \tag{6.42}$$

Van den Wollenberg provides simulation evidence that Q_1 has an asymptotic central chi-square distribution under the Rasch model, with degrees of freedom equal to that for R_{1c}. Glas and Verhelst (1995a) note that Q_1 can be regarded as an approximation to R_{1c} that ignores the off-diagonal elements of $\mathbf{A}_m$, $m = 1, \ldots, M$.

The foregoing R_{1c} and Q_1 test statistics evaluate the fit of the entire item set to the Rasch model. In some contexts, it may be of interest to evaluate the fit for specific items. The rationale for such tests is that while the bulk of the items fit the model, a small number of items may violate the parallelism assumptions, and these should be identified. Clearly, evaluations of fit for specific items only make sense if the majority of the items fit the model (Gustafsson, 1980). In addition, it may be useful in practice to introduce controls for potential inflation of the Type I error rate when conducting item-level fit evaluations, especially in long tests. False discovery rate procedures (Benjamini & Hochberg, 1995) may be helpful for this purpose.

The first item-level fit statistic to be described uses the deviations d_{mj} defined in Equation 6.40, following creation of M score intervals as described earlier. We can define the vector $\mathbf{d}'_j = (d_{1j}, d_{2j}, \ldots, d_{Mj})$ as a $1 \times M$ vector of deviations for the jth item in each of the M score groups. Then Verhelst and Eggen (1989) and Verhelst, Glas, and Verstralen (1994) define the fit statistic for the jth item as

$$S_j = \mathbf{d}'_j \mathbf{A}_j^- \mathbf{d}_j, \tag{6.43}$$

where $\mathbf{A}_j$ is an $M \times M$ covariance matrix for the elements of $\mathbf{d}_j$, with $\mathbf{A}_j^-$ the generalized inverse. Glas and Verhelst (1995a) discuss the creation of $\mathbf{A}_j$. The statistic S_j has a chi-square distribution in large samples with $df = M - 1$. This fit statistic is simply a reformulation of R_{1c} that considers the fit of a specific item across score groups.

Molenaar (1983) presented a different statistic that is intended to diagnose, for a specific item, whether the item tends to discriminate more or less than is expected under the Rasch model for the entire set of items. To create the statistic, we begin by splitting the range of T into low, middle, and high regions based on two cutpoints T_L and T_H chosen by the researcher. Values of $T \le T_L$ are considered "low," and values of $T \ge T_H$ are considered "high." A common practice is to choose cutpoints so that the low and high ranges correspond to the lower and upper quartiles of the sample distribution on T, but other choices are possible. Intermediate or middle values of T are omitted from the calculation of the fit statistic. The sample is partitioned into M score groups on the basis of T as previously described. In this case, score groups will be defined with consideration given to the choice of T_L and T_H. Groups that straddle these cutpoints are avoided. Let M_L and M_H denote the sets of score groups such that M_L includes groups with $T \le T_L$ and M_H includes groups with $T \ge T_H$. Then using the standardized deviation scores z_{mj} defined earlier, Molenaar proposed the fit statistic

$$U_j = \frac{\sum_{m \in M_L} z_{mj} - \sum_{m \in M_H} z_{mj}}{\sqrt{T_L + p - T_H}} \tag{6.44}$$

for the jth item. This fit statistic will have an approximate standard normal distribution in large samples. The U_j statistic will be positive when the item response function has less discrimination than expected under the Rasch model. Negative values for U_j indicate the reverse situation.

The R_{1c} and Q_1 statistics assume that the item parameter estimation proceeds using CML, eliminating the need to model the population distribution of W. If MML estimation is used, the test statistic R_{1c} must be modified. Under MML estimation, a distributional form for W is assumed as $g(W)$, with parameter ω that is usually vector valued. For example, if $g(W)$ is a normal density, then $\omega = (\mu_W, \sigma_W)$. These parameters must be estimated or stipulated. Let $\hat{\omega}$ represent their estimates. Considering both the item parameter estimates $\hat{b}$ and the estimates $\hat{\omega}$, we can evaluate the probability of any value for T and derive the expected number of examinees who score at any specific value of T. Let f_t be the number of examinees who actually score $T = t$, for $t = 0, 1, \ldots, p$. Then we can define the deviation

$$d_t = f_t - E(f_t \mid \hat{b}, \hat{\omega}) \tag{6.45}$$

as the discrepancy between the actual and expected numbers of examinees at a specific score level. There will be $p + 1$ of these deviations. As in the CML case, we can create score groupings based on the values of T, excluding the perfect scores $T = 0$ and $T = p$. The maximum number of these groups is $p - 1$, but fewer groups may be chosen. Let the number of groups again be $M \leq p - 1$. Then for a given item, we can define d_{mj} analogously to Equation 6.40, but now considering the estimates $\hat{\omega}$ as well

$$d_{mj} = f_{mj} - E(f_{mj} \mid \hat{b}, \hat{\omega}) \tag{6.46}$$

with f_{mj} as defined before. The interpretation of the d_{mj} is similar to that in Equation 6.40, except for the added structure on $g(W)$ required by MML estimation. Finally, we can define a vector $\mathbf{d}_m = (d_{m1}, d_{m2}, \ldots, d_{mp}, \mathbf{d}_{tm})$, where $\mathbf{d}_{tm}$ is a vector whose elements are the values of $\mathbf{d}_t$ from Equation 6.43 corresponding to the values of T that are included in the mth score group. The size of this vector varies depending on which values of T were used to form the mth score group. Then an MML test statistic is defined as

$$R_{1M} = r_0 + \sum_{m=1}^{M} \mathbf{d}'_m \mathbf{A}_m^- \mathbf{d}_m + r_T, \tag{6.47}$$

where $\mathbf{A}_m^-$ is the generalized inverse of $\mathbf{A}_m$, the covariance matrix of $\mathbf{d}_m$, and

$$r_0 = \frac{(f_0 - E(f_0 \mid \hat{b}, \hat{\omega}))^2}{E(f_0 \mid \hat{b}, \hat{\omega})}, \quad r_T = \frac{(f_p - E(f_p \mid \hat{b}, \hat{\omega}))^2}{E(f_p \mid \hat{b}, \hat{\omega})} \tag{6.48}$$

with f_0 and f_p being the number of examinees with $T = 0$ and $T = p$, respectively. Under the Rasch model with the assumed distribution $g(W)$, R_{1M} will have a central chi-square distribution in large samples. The degrees of freedom for R_{1M} are $M(p - 1) + 1 - v$, with v being the dimension of the vector $\hat{\omega}$. Ordinarily, $v = 2$. Descriptive measures of fit can be created by dividing elements by the square roots of the corresponding diagonal elements of $\mathbf{A}_m$. The resulting measures are essentially standard scores in large samples under the Rasch model. The structure of $\mathbf{A}_m$ is discussed in Glas (1988).

The fit procedures just described are designed to be sensitive to departures from parallelism in the item response functions for a set of items. These fit procedures are not necessarily sensitive to other violations of Rasch model assumptions. For example, departures from unidimensionality may occur that are undetected by the foregoing fit procedures (Gustafsson, 1980; Van den Wollenberg, 1979, 1982). Violations of unidimensionality are generally accompanied by violations of local independence in relation to the single, hypothesized latent variable. A different set of fit procedures are designed to evaluate whether the Rasch assumptions of local independence and unidimensionality hold for the data. These procedures generally use the pairwise relations among the items as a basis for evaluating the fit of the model. Procedures for evaluating the dimensionality of the latent space underlying a set of items are diverse (Hattie, 1985; Sijtsma & Molenaar, 2002; Stout, 1987, 1990; Wirth & Edwards, 2007). We focus here only on those procedures motivated by the Rasch model. More general methods that are either motivated by alternative models (e.g., factor analysis) or are essentially nonparametric (e.g., DIMTEST) could also be applied.

Van den Wollenberg (1982) proposed a test statistic Q_2 that is constructed by first partitioning the sample into M score groups as described earlier. Item parameter estimates are then obtained separately for each score group. Under the Rasch model, these estimates should vary only by estimation error, but this error may be substantial in modest samples or in long tests. Consider the bivariate frequency distribution for responses to the ith and jth items within the mth score group, which can be represented in a 2×2 table. This frequency distribution is illustrated in Table 6.1. In this table, f_{11ijm} represents the count of the number of examinees in the mth score group who respond positively to both the ith and jth items. The fit statistic Q_2 is based on the discrepancies between the expected frequencies

TABLE 6.1

2 × 2 Contingency Table for mth Score Group on ith and jth Items

	$X_j = 0$	$X_j = 1$
$X_i = 0$	f_{00ijm}	f_{01ijm}
$X_i = 1$	f_{10ijm}	f_{11ijm}

and the actual frequencies in Table 6.1. The expected frequencies are calculated conditionally, given the marginal frequencies and the parameter estimates in the mth score group. We can then define the deviation scores

$$d_{11ijm} = f_{11ijm} - E(f_{11ijm} \mid \hat{\mathbf{b}}_m), \tag{6.49}$$

where $\hat{\mathbf{b}}_m$ are the item parameter estimates obtained with the mth score group. Note that $E(f_{11ijm} \mid \hat{\mathbf{b}}_m) = N_m P_{ijm}(\hat{\mathbf{b}}_m)$, where $P_{ijm}(\hat{\mathbf{b}}_m)$ is the joint conditional probability under the Rasch model of responding positively to both the ith and jth items within the mth score group, evaluated using $\hat{\mathbf{b}}_m$. Deviations for the other three cells of the contingency table (d_{10ijm}, d_{01ijm}, d_{00ijm}) can be calculated analogously to d_{11ijm} in Equation 6.49. Then define

$$q_{ijm} = \frac{d_{11ijm}^2}{E(f_{11ijm} \mid \hat{\mathbf{b}}_m)} + \frac{d_{10ijm}^2}{E(f_{10ijm} \mid \hat{\mathbf{b}}_m)} + \frac{d_{01ijm}^2}{E(f_{01ijm} \mid \hat{\mathbf{b}}_m)} + \frac{d_{00ijm}^2}{E(f_{00ijm} \mid \hat{\mathbf{b}}_m)}$$

$$\tag{6.50}$$

for the mth score group. The statistic Q_2 is calculated as

$$Q_2 = \frac{p-3}{p-1} \sum_{m=1}^{M} \sum_{i=1}^{p-1} \sum_{j=i+1}^{p} q_{ijm}. \tag{6.51}$$

In large samples, the distribution of Q_2 is approximated by a chi-square distribution with $df = Mp(p-3)/2$. The adequacy of the chi-square approximation has been evaluated in simulations and has been found to be fairly good (Van den Wollenberg, 1982). A drawback of Q_2 is the need for M separate estimations of the item parameters in the M score groups. The available sample must be large enough to support these estimations within each score group.

Alternative fit statistics that do not require separate estimation by score group have been proposed by Glas (1988; Glas & Verhelst, 1995a). Let $f_{11ij} = \sum_{m=1}^{M} f_{11ijm}$ be the total number of examinees who respond positively to both the ith and jth items. We can then define the deviation score

$$d_{11ij} = f_{11ij} - E(f_{11ij} \mid \hat{\mathbf{b}}), \tag{6.52}$$

where $E(f_{11ij} \mid \hat{\mathbf{b}})$ is the expected value of f_{11ij} given the CML estimates $\hat{\mathbf{b}}$ defined earlier. We can then create a vector $\mathbf{d}_{11}$ of length $p(p-1)/2$ containing the values of d_{11ij} for all unique item pairs. Similarly, we can define the deviation

$$d_{1j} = f_{1j} - E(f_{1j} \mid \hat{\mathbf{b}}) \tag{6.53}$$

as the difference between the number of examinees who respond positively to the jth item and the expected number evaluated using the CML estimates. Let $\mathbf{d}_1$ be the $p \times 1$ vector containing the deviations in Equation 6.53 for each item. Then the R_{2c} statistic is

$$R_{2c} = \frac{1}{N} \mathbf{d}'_{11} \mathbf{A}_2^{-1} \mathbf{d}_{11} + \frac{1}{N} \mathbf{d}'_1 \mathbf{A}_1^{-1} \mathbf{d}_1 \tag{6.54}$$

which in large samples is distributed as a chi-square variate with $df = p(p - 1)/2$ under the Rasch model. The matrices $\mathbf{A}_2$ and $\mathbf{A}_1$ are the covariance matrices for $\mathbf{d}_{11}$ and $\mathbf{d}_1$, respectively. Although the large-sample distribution for R_{2c} is exact, a significant disadvantage of R_{2c} is the need to invert $\mathbf{A}_2$, whose dimension is determined by the number of pairs of items. This fact limits the use of R_{2c} to tests of modest length. Glas (1988; Glas & Verhelst, 1995a) give an alternative version of this statistic, called R_{2m}, that can be used with MML estimation.

Likelihood-Ratio Tests

An advantage of CML estimation within the Rasch model is that if the model fits an examinee population in relation to a set of items, we expect the CML estimates of the item parameters to be the same in all subpopulations created from that population, apart from sampling error. This result should hold whether the subpopulations are formed as score groups based on the total score T or are formed on the basis of other variables such as sex or ethnicity. Andersen (1973) used this property of the Rasch model to create an LR test of fit for the model when the subpopulations are defined by the total score T. This LR procedure can be extended to examine issues of measurement bias in the Rasch model, as discussed later. Here we focus on the use of the LR test with subpopulations defined by the total score.

Let $L_0(\mathbf{b})$ be the likelihood function using the conditional likelihood for the entire population, with $L_0(\hat{\mathbf{b}})$ its sample counterpart using CML estimates of the item parameters $\hat{\mathbf{b}}$. Suppose that the population is partitioned into M score groups based on the total score T as defined earlier. Let $L_1(\mathbf{b}_m)$ be the likelihood function for the mth score group, with $L_1(\hat{\mathbf{b}}_m)$ its sample counterpart. Then the Andersen LR is

$$L_A = \frac{L_0(\mathbf{b})}{\prod_{m=1}^{M} L_1(\mathbf{b}_m)} \tag{6.55}$$

with the numerator being the likelihood function for the entire population and the denominator being the joint likelihood in M score groups. If the Rasch model fits, we expect $L_A \cong 1.0$. Otherwise, we expect that the joint likelihood will exceed the likelihood in the numerator or that $L_A < 1.0$. The sample LR $\hat{L}_A$ is obtained by substituting the sample likelihood values in Equation 6.55. In large samples, it can be shown that

$$-2\ln(\hat{L}_A) = -2\left[\ln L_0(\hat{\mathbf{b}}) - \sum_{m=1}^{M} \ln L_1(\hat{\mathbf{b}}_m)\right] \qquad (6.56)$$

has a chi-square distribution with $df = (M - 1)(p - 1)$ under the Rasch model. The LR test statistic in Equation 6.56 will be sensitive to deviations from parallelism in the item response functions, as are the earlier R_{1c} and R_{1m} statistics. As noted by Andersen (1973), the separate sets of parameter estimates obtained within each score group can be plotted against the single set of estimates obtained from the likelihood for the entire sample. If the Rasch model fits, these plots should be roughly linear with slopes of 1.0 and intercepts of approximately zero. If the model fails to fit, the plots may give some indication about the source of the lack of fit, either with respect to individual items or specific score groups. For example, if the plots for the low score groups deviate significantly from linearity, Anderson suggests that guessing behavior may be an explanation.

The above LR procedure has several disadvantages, however. The procedure requires M separate sets of item parameter estimates, one set for each score group. Depending on the length of the test and the number of score groups M, large samples may be needed if stable parameter estimates are to be generated within each score group. The range of total scores to be included in each score group may need to be widened in smaller samples, reducing the resulting number of score groups. Another difficulty is that the method does not lead directly to any descriptive index for the size of the lack of fit to the model. In large samples, we would expect that even trivial departures from exact fit may lead to rejection of the model by a strictly statistical criterion. Furthermore, the LR procedure provides a global index of fit that is not easily translated into item-specific fit indices, unlike some of the procedures reviewed earlier. As noted above, however, one can use graphical plots to attempt to identify individual items that seem to depart from the model.

Polytomous Rasch Models

We now consider baseline fit evaluation methods for polytomous item response models belonging to the Rasch family, such as the partial-credit and rating-scale models. Because these models entail a sufficient statistic for the latent variable W, many of the fit evaluation methods described above for the dichotomous Rasch model will generalize to the polytomous case. From Equation 6.19, the total score statistic T is sufficient for W. As in the dichotomous case, we can partition the sample into M score groups based on examinee scores on T. The potential range of T is determined by C, the number of response categories per item, and p, the number of items. The maximum value of T is $p(C - 1)$. For large values of C and/or p, the range of T may be quite wide, and it will nearly always be the case that $M < p(C - 1)$. Some aggregation into score groups will usually be necessary to achieve adequate sample sizes for fit evaluation.

The R_{1c} test described earlier for the dichotomous item case is easily extended to the polytomous case. Let f_{jmc} be the number of examinees in the mth score group who responded in the cth category on the jth item. Under either the partial-credit or rating-scale models, we can evaluate the expected value of f_{jmc}, given the CML estimates of the item parameters $\hat{\beta} = (\hat{b}', \hat{\tau}')$ where $\hat{b}$ are the estimates of the location parameters and $\hat{\tau}$ are the estimates of the threshold parameters. Let these expected values be $E(f_{jmc} | \hat{\beta})$. Then we can define the deviation scores for each item, category, and score group. These deviation scores can be arrayed in a vector of length Cp as $\mathbf{d}_m = (d_{1m0}, d_{1m1}, \ldots, d_{1mC}, d_{2m0}, \ldots, d_{pmC})$. Then the fit statistic R_{1c} is defined

$$R_{1c} = N^{-1} \sum_{m=1}^{M} \mathbf{d}_m' \mathbf{A}_m^- \mathbf{d}_m, \tag{6.57}$$

where
   $\mathbf{A}_m$ is the covariance matrix for the Cp elements of $\mathbf{d}_m$
   $\mathbf{A}_m^-$ is its generalized inverse

The structure of $\mathbf{A}_m$ will depend on the definitions of the M score groups. Glas and Verhelst (1995) describe some examples. In large samples, R_{1c} in Equation 6.57 will have a chi-square distribution under the hypothesized model, with $df = \sum_{m=1}^{M} \text{rank}(\mathbf{A}_m) - q - 1$, where q is the number of independent parameters estimated in $\hat{\beta}$. As in the dichotomous case, R_{1c} is sensitive primarily to violations of parallelism, which in the polytomous case can be viewed as item differences in the discrimination levels associated with the category response functions.

The fit statistic R_{1c} can be specialized to yield an item-level statistic. Using the deviations defined in Equation 6.57, let $\mathbf{d}_j = (d_{j10}, d_{j11}, \ldots, d_{j1c}, d_{j20}, \ldots, d_{jMC})$ be a vector of length MC containing the deviations corresponding to the jth item. Then analogously to Equation 6.57, we can define a fit statistic for the jth item as

$$\mathbf{S}_j = N^{-1} \mathbf{d}_j' \mathbf{A}_j^- \mathbf{d}_j, \tag{6.58}$$

where $\mathbf{A}_j$ is the covariance matrix for $\mathbf{d}_j$, with $\mathbf{A}_m^-$ its generalized inverse. In large samples, this statistic will have a chi-square distribution under the hypothesized model with $df = \text{rank}(\mathbf{A}_j) - q_j - 1$, where q_j is the number of parameters estimated for the jth item.

The LR fit statistic used in the dichotomous case is also easily extended to polytomous Rasch models. Let $L_0(\boldsymbol{\beta})$ be the conditional likelihood function under the hypothesized model for the entire population, with $L_0(\hat{\boldsymbol{\beta}})$ its sample value based on parameter estimates $\hat{\boldsymbol{\beta}}$. After partitioning the sample into M score groups based on T as described earlier, let $L_1(\hat{\boldsymbol{\beta}})$ be the sample likelihood value within the mth score group under the hypothesized model, using group-specific parameter estimates $\hat{\boldsymbol{\beta}}_m$. Then as in the dichotomous case, the sample LR for testing the hypothesized model is

$$\hat{L}_A = \frac{L_0(\hat{\boldsymbol{\beta}})}{\prod_{m=1}^{M} L_1(\hat{\boldsymbol{\beta}}_m)}. \tag{6.59}$$

As before, we expect $\hat{L}_A \cong 1.0$ if the model fits. To the extent that the model gives substantially different estimates $\hat{\boldsymbol{\beta}}_m$ across score groups, we expect $\hat{L}_A < 1.0$, suggesting that the same model does not hold in all score groups. In large samples, the statistic $-2 \ln(\hat{L}_A)$ converges to a chi-square distribution under the hypothesized model, with degrees of freedom that are equal to the difference in the number of independent parameters estimated in $\hat{\boldsymbol{\beta}}$ and $(\hat{\boldsymbol{\beta}}_1, \hat{\boldsymbol{\beta}}_2, \dots, \hat{\boldsymbol{\beta}}_M)$. The degrees of freedom will depend on which polytomous Rasch model is chosen.

The LR statistic for the polytomous case suffers from the same disadvantages as in the dichotomous case. Although the statistic permits a hypothesis test, it does not lead directly to any simple index of lack of fit, nor does it reduce to an item-level statistic. Graphical plots of the location parameters for different score groups can be studied to detect items that deviate substantially across groups. Similar plots could be used for the category parameters in a given ordinal position. The sample size demands for the LR statistic in the polytomous case will meet or exceed those of the dichotomous case.

General Models

While useful statistical fit procedures with known asymptotic properties exist for models in the Rasch family, the situation is quite different for more general models. In the general case, fewer fit statistics with known properties are available. Instead, researchers rely on a variety of fit evaluation methods, ranging from tests oriented to specific assumptions (e.g., unidimensionality) to general omnibus fit statistics (e.g., Pearson chi-square).

Typically, researchers adopt a variety of approaches in a given application. Confidence in a model is enhanced to the extent that the model fits well by all criteria. Here we review several general fit evaluation procedures that can be adopted for most, if not all, models outside of the Rasch family.

Global Chi-Square Fit Statistics

The Pearson chi-square statistic in Equation 6.39 is potentially applicable to any IRT model for purposes of baseline model fit evaluation. In practice, however, the statistic is only applicable if the number of items p is small enough so that the expected frequencies for the different response patterns are meaningful in size. For example, a five-item test with dichotomous items will create 32 possible response patterns, a number that is small enough to make the use of Equation 6.39 feasible in moderate samples. The LR chi-square statistic provides another alternative in this case. This statistic is

$$G^2 = -2N \sum_{q=1}^{C^p} p_q \log \frac{P_0(\mathbf{X}_q)}{p_q},$$ (6.60)

where p_q is the observed proportion of N examinees who have response sequence $\mathbf{X}_q$, with $P_0(\mathbf{X}_q)$ the expected proportion under the hypothesized model. The G^2 statistic has the same asymptotic distribution as the Pearson chi-square, but the two statistics may give different results in finite samples. Agresti (2002) notes that the Pearson statistic appears to adhere more closely to the chi-square distribution when the expected frequencies are small. Fully general rules for when such frequencies are "small" are difficult to formulate (Cochran, 1954; Koehler, 1986; Koehler & Larntz, 1980). Mislevy and Bock (1993) suggest that the G^2 statistic should be used only for $p < 11$. Reiser and Vandenberg (1994) provide simulation evidence showing that G^2 performs poorly for $p > 5$, with the Pearson chi-square performing adequately up to $p = 10$. More research is needed on this question in relation to IRT applications.

The Pearson and LR chi-square statistics are based on a fit to the entire contingency table formed by the C^p possible response vectors. A logical alternative is to limit the assessment of fit to the first- and second-order marginal frequencies. With p items, there will be $p(p + 1)/2$ first- and second-order frequency tables to be fit. This limited information approach is most fully developed for the dichotomous case (Bartholomew & Leung, 2002; Cai, Maydeu-Olivares, Coffman, & Thissen, 2006; Maydeu-Olivares, 2001a, 2001b; Maydeu-Olivares & Joe, 2005), but work on the polytomous case is quickly catching up (Maydeu-Olivares & Joe, 2006). Reiser (1996) illustrates the use of one method under the 2PL model. Under this model for p items, Reiser shows that the statistic

$$\chi_W^2 = \hat{e}'\hat{\Sigma}_e^{-1}\hat{e} \tag{6.61}$$

will have an asymptotic chi-square distribution under fairly general conditions. The vector $\hat{e}$ is of length $p(p + 1)/2$ and contains the deviations

$$\hat{P}_j - P_j(\hat{\beta}), \qquad \hat{P}_{jj'} - P_{jj'}(\hat{\beta}), \tag{6.62}$$

where
   $\hat{P}_j$ is the sample proportion passing the jth item
   $\hat{P}_{jj'}$ is the sample proportion passing both items j and j'
   $P_j(\hat{\beta})$, $P_{jj'}(\hat{\beta})$ are the expected proportions under the model with estimated parameters $\hat{\beta}$

The degrees of freedom associated with χ_W^2 are $\min[p(p + 1)/2, 2^p - 2p - 1]$. Note that the parameter estimates may have been obtained through full information maximum likelihood. The matrix $\hat{\Sigma}_e$ is the estimated covariance matrix of $\hat{e}$ and is given in Reiser (1996). Rejection of the model using χ_W^2 can be followed by scrutiny of the standardized residuals corresponding to the deviations in Equation 6.62. The standardized residuals are calculated by dividing each deviation in Equation 6.62 by the square root of the corresponding diagonal element of $\hat{\Sigma}_e$. In large samples, we expect the standardized residuals to behave like standard normal deviates, although consideration of each residual in isolation ignores their correlations. The fit statistic χ_W^2 appears to perform well when the full 2^p contingency table is sparse, but further exploration of the performance of the statistic is needed.

While sparseness in the full C^p contingency table will degrade the performance of the traditional Pearson and LR chi-squares, the situation is improved if nested model comparisons can be conducted. Suppose that the baseline model of interest is Model A, and also suppose that this model is a restricted version of a more general Model B. A test of the restrictions leading from Model B to Model A can be performed using the difference statistic

$$G_{A|B}^2 = G_A^2 - G_B^2 \tag{6.63}$$

with degrees of freedom equal to the number of parameter restrictions needed to create Model A from Model B. An analogous difference can be defined for the Pearson chi-squares. Assuming that Model B fits adequately, the difference of chi-squares in Equation 6.63 will have a chi-square distribution in large samples under the null hypothesis that Model A also fits. Haberman (1977) established that the difference statistic converges in distribution to the chi-square distribution under the null hypothesis even if the contingency table is sparse. Agresti and Yang (1987) documented the performance of the difference statistic in sparse data using simulations.

Item-Level Chi-Square Statistics

Setting aside the global fit statistic in Equation 6.39, a general approach for assessing the fit of an IRT model to a binary test item following estimation of both item parameters **b** and the latent scores W is to (a) group individuals into intervals based on score estimates $\hat{W}$, (b) find the actual number of people passing the jth item within the mth score group f_{jm}, (c) calculate the expected proportion passing in each score group under the assumed model, and (d) calculate a chi-square statistic using the discrepancies between the actual and expected proportions passing across score groups. This approach is taken in some current software programs (e.g., BILOG). To define the chi-square statistic, let $E(P_{jm}|\hat{\mathbf{b}}, \hat{W})$ be the expected proportion of people who pass the jth item in the mth score group. Then a general Pearson fit statistic is

$$\chi^2_{sj} = \sum_{m=1}^{M} \frac{f_m[P_{jm} - E(P_{jm}|\hat{\mathbf{b}}, \hat{W})]^2}{E(P_{jm}|\hat{\mathbf{b}}, \hat{W})[1 - E(P_{jm}|\hat{\mathbf{b}}, \hat{W})]}, \tag{6.64}$$

where
   f_m is the number of people in the mth score group
   P_{jm} is the actual proportion of people who pass the jth item and are in the mth score group

There are several variations on this theme. For example, the expected values $E(P_{jm}|\hat{\mathbf{b}}, \hat{W})$ can be calculated in several ways, depending on how one represents W in the calculation. BILOG-MG (Zimowski et al., 2003) uses the mean $\hat{W}$ value in each score group. A different approach is to use posterior probabilities of W across the score groups, rather than point estimates of W, to calculate the expected proportion passing (Stone & Zhang, 2003). Yen (1981) used the average probability of passing across W values in a given score group. An additional source of variation in the application of the test statistic in Equation 6.64 concerns the appropriate degrees of freedom. BILOG-MG (Zimowski et al.) uses the number of score groups M as the degrees of freedom. Yen proposed using $M - q$, with q being the number of item parameters. Stone and Zhang estimated the degrees of freedom after using a resampling procedure to assess the distribution of the fit statistic, and hence there is no a priori value for the degrees of freedom in their case.

Two potential limitations of the procedure leading to the test statistic in Equation 6.64 are (a) the uncertainty in the estimates of the latent variable scores and (b) the choice of the number of score groups M. With short tests (e.g., $p < 20$), the uncertainty in assigning individuals to score groups based on their estimated latent scores becomes a problem. Given that very short tests can employ the global statistic in Equation 6.39, the problem is most severe for tests of medium length. Simulation studies suggest that the statistic in Equation 6.64 yields inflated Type I error rates when the number of items is less than 20 (McKinley & Mills, 1985; Orlando & Thissen, 2000; Stone & Hanson, 2000). The procedure developed by Stone (2000; Stone & Zhang, 2003) was designed to circumvent this problem by using the posterior density of potential score values, rather than point estimates, in calculating the expected number passing. Simulation evidence suggests that the procedure improves upon the point estimate approach, although computational complexity increases with the number of items (Stone; Stone & Zhang). The second problem of arbitrariness in the number of score groups M results in potential variation in fit results depending on the choice. Yen (1981) specified a fixed number of $M = 10$ groups, with an effort made to specify group boundaries to produce an equal number of groups. In contrast, BILOG-MG (Zimowski et al., 2003) varies the number of groups depending on the data at hand, resulting in variation in the degrees of freedom as well. The problem of choosing the number and boundaries of groups in goodness-of-fit testing in continuous distributions is a classic problem that predates IRT (Stuart & Ord, 1991). Two traditional approaches have been to either seek groupings that have equal probabilities under the assumed distribution or to seek intervals of equal width that then have unequal probabilities. This issue has not yet received systematic study in IRT applications.

All of the foregoing methods are based on forming groups on the basis of latent variable scores W. A different approach uses the total test score $T = \sum_{j=1}^{p} X_j$ as the basis for forming groups (Orlando & Thissen, 2000, 2003). The upper bound of the number of score groups is then fixed at pC, given item response categories $0, 1, \ldots, C$ for all items. For binary test items, the upper bound is p. The possible score vectors are limited at the highest and lowest score groups (i.e., in the highest score group, all items must be given response C). Excluding those groups, the Pearson version of the test statistic for binary items becomes

$$\chi^2_{Tj} = \sum_{t=1}^{pC-1} \frac{N_t[P_{jt} - E[P_{jt} \mid \hat{\boldsymbol{\beta}}]]}{E[P_{jt} \mid \hat{\boldsymbol{\beta}}][1 - E[P_{jt} \mid \hat{\boldsymbol{\beta}}]]}, \tag{6.65}$$

where

N_t is the number of people in the *t*th score group defined by the total
score T

P_{jt} is the proportion of people in the *t*th score group who pass the
*j*th item.

A likelihood version of this statistic can be formulated as well but has been
found to perform less well in simulations (Orlando & Thissen, 2000). The
Pearson statistic in Equation 6.65 has been found to work well across a range
of conditions (Orlando & Thissen, 2000, 2003). The statistic will be affected
by low frequencies in some total score groups, possibly requiring some col-
lapsing of score categories. In the polytomous case, this problem might be
more severe. The statistic has not been studied for that case. A clear advantage of the statistic in Equation 6.65 is the elimination of the need to classify
individuals based on their latent score estimates. The potential score groupings are also known in advance, apart from the need to collapse categories.

Factor Analytic Methods

The process of fit assessment commonly includes analyses that focus on
the dimensionality assumptions underlying the IRT model. Factor analysis is an important tool for this purpose. As reviewed in Chapter 5, factor analytic methods are available for both dichotomous and polytomous
items. An advantage of these methods is that a potentially rich variety
of fit statistics are available for factor analytic models under maximum
likelihood or weighted least squares estimation. These fit statistics include
both formal hypothesis-test procedures and indices of goodness-of-fit.

The relationships between the solutions produced by IRT models and single-factor models for ordered-categorical data are well known (Bartholomew,
1980, 1987; Kamata & Bauer, 2008; McDonald, 1999; Millsap & Yun-Tein,
2004; Muthén, 1984; Takane & de Leeuw, 1987). Takane and de Leeuw show
that the single-factor model and the normal ogive model provide equivalent
representations in dichotomous data, even given multiple factors or latent
variables. They also show the equivalence between Samejima's graded
response model and the single-factor model in polytomous data. It is reasonable to suggest that the fit of the factor model in dichotomous or polytomous data implies that *some* IRT model will also fit the data. The lack of fit
for the factor model is ambiguous, however, as some IRT models have no
precise factor analytic counterparts (e.g., the 3PL model).

The work on the equivalence between the single-factor model and certain IRT models in ordered-categorical data suggests that fitting a single-
factor model might be a useful precursor to IRT modeling. Confirmatory
factor analysis can be used for this purpose. Single-factor models can be
fit separately or simultaneously within each group defined by *V*. If the fit

of the single-factor model is rejected by the global chi-square fit statistic, residuals and other fit information can be used to evaluate the source of the lack of fit. For example, the root mean square residual with respect to the sample tetrachoric or polychoric correlation matrix can be calculated. McDonald & Mok (1995) illustrates the use of another fit index due to Tanaka (1993). Browne and Arminger (1995) suggest that the RMSEA index can be extended for use with factor models in ordered-categorical data, although they do not illustrate its use. The RMSEA statistic is now offered by both the LISREL (Jöreskog & Sörbom, 2003) and Mplus (Muthén & Muthén, 1998–2006) software programs for ordered-categorical data. Rejection of the single-factor model is inconclusive with respect to the larger class of IRT models, given that some IRT models have no factor analytic counterparts.

In the IRT context, exploratory factor analysis has been used primarily to provide descriptive information regarding how many factors might underlie the items. Much of this information is based on the eigenvalues of the matrix being analyzed (e.g., correlation or covariance matrix). Various approaches have been taken, including cutpoints for sample eigenvalues (e.g., eigenvalues greater than one, Kaiser, 1960), simulation methods in which the sample eigenvalues are compared to the eigenvalues for independent, normal variates (e.g., parallel analysis, Horn, 1965), graphical methods (e.g., scree plot, Cattell, 1966b), calculation of variance accounted for by the first r eigenvalues, and formal hypothesis tests (Bartlett, 1950). If the items are dichotomous or ordered-categorical, the eigenvalues should be based on the tetrachoric or polychoric correlation matrices. Scree plots of eigenvalues are often reported as descriptive information that is relevant to the decision about the number of factors.

Fit Evaluation in Bayesian Modeling

If the Bayesian approach described earlier is used for item parameter estimation, a natural next step is to evaluate the fit of the model using posterior predictive model checks (Sinharay, Johnson, & Stern, 2006). This approach compares the value of a chosen discrepancy index in the data at hand to the distribution of such values across replicated sets of data. Replications are created by first generating sets of item parameter values from the posterior distributions for the item parameters. Also, sets of latent variable scores are generated from the prior distributions for those scores. Once replicated sets of item parameter and latent variable scores are created, it is possible to generate replicates of actual item scores. In the final step of the cycle, the discrepancy index value is calculated from the replicated item scores. Let the value of this index in the replicated data in the kth cycle be π_k, and let the index value in the real data be π_0. A series of π_k values, $k = 1,\ldots,Q$, are generated by repeating the above steps Q times.

After the completion of the cycles, the value of π_0 is assessed relative to the distribution of the Q values of π_k. Inconsistencies between the model and the data are revealed if π_0 lies in the tail of the distribution of π_k. Plots of this distribution and of π_0 are usually enough to illustrate the results.

The choice of discrepancy index is important in determining which aspect of model fit will be examined. Sinharay et al. (2006) discuss a variety of approaches, some of which include multiple indices for different pairs of items. For example, one approach would calculate odds ratios for all pairs of items, given that different binary IRT models have different implications for these ratios. Graphical displays of the distribution of these ratios in the generated data versus the actual data may then reveal lack of fit. The Rasch model would generally imply less variability in the odds ratios across items than would the 2PL, for example. Another useful feature of this approach is that the theoretical distribution of the discrepancy index need not be known prior to the use of the method. Instead, the focus is on comparing the distributions between replicated and actual data.

Nonparametric Dimensionality Assessment

A drawback of model-based methods for evaluating unidimensionality is that the model itself may not provide a good representation of the relationship between item responses and W, even when W is unidimensional. For example, the factor model includes assumptions about the form of $P(\mathbf{X}|W)$ in addition to the unidimensionality assumption. An alternative approach is to weaken the assumptions about the form of $P(\mathbf{X}|W)$ and evaluate dimensionality within a nonparametric framework. Potentially testable consequences of a model that stipulates unidimensionality, conditional independence, and monotonicity for the item response functions are known (Ellis & Van den Wollenberg, 1993; Holland, 1981; Holland & Rosenbaum, 1986; Junker, 1993; Rosenbaum, 1984; Sijtsma, 1998; Stout, 1987, 1990). Practically useful test procedures are not yet available for some of these consequences, however.

One general approach that has led to practical nonparametric dimensionality assessment methods uses the conditioning principles adopted by Stout and colleagues in their work on dimensionality (Nandakumar, 1993a, 1994; Nandakumar & Stout, 1993; Stout, 1987, 1990; Stout et al., 1996; Zhang & Stout, 1999). These principles have roots in earlier work by Holland and Rosenbaum (Holland, 1981; Holland & Rosenbaum, 1986; Rosenbaum, 1984). The general conditioning idea is to evaluate the conditional covariance between pairs of items after conditioning on a sum score across a chosen subset of items. To the extent that the pair of items share a single latent dimension with the chosen conditioning subset, we expect the conditional covariance to be nonnegative (Rosenbaum). In this case, as the conditioning subset is lengthened, we expect the conditional covariance to approach zero. If the item pair together measure a single latent dimension different from the dimension underlying the conditioning subset, we expect the conditional covariance to be positive. Other outcomes are possible given other configurations of dimensions and items, as described in Stout et al. The sign and magnitude of the conditional covariance depend heavily on the choice of conditioning subsets. This choice can be based on substantive considerations or on empirical item-sorting procedures such as factor analysis or cluster analysis.

The conditioning logic is exploited in two dimensionality test procedures, DIMTEST and Poly-DIMTEST. DIMTEST (Nandakumar & Stout, 1993; Stout, 1987) applies to dichotomous items. The DIMTEST procedure provided a test statistic for the null hypothesis that the total set of items is unidimensional, given a division of the item set into a "partitioning" subset used to stratify the sample and an "assessment" subset chosen to measure a single common latent dimension. After stratifying the sample into subgroups based on the partitioning item subset, two variance estimates are calculated within each subgroup using scores on the assessment subset. One variance estimate is standard, while the other variance estimate assumes no covariances among the items in the assessment subset. Under the null hypothesis, these variance estimates should be approximately equal. The DIMTEST statistic is a function of the difference between the variance estimates, with some adjustments for bias due to varying item difficulties and the finite length of the partitioning subset. The statistic has a standard normal distribution in large samples. The DIMTEST procedure has been evaluated for Type I error performance and power, with good results (Hattie, Krakowski, Rogers, & Swaminathan, 1996; Nandakumar, 1993a, 1994). Note that while the DIMTEST procedure may lead to rejection of the null hypothesis of unidimensionality, the procedure does not determine the number of additional latent dimensions. Stout et al. (1996) suggest that DIMTEST should not be used with tests containing fewer than 18 items (15 in the partitioning subset, a minimum of 3 items in the assessment subset). Stout et al. also suggest that each examinee subgroup obtained through conditioning on the partitioning item subset should have a minimum of 20 examinees. This rule of thumb provides some indication of the required sample size for the use of the procedure, but more experience with the method is needed to give firmer guidelines.

The Poly-DIMTEST procedure (Li & Stout, 1995; Nandakumar, Yu, Li, & Stout, 1998) extends the conditioning approach to tests consisting of ordered-categorical items. The items need not all have identical numbers of response options. Poly-DIMTEST provides a test statistic whose development is similar to the DIMTEST statistic. The Poly-DIMTEST statistic again provides a test of the null hypothesis of unidimensionality. Nandakumar et al. studied the Type I error and power performance of the procedure in simulated data and found the procedure to perform well on both criteria. The sample sizes used in these simulations were large however (1,000, 1,500). It can be expected that with the potentially larger number of conditioned examinee subgroups due to the ordered-categorical response options, larger sample sizes would be required for Poly-DIMTEST than for DIMTEST. More study is needed on this question. Nandakumar et al. also found that preliminary factor analysis of Pearson correlations in selecting the item subsets performed as well as or better than factor analyses using polychoric correlations.

Neither of the above two procedures provide a descriptive index of the degree of multidimensionality in the total item set. For example, if the items depart from unidimensionality, to what extent would a unidimensional model provide an adequate approximation? Kim (1994) presented an index called DETECT that provides one answer to this question. DETECT was developed within the same conditioning framework that forms the basis for DIMTEST and Poly-DIMTEST. Suppose that each test item measures a dominant latent dimension, but with different item subsets measuring possibly different dimensions. In this multidimensional case, there will exist some partitioning of items into subsets that correspond to multiple dimensions underlying the test. In this ideal partitioning, each item is grouped with other items that measure the latent dimension for that group, with the multiple groups of items corresponding exactly to the multiple latent dimensions. Any other partitioning will misclassify at least one item. The DETECT index measures, for a given arbitrary partitioning, the extent to which the partitioning corresponds to an ideal multidimensional partitioning of items in the above sense. For the special case in which the test items are unidimensional, the DETECT index is zero when the items are simply grouped together. In the multidimensional case, the DETECT index is maximized when the items are partitioned into subsets corresponding to their appropriate latent dimensions. One use for the DETECT index is as a guide for actually implementing a partitioning. If no partitioning can be found that would raise the index beyond a certain threshold (Stout et al., 1996, suggest .10 as such a threshold), the item set can be considered essentially unidimensional. Larger values for the maximum of the DETECT index suggest increasing degrees of multidimensionality. Note that the logic of the index assumes that the items conform to a "simple structure" in the multidimensional case, with each item being related to one dominant latent dimension. When individual items are related to multiple latent dimensions, or when the multiple dimensions are sufficiently correlated, the interpretation of the index is clouded. The large-sample statistical theory for the DETECT index is not yet developed. One potentially useful yardstick for evaluating the index is to form a ratio of its sample value to the theoretical maximum value of the index for the data at hand (Stout et al., 1996). Values near one for this ratio indicate that the test items do exhibit approximate simple structure.

7

Item Response Theory: Tests of Invariance

This chapter assumes that a common baseline item response theory (IRT) model has been found to fit adequately in all groups of interest defined by **V**. This baseline model now becomes the starting point for further analyses that will investigate bias. This chapter describes a variety of approaches that can be taken in this investigation. We wish to not only determine if bias is present but also provide some estimate of the size of the bias. Bias "effect size" estimates are needed because simple hypothesis-testing methods are influenced by the available sample sizes. In large samples, bias that is trivial in absolute terms will still lead to rejection of the null hypothesis of no bias. Conversely, small samples may offer insufficient power to detect meaningful bias.

Given a common baseline model across groups, the bias investigation will examine group differences in the item parameter values in this model. If no group differences in parameter values are found, there is no evidence of bias. If some items are found to have parameter values that vary over groups, attention will then focus on describing these parameter differences, along with the implications of these differences for the size of the bias. The bias effect size need not be a simple function of the difference in parameter values (Linn, Levine, Hastings, & Wardrop, 1981).

Depending on the method used to study group differences in parameter values, it may be necessary to explicitly rescale the item parameter estimates in each group to place the estimates on a common metric. Recall that in any IRT model, some parameters must be constrained for model identification. In multiple-group applications, these constraints are usually placed on one or more item parameters. Even if there is no measurement bias with respect to these groups, we expect the item parameter estimates to vary across groups because of sampling error. Assuming that the IRT model fits, we should be able to find a simple (often linear) transformation that will put the item parameter estimates on a common scale (Lord, 1980). The process of finding and applying such transformations is known as parameter linkage. Linkage is needed when direct comparisons are to be made between item parameter estimates from different groups. When item bias is present, however, there may exist no simple linking transformation that will place all parameter estimates on a common scale. In this case, the best strategy may be to set aside the biased items through preliminary screening and then base the linkage on the items that remain. Strategies for addressing this problem are discussed in this chapter.

This chapter is organized as follows. Commonly used distinctions among different forms of bias in IRT-based bias investigations are described first. Likelihood-ratio (LR) methods for evaluating bias are presented next. These methods build upon the Pearson and LR chi-square methods of Chapter 6. In the following section, we turn to direct comparisons of item parameters across groups using Wald test statistics. Direct comparisons require some attention to the issues of parameter linkage, and so linkage methods are also discussed. We then describe different approaches to the estimation of bias effect size. Area indices that measure group differences in item response functions are useful for dichotomous items. Effect size measures for ordered-categorical items are also discussed. Next, the DFIT method of evaluating bias is described. An illustration of the use of IRT in item bias detection is given at the end of this chapter.

Forms of Bias

In IRT-based bias studies with dichotomous item data, it has become common to distinguish between *uniform* DIF or bias and *nonuniform* bias. As discussed by Hanson (1998), the precise meaning of uniform bias varies to some degree among authors. Mellenbergh (1989) originally defined uniform bias as holding when the relationship between group membership and the item score is the same at all levels of the variable used to match examinees across groups. In IRT applications, the matching variable is the latent variable score W. Since Mellenbergh, other authors have used a less restrictive definition of uniform bias. This definition simply requires the group difference in item response functions to have the same sign over the range of W (Shealy & Stout, 1993a; Uttaro & Millsap, 1994). For the reference and focal groups, for example, the definition is that there is no reversal in sign for the difference $P_{jr}(W) - P_{jf}(W)$ throughout the range of W. Shealy and Stout (1993a) denote this condition as *unidirectional* bias. Unidirectional bias need not be uniform in the sense of Mellenbergh because under unidirectional bias, the statistical relationship between the item score and group membership may vary over the range of the matching variable as long as there is no reversal in sign. A third type of "uniform" bias distinguished by Hanson is *parallel* bias in which the item response function for one group is simply shifted in location relative to the other group. In other words, for the reference and focal groups, we must have $P_{jr}(W) = P_{jf}(W + \varepsilon_j)$, with ε_j being a constant that may be unique to each item. If both item response functions are Rasch models, for example, any bias that is present is parallel bias because the functions may only differ in location. Parallel bias need not be uniform in the sense of Mellenbergh. For example, when both groups fit the 3PL model, the resulting bias may not be uniform yet may be parallel.

Given these distinctions, the definition of nonuniform bias is unclear unless one is careful to stipulate the definition of "uniform" bias. To avoid confusion, in this book, we will largely rely on the distinction between unidirectional bias as defined above and *bidirectional* bias that exists whenever the difference in item response functions reverses in sign over the range of the latent variable (Shealy & Stout, 1993a). Hanson (1998) notes that both uniform and parallel bias are forms of unidirectional bias. We will refer to these special cases as the need arises, but we will generally avoid the use of the phrase "nonuniform bias."

In polytomous item data, the category response functions are not ordinarily classified in terms of directionality or uniformity because they need not be monotonic. Instead, the directionality distinction can be applied to the item true-score functions across groups. From Chapter 6, it will be recalled that the true-score function for the jth item is the conditional expected value $E(X_j|W)$ given in Equation 6.11. Ordinarily, this function will be an increasing function of W. Once the category response functions have been estimated in each group, the true-score function can be estimated as well. With regard to these true-score functions, we will say that unidirectional bias exists if the difference between the true-score functions for two groups never reverses its sign throughout the range of W. In reference and focal groups, for example, directional bias means that the difference $E_r(X_j|W) - E_f(X_j|W)$ does not reverse its sign over the range of W. If sign reversals do occur, the bias that is present will be denoted as bidirectional bias. These distinctions will allow us to draw parallels between the dichotomous and polytomous cases.

Likelihood-Ratio Tests

Given either conditional maximum likelihood (CML) or marginal maximum likelihood (MML) estimation for the item parameters in each group, LR tests offer a general approach to the investigation of item bias (Thissen, Steinberg, & Gerrard, 1986; Thissen, Steinberg, & Wainer, 1988, 1993). In this approach, likelihood functions are evaluated under two models. The first model typically includes only the parameter constraints needed to identify the model. No attempt is made in this model to impose any invariance constraints on the item parameters, apart from constraints needed for identification. These identification constraints are discussed below.

This first model is essentially identical to the baseline model discussed in Chapter 6, except that the placement of identification constraints must be coordinated across groups. Let this first model be denoted M_1. The second model will add constraints to M_1 to achieve some degree of invariance in the item parameters across groups. One option is to constrain all item parameters to invariance in this second model. Alternatively, one can constrain a subset of these parameters, depending on the nature of the baseline model. For example, in ordered-categorical models, one may wish to constrain only a given type of parameter (e.g., category thresholds). Let the second model with invariance constraints be denoted M_0. Clearly, M_0 is nested within M_1. Suppose that one is able to obtain sample likelihood function values, L_0 and L_1, for the two models simultaneously across all groups. These likelihood values may be obtained via either CML or MML methods. Then under fairly general conditions, the test statistic

$$\chi^2_{LR} = -2\ln\left(\frac{L_0}{L_1}\right) \tag{7.1}$$

will have a chi-square distribution in large samples if M_0 fits in the population (Amemiya, 1985; Rao, 1973). The degrees of freedom for this test statistic are equal to the number of constraints needed to obtain M_0 from M_1. This test statistic provides an omnibus test statistic that can be used to jointly test an entire set of invariance constraints.

This LR test procedure is quite general. The choice of baseline model is flexible, as both dichotomous and ordered-categorical response models are potential candidates. More than two examinee groups may be compared at once. When more than two groups are studied, the M_0 model may incorporate constraints on parameters in only a subset of groups, permitting one or more other groups to differ from the constrained groups. Furthermore, the LR test statistic in Equation 7.1 may be used even when the C^p contingency table formed by the response patterns to the p items is sparse, as discussed in Chapter 6.

The LR test approach also has some weaknesses. Two evaluations of the likelihood are needed to obtain the test statistic in Equation 7.1, one under each of M_0 and M_1. For the restricted model M_0, the method of estimation must incorporate the invariance constraints. These constraints require a method of estimation that will use data simultaneously from all groups. Software for performing such analyses with general IRT models is limited at present. Furthermore, some consideration must be given to the placement of identification constraints in M_1, so that legitimate evaluations of invariance in M_0 will be possible. The typical approach to this problem is to designate one or more items as anchor items in M_1 (Thissen et al., 1993; Wang & Yeh, 2003; V. S. L. Williams, 1997; Woods, 2008). Finally, if the test statistic in Equation 7.1 leads to rejection of the model M_0, most investigators will wish to determine which item parameters differ across groups. Many individual post hoc tests are possible, and the best strategy for sequencing these tests is not obvious.

The next two sections provide a more detailed description of the use of the LR test procedure to detect bias in dichotomous and polytomous items.

Dichotomous Items

For the Rasch model, Andersen (1973) proposed an LR test that is easily adapted for the investigation of item bias. In this approach, M_1 represents a model that permits separate item parameter values among examinee groups defined by **V**. The likelihood L_1 is evaluated as a CML and can be calculated as the sum of the separate sample conditional likelihood values in K independent groups: $L_1 = \sum_{k=1}^{K} L_{1k}$. The likelihood L_0 is evaluated in the combined sample after pooling examinees across groups. Unlike other LR applications, Andersen's test does not require simultaneous multiple-group estimation under M_0. The test is limited to the global M_0 in which all items have invariant item parameters in all groups. Less constrained versions of M_0 cannot be tested using Andersen's test. Once L_0 and L_1 are calculated, the test statistic is given in Equation 7.1. With K groups and p items, the degrees of freedom will be $(K - 1)(p - 1)$. No explicit transformations to link parameters are needed in this test. Within each group under M_1, one constraint on the location parameters is needed to identify the model. One choice for this constraint is to identify a single item that will be an anchor item for all groups, fixing the location parameter for this item to a chosen value that is the same in all groups. The anchor item should have no measurement bias. If bias is present in this item, its use as an anchor will distort the estimates of the $p - 1$ other location parameters, as discussed in Chapter 6. Within the M_0 model, the location parameter for the same anchor item should be fixed to the same value used in M_1.

While the Andersen LR test is easily implemented, the test is limited to global invariance constraints in M_0. A more diverse array of constraints and M_0 models can be tested using MML under simultaneous multiple-group estimation. In this approach, L_1 represents the marginal likelihood for **X** after specification of the item response function and the prior distribution for W in the kth group, $g_k(W)$. The item response function need not be the Rasch function. Multiparameter models can be handled in this approach. Ordinarily, $g_k(W)$ will be taken as normal with an unspecified mean μ_{wk} and standard deviation σ_{wk}. In single-group applications, the mean and standard deviation for W are commonly taken as 0 and 1, respectively. In the multiple-group case, the standardized metric for W should not be uniformly imposed because there is generally no reason to suppose that the groups are identical in their prior distributions for W. A better approach is to require $\mu_{wk}=0$ and $\sigma_{wk}=1$ within one chosen group, and let μ_{wk} and σ_{wk} vary in the remaining groups. If this approach is adopted, some additional constraints are needed for the item parameters. A subset of items (perhaps only one item) will be designated as an anchor subset. These items are assumed to be free of bias. The item parameters for these items are constrained to be invariant over all groups. These invariance constraints, in addition to the fixed values of μ_{wk} and σ_{wk} for some choice of k, are sufficient to identify the remaining item parameters in L_1. All items are permitted to vary in their item parameter values in M_1, with the exception of the anchor items.

Under M_0, the item parameters for some further set of items are constrained to invariance. This additional set of items may include all items that are not anchor items or, alternatively, may include only a subset of the remaining items. In either case, no further constraints are introduced for the prior distribution parameters μ_{wk} and σ_{wk}. The likelihood L_0 is calculated under the invariance constraints on the item parameters of the additional set of items. If the item response functions are multiparameter models (e.g., 2PL), M_0 may incorporate invariance constraints on only some of the item parameters, rather than the entire set. For example, M_0 may first restrict the discrimination parameters in the 2PL to invariance, leaving the location parameters to vary over groups. Many possibilities exist for choices of which items and/or parameters to constrain in M_0.

Once M_0 and M_1 are specified, the sample likelihood values L_0 and L_1 can be calculated, and the LR test statistic in Equation 7.1 is found. The degrees of freedom for this test statistic correspond to the number of constraints needed to create M_0 from M_1. Note that unlike the Andersen test statistic described above, this test statistic requires some assumptions about the prior distributions $g_k(W)$. These assumptions are part of both M_0 and M_1 and are not directly tested by the LR statistic. In large samples, the LR statistic has a chi-square distribution under the null hypothesis that M_0 holds.

The MML LR approach is highly flexible, but if the test statistic leads to rejection of M_0, the test does not indicate which of the constraints in M_0 is responsible for the lack of fit. An obvious approach to obtaining additional information about individual constraints is to perform a set of additional LR tests, each with a single degree of freedom, by successively relaxing each invariance constraint in turn. This approach is unwieldy when the number of items is large. A more efficient approach would be to generate Lagrange multiplier (LM) statistics for each constrained item parameter (Glas, 1999). These statistics evaluate the expected drop in the LR chi-square in Equation 7.1 if the constraint under study is relaxed. Under M_0, the LM statistic just described is equivalent to the single degree of freedom chi-square from the LR test in large samples (Buse, 1982). The LM statistic is more easily calculated, however, because it does not require two likelihood evaluations and is based only on M_0. Unfortunately, it appears that no current IRT software package will produce the LM statistics for multiple-group MML estimation.

Polytomous Items

Under polytomous Rasch-family models, it is possible to develop an LR test procedure using CML estimation that parallels Andersen's (1973) procedure for dichotomous items. As in the dichotomous case, M_1 represents separate, group-specific models that introduce constraints needed for identification but that include no additional constraints. The choice of identification constraints will depend on which polytomous model is adopted for the items. For example, in the rating-scale model, one will need to impose one constraint on the location parameters in each group. An anchor item could be selected for this purpose, fixing the location parameter to a known value (e.g., zero). The anchor item should be selected to be an item that is thought to be free of bias, with the same item serving as an anchor in each group. The likelihood L_1 is then a sum of group-specific conditional likelihoods $\sum_{k=1}^{K} L_{1k}$. The model M_0 is based on the pooled sample that combines data from all K groups. As in M_1, an anchor item is chosen to carry the identification constraints. The conditional likelihood L_1 is based on the pooled sample. Once both L_0 and L_1 are available, the test statistic in Equation 7.1 can be calculated. Under the null hypothesis that no items are biased, this test statistic is distributed as a chi-square variate in large samples. The degrees of freedom are equal to $(K - 1)(h)$, where h is the number of free parameters in a single group under the chosen polytomous model.

The above test procedure has the same drawback found in the dichotomous LR procedure: Only global tests of "no bias" that apply to the entire set of items are possible. LR tests that focus on subsets of items require multiple-group simultaneous estimation procedures, and these procedures are available under MML estimation. The use of marginal likelihood methods also permits the extension of the LR test to models outside of the Rasch family. In this approach, M_1 represents a multiple-group model with identification constraints in each group, but without the invariance constraints that are the focus of interest. The prior distributions for W are permitted to vary across groups but commonly take the same form with varying parameter values (e.g., normal with varying means and variances). As in the dichotomous case, one approach to defining M_1 is to fix the mean and standard deviation of W in one group to known values (e.g., $\mu_{wk} = 0$, $\sigma_{wk} = 1$) and also to designate one or more items as anchor items whose parameter values will be invariant across groups. The combination of these two types of constraints should be sufficient to identify all remaining parameters in M_1. The anchor items must be carefully chosen to ensure that these items show no bias in relation to the groups under study.

The restricted model M_0 adds further invariance constraints to model M_1. Item parameters for some or all of the items outside of the anchor subset will be constrained to invariance in M_0. Using the likelihood values corresponding to M_0 and M_1, the test statistic in Equation 7.1 is calculated and is used to test whether the restricted model M_0 provides an adequate fit, given the fit of M_1. This test statistic has a chi-square distribution in large samples under M_0 with degrees of freedom equal to the number of independent constraints needed to create M_0 from M_1.

While M_1 may be initially structured to include invariance constraints only on the anchor items, other versions of M_1 could be created that include invariance constraints on items that are not anchor items. In the extreme case, M_1 may include invariance constraints on $p - 1$ items, permitting only a single item to vary in its parameters across groups. The restricted model M_0 would then add invariance constraints on this item to M_1. The resulting chi-square test examines whether the studied item displays bias, given invariance in the remaining $p - 1$ items. In theory, these tests on individual items could be conducted for each non-anchor item in turn. The presence of bias in more than one item, however, implies that many of the M_1 models in this sequence of tests are themselves incorrect. The typical response to this problem is to iteratively purify the test by dropping items that are initially flagged as biased, followed by further rounds of tests for the items that remain. This process is continued until no further items are found to be biased. An obvious difficulty with this iterative approach is that many hypothesis tests are required if the number of items is moderate or large, inflating the Type I error rate for the set of tests. One approach to reducing the inflation problem is to apply more stringent alpha levels to each individual test. Ideally, one could base decisions to flag an item on some measure of the size of the bias, in addition to the hypothesis test. The LR test statistic itself does not provide such an effect size measure. We will return to this problem below.

Evaluative Studies

The MULTILOG (Thissen, 1991) program gives information for calculation of the LR chi-square statistic once the M_0 and M_1 models have been run and works with all of the common binary models as well as the graded response and nominal polytomous model. The IRTLRDIF program (Thissen, 2001) makes the process of LR chi-square testing more convenient, however, because it will sequentially test all items automatically using a designated anchor set of items. CFA software can also be used for purposes of LR testing for any IRT model that is equivalent to a common factor model.

While the large-sample statistical theory underlying the LR test procedure is well understood, less is known about the small-sample behavior of the LR chi-square statistic in bias applications. Simulation studies have examined a number of potential influences on the Type I error and power performance of the LR chi-square statistic (Ankenmann, Witt, & Dunbar, 1999; Cohen, Kim, & Wollack, 1996; Edelen, Thissen, Teresi, Kleinman, & Ocepek-Welikson, 2006; Finch, 2005; Kim & Cohen, 1998; Wang & Yeh, 2003; Woods, 2008, 2009). These influences include sample size, size of the bias, direction of bias, type of model, test length, choice of anchor, and the presence of biased items in the anchor. Non-normality in the distribution of the latent variable is another possible influence, although fewer studies have examined this issue (Woods, 2006, 2007, 2008; Woods & Thissen, 2006).

Several large simulation studies have appeared that reported results on the Type I error performance of the LR chi-square statistic. Cohen et al. (1996) studied the test statistic in the dichotomous item case under the 2PL and 3PL models. Sample sizes studied were $N = 250$ and 1,000, with each sample size being applied to both the reference and the focal group. Test length was fixed at $p = 50$ items. Prior distributions for W in the two groups were both standard normal distributions, and MML estimation was used. The results showed that the LR test statistic adhered fairly closely to the nominal Type I error rate under the 2PL and 3PL models. Some inflation in the error rate was noted under the 3PL model, but the inflation was not large. Finch (2005) also examined the Type I error performance under either 2PL or 3PL models, with reference group sample sizes of 500 and focal group sample sizes of either 100 or 500. Either $p = 20$ or 50 items were used. Finch also manipulated whether biased items were used as anchor items, with either no biased items or 15% biased items. When no biased items were present in the anchor, the LR chi-square adhered to the nominal error rate. When biased items were present, the error rate was inflated. Kim and Cohen (1998) reported Type I error results for the LR chi-square, this time under the graded response model with five-category items. Sample sizes for the reference and focal groups were either 300 or 1,000, with a test length of $p = 30$ items. Normal prior distributions for W were used, either with identical means across groups or with different means. The results showed that the LR test procedure adhered closely to the nominal Type I error rate even in the smaller sample size condition. Wang and Yeh (2003) reported Type I error results under either a 2PL, 3PL, or graded response model with five-category items. Sample sizes were 1,000 per group, bias direction was either one sided or mixed, and the proportion of biased items was either 0%, 12%, 20%, or 32% of the test. Type of anchor was also manipulated, with either all items, 1 item, 4 items, or 10 items. The LR statistic adhered to the nominal error rate well except when the "all item" anchor method was used with higher proportions of the test items being biased and with one-sided bias. Ankenmann et al. (1999) examined Type I error performance in graded response model items with binary 3PL items in the anchor. No bias contamination in the anchor was introduced. Test length was $p = 26$ items with sample sizes of either 500 per group, 2,000 per group, or reference group with 2,000 and focal group with 500. Bias direction was either one or two sided. The LR statistic showed good adherence to the nominal rate throughout. Woods (2008) studied Type I error in the context of manipulating normality of the latent variable distributions. The latent distributions were normal in both the reference and focal groups, normal in one group but skewed in the other, or skewed in both groups. The reference group N was 1,500, with $N = 500$ in the focal group. Test length was $p = 24$ items. No biased items were present in the anchor set. All data were based on the 2PL model. It was found that the Type I error rate was higher than the nominal rate when only one group had a skewed latent variable distribution and the groups differed in latent means.

The general implications of the available simulation studies are that the LR chi-square statistic adheres well to the nominal error rate when the anchor items contain no biased items, or when the average bias across the biased anchor items is near zero (e.g., mixed directions for biased items). If the anchor contains a substantial proportion of biased items and those items tend to be one sided, the Type I error rate can be large. Also, non-normality of the latent distribution can inflate the error rate when the groups have different distributions and different means. Some effort is needed to remove biased items from the anchor through preliminary tests or through careful anchor choice. Alternatives to assuming normal prior distributions, such as those proposed by Woods (2006, 2007), are worth considering as well.

One question of interest about the anchor items, apart from the presence of biased items in the anchor, is the appropriate choice of length for the anchor: how many items are needed? Simulations have shown that even with only a single unbiased anchor item, the LR chi-square statistic adheres reasonably well to the nominal Type I error rate if other assumptions are met (Stark, Chernyshenko, & Drasgow, 2006; Wang, 2004; Wang & Yeh, 2003). In low sample size situations (e.g., combined N of 800 across groups), Woods (2009) found that the use of single anchor items produced low power to detect bias. Woods recommended that the anchor be chosen to be 10%–20% of the total number of items being studied and pointed to the trade-off between expanding the size of the anchor to improve validity of the anchor and running an increasing risk of including biased items in the anchor.

A few studies have examined the power of the LR chi-square statistic (Ankenmann et al., 1999; Finch, 2005; Wang & Yeh, 2003; Woods, 2008). Some indication exists that the power of the test is low at smaller sample sizes. Ankenmann et al. found lower power when $N = 500$ in both the reference and focal groups. Power is generally higher when longer anchor sets are used and when the bias is one sided rather than mixed (Wang & Yeh; Woods, 2009). Woods (2008) found fairly good power even with non-normal latent variable distributions, but the Type I error inflation under some conditions makes the power results difficult to judge in some cases. Further studies of the power of the LR chi-square statistic are needed, but the statistic seems to work well when the anchor is free of biased items, sample sizes are substantial, the latent distribution is normal, and the bias in the studied item is not too small in size.

Wald Statistics

Given that item bias within IRT is defined by group differences in item parameters, the most direct approach to investigating bias would seem to be to compare the values of the item parameter estimates across groups. Any such comparison must consider parameter estimate differences in relation to sampling error. Group differences that are larger than expected given the sample sizes and the IRT model under study are taken as evidence of bias. Generally speaking, statistical tests for group differences in item parameters in IRT are not exact in small samples. These tests instead rely on large-sample approximations provided by Wald (1943) and can be collectively denoted as Wald test statistics (Thissen et al., 1993).

To illustrate the principles underlying Wald statistics in a general context, suppose that scores on the measured variables **X** have a likelihood function $L(\boldsymbol{\Gamma})$, where $\boldsymbol{\Gamma}$ is an $s \times 1$ vector of parameters of interest. Let $\hat{\boldsymbol{\Gamma}}$ be the maximum likelihood estimator of $\boldsymbol{\Gamma}$, and assume that $\hat{\boldsymbol{\Gamma}}$ is distributed as multivariate normal in large samples. We wish to test a null hypothesis that places $t < s$ restrictions on $\boldsymbol{\Gamma}$ of the form $c(\boldsymbol{\Gamma}) = \mathbf{0}$, where $c()$ is a differentiable function. Then the Wald test statistic d^2 is

$$d^2 = -c(\hat{\boldsymbol{\Gamma}})'[\hat{\boldsymbol{\Delta}}\hat{\mathbf{H}}^{-1}\hat{\boldsymbol{\Delta}}']^{-1}c(\hat{\boldsymbol{\Gamma}}), \qquad (7.2)$$

where $\boldsymbol{\Delta}$ is an $s \times 1$ vector whose ith element is the first partial derivative of $c(\boldsymbol{\Gamma})$,

$$\Delta_j = \frac{\partial c(\boldsymbol{\Gamma})}{\partial \Gamma_i}, \qquad (7.3)$$

evaluated at Γ_i, and $\mathbf{H}$ is the $s \times s$ Hessian matrix for $\log L(\Gamma)$, whose ijth element is

$$H_{ij} = \frac{\partial^2 \log L(\Gamma)}{\partial \Gamma_i \partial \Gamma_j} \qquad (7.4)$$

evaluated at the ith and jth elements of Γ. The matrix $\widehat{\mathbf{H}}^{-1}$ in Equation 7.2 is the estimated covariance matrix for $\widehat{\Gamma}$ given the likelihood function $L(\Gamma)$. In large samples, d^2 will have a chi-square distribution under the null hypothesis with t degrees of freedom (Rao, 1973; Wald, 1943). Amemiya (1985) notes that d^2 will have the stated large-sample distribution under the null hypothesis even if the likelihood $L(\Gamma)$ is unspecified, as long as $\widehat{\Gamma}$ is multivariate normal in large samples and $\widehat{\mathbf{H}}^{-1}$ in Equation 7.2 is replaced by any consistent estimator of the covariance matrix for $\widehat{\Gamma}$. This fact is useful, as direct estimates of $\mathbf{H}^{-1}$ are sometimes difficult to obtain.

The above principles provide the basis for a variety of tests for group differences in item parameters, depending on the IRT model of interest and the number of item parameters to be investigated. An example will illustrate the application. Suppose that $L(\Gamma)$ represents a conditional likelihood under the Rasch model for two independent groups of examinees, with possibly different item location parameters for some of the p items in each group. Let $\Gamma = (\mathbf{b}_r, \mathbf{b}_f)$ be a $2p \times 1$ vector of item location parameters for the reference and focal groups, respectively. For the jth item, we wish to test the restriction $b_{jr} = b_{jf}$ or $b_{jr} - b_{jf} = 0$. This null hypothesis is represented as a simple linear restriction $c'\mathbf{T} = 0$, where c is a $2p \times 1$ vector with zeros in all positions except the jth and $(p + j)$th, which are 1 and –1, respectively. Note also that since the two groups are independent, the $2p \times 2p$ Hessian matrix $\mathbf{H}$ has a block diagonal structure

$$\mathbf{H} = \begin{vmatrix} \mathbf{H}_r & 0 \\ 0 & \mathbf{H}_f \end{vmatrix}, \qquad (7.5)$$

where $\mathbf{H}_r$ and $\mathbf{H}_f$ are each $p \times p$ matrices. The diagonal elements of $\mathbf{H}_r^{-1}$ and $\mathbf{H}_f^{-1}$ are the variances for the elements of $\hat{\mathbf{b}}_r$ and $\hat{\mathbf{b}}_f$, the CML estimates of $\mathbf{b}_r$ and $\mathbf{b}_f$. Then from Equation 7.2, the Wald statistic for testing the null hypothesis is

$$d^2 = (\hat{b}_{jr} - \hat{b}_{jf})[c' \, \widehat{\mathbf{H}}^{-1} \, c]^{-1}(\hat{b}_{jr} - \hat{b}_{jf}) = \frac{(\hat{b}_{jr} - \hat{b}_{jf})^2}{\mathrm{Var}(\hat{b}_{jr}) + \mathrm{Var}(\hat{b}_{jf})}, \qquad (7.6)$$

where $\mathrm{Var}(\hat{b}_{jr})$ and $\mathrm{Var}(\hat{b}_{jf})$ are the estimated variances of the location parameter estimates from the reference and focal groups, respectively.

In this case, d^2 has $df = 1$. Alternatively, we can regard $d = \sqrt{d^2}$ as a standard normal variate and refer d to the standard normal table. The above test is easily expanded to simultaneously consider restrictions on parameters for more than one item or to test hypotheses for more than two examinee groups.

The great advantage of the Wald statistic in comparison to the LR procedures considered earlier is that there is no need to evaluate the likelihood under restrictions. Only the unrestricted likelihood L_1 is needed to obtain the estimates Γ. It is necessary to estimate the covariance matrix for Γ, however, a requirement that is simple in principle yet often difficult in practice, depending on the model, sample sizes, and number of items. In multiparameter models, composite hypotheses that evaluate invariance jointly for different parameters (e.g., location and discrimination parameters) must consider both the variances and covariances among these parameters within each examinee group. The required estimates for this covariance structure may be inaccurate in small samples. The small-sample behavior of d^2 is not well understood in general, although simulations have been conducted for particular cases as discussed below.

A further difficulty facing applications of the Wald statistic in bias investigations is the need to achieve linkage across groups in the scales used for the item parameters, as noted earlier. Assuming that no bias exists, we expect the item parameter estimates to differ across groups both as a function of sampling error and as a function of any arbitrary scaling differences induced by group-specific standardizations. As an example of such a standardization, item parameters are commonly estimated in single-group applications under the restriction that $\mu_{wk} = 0$ and $\sigma_{wk} = 1$ in MML estimation. If this scaling is adopted in multiple-group applications, however, the resulting item parameter estimates will be artifactually different across groups whenever the latent variable distributions $g_k(W)$ have varying means and/or variances across groups. If these item parameter estimates are then compared across groups using the Wald statistic, spurious findings of bias may result. The traditional approach to this problem has been to place identification constraints on the item parameters, rather than on the parameters governing $g_k(W)$. For example, we could require that the average location parameter value be zero in each group in the Rasch model. It will still be true that sampling error, in combination with these constraints on the item parameters, will create group differences in the item parameter estimates even when no bias is present. If the average location parameter value is constrained to zero, for example, sampling error in one item's location parameter estimate will affect the parameter estimates for all other items. To surmount this difficulty, the location parameter estimates in each group are transformed to a common metric across groups prior to any direct comparisons. Various approaches to creating such "linkage" transformations exist.

The presence of bias in some items complicates the development of any linkage transformations. If the entire item set, including the biased items, is used to generate the linkage, no simple transformation may be found that will yield a common metric. The ideal approach in this case would be to weed out the clearly biased items using a preliminary screening and then base the linkage on the subset of unbiased (or less biased) items. The preliminary screening must identify the biased items using a method that does not require direct comparisons of parameter values. Once a linkage transformation is created and applied to the items that remain, these items are again evaluated for bias, now using direct comparisons via the Wald statistic. Some methods for developing linkage transformations in bias investigations are discussed below.

The next section describes the use of Wald statistics to evaluate bias in dichotomous items. The earliest applications of Wald statistics to investigate bias were developed for such items. Following this section, we discuss the use of Wald statistics in polytomous items. Applications to polytomous items are complex because the models include multiple item parameters. After the dichotomous and polytomous item sections, studies that have evaluated the Wald statistic approach in simulated data are described. Linkage transformations are discussed in the last section.

Dichotomous Items

The earliest application of the Wald statistic to the problem of item bias may be the statistic developed by Wright, Mead, and Draba (1976) for the Rasch model. This statistic is simply the square root of the Wald statistic, with the sign of the location parameter difference included:

$$d_j = \frac{\hat{b}_{jr} - \hat{b}_{jf}}{\sqrt{\text{Var}(\hat{b}_{jr}) + \text{Var}(\hat{b}_{jf})}}. \tag{7.7}$$

In large samples, the above statistic is distributed as a standard normal variate under the null hypothesis of invariance in the location parameter for the jth item. Separate values of d_j are calculated for each item, $j = 1, \ldots, p$. Items whose d_j values exceed a chosen threshold for significance are flagged as biased. Within the Rasch model, the sampling variance of b_j under CML estimation depends to some extent on the choice of identification constraints.

A general approach to obtaining large-sample standard errors or sampling variances $\text{Var}(\hat{b}_j)$ in the Wald statistic in Equation 7.7 is to use the appropriate diagonal elements of the inverse of the information matrix associated with the location parameter estimates b_j (Andersen, 1980). Under the Rasch model, the information matrix $\mathbf{I}_k(\mathbf{b})$ for the kth group is the $p \times p$ matrix whose element in the jth row and mth column is

$$-E\left[\frac{\partial^2 L(\mathbf{b})}{\partial b_j \partial b_m}\right], \tag{7.8}$$

where $L(\mathbf{b})$ is the conditional log likelihood function used to obtain estimates of $\mathbf{b}$. An estimate of the information matrix is obtained using estimates $\hat{\mathbf{b}}$. Assuming that the resulting estimate of the information matrix is positive definite, the information matrix is inverted and the appropriate diagonal element of the inverse is used in Equation 7.7. Separate estimates of the sampling variances are obtained for each group using that group's estimate of the information matrix.

Wright et al. (1976) developed the statistic in Equation 7.7 specifically for the two-group Rasch case. Other IRT models require different expressions for the sampling variances of $\hat{b}_j$ and would also incorporate Wald statistics for group differences in other parameters. Lord (1980) developed Wald statistics for use with the 2PL and 3PL models. In the 3PL case, Lord recommended that the test statistic be used only for hypotheses involving the location and discrimination parameters. The pseudo-guessing parameter c_j would be fixed to a common value across groups based on pooled data. The suggested sequence of steps in conducting Wald tests in the 3PL case began with the pooled sample, ignoring group membership. Item parameters are estimated in this pooled sample, with the scaling chosen to force the average location parameter value to zero and the standard deviation of the location parameters to one. The pseudo-guessing parameters are then fixed to their estimated values for this pooled analysis, and they retain those values in all subsequent steps. Next, the groups are separated and group-specific estimates of the location and discrimination parameters are obtained. The scaling used earlier for the location parameters is again adopted, this time imposed separately within each group. The resulting location and discrimination parameter estimates are then used in Wald tests to evaluate bias. For tests involving only location parameters, the statistic in Equation 7.7 is used. For tests on discrimination parameters, this statistic is simply modified as

$$d_j = \frac{\hat{a}_{jr} - \hat{a}_{jf}}{\sqrt{\mathrm{Var}(\hat{a}_{jr}) + \mathrm{Var}(\hat{a}_{jf})}}. \tag{7.9}$$

In large samples, d_j in Equation 7.9 is distributed as standard normal under the null hypothesis of invariance.

Lord (1980) also considered simultaneous tests for invariance in both location and discrimination parameters. This test requires estimates of the 2 × 2 covariance matrix for $(\hat{a}_j, \hat{b}_j)$ within each group. Let $\boldsymbol{\Sigma}_{jr}$ and $\boldsymbol{\Sigma}_{jf}$ be these covariance matrices within the reference and focal groups, respectively. Also let

$$\hat{\boldsymbol{\delta}}_j = [\hat{a}_{jr} - \hat{a}_{jf}, \ \hat{b}_{jr} - \hat{b}_{jf}]. \tag{7.10}$$

Then the test statistic is

$$d_j^2 = \hat{\boldsymbol{\delta}}_j' \, [\hat{\boldsymbol{\Sigma}}_{jr} + \hat{\boldsymbol{\Sigma}}_{jf}]^{-1} \hat{\boldsymbol{\delta}}_j. \tag{7.11}$$

This test statistic is distributed as a chi-square variate with $df = 2$ under the null hypothesis of invariance in both location and discrimination parameters for the jth item.

Polytomous Items

Wald statistics generalize easily to the case of polytomous items, apart from the difficulties created by the greater number of parameters found in models for such items. Each item will include multiple parameters. To fully evaluate bias in a given item, group differences in all of these parameters must be investigated. To illustrate, suppose that the partial credit model is found to fit the data in all groups and that we wish to compare parameters for the jth item across groups. Within the kth group, the vector of parameters for the jth item is $\boldsymbol{\Gamma}_{jk} = (\tau_{j1}, \tau_{j2} \ldots, \tau_{jC-1})$, a $(C - 1) \times 1$ vector of category location parameters. The estimates for these parameters will be correlated in general, regardless of the method of estimation. In the partial credit model, we could use CML estimates in the vector $\hat{\boldsymbol{\Gamma}}_{jk}$. Let $L(\boldsymbol{\Gamma})$ be the conditional log likelihood function to be maximized in obtaining $\hat{\boldsymbol{\Gamma}}_{jk}$. Also let the entire vector of parameters for p items in the kth group be $\boldsymbol{\Gamma}_k = (\boldsymbol{\Gamma}_{1k}, \boldsymbol{\Gamma}_{2k}, \ldots, \boldsymbol{\Gamma}_{pk})$. This vector is $p(C - 1) \times 1$. We can define the $p(C - 1) \times p(C - 1)$ information matrix $\mathbf{I}_k(\boldsymbol{\Gamma}_k)$ for the item parameters across p items in the kth group as having elements

$$-E\left[\frac{\partial^2 L(\boldsymbol{\Gamma})}{\partial \gamma_n \partial \gamma_m}\right], \tag{7.12}$$

in the nth row, mth column, with γ_n and γ_m being the nth and mth elements of $\boldsymbol{\Gamma}_k$. An estimate of the information matrix $\mathbf{I}_k(\boldsymbol{\Gamma}_k)$ is obtained by substituting estimates $\hat{\boldsymbol{\Gamma}}_k$ into the expressions in Equation 7.12. If the resulting matrix is positive definite, the matrix can be inverted to obtain an estimate of the large-sample covariance matrix for $\hat{\boldsymbol{\Gamma}}_k$.

In the two-group case with $\boldsymbol{\Gamma}_r$ and $\boldsymbol{\Gamma}_f$ being the item parameter vectors for the reference and focal groups, respectively, suppose that we wish to compare $\boldsymbol{\Gamma}_{jr}$ and $\boldsymbol{\Gamma}_{jf}$ for the jth item. Let the difference in the parameter vectors for the two groups be

$$\boldsymbol{\delta}_j = \boldsymbol{\Gamma}_{jr} - \boldsymbol{\Gamma}_{jf} = (\tau_{j1r} - \tau_{j1f}, \tau_{j2r} - \tau_{j2f}, \ldots, \tau_{jC-1r} - \tau_{jC-1f}), \qquad (7.13)$$

where τ_{jcr}, τ_{jcf} represent the cth category location parameters for the reference and focal groups, respectively. Then $\hat{\boldsymbol{\delta}}_j$ will represent the sample estimate of the difference vector in Equation 7.13 after the estimates $\hat{\boldsymbol{\Gamma}}_{jr}$ and $\hat{\boldsymbol{\Gamma}}_{jf}$ are substituted. Finally, let

$$\hat{\boldsymbol{\Sigma}}_{jr} = [\mathbf{I}_r(\hat{\boldsymbol{\Gamma}}_{jr})]^{-1}, \quad \hat{\boldsymbol{\Sigma}}_{jf} = [\mathbf{I}_f(\hat{\boldsymbol{\Gamma}}_{jf})]^{-1} \qquad (7.14)$$

be the sample estimates of the large-sample covariance matrices for the item parameter estimates in each group. We can then calculate the Wald statistic for the jth item as

$$d_j^2 = \hat{\boldsymbol{\delta}}_j' [\hat{\boldsymbol{\Sigma}}_{jr} + \hat{\boldsymbol{\Sigma}}_{jf}]^{-1} \hat{\boldsymbol{\delta}}_j. \qquad (7.15)$$

This statistic has $df = C - 1$, corresponding to the $C - 1$ restrictions imposed on $\boldsymbol{\Gamma}_{jr}$ and $\boldsymbol{\Gamma}_{jf}$. In large samples, d_j^2 will have a chi-square distribution under the null hypothesis that $\boldsymbol{\delta}_j = 0$, which corresponds to no bias in the jth item.

The above Wald statistic could be modified in several ways, depending on the needs of a particular investigation. For example, one could investigate group differences in the item parameters for an entire block of items, considered simultaneously. This extension would require that the large-sample covariance matrix be expanded to include elements for all parameters from the block of items under consideration. Alternatively, one could modify the statistic to compare parameters across more than two groups simultaneously. In a three group problem, for example, one could expand $\boldsymbol{\delta}_j$ to include pairwise contrasts across both groups 1 and 2, and groups 2 and 3. The dimension of this difference vector is then $2(C - 1) \times 1$. Analogously, the large-sample covariance matrix is expanded to a block diagonal matrix of dimension $2(C - 1) \times 2(C - 1)$, with each block being the sum of the appropriate pair of covariance matrices. In either of these extensions, the main difficulty would be that rejection of the null hypothesis would require further investigation to locate which set of item parameters are responsible for the rejection.

Evaluative Studies

A number of studies have evaluated the performance of Wald statistics in bias applications, in terms of Type I error behavior, Type II error behavior, or both (Cohen & Kim, 1993; Cohen, Kim, & Baker, 1993; Donoghue & Isham, 1998; Kim, Cohen, & Kim, 1994; Lim & Drasgow, 1990; McLaughlin & Drasgow, 1987). More evaluative studies of the Wald statistic have been performed in the dichotomous case than in the polytomous case. Kim et al. investigated the Type I error behavior of Lord's chi-square statistic in data simulated to fit either the 2PL or 3PL models. Two sample size conditions were created ($N = 250$ or $1,000$), with test length fixed at $p = 50$. Prior distributions for W were standard normal in both the focal and reference groups. The results showed that under the 3PL, the effective Type I error rate exceeded the nominal rate, even in the larger sample size condition. Conversely, under the 2PL model, the error rate was lower than the nominal rate, resulting in a conservative test. This result contradicts an earlier finding by McLaughlin and Drasgow, who found inflated Type I error rates under the 2PL. McLaughlin and Drasgow used joint maximum likelihood estimation in their study, while Kim et al. used MML. The error rate inflation for the 3PL found by Kim et al. was lessened if a 3PL model with a common pseudo-guessing parameter was used in the 3PL data, even though the data were generated under the unrestricted 3PL model. Kim et al. suggested that the distortions in the Type I error rates found in their study were probably due to inaccuracy in the estimation of the covariance matrix for the item parameter estimates, a problem noted by Thissen et al. (1993).

Cohen and Kim (1993) studied both the Type I and Type II error behavior of Lord's chi-square test under the 2PL model. Two sample size conditions ($N = 100$ or 500) were factorially combined with two test length conditions ($p = 20$ or 60). Bias was simulated for either no items, 10% of the items, or 20% of the items. The size of the bias, when present, was varied across items. Prior normal distributions for W were either invariant over groups or differed in means. The results were that in the null bias condition, the observed Type I error rate was held to the nominal rate, although the rate was higher when the prior distributions differed across groups. In the bias conditions, the false-negative rate (Type II error rate) was unacceptably high when $N = 100$ but was considerably better at $N = 500$, especially when no group differences existed in the prior distributions. The false-negative rate was higher when the percentage of biased items was higher. In general, the results supported the use of Lord's test under the 2PL when the sample size was at least 500.

Donoghue and Isham (1998) reported simulation results on the Type I error and power performance of Lord's test in the detection of item parameter drift. Item parameter drift refers to changes in the parameter values for an item across repeated measurement occasions. Item parameter drift differs from the bias phenomenon by being a within-group change, rather than a group difference. Formally, however, the use of Lord's test to detect drift is similar to its use in bias applications. Donoghue and Isham generated data to fit a 3PL model with a common value for the pseudo-guessing parameter across items. Sample size was varied (N = 300, 600, or 1,000), as was the test length (p = 30 or 60) and the number of items showing drift (0, 3, 6, or 12). Drift was manifested in changes in the difficulty parameters, changes in the discrimination parameters, or both. The results were that Lord's test performed well overall as long as no attempt was made to study group differences in the pseudo-guessing parameters. Lord's test adhered closely to the Type I error rate overall in the no-drift condition. When drift was present, Lord's test had fairly good power when $N > 300$.

In the polytomous item case, Cohen et al. (1993) studied Lord's test in data simulated to fit the graded response model. The sample size was fixed at N = 1,000, and the test length was fixed at p = 40. Each item was scored in five categories. Bias was simulated in six items by varying the discrimination parameters, the location parameters, or both. Prior distributions for W were standard normal in each group. The results showed that Lord's test detected bias in five of the six items simulated to be biased and (falsely) in one item that was simulated as unbiased. While limited in scope, these results suggest that Lord's chi-square test is feasible for polytomous items.

From this brief review, it is clear that Lord's test can be used effectively with the 2PL and 3PL models if the sample sizes are 300 or more, and if no group differences in pseudo-guessing parameters are sought under the 3PL. Attempts to evaluate bias in all three parameters of the 3PL do not seem effective, at least using current MML estimation methods. Further power studies that would focus specifically on the amount of bias that can reliably be detected for various sample sizes would be useful. Also, studies of the accuracy of estimates for parameter sampling covariance matrices are needed, as this accuracy affects the performance of the Wald statistic. It is also clear that much more work is needed for the polytomous item case.

Parameter Linkage

In any direct comparison of item parameter estimates across groups, preliminary adjustments to the parameter estimates are usually needed to remove the effects of any group-specific scaling adopted during the estimation process. These adjustments are especially important when the parameter estimation is done separately within each group defined by **V**. When estimation is done separately in this manner, constraints are placed on the item parameters within each group to achieve identification, as discussed in Chapter 6. For example, in the Rasch model for dichotomous items, we might require the location parameter estimates to have a mean of zero within each examinee group defined by **V**. Even if there is no bias present in any item in relation to **V**, sampling error will result in some group differences in the location parameter estimates. The group-specific identification constraints will combine with sampling error to widen group differences in parameter estimates for some items and to narrow group differences for other items. The net effect of these influences is that it becomes more difficult to accurately compare parameter estimates across groups for purposes of bias detection.

In the absence of any bias in the items, it should be possible to find a transformation to the item parameters that will place the estimates on a common scale across groups, removing the influence of any group-specific identification constraints. Lord (1980) illustrates the use of linear transformations for dichotomous item data under logistic models in two examinee groups. In this case, the objective is to find constants A and B to apply to the item parameter estimates in group one that will place these estimates on the scale used for group two. This strategy is based on the idea that the item parameters in the two groups are related as

$$b_{j2} = Ab_{j1} + B, \quad a_{j2} = \frac{a_{j1}}{A} \tag{7.16}$$

for location parameters (b_{j1}, b_{j2}) and discrimination parameters (a_{j1}, a_{j2}), $j = 1, \ldots, p$. Hence, knowledge of A and B will permit the transformation of the parameters in group one to the scale for group two (or the reverse). Note that A and B are not regression parameters but are scaling constants used to relate sets of item parameter values. In the 3PL model, the pseudo-guessing parameter c_j need not be transformed, as this parameter is not directly affected by the identification constraints. Methods for generating the needed constraints are discussed below. The problem of linkage transformations in polytomous items has received less attention. Methods are available for the graded-response model (Baker, 1992a; Cohen & Kim, 1998; Kim & Cohen, 1995). In polytomous Rasch models such as the rating scale or partial credit models, only the additive constant B is needed to link the metrics for the category location parameters.

In bias investigations, the development of the linkage transformation may be complicated by the presence of bias in some items. If bias is present, there will exist no linear transformation that will place the item parameter estimates on a common scale. If bias is ignored and a transformation is developed based on the entire item set, distortions may be produced in the transformed estimates for the unbiased items. The ideal strategy in this case is to base the generation of the linkage transformation on only the unbiased items. This strategy requires a preliminary screening for bias prior to development of the linkage transformation. Studies of linkage in the dichotomous case have generally found the optimal approach to be an iterative sequence in which a preliminary screening is followed by linkage based on the remaining items, followed in turn by another screening, and so forth (Candell & Drasgow, 1988; Kim & Cohen, 1992; Lautenschlager & Park, 1988; Lord, 1980; Marco, 1977; Park, 1988; Park & Lautenschlager, 1990; Segall, 1983). Presumably, this iterative strategy would be effective in the polytomous case as well.

We next describe some general methods for generating linkage transformations and then discuss their use in bias investigations.

Creating Linkage Functions

In the dichotomous item case, the linkage transformation is linear, and this linear transformation requires the constants A and B described above. Two broad methods exist for estimating these constants. The first method bases the constants on the means and standard deviations of the distributions of item location parameter estimates from the two groups under study (Linn et al., 1981; Loyd & Hoover, 1980; Marco, 1977; Vale, 1986; Warm, 1978). These methods will be denoted *moment methods* here. The second group of methods derive constants that minimize group differences in item or test response functions (Divgi, 1985; Haebara, 1980; Stocking & Lord, 1983). These methods will be denoted *response function methods* here.

The simplest moment methods take advantage of the fact that if the item location and discrimination parameters are related as in Equation 7.16, it should be true that

$$\bar{b}_2 = A\bar{b}_1 + B, \quad s_{b2} = \frac{S_{b1}}{A}, \tag{7.17}$$

where
  $\bar{b}_k$ is the average location parameter estimate in the kth group
  S_{bk} is the standard deviation of the location parameter estimates in the kth group (Marco, 1977)

Then we can choose

$$A = \frac{S_{b1}}{S_{b2}}, \quad B = \bar{b}_2 - A\bar{b}_1, \tag{7.18}$$

as the required constants. This approach would work perfectly if there is no sampling error in the item parameter estimates. Unfortunately, large sampling errors can strongly influence the means and standard deviations in Equation 7.18. In response to this problem, a number of modifications have been suggested that make the required means and standard deviations more robust. Linn et al. (1981) proposed that the item location parameter estimates be weighted to reflect their standard errors in the process of deriving A and B. Stocking and Lord (1983) applied a different weighting procedure. These weighting procedures are most useful when the available sample sizes for one or both groups are likely to lead to substantial estimation errors. No single method has been shown to be uniformly superior over variations in sample sizes, test lengths, and parameter values (Baker & Al-Karni, 1991; Candell & Drasgow, 1988; Kim & Cohen, 1992; Stocking & Lord).

Response function methods do not lead to simple formulas for A and B but instead find A and B values that will minimize some measure of distance between the item response functions in the two groups. The solution for A and B generally requires iterative numerical procedures. Divgi (1985) proposed that A and B be selected to minimize the sum, across items, of the quadratic forms

$$\delta_j^{*\prime} (\Sigma_{j1} + \Sigma_{j2})^{-1} \delta_j^*, \tag{7.19}$$

where

$$\delta_j^{*\prime} = (a_{j1} - a_{j2}^*, \ b_{j1} - b_{j2}^*) \tag{7.20}$$

with

$$b_{j2}^* = Ab_{j1} + B, \quad a_{j2}^* = \frac{a_{j1}}{A}. \tag{7.21}$$

The matrix Σ_{j1} is the 2×2 covariance matrix for (a_{j1}, b_{j1}), and Σ_{j2}^* is the analogous matrix for (a_{j2}^*, b_{j2}^*). These matrices are estimated as described in the earlier discussion of Wald statistics. The quadratic form in Equation 7.19 resembles the Wald statistic that would be used to test for parameter invariance under the 2PL model. As shown by Divgi (1985), minimization of the sum of the quadratic forms in Equation 7.19 across items leads to a simple expression for B in terms of A. The solution for A is found iteratively.

Stocking and Lord (1983) presented a response function method that selects A and B to minimize the difference between two estimates of the examinee's test true score. The first estimate uses the item parameter estimates from one examinee group. The second estimate uses the item parameter estimates from the second examinee group after linear transformation as in Equation 7.21. The objective is to find A and B to minimize the average squared difference between the two true-score estimates across examinees. Unlike the method of Divgi (1985), Lord and Stocking's method requires estimates of the latent trait values for the examinees, so that the true-score estimates can be calculated. This requirement makes Lord and Stocking's method more difficult to use, even though the minimization problem itself is not especially difficult.

Most of the research on linkage has addressed the dichotomous item case, but some work is available for the case of polytomous items. The available methods are simple extensions of the linkage methods used with dichotomous items. Baker (1992a) applied Stocking and Lord's response function method to the linkage problem for the graded response model. The extension modified the calculation of the true-score estimates to include the chosen scaling for the response categories. Baker (1993) provided a software program for implementing the method. Kim and Cohen (1995) modified Divgi's method for use with the graded response model. Cohen and Kim (1998) described the use of several moment methods with the graded response model. They evaluated three moment methods, along with the extensions of Divgi's method and Lord and Stocking's method, in simulated data from the graded response model. All of the methods performed well under MML estimation, suggesting that the simpler moment methods should be useful in the graded response model.

A general review of parameter linkage methods in IRT, apart from bias investigations, can be found in Kolen and Brennan (2010). Most of the linking methods described here can be implemented within the free R program plink (Weeks, 2010).

Bias Investigations

The presence of items that are biased in relation to the groups under study complicates the linkage problem. If the linkage transformation is based on the entire item set, the biased items may distort the transformation, leading to subsequent errors when bias is evaluated using the transformed parameters. McCauley and Mendoza (1985) showed that when biased items were included in the set that generates the linkage transformation, the bias investigation of the item set led to some items being falsely labeled as biased. In response to this problem, the ideal strategy would base the linkage transformation on only the unbiased items. This strategy is difficult to implement because the biased items cannot be identified a priori. Instead, an iterative scheme is introduced that alternates item screening for bias with generation of the linkage transformation based on the remaining items.

Lord (1980; Marco, 1977) presented one iterative scheme to be used with the 3PL model. The steps in this approach were as follows:

1. Combine data from all groups and estimate the item parameters. Use identification constraints that force the distribution of item location parameters to have a mean of zero and a standard deviation of one.

2. Fixing the pseudo-guessing parameters at the values estimated in step (1), separate the groups and estimate the location and discrimination parameters within each group, using the standardization from (1) separately within each group. Evaluate all items for bias.

3. Remove any biased items from the pool.

4. Combine all groups and estimate the latent trait values W using the remaining items.

5. Using the estimates of W from (4), estimate the item parameters for all items, including those dropped earlier, separately within each group.

6. Evaluate each item for bias using the item parameter estimates found in (5).

Note that only the location and discrimination parameters enter into the evaluations of bias in steps (2) and (6). The pseudo-guessing parameters are given the same values across groups in this approach. The bias evaluations in steps (2) and (6) could use Wald statistics or could be based on other approaches.

Lord's procedure conducts one initial screen for biased items, followed by a second estimation phase, and a final bias screen. Park and Lautenschlager (1990; Park, 1988) modified Lord's procedure by including additional iterations. The steps in this modified procedure are as follows:

1. Combine data from all groups and estimate latent trait values W.

2. Separate the groups and estimate all item parameters within each group using the latent trait estimates from step (1). Evaluate all items for bias.

3. Remove any biased items.

4. Working with the remaining items, combine data from all groups and reestimate the latent trait values W.

5. Separate the groups and estimate item parameters for all items within each group using the latent trait estimates from step (4). Evaluate the items for bias.

6. Repeat steps (3) through (5) until the same items are identified as biased on successive iterations.

The above method is not limited to the 3PL model and can potentially be used with any model. Both Park and Lautenschlager's method and Lord's method have the drawback that repeated estimation of latent trait values is needed. Given that latent trait estimates are generally not needed for bias investigations, the need for these estimates here is a significant inefficiency.

To avoid the need for repeated latent trait estimation, Segall (1983) suggested the following alternative:

1. Estimate the item parameters within each group separately.
2. Generate a linking function using the estimates from step (1), using one of the linking methods reviewed earlier.
3. After linkage, evaluate all items for bias. Remove any biased items.
4. Using the remaining items, generate new linking functions. Use these new functions to link the parameters for all items, including those removed earlier for bias.
5. Evaluate all items for bias and remove any biased items.
6. Repeat steps (4) and (5) until the same items are flagged as biased on successive iterations.

Segall's method has been used successfully in both real applications and simulations (Candell & Drasgow, 1988; Drasgow, 1987; Park & Lautenschlager, 1990). The available evidence suggests that the use of multiple iterations to establish the parameter linkage in bias investigations leads to better results in comparison to single linkage methods (Candell & Drasgow; Kim & Cohen, 1992; Lautenschlager & Park, 1988; Park & Lautenschlager). The use of multiple iterations may be especially advantageous when the samples are small (Kim & Cohen).

Effect Size Measures

A finding of statistically significant bias is simply the statement that the amount of bias is larger than we would expect to find by chance, given the sample size, number of items, and the model. The statistical significance does not tell us whether the bias found is of a magnitude that is meaningful in practical terms. To determine whether the bias is meaningful, it may be useful to create a measure of the "effect size" for the bias. Some approaches to developing such measures are described here. As will become clear, no fully general measure of effect size is yet available for IRT-based bias investigations. Measures of effect size that are useful with specific models and item formats are available, however. For example, measures for logistic models in dichotomous item data have received substantial attention. Measures that are useful in the polytomous case are less studied. We will begin with the dichotomous case, followed by the polytomous case.

Dichotomous Items

Assuming that estimates of the group-specific item response functions for the biased items are available, it is tempting to evaluate the size of the bias directly by calculating group differences in item parameters. In the case of the Rasch model, the group difference in the item location parameter is directly related to the log of the odds ratio. Letting $P_r(W)$ and $P_f(W)$ be the item response functions for the reference and focal groups, we have

$$\ln\left(\frac{P_r(W)/[1-P_r(W)]}{P_f(W)/[1-P_f(W)]}\right) = b_f - b_r. \tag{7.22}$$

In this case, the relative advantage of the reference group in the odds of passing the item can be written as a simple function of the group difference in location parameters, and it does not depend on W. When more than two groups are involved, each group can be compared to the one group that serves as a reference group, or each pair of groups can be compared. Given the familiarity of the log odds as a measure of effect size in other contexts, the relationship in Equation 7.22 is highly useful.

In multiple parameter models in which group differences exist in additional parameters, the use of the log odds to characterize the bias effect size is less successful. Under these models, the bias effect size will ordinarily depend on W. The bias will be larger within a certain range on the latent variable scale and will be smaller outside of that range. The direction of the bias may even reverse itself along the latent variable scale. The general approach to be taken under these multiple parameter models is to summarize the group difference in item response functions over the latent trait scale. The resulting measures are generically denoted as "area measures" of bias. The label denotes the idea that these measures gauge the magnitude of the bias by the area between the item response functions for a pair of groups.

In creating an area measure, several choices must be made regarding (a) the range on W to include, (b) whether a discrete approximation is to be used, and (c) whether absolute or signed measures of area will be used. For (a), the simplest choice is to use the full range of W. To do so, however, one must include regions of the latent variable scale in which very few examinees are found. Arguably, an area measure should focus on regions in which most examinees appear. For 3PL models, use of the full range for the latent variable leads to undefined (infinite) area measures whenever the pseudo-guessing parameter estimates differ between groups. The use of a bounded area measure that restricts W (e.g., $-3.0 < W < 3.0$) will eliminate these problems. Under (b), early area measures used discrete approximations to the true area (Ironson & Subkoviak, 1979; Linn et al., 1981; Rudner, Getson, & Knight, 1980). If the area between the item response functions is to be calculated without any differential weighting, discrete approximations are unnecessary because exact formulas are available for the Rasch, 2PL, and 3PL models (Kim & Cohen, 1991; Raju, 1988, 1990). The decision about (c) is only relevant when bidirectional bias is present, resulting in a reversal of the two groups in their rank-ordering on the probability of passing the item. Bidirectional bias can only arise in either the 2PL, normal ogive, or 3PL models. An unsigned area measure will gauge the area between the item response functions as an absolute quantity. A signed area measure will calculate the area between the item response functions as a sum of positive and negative areas, the sign reflecting which group is highest in the probability of passing in any given region of the latent variable scale. For example, a signed area index could have a value near zero even though the absolute area between the IRFs is substantial.

The general continuous area measure can be described for the jth item as

$$A_j = \int_S f[P_{jk}(W) - P_{jm}(W)] dW \qquad (7.23)$$

for item response functions from the kth and mth groups, $P_{jk}(W)$ and $P_{jm}(W)$, respectively, with $f[\ ]$ being a chosen function and S being a chosen range of integration. An unbounded measure will use $S = [-\infty, +\infty]$, while a bounded measure will pick $S = [W_L, W_U]$ for lower bound W_L and upper bound W_U. An unsigned measure might select

$$f = |P_{jk}(W) - P_{jm}(W)|, \qquad (7.24)$$

the absolute value of the difference in item response functions. A signed measure could use the simple difference

$$f = P_{jk}(W) - P_{jm}(W). \qquad (7.25)$$

For the unbounded case in which $S = [-\infty, +\infty]$, Table 7.1 gives expressions for both signed and unsigned area measures under the Rasch, 2PL, and 3PL

TABLE 7.1

Signed and Unsigned Unbounded Area Measures

Rasch model, jth item, comparing groups k and m

  Signed area: $b_{jk} - b_{jm}$

  Unsigned area: $|b_{jk} - b_{jm}|$

Two-parameter logistic model, jth item, comparing groups k and m

  Signed area: $b_{jk} - b_{jm}$

  Unsigned area, $a_{jk} = a_{jm}$: $|b_{jk} - b_{jm}|$

  Unsigned area, $a_{jk} \neq a_{jm}$:

$$UA_{2pl} = \left| \frac{2(a_{jk} - a_{jm})}{Da_{jk}a_{jm}} \ln\left[1 + \exp\left(\frac{Da_{jk}a_{jm}(b_{jk} - b_{jm})}{a_{jk} - a_{jm}} \right) \right] - (b_{jk} - b_{jm}) \right|$$

Three-parameter logistic model, jth item, comparing groups k and m (common c value)

  Signed area: $(1 - c)(b_{jk} - b_{jm})$

  Unsigned area, $a_{jk} = a_{jm}$: $(1 - c) |b_{jk} - b_{jm}|$

  Unsigned area, $a_{jk} \neq a_{jm}$: $(1 - c)UA_{2pl}$

---

models (Raju, 1988). The 3PL case in which the pseudo-guessing parameters vary over groups is omitted because the area measure is infinite in this case. In all three models, invariance in the discrimination parameters leads to area measures that are simple functions of the location parameter differences. In the 2PL and 3PL models, the signed area measures are zero when the discrimination parameters differ across groups. Given invariance in the discrimination parameters, we would expect the signed and unsigned measures to yield identical results for the size of the bias, apart from sign. In practice, the area measures in Table 7.1 are calculated by replacing the item parameters with their sample estimates. Raju (1990) provides large-sample standard errors for the resulting indices. These standard errors can be used to construct test statistics for testing the null hypothesis that the area measure is zero.

Expressions for the bounded area measures in the Rasch, 2PL, and 3PL models were given by Kim and Cohen (1991). The expressions assume that fixed boundary points $S = [W_L, W_U]$ are chosen by the investigator. The resulting area measures are more complex than those given in Table 7.1, especially when either the discrimination or pseudo-guessing parameters vary over groups. In these cases, the item response functions may intersect, and the formula for the area measure depends on whether the intersection points lie within the interval S or outside of this interval. Under the 3PL, the intersection points do not themselves have simple formulas when $c_{jk} \neq c_{jm}$ and $a_{jk} \neq a_{jm}$. Kim and Cohen suggest that the required intersection points be found using a Newton–Raphson algorithm. There may be zero, one, or two intersection points in this 3PL case. The same authors provide software for computing area measures (Kim & Cohen, 1992).

The few comparisons of performance between the unbounded and bounded continuous area measures have revealed few differences in the two types of measures (Kim & Cohen, 1991), apart from the 3PL case in which the unbounded measure is infinite. Bounded measures have a clear advantage in this case. On the other hand, the bounded measures employ bounds that are arbitrary to some extent, and their calculation requires greater effort. At present, the advantages of the bounded measures in comparison to the simpler unbounded measures have not been clearly demonstrated.

The choice between signed and absolute area measures depends on the item response functions in the groups being compared. The two types of area measures will be identical when the Rasch model holds, and when either the 2PL or 3PL models hold with invariant discrimination and pseudo-guessing parameters. When these parameters are not invariant, the signed and absolute area measures will differ, and the difference can be substantial. If the bias in the items is bidirectional, the signed measure may be close to zero while the absolute measure is substantial. For this reason, the two area measures can provide quite different pictures of the magnitude of the bias across items. The two types of measures have been compared in both real and simulated data (Cohen, Kim, & Subkoviak, 1991; Ironson & Subkoviak, 1979; Kim & Cohen, 1991; McCauley & Mendoza, 1985; Raju, 1990; Shepard, Camilli, & Averill, 1981; Shepard, Camilli, & Williams, 1984, 1985; Subkoviak, Mack, Ironson, & Craig, 1984). Neither measure has emerged from this research as uniformly better. The choice between them should depend on whether directional or bidirectional bias is found. If the bias is directional, the two measures should yield the same value. If bidirectional bias is present, the absolute measure provides a more realistic index of the difference in the item response functions.

All of the area measures discussed thus far have omitted any explicit differential weighting of the group differences in the item response functions. This weighting would assign varying weights to the differences as a function of W. The weights might reflect the relative frequencies or densities of examinees at a given W. Alternatively, the weights might be inversely related to the standard error associated with the estimated item response function at a given W. As Wainer (1993) emphasizes, a great advantage in weighting by the distribution of examinees is that bias in regions of low density will be given little weight because few examinees are affected by bias in this region.

Early weighting schemes were based on discrete approximations to various indices in Table 7.1 (Linn et al., 1981; Shepard et al., 1984, 1985). In practice, these investigators found that the weighted and unweighted versions of different area measures yielded similar results. Wainer (1993) proposed four weighted continuous area measures, in each case using weights based on the latent variable distribution in the focal group. He termed these area measures "standardized indices of impact." Two of the indices are unsigned measures, and two of them are signed. Letting N_f be the number of focal group examinees in the sample, the four indices are

$$T_{1j} = \int_{-\infty}^{+\infty} [P_{jf}(W) - P_{jr}(W)]g_f(W)\,dW \qquad (7.26)$$

$$T_{3j} = \int_{-\infty}^{+\infty} [P_{jf}(W) - P_{jr}(W)]^2 g_f(W)\,dW \qquad (7.27)$$

with $T_{2j} = N_f T_{1j}$ and $T_{4j} = N_f T_{3j}$. The inclusion of focal group sample sizes in T_{2j} and T_{4j} is intended to gauge "total impact" by multiplying the "average" impacts T_{1j} and T_{3j} by the number of focal group examinees. Indices T_{3j} and T_{4j} are unsigned measures. All four indices may be used with any dichotomous item IRT model.

Wainer's indices have clear advantages as measures of bias effect size. All of the indices are bounded yet do not require the use of arbitrary boundary values for W. Furthermore, it makes sense to downplay the bias in regions of W in which few examinees are found. At least three difficulties must be overcome before the measures will be widely used. First, it is unclear at present which values of the indices should be considered "large." Second, the relative performance of these weighted indices in comparison to the unweighted continuous indices is unknown. It may be true that in many applications, the weighted and unweighted yield similar rank-orderings of the items in terms of bias. Finally, no simple formulas for $\{T_{1j}, T_{2j}, T_{3j}, T_{4j}\}$ exist that are analogous to the continuous unweighted area measures. Wainer (1993) suggests several computational methods that use existing IRT software. These methods take advantage of the quadrature already performed in MML software such as BILOG-MG (Zimowsk, Muraki, Mislevy, & Bock, 2003). To date, none of the indices $\{T_{1j}, T_{2j}, T_{3j}, T_{4j}\}$ have been used extensively in bias research.

In addition to the direct area measures, some researchers have developed confidence region methods for either the item response functions or the group difference in item response functions (Hauck, 1983; Linn et al., 1981; Lord & Pashley, 1988; Pashley, 1992; Thissen & Wainer, 1990). Instead of summarizing the bias effect size with a single measure, these methods express the effect size as a function of W, graphically displaying the amount of bias as it varies over the latent variable scale. In addition, the confidence region methods incorporate statistical uncertainty into the display by creating confidence bounds on the item response functions or their differences, at any desired level of confidence. Pashley presents a method for creating confidence bands for the difference between item response functions under the 3PL model. The method relies on large-sample approximations to the standard errors of the item parameter estimates and also ignores variability associated with the estimation of the latent variable scores. Preliminary evidence using the method in real data showed consistency with the results of Mantel–Haenszel tests in the same data. Thissen and Wainer present methods for creating confidence "envelopes" for individual item response functions and suggest that in bias applications, the degree of overlap in the envelopes for each group's function can be used to informally assess the extent of the bias. None of these confidence region methods have yet been widely used in bias applications.

Polytomous Items

In the polytomous item case, area measures of bias are most easily defined in relation to the item true-score functions within each group: $E_k(X_j|W)$ for $k = 1, \dots, K$. These true-score functions are monotonically increasing in W under very general conditions (Molenaar, 1997). For commonly used polytomous IRT models such as the partial credit, rating scale, graded response, and generalized partial credit models, bias in the item true-score functions can exist if and only if the category response functions also exhibit bias (Chang & Mazzeo, 1994). Assuming that one of these models is an adequate baseline model for the data, we can evaluate the size of any bias by comparing the item true-score functions across groups.

As in the dichotomous case, we can distinguish two forms of bias in the true-score functions. Let $E_r(X_j|W)$ and $E_f(X_j|W)$ be the true-score functions for the jth item in the reference and focal groups, respectively. Directional bias will be said to exist for item j when

$$D_{Ej}(W) = E_r(X_j \mid W) - E_f(X_j \mid W) \tag{7.28}$$

is nonzero for some W and does not reverse its sign throughout the range of W. Bidirectional bias is present when $D_{Ej}(W)$ is nonzero for some W and reverses its sign across the range of W. The form of bias that is present is an important consideration in choosing an area measure. An absolute area measure for the jth item is

$$A_{Eaj} = \int_{-\infty}^{+\infty} | D_{Ej}(W) | \, dW. \tag{7.29}$$

This area measure will be positive if either directional or bidirectional bias is present in the jth item. A signed area measure is

$$A_{Asj} = \int_{-\infty}^{+\infty} D_{Ej}(W) \, dW. \tag{7.30}$$

This area measure need not be positive and may be close to zero when bidirectional bias is present. Both of these area measures are discussed by Cohen et al. (1993). Expressions for the large-sample standard errors for both area measures are given in that paper, but the expression for the standard error of A_{Eaj} requires distributional assumptions that are probably unrealistic in most applications. Cohen et al. note that A_{Esj} may be small when bidirectional bias is present. They suggest that other measures be used in such cases.

The evaluation of either area measure in Equations 7.29 and 7.30 requires that the true-score function be estimated in each group. For the *k*th group,

$$E_k(X_j \mid W) = \sum_{m=0}^{c-1} mP_k(X_j = m \mid W), \qquad (7.31)$$

with $P_k(X_j = m \mid W)$ being the category response function for the *m*th category of the *j*th item in the *k*th group. Then for the reference and focal groups, we have

$$D_{Ej}(W) = \sum_{m=0}^{c-1} m[P_r(X_j = m \mid W) - P_f(X_j = m \mid W)]. \qquad (7.32)$$

The value of $D_{Ej}(W)$ is easily calculated at any given value of W, given estimates for the category response functions in the reference and focal groups. It is then possible to graph $D_{Ej}(W)$ as a function of W for display purposes. The area measures A_{Eaj} and A_{Esj} are then calculable in theory, but in practice the required integral may be difficult to solve in closed form. Quadrature approximations will be necessary in such cases. Analytical formulas for A_{Esj} are available for the graded response model, as are formulas for a bounded version of A_{Eaj} (Cohen et al., 1993).

Summary

As the foregoing makes clear, a bias effect size measure can be defined for nearly any IRT model. It is fair to ask, however, whether any of the measures so defined are really useful in a practical sense. What is a "large" effect size in any of these cases? How should one judge whether an effect is large or small? Answers to these and other similar questions are not yet clear in general. In fact, it may not make sense to formulate a general rule for what constitutes a large effect size across all situations in which such effect sizes might be considered. Items are embedded in test forms, and the same effect size might be considered large or small depending on the length of a test. In short tests, a single item will have more influence on the resulting test score, and a given effect size will have more impact. In long tests such as those used in many educational settings, a single item ordinarily has less relative influence on the test score. The purpose of the test should also be considered. High-stakes tests used for selection in educational or employment settings may require stricter standards for exclusion of biased items, even when the bias effect size seems small. Remarkably, while much effort has gone into research on the development of IRT methods for detecting biased items, questions about the practical impact of item bias have not received much systematic attention within IRT (for an interesting exception, see Stark, Chernyshenko, & Drasgow, 2004). The next section describes a general method for item bias detection that explicitly considers the impact of item bias on the test score.

The DFIT Approach

Raju, Van der Linden, and Fleer (1995) proposed an IRT-based framework for evaluating bias at both the item and test levels for tests consisting of dichotomous items. This approach to bias evaluation is known by the acronym DFIT, which stands for *differential functioning of items and tests*. The DFIT approach provides effect size measures for bias at the level of the test item but also at the whole test level. The latter is an especially useful feature of the method, as the area measures described earlier have no simple extensions to the test level. The DFIT approach has been generalized to include polytomous items (C. P. Flowers, Oshima, & Raju, 1999) and dichotomous items modeled using multidimensional latent variables (Oshima, Raju, & Flowers, 1997). We first focus on the dichotomous, unidimensional application. The polytomous application is discussed below.

The DFIT approach begins with the assumption that a baseline IRT model has been found to fit in both the reference and focal groups, with separate group-specific estimates of all item parameters and latent variable scores W being available. It is also assumed that the metrics of the item parameter estimates have been linked using one of the methods discussed earlier. The DFIT method is not model specific. Any IRT model for dichotomous items may be used as a baseline model, providing that the model fits the data in both groups. The method is also flexible with regard to the estimation method chosen for the item parameters and latent variable scores. Raju et al. (1995) used MML estimation for the item parameters, with Bayesian maximum a posteriori estimation for the latent variable scores.

The DFIT method begins by defining a measure of differential test functioning (DTF) that applies to the p items taken as a whole. Assuming that the test score is calculated as an unweighted sum of the item scores, the conditional expected value for the test score T_i in the kth group for the ith person is

$$E_k(T_i \mid W_i) = \sum_{j=1}^{p} P_{jk}(W_i), \qquad (7.33)$$

where $k = r, f$ for the reference and focal groups, $j = 1, \dots, p$. Assuming that the item response functions in the reference and focal groups are known and that a score on W for the ith person is known, it is possible to evaluate the conditional expected value in Equation 7.33 for the ith person under *both* the reference and focal group models. If no bias exists in any of the p items, the expected test score is the same for the ith person regardless of which model is used because the models are identical across groups. On the other hand, if any of the p items are biased, the item response functions for these items differ across groups, and so the expected test score for the ith person may have different values depending on the group. To capture this difference, define

$$D_{i|W} = E_f(T_i \mid W_i) - E_r(T_i \mid W_i) \qquad (7.34)$$

as the difference in the conditional expected test scores for the ith person under the two item response functions. We can then define an index of DTF as

$$DTF = E_f(D_{i|W}^2) = \int D_{i|W}^2 g_f(W) \, dW, \qquad (7.35)$$

where $g_f(W)$ is the density function for W in the focal group. In practice, DTF is defined in relation to focal group members only, so that only persons who are members of the focal group receive values on $D_{i|W}$.

Several features of the DTF measure in Equation 7.35 should be noted. First, weighting by $g_f(W)$ will give more weight to values of $D_{i|W}$ in regions of the latent variable scale in which most focal group members are found. Second, the presence of item-level bias may, or may not, lead to meaningful bias at the test level as measured by DTF. As argued by Raju et al. (1995), item level biases that operate in different directions, with some items favoring the reference group and others favoring the focal group, may cancel out at the test level and yield low values for DTF. This compensatory feature of the DTF measure is useful when the test-level score is of inherent interest, as when an existing test is evaluated for bias.

In practice, the DTF measure in Equation 7.35 is estimated by replacing $P_{jk}(W_i)$ with $\hat{P}_{jk}(\hat{W}_i)$ in Equation 7.33, using estimated item parameters and latent variable scores. The integral in Equation 7.35 is avoided by realizing that

$$DTF = \sigma_D^2 + \mu_D^2. \tag{7.36}$$

Here $\mu_D = \mu_{Tf} - \mu_{Tr}$, and

$$\mu_{Tf} = \int E_f(T_i \mid W_i) g_f(W) dW, \tag{7.37}$$

$$\mu_{Tr} = \int E_r(T_i \mid W_i) g_f(W) dW. \tag{7.38}$$

The parameter σ_D^2 is the variance of $D_{i|W}$ in the focal group. Note that both μ_{Tr} and μ_{Tf} are defined with respect to the focal group also. We can estimate μ_D by estimating $D_{i|W}$ for every focal group member and then using the sample mean of $\hat{D}_{i|W}$ as $\hat{\mu}_D$. Similarly, the variance σ_D^2 is estimated using the sample variance of $\hat{D}_{i|W}$ within the focal group. Finally, DTF is estimated by substituting $\hat{\mu}_D$ and $\hat{\sigma}_D^2$ in Equation 7.36.

The DTF estimate indicates the magnitude of the test-level bias. Raju et al. (1995) suggest several alternative test statistics that might be used to test the null hypothesis that DTF is zero in the population from which the focal group sample is drawn. The proposed test statistics are preliminary and do not formally incorporate adjustments needed to acknowledge the degrees of freedom lost due to estimation of the item parameters and latent variable scores. The tests also assume a normal distribution for $D_{i|W}$ in the focal group, an assumption that will be difficult to verify in practice. In spite of these potential problems, simulation evidence for the proper Type I error and power behavior of the test statistics is promising (Raju et al.).

The DFIT approach extends to the item level in two ways, either by considering the bias for a given item in relation to the bias shown by other items in the test (compensatory DIF, or CDIF) or by considering bias in each item as if that item is the only item in the test that manifests bias (non-compensatory DIF, or NCDIF). The rationale for CDIF begins by noting that DTF can be expressed as

$$DTF = E_f\left[\left(\sum_{j=1}^{p} d_{ij}\right)^2\right]. \tag{7.39}$$

Here $d_{ij} = P_{jf}(W_i) - P_{jr}(W_i)$. But the expression in Equation 7.39 can be rewritten as

$$DTF = \sum_{j=1}^{p} [\text{Cov}(d_{ij}, D_{i|W}) + \mu_{dj}\mu_D].$$ (7.40)

Here $\text{Cov}(d_{ij}, D_{i|W})$ is the covariance between d_{ij} and $D_{i|W}$ in the focal group, and μ_{dj} is the expected value of d_{ij} in the focal group. Equation 7.40 suggests that DTF can be additively decomposed into a sum of DIF terms across p items. CDIF is then defined for the jth item as the term for that item in Equation 7.40

$$CDIF_j = \text{Cov}(d_{ij}, D_{i|W}) + \mu_{dj}\mu_D.$$ (7.41)

CDIF is unlike the standard definition of DIF in that it considers DIF for the jth item as it relates to the DIF in the other $p - 1$ items. The stronger the association between DIF on the jth item and DIF in the other items, the greater will be the CDIF for the jth item. Also, nonzero values for CDIF across items need not combine to yield nonzero DTF because the item-level DIF may go in different directions, with mutual cancellation at the test level.

NCDIF is defined as the special case of CDIF in which the other $p - 1$ items have no DIF, leading to

$$NCDIF_j = \sigma_{dj}^2 + \mu_{df},$$ (7.42)

where σ_{dj}^2 is the variance of d_{ij} in the focal group. We can rewrite $NCDIF_j$ as

$$E_f[(P_{jf}(W_i) - P_{jr}(W_i))^2] = \int (P_{jf}(W_i) - P_{jr}(W_i))^2 g_f(W) dW.$$ (7.43)

NCDIF is closely related to the unsigned weighted area measure suggested by Wainer (1993). Raju et al. (1995) described the relationship of $NCDIF_j$ to other standard indices of bias, such as Lord's chi-square index. Unlike $CDIF_j$, $NCDIF_j$ values for the p items do not sum to the DTF value for the set of items. The unsigned nature of $NCDIF_j$ removes any cancellation in this sum that would occur when the directions of the biases differ across items.

$NCDIF_j$ and $CDIF_j$ are estimated by first estimating $P_{jf}(W_i)$ and $P_{jr}(W_i)$ for every member of the focal group once parameter estimates and latent variable scores are available. Then $\hat{d}_{ij}$ and $\hat{D}_{i|W}$ can be calculated, and

$\text{Cov}(d_{ij}, D_{i|W})$ is estimated using these values. Similarly, μ_{dj} and μ_D are estimated as averages in the focal group. Finally, $NCDIF_j$ and $CDIF_j$ are estimated by substituting all of these quantities in Equations 7.41 and 7.42. Raju et al. (1995) did not develop any significance test procedures for $CDIF_j$. A test statistic is available for $NCDIF_j$. A chi-square statistic for the null hypothesis that the $NCDIF_j$ is zero for the jth item is

$$\chi^2_{NCDj} = \frac{\text{est}(NCDIF_j)}{\hat{\sigma}^2_{dj}/N_f}, \tag{7.44}$$

where $\text{est}(NCDIF_j)$ is the estimated $NCDIF_j$ for the jth item. This test statistic has $df = N_f$. The square root of the chi-square statistic can be regarded as a standard normal deviate and can be referred to the standard normal distribution.

When the bias investigation is focused on an intact test and interest lies in the total test score, Raju et al. (1995) suggest that DTF first be examined. If meaningful levels of DTF are found, Raju et al. suggest that $CDIF_j$ values be examined for the p items, with the item with the largest $CDIF_j$ value being dropped from the test. DTF is then reestimated for the shorter test. This iterative process is continued until the level of DTF falls below an acceptable limit. The $NCDIF_j$ values are useful if the individual items are specifically of interest. For example, when tests are being assembled from a larger item pool and the goal is to purge this larger pool of biased items, the $NCDIF_j$ values should be the focus of interest. The $NCDIF_j$ values will be less dependent than the $CDIF_j$ values on which other items were selected for the particular test form under study.

C. P. Flowers et al. (1999) describe the extension of the DFIT approach to ordered-categorical items. Any of the available polytomous IRT models may be used for the required calculations, assuming that the chosen model provides an adequate fit. It is also assumed that any needed parameter linkage has been achieved prior to the DFIT calculations. The first step begins with the item parameter estimates obtained within the reference and focal groups, along with the latent variable score estimates W_i for all focal group members. Let $P_{jmf}(W)$ and $P_{jmr}(W)$ be the category response functions for the jth item and mth category in the focal and reference groups, respectively. Assume that the item response categories are scored as $m = 0, 1, \ldots, C$ in each group. Then the conditional expected score for the ith focal person on the jth item in the reference group is

$$E_r(X_j \mid W_i) = \sum_{m=0}^{C} m P_{jmr}(W_i). \tag{7.45}$$

Similarly, the conditional expected score for the ith focal person in the focal group is

$$E_f(X_j \mid W_i) = \sum_{m=0}^{C} mP_{jmf}(W_i). \tag{7.46}$$

Then the difference d_{ij} is defined as

$$d_{ij} = E_f(X_j \mid W_i) - E_r(X_j \mid W_i). \tag{7.47}$$

At the test level, the conditional expected test score T_j for the ith person in the reference group is

$$E_r(T_i \mid W_i) = \sum_{j=1}^{p} E_r(X_j \mid W_i), \tag{7.48}$$

and for the ith person in the focal group, the conditional expected value is

$$E_f(T_i \mid W_i) = \sum_{j=1}^{p} E_f(X_j \mid W_i) \tag{7.49}$$

Given these definitions, the difference $D_{i\mid W}$ is

$$D_{i\mid W} = E_f(T_i \mid W_i) - E_r(T_i \mid W_i). \tag{7.50}$$

From this point on, the definitions of DTF, $CDIF_j$, and $NCDIF_j$ are identical to the dichotomous case. No other special formulas are needed for the polytomous item case. Test statistics are also identical in the dichotomous and polytomous cases.

Oshima et al. (1997) extend the DFIT framework to items that are fit by a multidimensional latent variable model. The dichotomous item case is illustrated in Oshima et al., although no barrier appears to exist that would prevent the application to polytomous items also. The multidimensional extension will not be described here.

An Example

To illustrate the use of IRT in the detection of measurement bias, we use data on a subtest within the College Basic Academic Subjects Examination (CBASE). CBASE is a set of achievement tests in four subjects: mathematics,

English, science, and social studies. The tests are intended for students enrolled in college and designed to assess knowledge and skills of the sort that would be part of most undergraduate general curricula. The entire exam consists of 180 multiple-choice items, along with an additional essay portion for writing assessment. For more information on CBASE, see Osterlind, Robinson, and Nickens (1997), L. Flowers, Osterlind, Pascarella, and Pierson (2001), and Pike (1992).

The analyses to be described here used 11 items from the geometry section of the mathematics portion of CBASE. The mathematics test contains three subtests: general mathematics, algebra, and geometry. We will compare males and females on the geometry items. A total of 5,486 examinees provided data, with 1,034 males and 4,452 females. Table 7.2 gives the proportions passing each of the 11 multiple-choice items by gender. Males show a consistently higher proportion passing, although the gap between males and females varies considerably across items. The geometry subtest was selected for these analyses in preference to the entire mathematics test in hopes that the subtest would more closely adhere to unidimensionality for purposes of IRT analyses.

The first set of analyses examined the dimensionality of the 11 items using CFA in Mplus 5.21 (Muthén & Muthén, 1998–2006). A single-factor model was fit simultaneously within the male and female groups using the factor model for ordered-categorical data (see Chapter 5). In these analyses, no invariance constraints were imposed apart from those needed for identification.

Given that the items are scored as binary, all threshold parameters were initially constrained to invariance. The loading for item Q87 was

TABLE 7.2

Proportions Passing the CBASE
Geometry Items by Gender

Item Number	Males ($N = 1,034$)	Females ($N = 4,452$)
Q83	.766	.618
Q84	.601	.488
Q85	.813	.742
Q86	.618	.496
Q87	.860	.809
Q88	.653	.583
Q89	.590	.387
Q90	.544	.375
Q91	.808	.728
Q92	.837	.784
Q93	.779	.642

fixed to one in both groups, with the remaining loadings free. This item was selected because of the small group difference in proportion passing for that item. The factor mean for males was fixed to zero, with the factor mean in the female group being free. Factor variances were also free. In addition, the scaling parameter for item Q87 was fixed to invariance at 1.0 (Millsap & Yun-Tien, 2004). This model led to numerical problems due to the constraints on the thresholds for items Q88 and Q89. To circumvent this problem, the thresholds were permitted to vary across groups for these two items, and the scaling constants for the items were constrained to invariance instead. The new model produced convergence on a solution. The global fit statistics suggest that while the model is wrong, the approximate fit is reasonably good. The chi-square is 346.69 with $df = 82$. The CFI value is .977 and the RMSEA value is .034. Examining the residuals for the sample tetrachoric correlation matrices in each group reveals that for the male group, 9 of 55 residuals exceed .05 in absolute value, and in the female group, 12 of 55 residuals exceed .05 in absolute value. The largest residual in the male group is $-.123$ for the correlation between Q86 and Q92. The largest residual in the female group is .135 for the correlation between Q92 and Q93. The approximate fits afforded by the single-factor model in each group are good enough to proceed to the next stage. The results also suggest that a 2PL model might fit the data in each group.

In the next step, the IRTLRDIF (version 2.0b, Thissen, 2001) program was used to provide LR tests of invariance for each item under the 2PL model. Given no prior research on which of the 11 items might violate invariance over gender, we begin with a procedure that evaluates each item for possible bias, using all other items as the anchor. Items that were flagged for bias using this procedure and anchor definition were dropped from the anchor before the next step. The next step used a designated anchor consisting only of items that had not been flagged as biased in the first round. All items were again evaluated for bias using this designated anchor. This process was repeated until all of the 11 items were divided into two categories: anchor items showing no evidence of bias and items that were flagged for evidence of statistically significant bias. For the 2PL model, an item is flagged for bias if the LR chi-square exceeds the critical value at an alpha of .05 with $df = 2$. Once flagged, separate $df = 1$ tests were performed for invariance in the difficulty and discrimination parameters separately.

Table 7.3 provides the parameter estimates under the 2PL model for each of the 11 items in the male and female groups. These estimates were actually provided by MULTILOG 7.0 (Thissen, 1991), following completion of the IRTLRDIF analyses. At the end of those analyses, items Q83, Q84, Q90, Q91, and Q93 were designated anchor items. Their parameters were estimated in MULTILOG under invariance constraints across gender. The IRTLRDIF analyses found statistically significant group differences

TABLE 7.3

Item Parameter Estimates for the CBASE Geometry
Items by Gender

Item Number	Males ($N = 1,034$)		Females ($N = 4,452$)	
	a_j	b_j	a_j	b_j
Q83	1.97	−.42	1.97	−.42
Q84	1.21	.06	1.21	.06
Q85[a]	1.73	−.70	1.73	−.92
Q86[a]	1.35	.11	1.35	.01
Q87[a]	1.62	−1.03	1.62	−1.27
Q88[a]	1.14	−.11	1.14	−.38
Q89[a]	1.03	.16	1.03	.54
Q90	1.22	.51	1.22	.51
Q91	1.21	−1.02	1.21	−1.02
Q92[a]	1.51	−.93	1.01	−1.53
Q93	1.40	−.59	1.40	−.59

[a] Statistically significant group differences at $p < .05$.

in difficulty parameters for items Q85, Q86, Q87, Q88, Q89, and Q92. Significant group differences in discrimination parameters were found only for item Q92, and those differences were marginally significant. The estimates in Table 7.3 reflect the corresponding pattern of group differences. For items in which group differences in difficulty parameters and no group differences in discrimination parameters were found, separate difficulty estimates by group are given, with invariant discrimination parameters. Only item Q92 shows group differences on both parameters. Finally, the estimates in Table 7.3 were obtained assuming that the latent variable is distributed normally in both groups, with $\mu_f = 0$, $\sigma_f = 1.0$ for females and $\mu_m = 60$, $\sigma_m = 1.0$, for males.

Among the items showing group differences in Table 7.3, items Q88 and Q89 had the largest chi-square statistics from IRTLRDIF for the test of invariance in difficulty parameters (9.5 and 14.1, respectively, at $df = 1$). For item Q89, the item is considerably harder for females than males of equal status on the latent variable. This result is consistent with the proportions passing the item in Table 7.2. On the other hand, the difficulty estimates for Q88 show that it is actually easier for females than we would expect, even though males pass the item at a higher rate overall. In other words, we expect to see an even larger gap in the proportion passing the item if the item is functioning identically across gender. In fact, five of the six items flagged as biased show bias against males, a surprising result. The item with the largest bias, however, is item Q89, and it is harder for females than males.

8

Observed Variable Methods

This chapter reviews measurement bias detection methods that collectively are classified as *observed variable methods*, using the distinction developed in Chapter 3. These methods do not formally model the relationship between the measured variables X and the latent variables W that might underlie X. Instead, a set of measured variables Z are used as substitutes or proxies for W. The variables Z are used to match examinees prior to any group comparisons on the studied variables X. This matching is intended to adjust for any group differences in the distributions of the target latent variable W_t, as these group differences may confound the comparisons on the studied variables X. The observed variable methods described in this chapter vary in their use of Z as a matching variable and in the statistical model used to relate X, Z, and the grouping variable V.

The observed variable methods to be described provide tests of observed conditional invariance (OCI) or weaker forms of this invariance. The distinction between OCI and the forms of measurement invariance defined in Chapter 3 lies in the adequacy of Z as a proxy for W_t. In all of the methods to be reviewed here, the variable Z is a scalar and is typically a function of the studied variables X. Ordinarily, Z is the total score $Z = T = \sum_{j=1}^{P} X_j$. In principle, it would be possible to use a multivariate matching variable Z. If W_t is believed to be multidimensional ($r_t > 1$), the use of a multivariate Z would probably be necessary. Chapter 3 presents general results on the conditions for equivalence between OCI and measurement invariance. We examine some of these conditions in this chapter as they apply to the particular methods reviewed here.

Apart from the issue of equivalence between OCI and measurement invariance, observed variable methods have several clear advantages. First, most observed variable methods do not require complex software for their use and are relatively easy to implement. If bias detection methods are to be routinely applied in practice, ease of use becomes a significant issue. Second, several of the observed variable methods offer effect size measures that are useful and understandable, at least with respect to the observed score metric. The availability of clear measures of bias effect size greatly enhances the practical value of the method. Finally, the sample size demands of most of the observed score methods are modest in comparison to some latent variable methods.

The present chapter divides the methods to be reviewed into two groups based on whether **X** contains dichotomous or polytomous measures. A few methods are applicable in both cases, but most methods were developed for one of the two cases. The chapter confines discussion to methods that employ a matching variable **Z**. Older methods that do not match examinees prior to group comparisons are omitted (see Berk, 1982, for a discussion of these). We begin with methods for dichotomous measures **X**, followed by the polytomous case.

Dichotomous Item Methods

We begin by defining notation, or reviewing notation in some cases, that will be useful in what follows. Let N_k be the sample size for the examinee sample from the kth population under study. Often, $k = 1, 2$ with a focal and a reference group. The dichotomous item scores for p items are the variables $\mathbf{X} = (X_1, X_2, \ldots, X_p)$ with $X_j = \{0, 1\}$, $j = 1, \ldots, p$. A matching variable Z is created as the total score across the p items: $Z = \sum_{j=1}^{P} X_j$. Scores on Z partition the samples into $M < p$ score groups, ignoring groups defined by the perfect scores $Z = 0$ or $Z = p$. In some applications, fewer than $p - 1$ score groups are formed because adjacent scores are combined to achieve sufficient sample sizes for the analysis. Let F_{mk}, $m = 1, \ldots, M$, $k = 1, 2, \ldots, K$, be the number of examinees who belong to the mth score group on Z and who are sampled from the kth population. Let $F_m = \sum_{k=1}^{K} F_{mk}$ be the total frequency in the mth score group across the K studied populations. Also, let f_{1jmk} be the number of examinees who pass the jth item (e.g., $X_j = 1$) and who are in the mth score group and kth examinee population. Similarly, let f_{0jmk} be the number of examinees who fail the jth item and who are in the mth score group and kth population. Finally, we have $F_{1jm} = \sum_{k=1}^{K} f_{1jmk}$ as the number of examinees who pass the jth item and who are in the mth score group. Similarly, we have the number of examinees who fail the jth item and are in the mth score group: $F_{0jm} = \sum_{k=1}^{K} f_{0jmk}$. These definitions are illustrated in the 2×2 contingency table for the jth item and the mth score group, as given in Table 8.1.

The Mantel–Haenszel Method

The Mantel–Haenszel (MH) method applies a well-known test procedure for a uniform odds-ratio in an $M \times 2 \times 2$ table to the problem of detecting item bias in dichotomous item data (Holland & Thayer, 1988; Mantel & Haenszel, 1959). The MH method is widely used in bias studies, both

TABLE 8.1

2 × 2 Contingency Table for mth Score
Group on Matching Variable Z

	$k = 1$	$k = 2$
$X_j = 0$	f_{0jm1}	f_{0jm2}
$X_j = 1$	f_{1jm1}	f_{1jm2}

because of its ease of use and because its properties are well understood. Furthermore, the MH method leads to a useful measure of the bias effect size in addition to a test statistic.

To understand the calculation of the MH test statistic, consider the $M \times 2 \times 2$ contingency table for the jth item formed by the M score groups defined by Z, two examinee groups (i.e., reference and focal groups), and the jth item score (i.e., pass or fail). The mth "slice" of this table is shown in Table 8.1. The number of score groups M has a maximum value of $p - 1$ because the extreme score groups are ignored. Fewer than $p - 1$ score groups may be formed to achieve adequate sample sizes F_{mk} as needed. The odds-ratio for the mth score group is defined as

$$\alpha_m = \frac{P_m(X_j = 1 \mid k = 2) / P_m(X_j = 0 \mid k = 2)}{P_m(X_j = 1 \mid k = 1) / P_m(X_j = 0 \mid k = 1)}, \tag{8.1}$$

where $P_m(X_j=1 \mid k=2)$ is the conditional probability of passing the jth item given that the examinee is from the reference group (denoted here as population 2) and is in the mth score group. The MH chi-square statistic is used to test the null hypothesis that

$$H_0: \alpha_m = \alpha = 1, \quad m = 1, \dots, M \tag{8.2}$$

against the alternative hypothesis

$$H_1: \alpha_m = \alpha \neq 1, \quad m = 1, \dots, M. \tag{8.3}$$

The null hypothesis asserts that within all score groups, the probability of passing the item is the same for the two examinee populations. This odds-ratio is therefore equal to one uniformly over score groups. This null hypothesis represents a hypothesis of OCI as defined in Chapter 3. The conditional probabilities of passing the item (and therefore of failing the item), given the value of Z, are identical across examinee populations. The null hypothesis also represents conditional independence between the item score and examinee group membership within each score group.

The alternative hypothesis retains the restriction that the odds-ratios are the same across score groups but asserts that the common odds-ratio has a value other than one. From the definition of the odds-ratio in Equation 8.1, values of $\alpha > 1$ mean that the conditional probability of passing the item is higher in the reference group. Values of $\alpha < 1$ indicate the reverse ordering. An important point is that under the alternative hypothesis, one examinee group is consistently favored by the item regardless of the score group. This condition is analogous to the unidirectional bias defined in Chapter 3 for latent variable approaches to bias detection, with the difference that in the MH procedure, the observed variable Z is used to match examinees. The MH procedure does not explicitly test for the possibility of bidirectional bias. We return to this point below.

Under the assumption of independence among examinees, the MH null hypothesis can be tested using the statistic

$$\chi^2_{\text{MH}} = \frac{\left[\left|\sum_{m=1}^{M} f_{1jm2} - \sum_{m=1}^{M} E(f_{1jm2})\right| - .5\right]^2}{\sum_{m=1}^{M} \sigma^2(f_{1jm2})}. \tag{8.4}$$

Here we define

$$E(f_{1jm2}) = \frac{F_{m2}F_{1jm}}{F_m}, \tag{8.5}$$

$$\sigma^2(f_{1jm2}) = \frac{f_{1jm1}f_{0jm1}f_{1jm2}f_{0jm2}}{F_m^2(F_m - 1)} \tag{8.6}$$

as the expected value and variance of f_{1jm2}, respectively, under the null hypothesis in Equation 8.2. Under this hypothesis, the test statistic in Equation 8.4 is distributed in large samples as a central chi-square statistic with $df = 1$. The null hypothesis is rejected if the test statistic exceeds the critical value of the central chi-square at the chosen significance level.

Holland and Thayer (1988) state that the chi-square statistic in Equation 8.4 provides a uniformly most powerful unbiased test of the null hypothesis in Equation 8.2 against the alternative in Equation 8.3. As long as the odds-ratio is common across score groups, no other statistical test of H_0 will have better power than MH over all values of $\alpha \neq 1$. While the MH test requires adequate sample sizes for the chi-square approximation to hold, the sample sizes within score groups F_m need not be large as long as the number of score groups is large (Agresti, 2002). Evidence for the sample sizes needed to achieve adequate power is based largely on simulations. This evidence is reviewed below.

Assuming a common value for the odds-ratio across the M score groups, Mantel and Haenszel (1959) gave an estimator for α as

$$\hat{\alpha} = \frac{\sum_{m=1}^{M} [f_{1jm2}f_{0jm1}/F_m]}{\sum_{m=1}^{M} [f_{1jm1}f_{0jm2}/F_m]}. \tag{8.7}$$

This estimator ranges from 0 to ∞ in value. In bias applications, a more useful descriptive statistic uses a logarithmic transformation

$$\hat{D}_\alpha = -2.35\ln(\hat{\alpha}). \tag{8.8}$$

If $\hat{\alpha} > 1$ so that the reference group is favored, then $\hat{D}_\alpha < 0$. The focal group is favored when $\hat{D}_\alpha > 0$. The estimator in Equation 8.8 provides a useful measure of the bias effect size in that values of $\hat{D}_\alpha$ that are substantially different from zero would indicate substantial violations of OCI. For example, the Educational Testing Service, as reported in Dorans and Holland (1993), uses the point estimate of $\hat{D}_\alpha$ in combination with the results of the chi-square test in Equation 8.4 to classify items as either showing "negligible DIF," "intermediate DIF," or "large DIF."

Approximate estimators for the standard error of $\ln(\hat{\alpha})$ are available (Philips & Holland, 1987; Robins, Breslow, & Greenland, 1986). Philips and Holland give the estimator for the sampling variance as

$$\sigma^2_{\ln\hat{\alpha}} = \frac{1}{2A^2}\left(\sum_{m=1}^{M} F_m^{-2}[(f_{1jm2}f_{0jm1} + \hat{\alpha}f_{0jm2}f_{1jm1})(f_{1jm2} + f_{0jm1} + \hat{\alpha}f_{0jm2}f_{1jm1})]\right). \tag{8.9}$$

Here we have $A = \sum_{m=1}^{M} [F_m^{-1}(f_{1jm2}f_{0jm1})]$. To obtain the standard error of D_α, the square root of the variance estimate in Equation 8.9 can be multiplied by 2.35. We can evaluate the departure of $\hat{D}_\alpha$ or $\ln(\hat{\alpha})$ from zero using the ratio of either $\hat{D}_\alpha$ or $\ln(\hat{\alpha})$ to the appropriate standard error. In large samples, this ratio could be referred to the standard normal distribution for hypothesis testing. Alternatively, the standard errors could be used to set confidence intervals around either $\hat{D}_\alpha$ or $\ln(\hat{\alpha})$ using a normal approximation. Neither of these uses for the standard error in Equation 8.9 appears to be widespread in bias applications. Furthermore, there appear to have been few comparisons between such uses for the standard error and the traditional chi-square test. Camilli and Smith (1990) compared the MH chi-square test to both a randomization test and the use of a standard error for $\ln(\hat{\alpha})$ obtained from a jackknife procedure. In both real and simulated data, the two resampling procedures gave results that were comparable to the MH chi-square test and to the standard error formula in Equation 8.9. The results suggest that the traditional test and standard error are fairly robust, at least with respect to the conditions examined in the study.

A number of researchers have noted the relationship between the MH odds-ratio and the item location parameters in the Rasch model (Fischer, 1995a; Holland & Thayer, 1988; Meredith & Millsap, 1992; Zwick, 1990). Suppose that p items fit a Rasch model in each group, with invariant location parameters for all items except possibly the jth item, which is under study. Then it can be shown that the MH odds-ratio for the jth item is equal to

$$a_j = \exp(b_{j1} - b_{j2}), \tag{8.10}$$

where b_{jk} is the Rasch location parameter for the jth item in the kth group, $k = 1, 2$. Under these conditions, OCI for the jth item as evaluated by the MH procedure is equivalent to measurement invariance as defined in Chapter 3. Given the Rasch model, each of the M 2×2 subtables for the jth item must have the same population odds-ratio. This common odds-ratio is simply a monotonic function of the group difference in the location parameters. When measurement invariance holds for the jth item, this difference is zero and the odds-ratio is one. If the item disadvantages the focal group so that $b_{j1} > b_{j2}$, the odds-ratio will exceed 1.

The mathematical correspondence between the Rasch location parameters and the MH odds-ratio breaks down under either of two conditions. First, measurement invariance may fail to hold for some of the $p - 1$ items that are used to create Z. In this case, the matching variable itself may be biased due to bias in the other $p - 1$ items. Second, some or all of the p items may not fit the Rasch model. As discussed in Chapter 3, Bayes sufficiency no longer holds for Z in relation to W in this case. Depending on the underlying latent variable model, a common odds-ratio for the M score groups may no longer exist. Consequently, the difference between the focal and reference groups in the probability of passing the item within each score group may vary across score groups, possibly leading to bidirectional bias.

While the conditions for correspondence between the Rasch location parameters and the MH odds-ratio are well understood, the practical question of interest is as follows: Under what conditions will the MH procedure be accurate in the detection of measurement bias, or invariance? The MH procedure may function effectively in practice even under conditions that do not support the correspondence mentioned above. Interest in this practical question has led to intensive research on the performance of the MH procedure in simulated data (Donoghue, Holland, & Thayer, 1993; Narayanan & Swaminathan, 1994, 1996; Rogers & Swaminathan, 1993; Uttaro & Millsap, 1994). In the typical study, item data are simulated to fit a latent variable model that either incorporates bias for one or more items, or includes no bias. The data are then examined using the MH procedure to flag items as biased or not, using a given decision rule (e.g., MH chi-square that is significant at the .05 alpha level). The Type I error rate or power for the MH procedure can then be studied, depending on whether the items under study are unbiased or biased. In addition to manipulating the latent variable model in these studies, other performance influences such as sample size, test length, proportion of biased items in Z, or the form of the bias can be studied. This research has led to a number of conclusions about the performance of the MH procedure in practice.

1. Both theoretical and simulation evidence underscores the importance of including the studied item score in the total score that defines Z, the matching variable (Donoghue et al., 1993; Lewis, 1993; Meredith & Millsap, 1992; Zwick, 1990). If the studied item is excluded from Z and the examinee groups differ in their distributions on W, the MH procedure is likely to indicate bias in the studied item even if no bias is present. Donoghue et al. illustrated this phenomenon in their simulations. The explanation for this effect lies in Theorem 3.3. If the studied item score X_j is omitted from Z, then X_j and Z are conditionally independent given the latent variable W that presumably underlies both X_j and Z. The regression of X_j on Z will then tend to vary across groups even though both X_j and Z are unbiased. These group differences in regressions imply rejection of the MH null hypothesis. The entire problem is avoided by including X_j in the calculation of Z.

2. The number of items used to form the matching variable Z has an impact on the performance of the MH procedure. There are several aspects to this problem. When the number of items p is small, the MH procedure tends to function poorly. The operational definition of "small" seems to be $p < 20$. Donoghue et al. (1993) found that when $p < 20$, the performance of the MH procedure was substantially influenced by characteristics of the studied item such as the difficulty and discrimination levels. Uttaro and Millsap (1994) found in simulations that when $p = 20$ and the examinee groups differed in their distributions on W, the MH procedure tended to indicate bias in the studied item when no bias was present. The data in these simulations were generated from 3PL models, with discrimination and pseudo-guessing parameters varying over

items. The false-positive problem largely disappeared when the test length was increased to $p = 40$. This finding leads to the second aspect of test length, which is that in longer tests, the MH procedure adheres to the nominal Type I error rate fairly well regardless of the underlying model for the items. The definition of a "long" test is not clear, but the available evidence suggests that $p > 40$ is adequate (Donoghue et al.; Narayanan & Swaminathan, 1994, 1996; Uttaro & Millsap). Theoretical results suggest that in long tests, tests of OCI using the proxy variable Z should provide adequate tests of measurement invariance (Meredith & Millsap, 1992; Shealy & Stout, 1993b). These theoretical results do not identify the value of p that can be considered "long" in practice, however. In particular, the performance of the MH procedure in the intermediate range $20 < p < 40$ with regard to false positives has not been fully explored.

3. The power of the MH procedure for detecting bias is affected strongly by the form of the bias, or whether the bias is unidirectional or bidirectional. In adequate samples, the MH procedure has sufficient power to detect unidirectional bias if the degree of bias is not too small (Narayanan & Swaminathan, 1994; Rogers & Swaminathan, 1993; Uttaro & Millsap, 1994). The sample size issue is discussed below. The unidirectional bias case includes situations in which the IRFs are not strictly parallel, as long as the ordering of the IRFs does not reverse across the range of W. When the bias is bidirectional, the MH procedure can have low power even in large samples (Narayanan & Swaminathan, 1996; Rogers & Swaminathan; Uttaro & Millsap). The lowest power appears for studied items of medium difficulty, where the IRFs cross in the middle of the range of W (Rogers & Swaminathan). In this case, the MH assumption that the odds-ratio is constant across score groups is violated. If the item is either quite low or quite high in difficulty, the MH procedure can maintain power to detect moderate levels of bias in spite of the bidirectionality.

What sample sizes are needed for the MH procedure to achieve adequate levels of power to detect bias? The required sample sizes depend on the size of the bias and whether the bias is unidirectional or bidirectional. In the unidirectional case, Narayanan and Swaminathan (1994) found that sample sizes of 300 individuals in each examinee group were enough to give adequate power, given that the area between the IRFs is .80 or larger, using the area measures from Raju (1988). This effect size level is moderate to large. When the focal group sample size was smaller than the reference group sample size, increases in the focal group sample size had a greater impact on power. Rogers and Swaminathan

(1993) report an average power of 68% with sample sizes of 250 in each examinee group. At $N = 500$ per group, the average power increases to 83%. Both figures are averaged across levels of the factors manipulated in the simulations, including the bias effect size levels. Bias effect size levels of .40 or less appear to be difficult to detect with adequate power (Narayanan & Swaminathan; Rogers & Swaminathan; Uttaro & Millsap, 1994).

A further influence on the power of the MH procedure in the unidirectional case is the group difference in prior distributions on W (Narayanan & Swaminathan, 1994; Uttaro & Millsap, 1994). Power is somewhat higher when no group differences exist in the prior distributions. As the prior distributions separate in their means, power decreases to some extent. We would expect this effect to dissipate in longer tests, where the reliability of Z is high and the matching afforded by Z is more accurate.

In the bidirectional case, the MH procedure appears to have low power even with relatively large samples (Narayanan & Swaminathan, 1996; Uttaro & Millsap, 1994). Narayanan and Swaminathan found that even with a sample of 1000 in the reference group and 500 in the focal group, the MH procedure showed an average power of less than 50% across all study conditions. Power was especially low when the studied item was of medium difficulty, with the IRFs crossing in the middle range of W. The MH procedure is not designed to detect this form of bias, and so large sample sizes will not bring the power to an acceptable level in such cases.

4. A number of studies have examined the impact of bias in the items used to create Z apart from the studied item (Donoghue et al., 1993; Narayanan & Swaminathan, 1994, 1996; Rogers & Swaminathan, 1993). This influence is usually modeled in terms of the proportion of the items in Z that are biased, rather than a simple count of the number of such items, which might be confounded with test length. Holland and Thayer (1988) suggested that the MH procedure should be done in two stages to filter out biased items from the matching variable Z. In the first stage, the usual MH procedure is performed on all items using Z as the total score across all items. In the second stage, items flagged as biased in the first stage are removed from the calculation of Z, except where one such item is the studied item in the second stage. The MH procedure is then repeated using the purified Z, possibly redefining Z depending on which item is studied. Items detected as biased at this second stage are declared biased. This two-stage procedure has been adopted in some simulation studies that have examined the effects of biased items in Z (Narayanan & Swaminathan, 1994, 1996; Rogers & Swaminathan).

Perhaps as a consequence, these studies have not found that the proportion of biased items in Z has a substantial effect on either the Type I error rates or the power of the MH procedure. Donoghue et al. did not use the two-stage procedure, however, yet did not find meaningful effects for the number of biased items in Z. Unlike other studies in this area, Donoghue et al. manipulated the actual number of biased items (0, 1, 2, or 4 items), along with the test length (5, 10, 20, or 40 items). Other studies have confined levels of the proportion of biased items to a maximum of 20%. Studies examining higher proportions of biased items do not appear to have been done. Intuitively, it can be expected that the power of the MH procedure would deteriorate when the proportion of biased items is high. The lack of simulation evidence on this point is probably based on the belief that in practice, the proportion of biased items should be relatively small.

5. A practical issue in the application of the MH procedure is the definition of the score groups to be used in matching examinees on Z. In theory, if p items are used to define the total score Z, there are $p + 1$ possible scores on Z. Perfect scores must be dropped from consideration, leaving $p - 1$ potential score groups. The use of $M = p - 1$ score groups will result in the most fine-grained analysis, but small samples may mean that the $2 \times 2 \times (p - 1)$ contingency table is sparse, with many zero frequencies. To reduce this sparsity, score groups may be combined prior to the MH analysis. If score groups are to be combined, the question of how this combination should best be done becomes important.

Several studies have examined the effects of score group combination on the results of the MH procedure in bias applications (Donoghue & Allen, 1993; Raju, Bode, & Larsen, 1989; Wright, 1986). Among these, Donoghue and Allen's application is the only one in simulated data for which the true biases were known. This study compared 11 different score group combination methods (thick matching), including one method that simply used the full Z without any combination of score groups and one in which all examinees were combined, eliminating all matching. The study varied other features of the data besides the thickness of the matching: test length, sample size, size of bias, and the values of the 3PL discrimination and location parameters. Bias was evaluated using both the MH chi-square and the estimated odds-ratio. The results showed that some forms of thick matching could improve the performance of the MH procedure, depending on the data conditions and whether the chi-square or odds-ratio estimator was used. With large samples and long tests (e.g., 40 items), the use of the original total score without score group combination was best. Thick matching was more useful with short tests. When the MH chi-square was the measure of interest, score group combination to either yield approximately equal focal group percentages for each score group, or equal total group percentages for each table, were effective. When the odds-ratio estimator was of interest, combination to achieve equal score intervals on Z, or to eliminate zero frequencies at extreme score levels, were effective. In both cases, effectiveness was gauged by fewer false negative and fewer false-positive flags for bias.

The general conclusion is that the thickness of the matching on Z can have a substantial impact on the performance of the MH chi-square and odds-ratio estimator. The impact depends on the sample size, test length, and the characteristics of the items under study. Thick matching is more beneficial for short tests, yet short tests imply fewer score groups on Z and consequently less need for a thick matching from the perspective of sparsity.

6. The MH method makes no explicit assumptions about the dimensionality of the latent variables that underlie $\mathbf{X}$. The use of the total score Z as a matching variable in the MH procedure is consistent with unidimensionality, and the connection drawn between the MH procedure and the Rasch model is also based on unidimensionality. What happens to the performance of the MH statistic in the multidimensional case? The fact that the MH procedure makes no dimensionality assumptions does not mean that the procedure is unaffected by the number of latent variables underlying $\mathbf{X}$.

The impact of multidimensionality on the performance of the MH has been studied (Ackerman & Evans, 1994). Ackerman and Evans simulated item scores using a two-dimensional compensatory IRT model that is a simple generalization of the 2PL model. Items were specified as measuring primarily the first dimension, the second dimension, or both dimensions to a similar extent. Reference and focal groups were simulated to differ in means on the two latent dimensions, with the reference group higher on one dimension and the focal group higher on the other dimension. The item response functions were invariant over groups (i.e., no measurement bias). When the matching variable was defined as the usual total score across the entire 30-item test, the MH procedure tended to flag items as biased that primarily measured a single dimension. The direction of the bias depended on the dimension involved and on which group was favored on the dimension. The net effect was that subsets of items demonstrated bias in different directions, with one set favoring the reference group and another set favoring the focal group. The interpretation to be placed on this result would depend on which of the two latent variables is regarded as the target latent variable of interest. One could also regard both latent variables as target latent variables, with the test being intentionally multidimensional. In all cases, however, the results show that some items are falsely flagged as biased by the MH procedure when the total score is used as the matching variable. Ackerman and Evans also found that if the matching variable is defined differently, using either a unidimensional conditioning score or a conditioning score created by considering the joint distribution of the two latent variables, the MH procedure performed as expected by theory. When the matching variable Z was defined by items measuring mostly dimension one, items measuring dimension two were flagged as biased. If the matching variable Z is defined by the joint distribution of the latent variables, no items were flagged as biased.

One conclusion clearly suggested by the multidimensional perspective is that spurious findings of bias using the MH procedure are expected in the multidimensional case, depending on the relative standing of the groups on the latent variables and on the definition of the matching variable. In contrast, the conditions that would lead to false-negative findings are less clear. One scenario leading to false negatives would use a matching variable Z consisting of items that primarily measure the nuisance latent dimension. If Z is the total test score, this scenario implies a pervasive bias across the entire item set or at least a substantial portion of the item set. Assuming a pervasive bias of this sort is unrealistic, are there more realistic conditions that would lead to false negatives?

The Standardization Method

The standardization method (Dorans & Holland, 1993; Dorans & Kulick, 1983, 1986) provides both an effect size measure and a test statistic for evaluating bias in dichotomous items. The method is based on the idea that under OCI, the conditional expected value of the item score given the matching variable Z should be identical across the reference and focal groups, at all values of Z. In other words, it should be true that

$$D_j(Z) = E_f(X_j \mid Z) - E_r(X_j \mid Z) \tag{8.11}$$

for all values of Z, given OCI for X_j in relation to Z. In fact, with X_j being dichotomous in scale, Equation 8.11 is equivalent to OCI. We expect that in sample data, the empirical item-total score regressions may not be identical across groups, even when Equation 8.11 holds. The standardization method creates an index to measure the group difference in the empirical regressions. The index is a weighted average of the sample differences in the regressions, averaged over the possible values of Z and weighted by the focal group sample sizes within each score group. The weighting by the focal group sample size is designed to weight most strongly the differences in regions on Z where most focal group members are found. The resulting index is

$$STNDP\text{-}DIF = \sum_{m=0}^{M} \frac{F_{m1}D_j(m)}{N_1},$$ (8.12)

where the matching variable Z has $M + 1$ values $(0, 1, \ldots, M)$, and F_{m1} is the sample frequency of the focal group at $Z = m$, and $N_1 = \sum_{m=1}^{M} F_{m1}$. Positive values of *STNDP-DIF* indicate that the item favors the focal group, and negative values suggest the reverse. The index ranges between −1 and +1. Dorans and Holland (1993) suggest that values of *STNDP-DIF* between −.05 and +.05 indicate negligible bias. Values between −.10 and −.05, or between .05 and .10, indicate that the item should be studied to examine possible bias. Values less than −.10 or greater than .10 indicate possibly substantial bias. Dorans, Schmitt, and Bleistein (1988) report that these values work well in practice.

Dorans and Holland (1993) presented an estimator of the standard error of *STNDP-DIF*. The estimator is

$$\sigma_{jST} = \left(\frac{P_{jf}(1 - P_{jf})}{N_1} + \sigma_{pj}^2 \right)^{1/2},$$ (8.13)

where

$$\sigma_{pj}^2 = \sum_{m=1}^{M} \frac{F_{m1}^2 P_{jr}(1 - P_{jr})}{F_{m2}N_1^2}.$$ (8.14)

In theory, the standard error in Equation 8.13 could be used to develop hypothesis testing procedures for *STNDP-DIF* in Equation 8.11. The estimate of *STNDP-DIF* would be divided by its standard error estimate, and the ratio would be regarded as a standard normal score in large samples. Alternatively, the standard error estimate could be used to set a confidence interval around the estimate of *STNDP-DIF*. In practice, these inferential procedures are rarely used. The standardization method as used in practice is largely descriptive, with the point estimate of *STNDP-DIF* being combined with graphical displays of $D_j(m)$ or group-specific plots of $E_f(X_j|Z)$ and $E_r(X_j|Z)$.

The *STNDP-DIF* index is closely related to the MH odds-ratio estimator as a measure of bias. *STNDP-DIF* is a weighted average of the differences between the regression functions in the two groups, the regressions being the studied item score regressed on the value of the matching variable. The regression differences are averaged across values of the matching variable. The MH odds-ratio estimator is a weighted average of the conditional odds-ratios for the two groups, averaged over values of the matching variable. Hence, the relationship between the two indices turns on the relation between the conditional odds-ratio and the item regressions. Dorans and Holland (1993) note that under conditions representing OCI, it is true that $D_j(m) = 0$ for $m = 0, 1, \ldots, M$ and also that $\alpha_m = 1$ for $m = 0, 1, \ldots, M$, where α_m is the conditional odds-ratio

$$\frac{P_m(X_j = 1 \mid k = 2) / P_m(X_j = 0 \mid k = 2)}{P_m(X_j = 1 \mid k = 1) / P_m(X_j = 0 \mid k = 1)}. \tag{8.15}$$

Given that $E_k(X_j \mid Z) = P_m(X_j = 1 \mid k)$ for $Z = m$ in this dichotomous case, it is clear that $D_j(m) = 0$ in Equation 8.10 if and only if $P_m(X_j = 1 \mid k = 1) = P_m(X_j = 1 \mid k = 2)$, leading to $\alpha_m = 1$. Hence, when OCI holds, the MH odds-ratio estimator and *STNDP-DIF* should yield equivalent answers. When invariance fails, however, the two indices measure the size of the bias in different ways due to the contrast between the "difference" metric in *STNDP-DIF* in comparison to the ratio metric in MH. The weighting of the contributions of each score group to the overall index value also differs for the two indices. Dorans and Holland argue, however, that the values of *STNDP-DIF* and the MH odds-ratio estimators are usually highly correlated across items, with correlations well above .90 in most cases. This strong relationship between the two indices may explain why the standardization index is not more widely used in dichotomous item applications.

The *STNDP-DIF* index has been studied less intensively than the MH procedure, but the available findings indicate that the index performs similarly to the MH odds-ratio estimator, with strengths and weaknesses that parallel the odds-ratio estimator. Donoghue et al. (1993) examined both the *STNDP-DIF* index and its standard error in Equation 8.13 in simulated data. They found that like the MH odds-ratio estimator, *STNDP-DIF* can yield spurious findings of bias when the studied item is excluded from the matching variable. Also, the effects on *STNDP-DIF* of the difficulty of the studied item are similar to those found for the MH procedure: it is harder to detect bias in highly difficult items. Of the six factors studied by Donoghue et al., those that were statistically significant influences on MH were also significant influences on the performance of *STNDP-DIF*. With regard to the standard error estimator in Equation 8.13, Donoghue et al. found the estimator to have a positive bias of about 8% on average across the conditions studied. This bias is modest in size, but its direction would tend to reduce the power of any formal hypothesis test that uses the estimator. Given that such tests are infrequently used in standardization applications, the accuracy of the standard error estimator is not especially important in practical terms.

Although some aspects of the performance of the *STNDP-DIF* have not been studied via simulations, theory suggests that *STNDP-DIF* will be vulnerable to some of the same problems faced by the MH procedure. For example, items that exhibit bidirectional bias may not be detected with adequate power because the *STNDP-DIF* index in Equation 8.12 permits some cancellation. Multidimensionality in the latent space underlying the item pool should influence *STNDP-DIF* in a manner that parallels the behavior of the MH odds-ratio estimator under multidimensionality.

Logistic Regression

An observed score method that is more general than the MH procedure is the use of logistic regression (Swaminathan & Rogers, 1990). Logistic regression is a widely used method for modeling the probability of a binary outcome as a logistic function of one or more predictor variables (for general references, see Agresti, 2002; Christensen, 1997; Hosmer & Lemeshow, 2000). Predictor variables may be continuous or discrete in scale and, if discrete, may be ordered or purely categorical. In the item bias context, the predictors of interest are typically (a) the group membership variable **V**, (b) the matching variable Z, usually defined as the total score across items, and (c) an interaction term formed as the product of (a) and (b). When the group membership V assumes only two values corresponding to two populations of interest, only a single-group membership indicator is needed. In multiple-group studies with three or more groups, multiple-group membership indicators are needed. The coding for the indicators is discussed below. The matching variable Z could be defined as any variable or set of variables that are appropriate substitutes for the target latent variable W_t. In practice, Z is usually the total score across items, including the studied item. Instead of using the total score, a total score based on a subset of items that passed a preliminary screen for bias may be used (again including the studied item). Most applications use a single matching variable, but there is no theoretical barrier to using multiple matching variables. Finally, the interaction predictor may also include more than one variable, depending on the status of the group membership indicators and the matching variables.

To describe the logistic regression model, let $P(X_j = 1 | Z, V)$ be the conditional probability of passing the jth item given the score on the matching variable Z and the group membership indicator V. Under the logistic regression model, this conditional probability is

$$P(X_j = 1 \mid Z, V) = \frac{\exp[B_0 + B_1 Z + B_2 V + B_3(ZV)]}{1 + \exp[B_0 + B_1 Z + B_2 V + B_3(ZV)]}, \qquad (8.16)$$

where
B_0 is an intercept parameter
B_1 is the regression coefficient for the matching variable
B_2 is the regression coefficient for the group membership indicator
B_3 is the regression coefficient for the interaction

Equation 8.16 implies that the logit for the conditional probability of passing the jth item is

$$\ln\left[\frac{P(X_j = 1 \mid Z, V)}{1 - P(X_j = 1 \mid Z, V)}\right] = B_0 + B_1 Z + B_2 V + B_3(ZV). \qquad (8.17)$$

Equation 8.17 shows that under the model, the log odds of passing the item is a linear function of the matching variable, the group membership indicator, and their interaction. OCI for the jth item implies that the logit depends only on Z or that $B_2 = B_3 = 0$. This hypothesis is testable, using either a likelihood-ratio test or a Wald test involving the parameter estimates and their standard errors. Parameters in the model can be estimated using maximum likelihood. Estimation theory for the logistic regression model is well known and will not be discussed here. For extensive descriptions of the theory, see Agresti (2002), Christensen (1997), or Hosmer and Lemeshow (2000).

The likelihood-ratio approach to evaluating OCI proceeds by fitting three models. The first model uses only the matching variable Z as a predictor, excluding both the group membership indicator and the interaction term. This highly constrained model represents the OCI hypothesis: the probability of passing the item depends only on Z. The second and third models each represent violations of OCI. Model Two adds the group membership indicator to Model One. Under this model, different groups have systematically different probabilities of passing the item, with the difference being independent of Z. This model represents the counterpart of unidirectional bias in the latent variable definition of bias. Model Three adds the interaction between the matching variable and group membership to Model Two. Model Three permits group differences in the relationship of Z to the probability of passing the item, with the group difference in passing permitted to vary depending on the value of Z. This latter feature permits bias that is bidirectional. Model Three is the full model in Equation 8.16. Model Two is obtained from Model Three by setting $B_3 = 0$, and Model One is in turn obtained from Model Two by setting $B_2 = 0$.

The full Model Three is saturated and cannot be directly tested using a likelihood-ratio test, but it is possible to test either Model One or Model Two against Model Three using a likelihood-ratio test. The sample likelihood under Model Three for the jth item, using previously defined notation, is

$$L_3 = \prod_{m=1}^{M} \prod_{k=1}^{K} [P(X_j = 1 \mid Z, V)]^{f_{1jmk}} [1 - P(X_j = 1 \mid Z, V)]^{F_{mk} - f_{1jmk}}, \quad (8.18)$$

with the definition of $P(X_j = 1 \mid Z, V)$ given in Equation 8.16. Likelihood expressions for Models One and Two are created as special cases of the likelihood in Equation 8.18. In bias applications, the typical procedure is to evaluate Model One in comparison to Model Three using the log-likelihood-ratio

$$G_1^2 = -2\ln\left(\frac{L_1}{L_3}\right) = 2\ln(L_3) - 2\ln(L_1), \quad (8.19)$$

where G_1^2 is the likelihood-ratio chi-square statistic for testing Model One against the saturated Model Three. Given that two parameters were eliminated in creating Model One from Model Three, the statistic in Equation 8.19 will have $df = 2$. In large samples, G_1^2 is distributed as a central chi-square variate under the null hypothesis that $B_2 = B_3 = 0$ in Equation 8.16. This test statistic evaluates whether OCI is violated, either through unidirectional or bidirectional bias (Swaminathan & Rogers, 1990).

Some researchers recommend that the $df = 2$ test just described should be split into two $df = 1$ tests, each test focusing on a particular form of bias (Camilli & Shepard, 1994; Zumbo, 1999). Zumbo views the logistic regression as a hierarchical regression consisting of three steps: (1) matching variable predictor is entered, (2) group membership indicator is added next, and (3) the interaction term is added last. The $df = 2$ test described above examines the model at (3) in comparison to (1). This test combines two $df = 1$ tests that are separable. The first test would compare the model at step (2) to the model at step (1). This test examines whether unidirectional violations of OCI are present. Rejection of the null hypothesis suggests that unidirectional violations are present. The second test would compare the model at step (3) to the model at step (2). This comparison evaluates whether bidirectional violations of OCI are present, given a model that already permits unidirectional violations. Standard practice would suggest that the comparison between the models in steps (2) and (3) should be conducted first, given that step (3) includes the interaction. If the interaction term is needed, the second test for the "main effect" of the grouping variable is optional. If the interaction term is not needed, the next step compares the step (2) and step (1) models.

The logistic regression approach offers several options for creating effect size estimates, depending on whether the interaction term is needed. If no interaction is present but the grouping variable is needed, the regression coefficient B_2 for the grouping variable can be interpreted as the adjusted log odds-ratio for passing the item under study. The odds-ratio is "adjusted" for group differences in the distribution of the matching variable Z. This estimate for B_2 should be close to the estimate of the MH log odds-ratio estimator. Large-sample standard errors for the estimate are available and can be used to construct confidence intervals for B_2 (Agresti, 2002).

When the full Model Three is needed, the coefficient estimate B_2 no longer has a simple interpretation as the log odds-ratio. A different approach to documenting the bias effect size in this case uses one of several R^2 measures (Arminger, 1995; Christensen, 1997; Zumbo, 1999). The general intent of such measures is to assess the incremental variance explained by the grouping and interaction variables in relation to a model that includes the matching variables only. A difficulty with these measures, however, is that the cutpoints for distinguishing bias that is meaningful in size are not yet clear. In the general context, Agresti (2002) notes that R^2 measures in logistic regression are not yet as useful as their counterparts in linear regression.

Although the logistic regression procedure has not been as extensively studied as the MH procedure, simulation studies have been conducted of its performance across variations in factors thought to influence this performance (Narayanan & Swaminathan, 1996; Rogers & Swaminathan, 1993; Swaminathan & Rogers, 1990). Theoretical work on the properties of methods for testing OCI in relation to measurement bias also has implications for the logistic regression procedure. Two immediate conclusions follow from simulations that have compared the logistic regression procedure to the MH method:

1. The logistic regression method performs as well as the MH procedure when the bias in the studied item is unidirectional (Rogers & Swaminathan, 1993; Swaminathan & Rogers, 1990). When no interaction term is needed in the logistic regression model because the group difference in the conditional probability of passing the item given the total score always has the same sign across score groups, it was noted earlier that the MH and logistic regression methods should yield similar results. This prediction is supported

by the available simulation evidence. In this unidirectional case, the logistic regression procedure has fairly good power even with only 250 examinees per group (Rogers & Swaminathan).

2. When the bias is bidirectional, the logistic regression method has greater power than the MH method (Narayanan & Swaminathan, 1996; Rogers & Swaminathan, 1993; Swaminathan & Rogers, 1990). This finding is understandable given that the logistic regression equation includes an interaction term between the examinee group and the score group. Rogers and Swaminathan found that the logistic regression method had around 20% more power than the MH method, depending on the size of the bias. Narayanan and Swaminathan reported similar results.

The available methodological research on the logistic regression method leaves some unanswered questions about the performance of the method. These questions are potentially answerable, either via theory or using simulation approaches. First, how does the performance on the logistic regression method vary with test length? The available studies have varied test length but have used lengths that are at least 40 items. What happens in shorter tests? Research on the MH has shown the method to be weak in short tests due to the inaccuracy in the matching variable as a proxy for the target latent variable. We can predict similar inaccuracy in the logistic regression method in short tests, but the degree of inaccuracy could be studied in simulations. Second, what is the impact of multidimensionality in the target latent variable on the performance of the logistic regression procedure? This question has several distinct parts. One part concerns the effect of ignoring multidimensionality when the matching variable Z is univariate. This situation has been studied with respect to the MH procedure, as noted earlier. We might expect similar distortions in the performance of the logistic regression procedure. A second part to the multidimensionality problem concerns the use of multiple matching variables Z for purposes of capturing a multidimensional target latent variable. In principle, there is no barrier to using multiple matching variables in logistic regression, but this possibility has not received much attention in applications.

A further question of interest for the logistic regression procedure concerns the impact of biased items in the matching variable Z on the performance of the method. As noted earlier, this problem is handled in the MH procedure by attempting to "purify" the matching total score using preliminary item screening. The purification process is fairly routine in applications of the MH procedure, but preliminary screens are not often used in logistic regression applications, for reasons that are unclear. Narayanan and Swaminathan (1996) found that variations in the percentage of biased items in the matching criterion had a significant effect on the performance of logistic regression. Power was reduced and the Type I error rate became larger as the percentage of biased items increased. The same factor did not influence the performance of the MH, presumably because iterative purification was included as part of the MH method. The use of preliminary screening as part of the logistic regression procedure should improve the power of the method.

Log-Linear Models

Given the use of logistic regression in detecting bias, it is not surprising that log-linear modeling methods have also been used in this application. As reviewed earlier, the use of the total score as a matching variable leads to a multiway contingency table for the response frequencies to each item, for each group under study. Log-linear models provide a natural basis for studying such contingency tables. In addition, a close connection exists between the log-linear model for the multiway contingency table and the Rasch model in the dichotomous case (Cressie & Holland, 1983; Duncan, 1984; Kelderman, 1984; Tjur, 1982). One can show that the item parameters of the Rasch model can be expressed as a function of the parameters in a restricted log-linear model for the contingency table. From this standpoint, the log-linear approach to bias detection can be viewed as an observed-score method, but one that should yield results similar to those found using the Rasch model when the Rasch model is appropriate.

To describe the log-linear approach in the dichotomous item case, we first expand the three-way contingency table for the jth item (total score × group × item score) to include all p test items under study: total score × group × item 1 × item 2 × ... × item p. This larger multiway contingency table permits one to uniquely locate any specific response sequence across the p items. The table is necessarily incomplete, however, because some response sequences are inconsistent with some values for the total score. If $p = 4$, the sequence $(0,1,0,1)$ corresponds to a total score $Z = 2$ but is inconsistent with other values of Z. Hence, the contingency table will contain structural zero cells (Agresti, 2002; Bishop, Fienberg, & Holland, 1975; Christensen, 1997). Incomplete contingency tables of this sort are represented by quasi-log-linear models (Bishop et al.). Kelderman (1984, 1989) provided a complete treatment of such models in item data for bias detection applications.

The description of the log-linear model will require some alterations in the notation used earlier. We will assume that two examinee populations are to be compared ($k = 1, 2$). Let each response sequence across the p items $(X_1, X_2, ..., X_p)$ be indexed by the subscript s, with $s = 1, 2, ..., 2^p$. Let f_{smk} be the frequency of examinees with the mth total score ($m = 0, 1, ..., p$) from the kth group who gave the sth response sequence. Then $F_{mk} = \sum_s f_{smk}$

is the total number of examinees from the kth group who have a total score equal to m, and $F_m = F_{m1} + F_{m2}$, as before. Note that $f_{smk} = 0$ for many values of m because a given response sequence corresponds to a unique total score. In what follows, we adopt notational conventions that parallel Kelderman (1984) and rely heavily on that source for development of the models of interest.

The saturated log-linear model expresses the log of the expected value of f_{smk} as a linear function of a set of unknown parameters

$$\ln E(f_{smk}) = \mu + \mu_1(k) + \mu_2(m) + \mu_3(X_1) + \cdots + \mu_{p+2}(X_p)$$
$$+ \mu_{12}(km) + \mu_{13}(kX_1) + \cdots + \mu_{p+1,p+2}(X_{p-1}X_p)$$
$$+ \mu_{123}(kmX_1) + \cdots + \mu_{123\ldots p+2}(kmX_1\ldots X_p), \tag{8.20}$$

where X_j represents the jth item, $j = 1,\ldots,p$. Each term in Equation 8.20 is either a constant, a main effect parameter, or an interaction parameter. The saturated model includes all possible interactions, but our interest will be in restricted versions of this model that omit most of the interaction terms. The parameters in the saturated model are not identified without further constraints. We will delay the discussion of the constraints until we have defined the restricted models of interest below.

By eliminating all of the interaction terms that involve the item scores, we create a model that represents the conditional Rasch model, conditioned on a given total score. This model is

$$\ln E(f_{smk}) = \mu + \mu_1(k) + \mu_2(m) + \mu_{12}(mk) + \mu_3(X_1) + \cdots + \mu_{p+2}(X_p). \tag{8.21}$$

This restricted model permits an interaction term for total score × group, corresponding to group differences in total score distributions. The omission of all other interaction terms means that item performance is unrelated to group membership or to performance on other items, given the total score. This model represents OCI for all items jointly. Weaker models that represent different violations of OCI will be intermediate in restrictions between the saturated model in Equation 8.20 and the Rasch model in Equation 8.21. Different types of violations are created depending on which parameters are added to the model in Equation 8.21. A model that includes one or more of these additional parameters can be evaluated for fit in comparison to the more restrictive Rasch model in Equation 8.21. If the fit of the weaker model is better, we conclude that OCI is violated as represented by the weaker model. A series of such models can be formulated to represent possible biases in different sets of items or different forms of bias.

To illustrate these possibilities, we begin with a model that permits uni-directional bias in the first item. The item difficulty is allowed to vary over examinee groups by including an interaction term between group membership and the item score: $\mu_{23}(kX_1)$. The interaction term is included in the Rasch model in Equation 8.21 to create a single-item unidirectional bias model

$$\ln E(f_{smk}) = Rasch + \mu_{23}(kX_1), \tag{8.22}$$

where *Rasch* represents all parameters needed for the model in Equation 8.21. The comparison of fit between this single-item unidirectional bias model and the Rasch model reveals whether the additional interaction term is needed. If not, there is no evidence for unidirectional bias in the first item. The model in Equation 8.22 limits the added term to a single item. Simultaneous tests of unidirectional bias in multiple items are achieved by expanding the model in Equation 8.22 to include interaction terms between group membership and other item scores. Comparisons of fit between this expanded model and the Rasch model provide evidence on whether the selected block of items shows unidirectional bias. A posi-tive result in this case would probably lead to follow-up tests on items within the block.

The investigator may hypothesize that a biasing influence exists in com-mon between a pair of items. Kelderman (1989) uses the example of an added nuisance latent variable that is shared between the items and that differs across examinee groups. This hypothesis may be tested by includ-ing interaction terms between the pair of items and a three-way interac-tion between the pair and group membership. For example, suppose that the pair of items includes the first and second items. The model of interest then is

$$\ln E(f_{smk}) = Rasch + \mu_{34}(X_1, X_2) + \mu_{234}(kX_1X_2). \tag{8.23}$$

The first term $\mu_{34}(X_1, X_2)$ introduces a dependency between the pair of items that violates the Rasch model. This dependency could be gener-ated by an added latent dimension common to the pair. The second term $\mu_{234}(kX_1X_2)$ permits the dependency to vary across groups. The joint impact of the added terms represents a shared unidirectional bias between the pair. The fit of this shared unidirectional bias model can be compared to the fit of the Rasch model to evaluate the significance of the added terms. This form of bias cannot be tested using methods that evaluate items sequentially, rather than jointly as in the log-linear approach. In theory, the model illustrated here could be expanded to consider item triplets or even larger clusters. All lower order interaction terms would be included in such models.

The above models represent different forms of unidirectional violations of OCI. Bidirectional violations could be represented by models that permit interactions with both group membership and the matching variable. The simplest example would focus on a single item and the possible bidirectional bias in that item. If the focus is the first item, the model of interest is

$$\ln E(f_{smk}) = Rasch + \mu_{13}(mX_1) + \mu_{123}(mkX_1). \tag{8.24}$$

The first term permits a dependence between the matching score level and the item score. This dependence violates the Rasch model by permitting the relative difficulty of the first item to vary depending on the matching score. The second term allows this dependence to vary over examinee groups, representing the potential for bidirectional violations of OCI. Comparisons between the fit of this single-item bidirectional model and the Rasch model will assess the significance of the violation. The model in Equation 8.24 can be expanded to include analogous terms for additional items, providing a joint test for bidirectional violations for the block of items. Kelderman (1989) also describes how such models may be combined with the inter-item interaction models discussed earlier.

Parameter estimation for any of the quasi-log-linear models will generally employ maximum likelihood methods. The details of these methods will not be reviewed here, as they can be found in texts on log-linear models or categorical data analysis (Agresti, 2002; Bishop et al., 1975; Christensen, 1997). Estimation requires iterative numerical methods, as the likelihood equations cannot be solved analytically. Kelderman and Steen's (1988) LOGIMO software program will perform estimation for all of the previously discussed models for bias detection applications. This program uses an iterative proportional fitting algorithm to estimate model parameters. Standard constraints must be imposed on the parameters before estimation is possible. In the Rasch model in Equation 8.21, for example, the constraints can be

$$\mu_a(+) = 0, \quad a = 1, 2, \ldots, p+2 \tag{8.25}$$

$$\mu_{12}(+k) = \mu_{12}(m+) = 0, \quad k = 1, 2 \quad m = 0, 1, \ldots, p, \tag{8.26}$$

where "+" indicates summation over the index replaced by "+." Kelderman (1990) notes that these constraints are not sufficient to fully identify the model and suggests that one item score main effect parameter be fixed to zero in addition to the above constraints. Given the full-information nature of the estimation method, estimation requires extensive storage. Kelderman reports that LOGIMO can handle up to 40 items without difficulty.

Fit evaluation for any of the models described earlier can be based on the likelihood-ratio chi-square statistic that is used widely in log-linear modeling (Agresti, 2002; Bishop et al., 1975; Christensen, 1997). This statistic can be used to either compare two nested restricted models or to compare a given model to the saturated model. Let L_s be the likelihood value for the saturated model, L_0 be the likelihood value for the most restricted model of interest (e.g., the Rasch model), and L_1 be the likelihood function for a less restricted model. Then the chi-square statistic for comparing the model corresponding to L_0 to that of is

$$G_{01}^2 = -2[\ln(L_0) - \ln(L_1)] \tag{8.27}$$

which under the null hypothesis that the model corresponding to L_1 fits is distributed as central chi-square in large samples. The degrees of freedom are calculated as the difference in the number of independent free parameters in the two models being compared. To evaluate the fit of any individual restricted model, the test statistic in Equation 8.27 is modified to compare this model to the saturated model

$$G_{1s}^2 = -2[\ln(L_1) - \ln(L_s)]. \tag{8.28}$$

The calculation of degrees of freedom here is complicated by the presence of structural zero frequency cells in the model. These cells are not included in the cell count needed to calculate the degrees of freedom. Furthermore, the parameter count must consider the zero cells also, given that fewer parameters are needed for the saturated model in this case. The number of structural zero cells will vary systematically with the number of items under discussion. Kelderman (1984) describes this relationship.

The log-linear modeling approach described here can be generalized in several ways. More than two examinee groups can be studied simultaneously for item bias using the log-linear model. The model can also be extended to the polytomous item case without great difficulty, as discussed below (Kelderman, 1997; Kelderman & Rijkes, 1994). A particularly interesting extension lies in the consideration of examinee groups defined by latent variables, rather than observed variables (Kelderman & Macready, 1990; see Samuelsen, 2008, for a general treatment of this topic). The examinee groups are defined as latent classes in this approach. The latent class model might be useful in situations in which the real basis for distinguishing examinee groups is not fully captured by the measured variables. For example, "culture" as a basis for defining examinee groups may be imperfectly measured and may be usefully conceived as a set of latent classes.

Unlike some of the other observed-score methods reviewed in this chapter, the general properties of the log-linear modeling approach to bias detection do not appear to have been extensively studied. For example, an obvious question concerns the performance of the method when the data do not meet the assumptions of the Rasch model, both in the biased and unbiased cases. Kelderman (1989) reports the results of a small simulation study of the performance of the method when the data are generated under a 2PL model. The departure from the Rasch assumptions did not significantly affect the performance of the method in these simulations. The simulations are too limited to support general conclusions, however. A more detailed study of the method is needed. Topics that should be examined include (a) the performance of the method at varying test lengths in the biased and unbiased cases, (b) the power of the method to detect unidirectional and bidirectional bias, (c) Type I error performance under different violations of Rasch assumptions, and (d) the impact of multidimensionality in the latent variable that underlies the items.

A further topic that needs attention within the log-linear approach concerns the proper measure of effect size for bias within the log-linear approach. The log-linear approach to detection relies heavily on significance tests in deciding whether bias is present. In real applications, one would want to supplement these tests with an estimate of the size of the bias, so that the practical significance of the bias can be judged. More work is needed on developing an appropriate effect size measure whose interpretation is clear.

Polytomous Item Methods

We turn now to observed-score methods for the detection of bias in polytomous measures. The polytomous case raises several problems for observed-score methods that were not serious in the dichotomous case. The first problem lies in the creation of the matching variable for the observed-score methods. The number of polytomous measures within the test under study may be small in some applications. In cognitive testing, several polytomous items may be included in a longer exam consisting largely of dichotomously scored items. If the total score used for matching purposes is confined to only the polytomous items, the number of items will be too small to have confidence in the matching. An alternative in this case would be to define the matching variable as the total score across both the dichotomous and polytomous items. It is assumed here that the same target latent variable underlies both types of items, an assumption that may be doubtful in some cases. Taking the assumption at face value, however, we still have a potential problem related to the varying item scale ranges for the dichotomous versus polytomous items. It is not clear whether the polytomous items should be rescaled prior to summation to render their ranges to be more similar to the dichotomous items. The scaling question can be avoided entirely by confining the matching variable to just the dichotomous items or some alternative external source of data. Exclusion of the polytomous items from the matching variable may lead to other difficulties, however, due to Theorem 3.3, which implies that exclusion of the studied item from the matching variable may lead to spurious conclusions of bias (Meredith & Millsap, 1992).

The second problem that runs through all of the methods for polytomous measures is the lack of clearly interpretable bias effect size measures. The dichotomous case permitted some progress on this question using odds-ratio formulations, especially for the case of unidirectional bias. No unique generalization of this idea to the polytomous case seems possible. Instead, there are a variety of potential effect size measures in this case. Furthermore, heuristic guidelines for interpreting these measures in terms of practical significance have not yet appeared (Zwick, Thayer, & Mazzeo, 1997). As experience with these measures grows, consensus on the thresholds for meaningful degrees of bias should emerge.

Generalizations of the Mantel–Haenszel

Two extensions of the MH procedure for the polytomous case have been studied: the Mantel (1963) procedure and the generalized Mantel–Haenszel (GMH; Mantel & Haenszel, 1959; Somes, 1986) procedure. Both procedures assume that two examinee groups are to be compared and that the data are stratified according to some matching variable Z as in the dichotomous case. The matching variable will ordinarily be a total score across all items, but other definitions of the matching variable are possible.

To describe each of these procedures, we introduce a slight generalization of the previous notation to accommodate the polytomous response scale. For simplicity, we will assume that all studied items have C ordered response categories, numbered $(0, 1, 2, \ldots, C-1)$. As before, let F_{mk}, $m = 1, \ldots, M$, $k = 1, 2$, be the number of examinees who belong to the mth score group on the matching variable and are in the kth examinee group. Note that the number of score groups M is determined by the number of items that are included in the matching variable. Then $F_m = F_{m1} + F_{m2}$ is the total number of examinees in the mth score group. Let f_{cjmk} be the number of examinees from the mth score group and kth examinee group who score in response category c on the jth item, $c = 0, 1, \ldots, C - 1, j = 1, \ldots, p$. Then $F_{cjm} = f_{cjm1} + f_{cjm2}$ is the total number of examinees from the mth score group who scored in response category c on the jth item.

The Mantel (1963) test assumes that the C response categories on the studied item are ordered and that numbers can be assigned to the response categories to reflect this ordering. Let those numbers be indexed by $c = 0, 1, \ldots, C - 1$. The Mantel test compares the conditional sum of item scores in the focal group to the sum of item scores that would be expected under the null hypothesis of no conditional association between item score and examinee group membership. To illustrate this test, let $S_{jm1} = \sum_{c=0}^{C-1} cf_{cjm1}$ be the sum of item scores for the jth item in the mth score group within the focal group. We define the expected value of this sum under the null hypothesis of no conditional association as

$$E(S_{jm1}) = \frac{F_{m1}}{F_m} \sum_{c=0}^{C-1} cF_{cjm}. \tag{8.29}$$

Another way of expressing this expected value is as

$$E(S_{jm1}) = F_{m1} \left[\frac{\sum_{c=0}^{C-1} cF_{cjm}}{F_m} \right] = F_{m1}\bar{X}_{jm}, \tag{8.30}$$

where $\bar{X}_{jm}$ is the average item score in the mth score group for the jth item. In this way, $E(S_{jm1})$ can be viewed as the sum we expect to see if everyone in the focal group scored at the grand mean within the mth score group. The Mantel statistic is then

$$\chi^2_{Mj} = \frac{\left[\sum_m S_{jm1} - \sum_m E(S_{jm1}) \right]^2}{\sum_m \text{Var}(S_{jm1})}, \tag{8.31}$$

where

$$\text{Var}(S_{jm1}) = \frac{F_{m1}F_{m2}}{F_m^2(F_m - 1)} \left[\left(F_m \sum_{c=0}^{C-1} c^2 F_{cjm} \right) - \left(\sum_{c=0}^{C-1} cF_{cjm} \right)^2 \right]. \tag{8.32}$$

Under the null hypothesis of no conditional association between item score and group membership, the test statistic in Equation 8.31 has a central chi-square distribution with $df = 1$ in large samples.

The numerator of the test statistic in Equation 8.31 accumulates the differences $[S_{jm1} - E(S_{jm1})]$ across levels of the matching variable. If these differences do not all have the same sign, some cancellation of values will occur and the resulting numerator in Equation 8.31 may be small even if the absolute differences at each score group are large. Like the MH procedure, the Mantel test procedure assumes that violations of OCI are unidirectional, eliminating the cancellation problem.

While the Mantel test focuses on group differences in conditional means on the studied item, the GMH test provides a test for group differences in the entire conditional distribution of scores on the studied item. The GMH procedure does not require that the item response categories be ordered. The procedure could be used with purely categorical response scales, but it is still applicable to the ordered-categorical case.

To calculate the GMH statistic, define $\mathbf{A}_{jm2}$ as the $(C - 1) \times 1$ vector of conditional reference group response frequencies

$$\mathbf{A}'_{jm2} = [f_{0jm2}, f_{1jm2}, \ldots, f_{(C-2)jm2}]. \tag{8.33}$$

Let $\mathbf{A}_{jm}$ be the $(C - 1) \times 1$ vector

$$\mathbf{A}'_{jm} = [F_{0jm}, F_{1jm}, \ldots, F_{(C-2)jm}], \tag{8.34}$$

and let $\mathbf{D}_{Ajm}$ be a $(C - 1) \times (C - 1)$ diagonal matrix whose diagonal elements are the elements of $\mathbf{A}_{jm}$. Then if

$$E(\mathbf{A}_{jm2}) = \frac{F_{m2}}{F_m} \mathbf{A}_{jm}, \tag{8.35}$$

$$\mathbf{S}_{jm1} = \frac{F_{m1}F_{m2}}{F_m^2(F_m - 1)} [F_m \mathbf{D}_{Ajm} - \mathbf{A}_{jm}\mathbf{A}'_{jm}], \tag{8.36}$$

the GMH test statistic is the quadratic form

$$\chi^2_{\text{GMHj}} = \left[\sum_{m=1}^{M} \mathbf{A}_{jm2} - \sum_{m=1}^{M} E(\mathbf{A}_{jm2}) \right]' \left[\sum_{m=1}^{M} \mathbf{S}_{jm2} \right]^{-1} \left[\sum_{m=1}^{M} \mathbf{A}_{jm2} - \sum_{m=1}^{M} E(\mathbf{A}_{jm2}) \right]. \tag{8.37}$$

Under the null hypothesis of OCI, this test statistic is distributed in large samples as central chi-square with $df = C - 1$. As in the MH and Mantel test statistics, the GMH test statistic accumulates the differences $[\mathbf{A}_{jm2} - E(\mathbf{A}_{jm2})]$ across levels of the matching variable, permitting cancellation to occur if the differences have opposite signs. The GMH test statistic could be small even though bidirectional bias is present.

One contrast between the Mantel and GMH procedures that may be important concerns their treatment of group differences in relative frequencies across response categories. The Mantel test is sensitive to group differences in conditional means on the studied item. It is possible, however, that the pattern of response frequencies will differ between groups even though the means do not differ. The same conditional mean could be produced by two different response patterns. The GMH procedure is sensitive to group differences in response patterns even if the conditional means are identical between groups. Zwick, Donoghue, and Grima (1993) illustrated both of these phenomena using simulations. The choice between the GMH and Mantel procedures in practice should consider whether the conditional mean difference is of primary interest or whether more general differences are likely.

Research on the properties of the Mantel and GMH procedures in bias applications is sparse relative to the volume of such research for the dichotomous MH procedure. The available evidence does suggest several conclusions, however. Most of these are consistent with results found in the dichotomous case. First, the studied item should be included in the total score used as the matching variable (Zwick et al., 1993). Exclusion of the studied item can lead to Type I error inflation in the case of an unbiased studied item. Second, if the items used in the matching variable do not fit a Rasch-family model and the target latent variable distributions differ across groups, Type I error rate inflation is likely unless the number of items in the matching variable is sufficiently large (Zwick et al., 1997). With regard to test length, Zwick et al. found that problems arose with a 20-item matching test and the problems largely disappeared with a 50-item test. Intermediate values do not appear to have been studied. Another open question concerns the impact of different violations of the Rasch-family assumptions on the error rate. The situation is more complex than in the dichotomous case because of the greater complexity of the item response functions for polytomous items. Ideally, we would want to know which violations of the Rasch assumptions are most serious in their consequences for the error rate problem. Finally, neither the Mantel nor the GMH procedures are especially powerful when bidirectional bias in present (Zwick et al.). This finding is expected given the nature of the test statistics in each case.

Extensions of Logistic Regression

In the polytomous case, several different extensions of logistic regression analysis are possible, depending on whether the categories of the studied item are regarded as ordered or purely nominal. We consider only the ordinal case here, as this case is far more common in bias studies. Within this ordinal case, several possible extensions can be applied to the bias detection application. These extensions differ in their definitions of the logits to be modeled. Agresti (2002) describes three procedures for ordinal variables. *Adjacent-categories logit* models use the logit of the conditional probabilities of responding in adjacent categories on the studied item. *Continuation-ratio logit* models use the logit of the conditional probability of responding in a category, given that the response is in that category or one that is higher. *Cumulative logit* models use the logit of the cumulative probability of responding up to or including a given category. All of these models share the property that multiple logistic curves are fit to a given studied item. For C response categories, $C - 1$ logistic curves will be needed. It is not clear that any one of the alternative approaches is superior for bias applications. We discuss the cumulative logit approach here. Miller, Spray, and Wilson (1992) explored the continuation-ratio model in the bias context.

In the cumulative logit model, we first define the conditional cumulative probability of responding in the cth category, $c = 0, 1, \ldots, C - 1$, as

$$P(X_j \leq c \mid Z, V) = \sum_{m=0}^{c} P(X_j = m \mid Z, V) \qquad (8.38)$$

with Z the value of the matching variable and V the group membership indicator. The logit of interest is then

$$l_{jc} = \ln\left[\frac{P(X_j \leq c \mid Z, V)}{1 - P(X_j \leq c \mid Z, V)} \right] \qquad (8.39)$$

for $c = 0, 1, \ldots, C - 2$, given that only $C - 1$ logits are independent. Interest then lies in the same regression formulation as in the dichotomous case

$$l_{jc} = B_{0jc} + B_{1j}Z + B_{2j}V + B_{3j}(ZV). \qquad (8.40)$$

A new question arises in the polytomous case, however: Which of the model parameters, if any, will vary with the response category? Arguably, the intercept term B_{0jc} should vary with the category, given the ordinality assumed for these categories. The answer for the remaining parameters is less obvious. The simplest approach is to require that (B_{1j}, B_{2j}, B_{3j}) be invariant over categories, leading to the *proportional odds* model. This label stems from the idea that expected value for l_{jc} at two distinct values of Z, say Z_1 and Z_2, will be proportional to the distance $Z_1 - Z_2$. Under the proportional odds restriction, the $C - 1$ logistic curves will all have the same shape, with shifts in location determined by the intercepts B_{0jc}.

Estimation under the proportional odds model will employ maximum likelihood, using a multinomial likelihood. The constraints on the model parameters needed to implement proportional odds must be introduced. More details regarding estimation can be found in Agresti (2002) and McCullagh and Nelder (1989). Johnson and Albert (1999) describe an estimation algorithm using a Markov Chain Monte Carlo approach.

A sequence of models can be tested using likelihood-ratio statistics as in the dichotomous case. The same sequence can apply in both the polytomous and dichotomous cases. Effect size estimation is more complex in the polytomous case, however, and no single measure has yet emerged as an accepted choice. Zumbo (1999) recommends the use of an R-squared measure presented by McKelvey and Zavoina (1975). More research is needed on this measure in bias applications and on the issue of effect size calculation generally. The proportional odds restriction itself can be tested. Long (1997) discusses the use of score tests and Wald statistics in testing the proportional odds restriction.

Until recently, few investigations of the properties of the polytomous logistic regression extension in bias applications had been published. Miller et al. (1992) found in simulated data that logistic regression could detect bidirectional bias, while the GMH procedure did not reliably detect this type of bias. They used a continuation ratio logit model in this study, instead of the cumulative logit model described above. Their results parallel the results found in the dichotomous case, where logistic regression is found to be more powerful than MH for detecting bidirectional bias. A different direction for extending logistic regression to the ordinal case was taken in Crane, Gibbons, Jolley, and van Belle (2006; Crane, van Belle, & Larson, 2004). Crane et al. replaced the use of the total score matching variable Z with IRT-based estimates of the latent variable W. These estimates were based on the graded response model in the ordinal case (see Chapter 6 for more on this model). Tests of B_{3j} are done using the usual chi-square LR procedure, but tests of B_{2j} use the change in the value of the B_{1j} coefficient with or without V in the equation as the criterion for deciding whether B_{2j} is nonzero. No statistical test is involved here, and instead the judgment is based on the magnitude of the change in coefficient. The method developed by Crane et al. can be implemented using the DIFdetect software package, which can be downloaded from the Web site ww.alz.washington.edu/DIFDETECT/welcome.html.

Extensions of the Standardization Method

The standardization method generalizes easily to the polytomous case. The method again considers the regression of the score X_j on the matching variable score Z and compares these regressions between groups. The difference in these regressions is the focus of interest:

$$D_j(Z) = E_f(X_j \mid Z) - E_r(X_j \mid Z). \qquad (8.41)$$

In the polytomous case, the regressions are based on some choice for scaling of the C response categories. For example, we could use the numbers $0, 1, \ldots, C - 1$ as the possible values for X_j. Then define

$$E_f(X_j \mid Z) = \sum_{c=0}^{C-1} \frac{cf_{cm1}}{F_{m1}}, \quad E_r(X_j \mid Z) = \sum_{c=0}^{C-1} \frac{cf_{cm2}}{F_{m2}} \qquad (8.42)$$

as the regression functions in the focal and reference groups. The standardization index is then calculated as

$$STNDES\text{-}DIF = \sum_{m=0}^{M} \frac{F_{m1}D_j(m)}{N_1} \qquad (8.43)$$

which parallels the dichotomous case, using a weighting based on focal group frequencies. Under OCI, we expect this index to be zero because the regressions must be identical across groups. Sample values of the index will have nonzero values by chance even under OCI.

The range of *STNDES-DIF* will depend on the scaling chosen for X_j. For the choice $(0, 1, \ldots, C - 1)$, the range of the index is $(1 - C, C - 1)$. The varying range for the index complicates the question of deciding on a cutpoint for meaningful departures from OCI. Dorans and Schmitt (1993) suggest that the obtained value for *STNDES-DIF* be compared to its maximum possible value under the chosen scaling for X_j. For example, suppose that $C = 5$ and the range for the index is $(-4, 4)$. If the obtained value is .50, we would calculate $.5/4 = 1/8$. Given that a 10% cutpoint is recommended for the dichotomous case, the obtained value of .50 would represent an effect size that is larger than 10% (i.e., departs from 0 by more than 10% of the range from 0 to 4).

Estimators for the standard error of *STNDES-DIF* have been investigated by Zwick and Thayer (1994), who present three different estimators that are generated from varying assumptions. Two of these were examined in simulations and seemed to perform well generally (see also Zwick et al., 1993). The availability of an estimator for the standard error leads to a large-sample test statistic for the null hypothesis that *STNDES-DIF* is zero. The value of *STNDES-DIF* is divided by the standard error estimate to provide a Z-statistic. Zwick and Thayer (1994) describe a close connection between this test statistic and the Mantel statistic described earlier.

Random Effects Models

The detection methods reviewed thus far have treated the set of measures at hand as a fixed set of measures whose bias properties are to be estimated based strictly on the information in the sample. In this approach, the amount of bias in each measure is determined as a fixed property of that measure. The bias is defined within a particular detection method, with the amount of bias being a parameter whose value is to be estimated from the data. We can characterize this point of view as a "fixed effects" approach to the detection of bias.

In contrast to this fixed effects approach, we might regard the amount of bias in a given measure as a random variable. For example, a set of test items might be regarded as a random sample from a larger domain of potential test items. Within this larger domain, there is a distribution of bias parameters, with different items manifesting more or less bias. Our task might then be to use the data at hand to evaluate this distribution of bias parameters. Alternatively, we could forgo any formal notion of a wider domain of measures, while still regarding the item-level bias within a Bayesian framework. Here we will suppose that prior uncertainty about the level of bias in a given item can be represented as a prior distribution. This prior distribution can then be combined with sample estimation to yield a posterior distribution for the bias in a given measure.

A number of researchers have developed bias detection procedures based on random effects notions, either as variance components methods (Longford, 1995; Longford, Holland, & Thayer, 1993) or as empirical Bayes methods (Zwick, Thayer, & Lewis, 1999, 2000). The common thread that links these methods is the use of additional information beyond the sample data on a given measure in estimating the amount of bias in that measure. This approach has the advantage that in small samples, unstable sample estimates of bias parameters can be improved by weighting other sources of information more heavily. The random effects approaches do require that the size of the bias in an item be characterized by an effect size statistic whose distributional properties are known, at least asymptotically. The MH odds-ratio estimator fulfills this requirement, and so the two methods reviewed here have focused on this estimator. In theory, the random effects approach could be applied to any detection method that produces a bias effect size estimator.

Variance Components

Longford (1995; Longford et al., 1993) argues that instead of studying bias at the level of an individual item or measure, we should model the distribution of bias effect sizes for a set of measures as a sample from a larger domain of such measures. The items on a specific test, for example, can be viewed as a selection of items from a larger item pool. Items in this larger pool are all measures of a target latent trait. The bias effect sizes associated with the test items can also be viewed in this way, with each item in the larger pool of items having a bias parameter value. Our interest lies in the distribution of these bias parameter values in the pool of items.

A given test form will select a subset of the items. We can then use the sample data to estimate the parameters governing the distribution of bias effect sizes in the larger item pool.

To make these ideas concrete, suppose that the MH odd-ratio estimator for the jth item is $D_{\alpha j}$ in Equation 8.8. We assume that in the item pool, the estimator $D_{\alpha j}$ has a distribution across items with a mean of μ_D and a standard deviation of σ_D. We can then write

$$\hat{D}_{\alpha j} = \mu_D + \Delta_{Dj} + E_j. \tag{8.44}$$

Here $\Delta_{Dj} = D_{\alpha j} - \mu_D$ and E_j reflect estimation error in estimating $D_{\alpha j}$ from $\hat{D}_{\alpha j}$. An estimator for the variance of E_j can be obtained as a simple rescaling of the estimator in Equation 8.9. Assuming independence between Δ_{Dj} and E_j, we can then estimate σ_D^2 using the observed variance of $\hat{D}_{\alpha j}$ in combination with Equation 8.9. The variance σ_D^2 is the key indicator of bias in the items under study. For the MH odds-ratio estimator using an internal matching variable (e.g., total item score), we expect that $\mu_D = 0$, and so if $\sigma_D^2 = 0$, there can be little bias in the pool. If $\sigma_D^2 > 0$, we must have some items that violate OCI and may be biased.

Longford (1995) extends the above model by replacing μ_D in Equation 8.44 with $\mathbf{X}_j'\mathbf{B}$, where $\mathbf{X}_j$ is a vector of predictors of bias for the jth item and $\mathbf{B}$ is a vector of regression weights. The predictors might represent item-level features that are believed to be associated with bias, for example. The vector $\mathbf{X}_j$ will ordinarily include a unit element to obtain the additive constant μ_D in Equation 8.44.

As described in Longford (1995), estimation for the parameters σ_D^2 and $\mathbf{B}$ proceeds by assuming that the variables Δ_{Dj} and E_j are independent and that each variable has a normal distribution across items. The variances of the E_j are assumed to be known, although in practice, sample estimates will be used. Longford presents a Fisher scoring algorithm that solves the likelihood equations for $\hat{\sigma}_D^2$ and $\hat{\mathbf{B}}$. The method leads to estimates for the sampling variances or covariance matrices for $\hat{\sigma}_D^2$ and $\hat{\mathbf{B}}$. A likelihood-ratio test can be constructed for the null hypothesis that $\sigma_D^2 = 0$, leading to a chi-square statistic with $df = 1$. Longford notes that normal theory-based confidence intervals for σ_D^2 are likely to be poor due to non-normality in the sampling distribution for $\hat{\sigma}_D^2$.

A logical sequel to the above analysis is to obtain shrinkage estimates of the individual bias parameters $D_{\alpha j}$ under the model. The variation across items in the usual sample estimates $\hat{D}_{\alpha j}$ is likely to exceed σ_D^2 due to the variation contributed by the estimation errors in E_j. Shrinkage estimates of the $D_{\alpha j}$ will tend to pull extreme values of the usual estimates $\hat{D}_{\alpha j}$ toward the mean μ_D, resulting in smaller variation in the shrinkage estimates relative to the usual estimates. The degree of shrinkage will depend on the relative sizes of the variance σ_D^2 and the variance σ_{Ej}^2 of E_j. When σ_D^2 is large relative to σ_{Ej}^2, the shrinkage estimates will be close to the usual sample estimate of $D_{\alpha j}$. Conversely, small values for σ_D^2 lead to greater shrinkage.

The foregoing model makes a number of strong assumptions that may not hold in practice, but the impact of violations of these assumptions on the estimates is not obvious. For example, the assumption of normal distributions for the parameters $D_{\alpha j}$ and residuals E_j over items is unlikely to hold precisely. The robustness of the method to non-normality is not known. Longford (1995) describes how the assumption of independence between $D_{\alpha j}$ and E_j could be relaxed through modifications to the estimation algorithm that permit nonzero covariances. A more fundamental issue concerns the use of σ_D^2 as a summary indicator of bias. When $\mu_D \cong 0$, it makes intuitive sense that the size of σ_D^2 bears a strong relationship to the extent of violations of OCI. In the MH procedure with an internal matching variable such as the total item score, the condition $\mu_D \cong 0$ is plausible. Applications of MH that use external anchors need not have $\mu_D \cong 0$, however. Also, the practice of using initial item screens with the MH under an internal matching criterion could also lead to $\mu_D \cong 0$. Investigators should check the estimate of μ_D to evaluate whether σ_D^2 can be taken as a useful summary.

Empirical Bayes

Zwick and colleagues (Zwick et al., 1999, 2000) have described an alternative approach to modeling the distribution of bias effect size measures that is based on an empirical Bayes estimation procedure. This modeling approach, like the variance components method just described, is developed for immediate application to the MH bias statistic, but the model could be applied more generally to any bias effect size statistic if enough is known about the distribution of the statistic. The description of the model below will use the MH effect size statistic as an illustration.

The MH odds-ratio estimator in Equation 8.8 is known to have a normal sampling distribution in large samples, with a standard error estimator that is proportional to the expression in Equation 8.9. The empirical Bayes model assumes that for the jth measure, $\hat{D}_{\alpha j}$ is distributed normally with a mean of $D_{\alpha j}$ and a variance of σ_{Ej}^2. In practice, a rescaled version of the estimator in Equation 8.9 will replace σ_{Ej}^2, and this variance will be regarded as known. Zwick et al. (2000) argue that little distortion is introduced by this assumption. The true effect sizes $D_{\alpha j}$ can in turn be given prior distributions for the set of measures at hand. A normal prior is assumed: $D_{\alpha j} \sim N(\mu_D, \sigma_{Ej}^2)$, with μ_D being the average bias effect size and σ_D^2 the variance of these effect sizes. Combining this prior distribution with the conditional distribution of the effect size estimates for the various items leads to posterior distributions for $D_{\alpha j}$, the true bias effect size for the jth item. This posterior distribution is normal, with a mean equal to $w_j(\hat{D}_{\alpha j}) + (1 - w_j)\mu_D$ and a variance of $w_j^2 \sigma_{Ej}^2$, with the weight w_j being

$$w_j = \frac{\sigma_D^2}{\sigma_D^2 + \sigma_{Ej}^2}. \tag{8.45}$$

The posterior mean will be close to $\hat{D}_{\alpha j}$, the sample odds-ratio estimator, when σ_{Ej}^2 is small. This situation would arise in large samples, for example. When the variance σ_{Ej}^2 is large, however, the posterior mean moves closer to the overall mean μ_D, and Bayesian shrinkage occurs. This shrinkage is essentially the same phenomenon noted earlier under the variance components method.

Zwick et al. (2000) suggest that estimates of μ_D and σ_D^2 be substituted into the above formulas for the posterior parameters. The resulting normal distribution can then be used together with the ETS DIF classification cutpoints to obtain a classification probability for each item. These probabilities are obtained by calculating the areas under the appropriate normal curve between the cutpoints of interest. For example, the probability of a "*B*" classification under the ETS guidelines would be found as the area under the appropriate normal curve between the cutpoints of 1.0 and 1.5. Using this approach, each item is given a probability of classification within each of the ETS DIF categories.

Estimates of μ_D and σ_D^2 are calculated using the observed distribution of effect size estimates $\hat{D}_{\alpha j}$, together with the estimate of the sampling variance $\hat{\sigma}_{Ej}^2$. The estimate $\hat{\mu}_D$ is taken as the sample mean of $\hat{D}_{\alpha j}$ over items. The estimate $\hat{\sigma}_D^2$ is taken as the difference between the variance of the estimates $\hat{D}_{\alpha j}$ and the average value of $\hat{\sigma}_{Ej}^2$ across the items. In many applications, $\hat{\mu}_D$ will be near zero, but the use of the average avoids the practice of fixing this mean to zero a priori. These choices for the estimators $\hat{\mu}_D$ and $\hat{\sigma}_{Ej}^2$ can be justified through a simple linear additive model $D_{\alpha j}$ (Zwick et al., 2000).

SIBTEST

The SIBTEST procedure (Shealy & Stout, 1993b) represents a hybrid approach to bias detection in that it combines elements of latent variable modeling with a conditioning on adjusted observed scores for matching purposes. The procedure is conceptually based on a multidimensional latent variable definition of item performance (Shealy & Stout, 1993a).

Item performance is assumed to depend on a person's status on a target latent dimension and one or more nuisance latent dimensions. In the complete latent space that includes both target and nuisance dimensions, there are no group differences in measurement response functions (see Chapter 2 for more discussion of the target versus nuisance dimension distinction). Informally, the potential for item bias exists whenever an item depends on one or more nuisance latent variables, and the groups differ in their conditional distributions on the nuisance variables, given their standing on the target latent dimension. This potential comes about when we examine the conditional distribution for the item scores, given the target latent dimension but ignoring the nuisance variables. The resulting conditional probabilities for the item scores will not be identical across groups because of the group differences in the nuisance variable distributions. Hence, SIBTEST methods are based on a view of bias that attributes bias to the operation of nuisance latent variables, a point of view that is accepted by many researchers (Kok, 1988). While the origin and definition of item bias for SIBTEST rest on a latent variable conception, the method does not pursue the estimation of measurement response functions or group comparisons of model parameters. In this sense, the method departs from the latent variable approach as typically conceived. As we will see, the basic SIBTEST idea has expanded to include a variety of bias detection approaches for different measurement situations.

Consider the case of a single nuisance dimension $\mathbf{W_n}$ and a single target latent dimension $\mathbf{W_t}$. Let the jth dichotomous item score variable X_j have a multidimensional item response function $P_k(X_j|\mathbf{W_t},\mathbf{W_n})$ in the kth group. We then define the marginal probability of passing the item X_j given $\mathbf{W_t}$ as

$$P_k(X_j \mid \mathbf{W_t}) = \int P_k(X_j \mid \mathbf{W_t}, \mathbf{W_n}) f_k(\mathbf{W_n} \mid \mathbf{W_t}) d\mathbf{W_n}. \qquad (8.46)$$

Here $f_k(\mathbf{W_n}|\mathbf{W_t})$ is the conditional density function for the nuisance variable $\mathbf{W_n}$ given $\mathbf{W_t}$. At any given target latent variable value, we can compare the reference and focal groups on the probabilities in Equation 8.46 as

$$\beta_j(\mathbf{W_t}) = P_R(X_j \mid \mathbf{W_t}) - P_F(X_j \mid \mathbf{W_t}). \qquad (8.47)$$

This quantity $\beta_j(\mathbf{W_t})$ represents a theoretical local measure of bias at the item level. Analogous quantities can be defined at the subtest or even whole test level, given a choice for a subtest or test scoring function. SIBTEST methods in general have an advantage in applying at both the item and higher aggregate levels, unlike some detection methods that operate strictly at the item level.

The practical use of the SIBTEST approach requires the identification of a valid subtest or a subset of the total set of test items that can be assumed to measure only the target latent variable $\mathbf{W_t}$. These items are not influenced by the nuisance latent variable and therefore have no potential for bias. The method for identifying such items is not part of SIBTEST per se. Other tools must be used, including factor analysis, prior research with the items, or any theory that might be relevant. In using factor analysis, the goal would be to confirm that the chosen subset of items fits a single-factor model. If a subset of items was first identified via available theory and it was then found that the subset fit a single-factor model, the choice of the items as the valid subset would have support. Once the valid subtest is identified, some or all of the remaining items become the studied subtest. Items in the studied subset are those for which the question of item bias is at issue. These studied items may be considered one at a time in the analysis or may be bundled into subsets and scored together for analysis.

The index $\beta_j(\mathbf{W_t})$ in Equation 8.47 is conditional on a particular latent variable value $\mathbf{W_t}$, but we are more interested in the index across all possible values of $\mathbf{W_t}$. Shealy and Stout (1993a) define a global bias index for the jth item as

$$B_j = \int \beta_j(\mathbf{W_t}) f_F(\mathbf{W_t}) d\mathbf{W_t}. \tag{8.48}$$

Here $f_F(\mathbf{W_t})$ is the density function for the target latent variable in the focal group. Weighting by the reference group density is also an option, or even the pooled group density. An assumption needed to make B_j a useful index is that any bias is unidirectional: the sign of $\beta_j(\mathbf{W_t})$ does not reverse itself across the values of the target latent variable. The original SIBTEST procedure was designed for the detection of unidirectional bias. Extensions that permit detection of bidirectional bias are discussed below. The definition of the global index in Equation 8.48 is specified for a single item. The same index can be defined for the unweighted sum of m item scores as

$$B = \sum_{j=1}^{m} B_j. \tag{8.49}$$

This index denotes the bias in the total score based on a particular set of items. At this level, cancellation or amplification of bias in the sum of items as a function of the item level biases becomes possible (Nandakumar, 1993b).

The SIBTEST procedure defines an unweighted sum of items in the studied subset of items as

$$X = \sum_{j=1}^{m} X_j. \qquad (8.50)$$

We can define an analogous sum for the valid subset of items as

$$Z = \sum_{j=m+1}^{p} X_j. \qquad (8.51)$$

The valid subtest score Z could in theory be used as the matching variable for comparisons of the studied subtest score X across groups. Shealy and Stout (1993b) show why a simple matching scheme of this type could lead to incorrect results in the usual case in which the groups differ in their target latent variable distributions. To surmount this problem, SIBTEST departs from the usual observed score procedure and takes advantage of the latent variable conceptualization.

The key notion in SIBTEST is that the group comparisons of the studied subtest scores X should not be done by simply matching examinees on their valid subtest scores but rather by matching on adjusted valid subtest scores. The adjustment is designed to remove the influence of the group difference in target latent variable distributions, and in this way, it will reduce the rate of false positive findings of bias. The null hypothesis tested by the SIBTEST procedure is

$$H_0: B = 0. \qquad (8.52)$$

A unidirectional alternative is usually chosen, as in bias against the focal group. Let $\bar{X}_F^*$ and $\bar{X}_R^*$ be the adjusted average studied subtest scores in the focal and reference groups, respectively. The global test statistic is then

$$\hat{B} = \frac{\sum_{q=0}^{n_x} h_q(\bar{X}_{Rq}^* - \bar{X}_{Fq}^*)}{s_B}. \qquad (8.53)$$

Here
s_B is the pooled standard deviation across the reference and focal groups
h_q is the weight applied to each difference between the reference and focal groups average studied subtest score, taken for people having the valid subtest score $Z = q$
The numerator is a summation across all valid subtest scores from 0 to n_x

The test statistic in Equation 8.53 is referred to the standard normal distribution to determine the decision about the null hypothesis. The critical values depend on whether a one- or two-tailed rejection region is chosen. Details about the calculation of the test statistic $\hat{B}$ can be found in the Appendix in Shealy and Stout (1993b). That reference also contains a detailed explanation of the regression adjustment leading to $\bar{X}_{kq}^{*}$ in the kth group.

Simulation studies comparing the Type I error performance of SIBTEST to the MH procedure have shown SIBTEST to be as good as or better than the MH procedure in its Type I error properties and generally as good as MH in terms of power (Douglas, Stout, & DiBello, 1996; Narayanan & Swaminathan, 1994; Roussos & Stout, 1996b; Shealy & Stout, 1993b). Narayanan and Swaminathan compared SIBTEST and the MH method on both Type I error performance and power to detect unidirectional bias. SIBTEST's Type I error rates were slightly higher than the nominal levels, even when the groups did not differ in their target latent variable distributions. SIBTEST showed good power to detect unidirectional bias with a sample size of at least 300 per group. SIBTEST had greater power than MH when the target latent variable distributions differed across groups. Power for both procedures was weakened to some extent when a larger proportion of the items were biased.

As the above study found, the SIBTEST Type I error rates depart from the nominal rate and are larger under some circumstances, particularly for items with high discrimination values. This phenomenon led Jiang and Stout (1998) to propose a more accurate adjustment method for the studied subtest scores $\bar{X}_{kq}^{*}$. The new method uses a piecewise linear regression that better captures the nonlinearity in the regression of the valid subtest true score on the observed valid subtest score. Simulations reported in Jiang and Stout support the conclusion that the new adjustment method improves Type I error performance and that the new procedure performs better than the MH method under the conditions studied.

One clear weakness of the SIBTEST procedure that it shares with the MH procedure is that it does not have power to detect bidirectional bias. As noted earlier in defining the test statistic $\hat{B}$, the statistic assumes that across levels of the target latent variable, the difference in the measurement response functions across groups does not change sign. Biased items that show bidirectional bias will therefore be likely to go undetected. To address this problem, Li and Stout (1996) extended the SIBTEST procedure to enable the detection of bidirectional bias, assuming only one sign reversal for the difference in the measurement response functions. To make this idea concrete, suppose that for the difference $\beta_j(\mathbf{W}_t)$ in Equation 8.47, there exists a target latent variable value w_c such that the sign of $\beta_j(\mathbf{W}_t)$ changes from one value for all $\mathbf{W}_t < w_c$ to the other value for all $\mathbf{W}_t < w_c$.

In other words, the item favors one group below w_c and the other group above w_c. If such a value w_c exists, it then makes sense to define a new global bias index for the jth studied item as

$$B_{jc} = \int_{W_t > w_c} \beta_j(W_t) f_p(W_t) dW_t - \int_{W_t < w_c} \beta_j(W_t) f_p(W_t) dW_t. \tag{8.54}$$

Here $f_p(W_t)$ is a density function for the pooled target latent variable distribution across groups. The index in Equation 8.54 can be positive or negative, depending on which group's measurement response function is higher at low values of W_t and lower at high values of W_t. The null and alternative hypotheses to be tested are

$$H_0: B_{jc} = 0 \quad H_1: B_{jc} \neq 0. \tag{8.55}$$

The above test procedure is easily extended to bundles of items by creating the sum of the statistics in Equation 8.54. The actual use of the test statistic will require calculation of the adjusted studied subtest score average $\bar{X}_{kcq}^*$ as in the original SIBTEST approach. An additional requirement is that we must estimate x_c, the value of the studied subtest corresponding to the latent crossing point w_c. We then define

$$\hat{B}_c = \sum_{q=0}^{x_c} h_q(\bar{X}_{Fcq}^* - \bar{X}_{Rcq}^*) + \sum_{q=x_c+1}^{n_x} h_q(\bar{X}_{Rcq}^* - \bar{X}_{Fcq}^*). \tag{8.56}$$

The actual test statistic is then

$$B = \frac{\hat{B}_c}{s_{Bc}}. \tag{8.57}$$

Here s_{Bc} is the standard error, as given in Li and Stout (1996).

The above calculation of the test statistic requires knowledge of x_c, the crossing point on the studied subtest scale corresponding to w_c. The point is estimated using a weighted linear regression of the studied subtest score difference $\bar{X}_R^* - \bar{X}_F^*$ on the valid subtest scores Z. The rationale for the identification of x_c is given in Li and Stout (1996). A second difficulty is that the final test statistic B has a distribution under the null hypothesis that is unknown. A randomization procedure is therefore used to establish the significance of the sample value of B. This is done by randomly changing the signs of the differences $\bar{X}^*_{Rq} - \bar{X}^*_{Fq}$ at all values $q = 0, 1, \dots n_x$, reestimating the crossing point score and then recalculating the test statistic. Given at least 1000 iterations, it becomes possible to estimate the significance probability associated with the original sample test statistic value.

Li and Stout (1996) evaluated the Type I error and power performance of the crossing SIBTEST procedure. Comparisons were made with the usual SIBTEST procedure, the MH procedure, and the logistic regression procedure. Crossing SIBTEST was found to adhere well to the nominal Type I error rate. The procedure had adequate power to detect unidirectional bias, compared to the MH and ordinary SIBTEST methods. Crossing SIBTEST had good power to detect bidirectional bias as well. The logistic regression procedure had better power than crossing SIBTEST to detect bidirectional bias when the 2PL model generated the data. This advantage did not hold for data generated under a 3PL model. The logistic regression method had higher Type I error than did the crossing SIBTEST method, however, rendering power comparisons difficult. Li and Stout also argue that crossing SIBTEST has an advantage in being able to estimate the crossing point, and in this way allowing the investigator to distinguish unidirectional and bidirectional bias.

In a different extension of the SIBTEST procedure, Chang, Mazzeo, and Roussos (1996) consider polytomously scored items. The extension to the polytomous case does not require any radical changes because local bias can simply be defined by expectation. Let X_j be the jth polytomous studied item with possible scores $(0, 1, \dots, c_j)$. Let Z_j be the jth valid subtest item, also polytomous. The studied subtest score is

$$X = \sum_{j=1}^{m} X_j. \tag{8.58}$$

The subtest score can assume values $(0, 1, \dots, n_x)$. Define the local bias for X_j as

$$\beta_j(\mathbf{W_t}) = E_R(X_j \mid \mathbf{W_t}) - E_F(X_j \mid \mathbf{W_t}). \tag{8.59}$$

Here $E_k(X_j \mid \mathbf{W_t})$ is just the conditional expectation of X_j given $\mathbf{W_t}$ in the kth group. Then the global bias measure is just B_j in Equation 8.48. This definition specializes to the usual SIBTEST statistic when the items are dichotomous because the expected values in Equation 8.59 reduce to the usual item response functions in that case.

In practice, the local bias measure will use the sample averages for X_j after matching on the valid subtest score, followed by the usual regression adjustment. Let $\bar{X}^*_{kjq}$ be the adjusted average studied item score for the *j*th item in the *k*th group for individuals whose valid subtest score is *q*. Then the adjusted local bias index is

$$B_j^* = \bar{X}_{Rjq}^* - \bar{X}_{Fjq}^*.$$
(8.60)

The global index is then

$$B^* = \sum_{q=0}^{n_z} h_q B_j^*.$$
(8.61)

Here h_q is a weight that reflects the number of individuals whose value subtest score is *q*. We can test the null and alternate hypotheses

$$H_0: B^* = 0 \quad H_1: B^* \neq 0.$$
(8.62)

We refer the test statistic to the standard normal distribution in deciding whether to reject the null.

One objection that could be raised about the use of the definition of bias based on expectation in Equation 8.59 is whether invariant expected values really imply invariant category response functions. Chang and Mazzeo (1994) established, however, that for most of the commonly used polytomous IRT models, the expected score function corresponds to a unique set of category response functions. Hence, we can evaluate the expected values in Equation 8.59 knowing that for most polytomous IRT models, invariance in the expected score function is equivalent to measurement invariance in the usual sense.

Chang et al. (1996) compared the polytomous SIBTEST procedure to both the Mantel (1963) procedure and the standardization procedure (Dorans & Kulick, 1983, 1986) using simulated data in two studies. The first study used some polytomous item data generated from the partial credit model (Masters, 1982) and more dichotomous item data generated from a 3PL model. Both Type I error and power performance were studied. The studied item data were generated using the partial credit model. Unidirectional bias was simulated except for a single condition in which bidirectional bias was created. The Mantel and standardization procedures adhered to the nominal Type I error rate well, while the polytomous SIBTEST procedure had a slightly inflated error rate. The three procedures each had good power for detecting unidirectional bias, with none of the methods detecting bidirectional bias. This first study included items whose discrimination parameters were not highly variable across items. The second study used simulated studied items with higher variability in their discrimination parameters. As a result, the discrimination parameter values for the studied items were different from the average discrimination values in the valid subtest. The results showed substantial Type I error rate inflation for the Mantel and standardization methods. The polytomous SIBTEST method showed minimal inflation. SIBTEST also showed good power for detecting the unidirectional bias simulated in this study. The inflated Type I error rates for the Mantel and standardization procedures precluded meaningful power comparisons with SIBTEST.

As a final extension of SIBTEST to be considered here, Stout, Li, Nandakumar, and Bolt (1997) examined tests that are intentionally designed to measure two latent variables, creating two target latent variables W_{t1} and W_{t2}. A biased item in this case is one that is influenced by one or more nuisance latent variables beyond W_{t1} and W_{t2}, with group differences in the conditional nuisance distribution as discussed earlier. For this two-dimensional case, a single matching score is insufficient. Two matching subtests will be employed. The items Z_{1j} are assumed to primarily measure W_{t1}, and the items Z_{2j} are assumed to primarily measure W_{t2}. Individuals will be matched based on their scores on functions of the two sets of valid subtest items Z_{1j} and Z_{2j}. The multiple matching places greater demands on sample size and increases the potential for sparsity in the contingency table formed from the cross-classification of the score ranges for the two matching variables. To address this problem, a smoothing approach is adopted in which individuals from immediately adjacent cells in the contingency table are used in the calculation of the variance of the test statistic.

The actual test statistic is defined in a manner that is analogous to the usual SIBTEST statistic. The studied score X can be either a single item score or a score based on a set of items (item bundle). Reference and focal group average scores on X are again compared locally after matching, now based on the bivariate matching score. A regression adjustment is again made to X prior to calculating the group difference. The adjustment is now based on a regression on both subtest scores and is linear. The final global test statistic is defined in the usual way once the regression adjustment is done.

Stout et al. (1997) conducted a series of simulation studies to examine the power and Type I error performance of the two-dimensional SIB method (MULTISIB). Several other research questions were examined as well. For example, the studies established that matching on only a single score in two-dimensional data led to inflated Type I error rates. The Type I error rate for matching on two subtest scores appeared to adhere well to the nominal error rates across the study conditions. Power simulations revealed that MULTISIB can detect reasonably large biases at sample sizes of 300 per group. Power at the size of 1000 per group is needed for small biases.

An Example

To illustrate some of the observed variable methods described in this chapter, we again use the CBASE Geometry item data from Chapter 7. These data consist of scores on 11 geometry multiple-choice items. All items are scored dichotomously. The data were provided by 5,486 college student examinees, with 1034 males and 4452 females. These data were already analyzed using IRT models in Chapter 7. Those analyses identified a subset of the 11 items as showing statistically significant bias. The analyses reported below will show a different perspective on the same data.

The first set of analyses applied the MH procedure using SPSS Version 17.0.1 (SPSS Inc., 2008). We again begin by using a matching variable Z that is the sum of the 11 item scores. This total sum was used in the first round of analyses for each of the 11 items. That set of analyses flagged a subset of items as showing differential functioning. An item was flagged if the estimate of the common odds-ratio was significantly different from 1.0 at an alpha level of .05. The flagged items were then dropped from the matching sum, and a new matching variable was defined. The new matching variable was then used in a second round of analyses, producing another set of flagged items. This process was repeated until the 11 items were divided into two sets: items that were not flagged for bias and items that were flagged. The items that were flagged were Q83, Q89, Q90, and Q93. In addition, item Q88 was very close to being significant ($p = .054$) and was therefore dropped as well. The items that were not flagged and that therefore served as a designated anchor were Q84, Q85, Q86, Q87, Q91, and Q92.

Table 8.2 gives the estimates of the common odds-ratios for the flagged items and also gives the estimate from Equation 8.8 as an effect size measure for each item. None of these items show group differences that would reach beyond Category *B* in the ETS DIF classification system (Zieky, 1993). Item Q89 is the largest in effect size, consistent with the

TABLE 8.2

Mantel–Haenszel Odds-Ratio Estimates for Flagged CBASE Items

Item	Odds-Ratio Estimate	Delta Estimate[a]
Q83	.706	.818
Q89	.617	1.135
Q90	.738	.714
Q93	.727	.749

[a] $-2.35 \ln(\hat{\alpha})$.

IRT analyses in Chapter 7. Comparing those results with the MH results, only item Q89 was found to be biased by both methods, although Q88 was nearly significant under MH and was flagged by the IRT methods also. Items Q83, Q90, and Q93 were flagged by MH but were part of the anchor set for IRT. With regard to the anchor sets in each method, only items Q84 and Q91 were designated as anchors by both methods. Hence, the overall agreement between the MH and IRT methods was modest in these data. The relatively short item set may have contributed to this problem. Although the presence of bidirectional bias would be another explanation, only item Q92 shows this pattern in the IRT analyses. This item was flagged as biased in the IRT analyses but was not flagged in the MH analyses.

Next, logistic regression methods were applied to the data to evaluate bias. All analyses were again performed using SPSS (SPSS Inc., 2008). The fit of the 2PL model to the data in Chapter 7 suggests that the logistic regression approach might be a good choice for these items. The initial regression used the total sum of the 11 item scores as the matching variable $\mathbf{Z}$. An interaction variable was then created as the product of the binary gender indicator and the sum. Three predictors were then used in the regression: the matching sum variable, the gender indicator, and the interaction term. For each of the 11 items, a three-step hierarchical regression was performed. The first step entered the matching sum variable as the sole predictor. The second step added the gender indicator as the second predictor. The final step entered the interaction term. Consideration of the significance of the predictors began with the third step. If the interaction term produced a significant regression coefficient estimate ($p < .05$), the item was flagged. If not, the focus shifted to the second step results in which no interaction term was entered. The regression coefficient estimate for gender was evaluated for significance in the second step. If the coefficient reached significance, the item was flagged. If not, the analysis for the item was complete.

TABLE 8.3

Logistic Regression Coefficient Estimates for Flagged CBASE Items

Item	Matching Sum Variable	Gender
Q83	1.026	−.356
Q88	.759	.177
Q89	.660	−.480
Q90	.679	−.323
Q93	.839	−.332

Note: All coefficients significant at $p \leq .001$ except gender for Q88, which has $p = .054$.

In the above initial analyses, any item that was flagged was subsequently removed from the matching sum. A second set of analyses was then performed with a reduced sum for matching purposes that included only items that were not flagged in the first round. All items were then reevaluated for bias using the steps described above. If an item had been flagged in the first set of analyses, the item was temporarily added to the matching sum for reevaluation. This set of analyses only confirmed the results of the initial set. The items that were flagged for bias were Q83, Q88, Q89, Q90, and Q93. This set is identical to the items flagged by the MH analyses. All of these items revealed significant effects for gender, but no significant interactions. The gender effect for Q88 was marginally significant. Table 8.3 gives the regression coefficient estimates for each of the flagged items. Interaction coefficients are not shown as none of these reached significance. With the exception of Q88, all of the gender coefficients are negative, indicating that females are disadvantaged by the item after controlling for the sum. These results are consistent with the MH results. Item Q89 is again the item showing the largest bias effect size.

9

Bias in Measurement and Prediction

One of the most common applications of psychological testing is in the use of such tests to predict other variables. Admission tests in higher education are used to predict academic performance in college, either in terms of grade point average or the binary variable of degree completion. Employment selection tests are used to predict job performance, with performance being measured in a variety of ways. Employment tests themselves cover a wide variety of types, including cognitive tests, personality measures, or integrity tests. Clinical tests are used to predict response to treatment, readiness for treatment, or specific behaviors (e.g., suicide attempts). In the legal context, these tests might be used to predict recidivism, as an adjunct to parole decisions. In all of these applications, the test score serves as a "predictor," with the variable being predicted serving as the "criterion." Multiple predictors may be used, as in the use of a battery of tests. In nearly all cases, the scale for the test score predictors is discrete, but with many possible values, given that total test scores are used rather than item-level scores. Most prediction procedures treat these predictors as continuous. The criterion scores are more varied in scale, ranging from binary to nearly continuous criteria.

Group differences in prediction have been of long-standing interest in psychology, both for scientific reasons and for reasons arising from concerns about equitable treatment (Humphreys, 1952). The phrase "differential prediction" has been used to describe group differences in the regression of a criterion on one or more predictors of interest (Linn, 1978). Let $\mathbf{X}'_k = (Y_k, \mathbf{Z}'_k)$ be a $1 \times (p + 1)$ vector of measured criterion (Y_k) and predictor ($\mathbf{Z}_k$) variables in the kth group, with $\mathbf{Z}_k$ being a $p \times 1$ vector. The regression of interest in differential prediction is $E(Y_k | \mathbf{Z}_k) = \hat{Y}_k$, where E is the expectation operator. In the most common case, this regression is linear, as in

$$Y_k = B_{0k} + \mathbf{B}'_{1k}\mathbf{Z}_k + e_k. \tag{9.1}$$

We also have $E(e_k | \mathbf{Z}_k) = 0$ and $\mathrm{Var}(e_k | \mathbf{Z}_k) = \sigma^2_{ek}$ by assumption. Differential prediction is then said to exist when the parameters $(B_{0k}, \mathbf{B}_{1k}, \sigma^2_{ek})$ depend on k, or when for at least one value of k,

$$(B_{0k}, \mathbf{B}_{1k}, \sigma^2_{ek}) \neq (B_0, \mathbf{B}_1, \sigma^2_e). \tag{9.2}$$

In practice, interest usually focuses on either the regression intercept B_0 or the regression slopes $\mathbf{B}_1$. An implication of differential prediction as manifested in different intercepts or slopes is that two individuals with identical predictor scores $\mathbf{Z}_k$, but who are from different groups, will receive different predictions $\hat{Y}_k$ as a function of group membership. A related implication is that the use of a common regression equation for individuals from both groups would lead to systematic errors of prediction as a function of group membership. In other words, if we ignore the group differences in the regression lines and try to use a single line across both groups, we will consistently under- or overpredict for members of one or both groups. In this sense, differential prediction leads to biased and inaccurate predictions as a function of group membership.

In the context of using test scores to select individuals for educational programs or for employment, differential prediction has been studied for its implications for fairness and equitable treatment. Cleary (1968) formulated a definition of fair selection using the concept of invariant regression lines as the key consideration in fairness. Other fairness definitions exist however. The general view at present is that no definition of fairness based on purely statistical considerations is fully adequate (Peterson & Novick, 1976). From the viewpoint of prediction accuracy, however, the implications of differential prediction are clear: systematic errors of prediction, or predictive bias, result from reliance on a single prediction equation across groups in this case. If we want to maximize prediction accuracy, we will want to know whether differential prediction exists for the prediction problem at hand.

In this chapter, we begin by examining predictive bias, its definition, and the methods used to identify it statistically. We then examine the relationship between measurement bias and predictive bias under various measurement models. As will become clear, these two forms of bias have a complex relationship that has often been misunderstood.

Predictive Bias

We can formulate a very general definition of predictive bias that parallels our earlier definition of measurement bias. Using Y, $\mathbf{Z}$, and V as defined earlier, we can let $P(Y|\mathbf{Z}, V)$ be the probability distribution for the criterion variable Y, conditional on the predictors $\mathbf{Z}$ and the group membership indicator V. This conditional distribution forms the basis for any statistical prediction system, linear or otherwise. We can define predictive invariance as holding if and only if for all values of $\mathbf{Z}$ and V,

$$P(Y \mid \mathbf{Z}, V) = P(Y \mid \mathbf{Z}). \tag{9.3}$$

Conversely, we will say that predictive bias exists when the equality in Equation 9.3 does not hold. This formulation includes many special cases. In the context of linear regression, differential prediction is a violation of invariance in Equation 9.3 and is therefore an example of predictive bias. If Y is a binary criterion variable, we can translate Equation 9.3 into a statement about invariance of the logistic regression of Y on $\mathbf{Z}$ (Raju, Steinhaus, Edwards, & DeLassio, 1991). Violations of invariance in Equation 9.3 could exist yet have little practical impact. For example, slight group differences in the tails of the conditional distributions may not matter, particularly if these differences concern the side of the distribution that is of little interest. Furthermore, as we will see, violations of predictive invariance can arise simply as a function of unreliability in $(Y, \mathbf{Z})$, combined with group differences in the means of $(Y, \mathbf{Z})$.

Linear Regression

We begin with the simplest case of a linear regression of Y on $\mathbf{Z}$ at all values of V. It is possible that this regression is linear for some groups and not others, but we will assume linearity for all groups at this point. Equation 9.1 provided the regression equation, with parameters $(B_{0k}, \mathbf{B}_{1k}, \sigma_{ek}^2)$. If Y is conditionally normal, invariance in these parameters is equivalent to predictive invariance in Equation 9.3 because these parameters fully determine the shape of the distribution $P(Y \mid \mathbf{Z}, V)$. If the conditional distribution of Y is not normal, invariance in the parameters $(B_{0k}, \mathbf{B}_{1k}, \sigma_{ek}^2)$ is not sufficient for predictive invariance, but we may be interested in this form of invariance for practical reasons. More specifically, we may be interested primarily in whether the regression itself is invariant across groups or whether for all $\mathbf{Z}$ and V

$$E(Y \mid \mathbf{Z}, V) = E(Y \mid \mathbf{Z}). \tag{9.4}$$

We will say that regression invariance holds if and only if the equality in Equation 9.4 holds. For linear regression, regression invariance holds when for $k = 1, \ldots, K,$

$$B_{0k} = B_0, \quad \mathbf{B}_{1k} = \mathbf{B}_1. \tag{9.5}$$

Regression invariance is at issue in most studies of differential prediction. It is possible that $\mathbf{B}_{1k} = \mathbf{B}_1$ for all k, yet $B_{0k} \neq B_0$ for some k. In this case, we will say that slope invariance holds but intercept invariance does not. The converse situation ($B_{0k} = B_0$ but $\mathbf{B}_{1k} \neq \mathbf{B}_1$ for some k) is possible but unlikely in practice.

Procedures for testing whether regression invariance holds in practice are well known for the normal distribution case (Gulliksen & Wilks, 1950;

Pearson & Wilks, 1933; Potthoff, 1966). Aguinis (2004) provides a recent treatment of the topic. The most common approach to this problem is to employ moderated multiple regression (MMR) under an additional assumption that $\sigma_{ek}^2 = \sigma_e^2$ for all k. In this approach, a regression model is fit to the combined group data. Assume that we have two groups ($K = 2$) with a single predictor ($p = 1$). Representing the grouping variable with V, the predictor variable with Z, and their product as ZV, the model is

$$Y = \Gamma_0 + \Gamma_1 Z + \Gamma_2 V + \Gamma_3 (ZV) + \epsilon. \tag{9.6}$$

After fitting this model, invariance in the regression slopes across groups ($B_{1k} = B_1$ for $k = 1, 2$) is evaluated by testing

$$H_0 : \Gamma_3 = 0. \tag{9.7}$$

Rejection of this null hypothesis would imply that the B_{1k} are not invariant. Failure to reject H_0 would support invariance in the slopes. For the case of $p > 1$, Γ_3 is a vector, and we can test the null hypothesis in 9.7 for some or all elements of this vector. If slope invariance holds, the next step is to test the hypothesis

$$H_0 : \Gamma_2 = 0. \tag{9.8}$$

This hypothesis implies that the regression intercepts are invariant, given invariance in the slopes. If we reject this hypothesis, we conclude that the regression intercepts are not invariant. Hence, the combined tests of the hypotheses in Equations 9.7 and 9.8 will permit us to distinguish three different regression invariance scenarios: regression invariance ($B_{0k} = B_0$, $B_{1k} = B_1$ for $k = 1, 2$), group differences in regression slopes ($B_{1k} \neq B_1$), or group differences in intercepts with no differences in slopes ($B_{0k} \neq B_0$, $B_{1k} = B_1$ for $k = 1, 2$).

The MMR strategy is effective given adequate sample sizes and some distributional assumptions. These assumptions include normality of the residuals ϵ in Equation 9.6, homoscedasticity of these residuals, and homogeneity of their variances across groups as noted earlier. Recent interest has focused on the impact of violations of homogeneity in the variance of the residuals (Alexander & DeShon, 1994; DeShon & Alexander, 1996; Dretzke, Levin, & Serlin, 1982). It has been shown that the violations will affect both the Type I error rate and power for testing, depending on the sample sizes of the groups and the rank ordering of the variances across groups (see Aguinis, 2004, for a review of these findings). Alternative methods for testing regression invariance that are more robust are available (Aguinis; Alexander & Govern, 1994; DeShon & Alexander; Overton, 2001). Tests of the hypotheses in (9.7) and (9.8) could also be performed using path analysis software within a multiple-group analysis (see, e.g., Millsap, 1998). Using this method, it is also possible to test for homogeneity of variance prior to testing invariance constraints on the regression slopes or intercepts.

Measurement error in the predictors $\mathbf{Z}$ or the criterion Y can affect the outcomes of the tests of regression invariance in the sense that these outcomes may differ from what would have been found using error-free measures. For example, measurement error in some elements of $\mathbf{Z}$ can lead to rejection of the hypothesis (9.7) and/or the hypothesis (9.8), even though both hypotheses would be true for the error-free versions of $\mathbf{Z}$ (e.g., the true scores). This fact is widely known (Peterson, 1986) and is just one example of the general theory of measurement error in regression (Fuller, 1987). The classical model for measurement error can be viewed as a special case of the more general common factor model, however, and we can explore both the impact of measurement error and measurement bias in that context, as described next.

Prediction Within the Factor Analysis Model

We begin by supposing that a factor analysis model holds for $\mathbf{X} = (Y, \mathbf{Z})$ in each group. Note that the model holds jointly for the criterion Y and the predictors $\mathbf{Z}$. Suppose that the factor model in the kth group is

$$\mathbf{X}_k = \mathbf{\tau}_k + \mathbf{\Lambda}_k \mathbf{W}_k + \mathbf{u}_k. \tag{9.9}$$

Here
  $\mathbf{W}_k$ is an $r \times 1$ vector of factor score random variables
  $\mathbf{u}_k$ is a $(p + 1) \times 1$ vector of unique factor score random variables
  $\mathbf{\tau}_k$ is a $(p + 1) \times 1$ vector of measurement intercept parameters
  $\mathbf{\Lambda}_k$ is a $(p + 1) \times r$ factor pattern matrix

All random variables and parameters are subscripted to permit group differences. In the simplest case, a single common factor underlies both the predictors and the criterion ($r = 1$). As noted in Chapter 4, the unique factor scores $\mathbf{u}_k$ can include both measurement error and specific portions, permitting us to consider the impact of measurement error on the regression of Y on $\mathbf{Z}$.

The partitioning $\mathbf{X} = (Y, \mathbf{Z})$ extends to the parameter matrices and vectors as well. We make the following definitions and assumptions:

$$E(\mathbf{W}_k) = \mathbf{\kappa}_k \qquad \text{Cov}(\mathbf{W}_k) = \mathbf{\Phi}_k, \tag{9.10}$$

$$E(\mathbf{u}_k) = \mathbf{0} \qquad \text{Cov}(\mathbf{u}_k) = \mathbf{\Theta}_k, \tag{9.11}$$

$$\text{Cov}(\mathbf{W}_k, \mathbf{u}_k) = \mathbf{0}. \tag{9.12}$$

We further assume that Θ_k is a diagonal matrix with nonnegative elements, implying that the unique factors are mutually uncorrelated. We can partition the parameter matrices $(\tau_k, \Lambda_k, \Theta_k)$ as

$$\tau_k = \begin{bmatrix} \tau_{yk} \\ \tau_{zk} \end{bmatrix} \qquad \Lambda_k = \begin{bmatrix} \lambda_{yk} \\ \Lambda_{zk} \end{bmatrix}, \tag{9.13}$$

$$\Theta_k = \begin{bmatrix} \theta_{yk} & 0 \\ 0 & \Theta_{zk} \end{bmatrix}. \tag{9.14}$$

Here
τ_{yk} and θ_{yk} are each scalars
λ_{yk} is a $1 \times r$ vector
τ_{zk} is $p \times 1$
Λ_{zk} is $p \times r$
Θ_{zk} is a $p \times p$ diagonal matrix

Under this factor model, it becomes possible to reformulate the original regression parameters $(B_{0k}, B_{1k}, \sigma_{ek}^2)$ in terms of the factor model parameters. This reformulation is an extension of the model developed by Lawley and Maxwell (1973) (see also Scott, 1966) to permit multiple oblique factors in multiple groups with mean structure. We can express the regression intercept and slopes as

$$B_{0k} = (\tau_{yk} - \mathbf{B}'_{1k}\tau_{zk}) + (\lambda_{yk} - \mathbf{B}'_{1k}\Lambda_{zk})\kappa_k, \tag{9.15}$$

$$\mathbf{B}_{1k} = (\Lambda_{zk}\Phi_k\Lambda'_{zk} + \Theta_{zk})^{-1}\Lambda_{zk}\Phi_k\lambda_{yk}. \tag{9.16}$$

Furthermore, it can be shown that

$$\sigma_{ek}^2 = \lambda'_{yk}\Phi_k[\Phi_k^{-1} - \Lambda'_{zk}(\Lambda_{zk}\Phi_k\Lambda'_{zk} + \Theta_{zk})^{-1}\Lambda_{zk}]\Phi_k\lambda_{yk} + \theta_{yk}. \tag{9.17}$$

From this expression, it is clear that heterogeneity in σ_{ek}^2 over groups can have several sources in the factor model. Group differences in the unique factors on either $\mathbf{Z}$ or Y will generally lead to heterogeneity. We can use the results in Equations 9.15 and 9.16 to study the impact of group differences in factor model parameters on regression invariance. We will begin with the single factor case ($r = 1$).

The Single Factor Case

Suppose that a single factor underlies both the predictors and the criterion, so that $r = 1$. This single factor case has been studied in the literature (Birnbaum, 1979; Humphreys, 1986; Linn, 1984). Birnbaum examined it in the context of salary equity studies in which $p = 1$ (only a single predictor). Within the single factor case, the situation that has been most often studied is when $\mathbf{X} = (Y, \mathbf{Z})$ is factorially invariant, with the additional restriction of no group differences in common factor variances:

$$\Lambda_k = \Lambda \qquad \Theta_{zk} = \Theta \qquad \tau_k = \tau \qquad \Phi_k = \Phi. \qquad (9.18)$$

Here invariance in the criterion unique variances θ_{yk} is not strictly required for the results to follow. In this highly restricted model, it can be shown (Millsap, 1998) that the regression slopes are invariant, but the regression intercepts are not invariant:

$$\mathbf{B}_{1k} = \mathbf{B}_1 \qquad B_{0k} \neq B_0. \qquad (9.19)$$

Furthermore, the relative sizes of the intercepts across groups are a function of the relative sizes of the common factor means. If $\kappa_1 > \kappa_2$, we then must have $B_{01} > B_{02}$. If $\kappa_1 < \kappa_2$, we have $B_{01} < B_{02}$. As a result, the group with the higher average test and criterion scores will have a regression line that is above the line of the lower scoring group. This relative placement of the lines implies under-prediction for members of the higher scoring group if a common regression line is used. Hence, the predictive bias in this situation penalizes the higher scoring group.

This situation has been noted in the literature in part because it is consistent with many empirical studies of differential prediction (Gottfredson, 1994; Hartigan & Wigdor, 1989; Jensen, 1980; Sackett & Wilk, 1994; Schmidt, Pearlman, & Hunter, 1980). In these studies, it is found that the predictive bias works against the higher scoring group, contrary to the expectation that such bias would penalize the lower scoring group. As noted above, this finding could be consistent with no measurement bias in either the predictor or the criterion. The above model therefore serves as a convenient and parsimonious explanation for the empirical findings. Unfortunately, studies of predictive bias do not generally examine the data for evidence of measurement bias. Hence, the restrictive measurement implications of the above model are seldom tested empirically in studies of differential prediction.

The restrictiveness of the model in Equation 9.18 can be appreciated by considering its implications. First, the model implies that the covariance matrices for $\mathbf{X} = (Y, \mathbf{Z})$ are invariant, apart from the variance of Y, which can be affected by possible group differences in criterion unique variances. Second, this invariance in turn implies that the variance explained in predicting Y from $\mathbf{Z}$ is also invariant. Finally, the expected values for $\mathbf{X}$ are ordered by the factor means κ_k. The group with the largest factor mean will have the largest means on each of the variables in $\mathbf{X}$. Apart from sampling error, this implication rules out any reversals of the ordering in the groups across the means on the elements of $\mathbf{X}$.

   All of the above implications can be checked empirically, but it is more direct to test the model itself using confirmatory factor analysis (CFA) (Millsap, 1998). The degrees of freedom for the model can be shown to be $df = p(p + 2)$, after additional constraints needed to identify the model are imposed and also after imposing invariance on the criterion unique factor variances. This latter constraint produces homogeneity of error variances for the regressions across groups (see Equation 9.17). This $df = 3$ when $p = 1$ and only a single predictor is used. The model is testable even in this case. If the model is rejected in the $p = 1$ case, no further relaxations of any constraints are possible, and so it may be difficult to pinpoint the source of the problem. When $p > 1$, further modifications to the model are possible. Any CFA software program that can analyze multiple groups can be used to test the model. Examples are given in Millsap.

   The model in Equation 9.18 has received attention in the literature, but alternative models exist. Some of these alternative models imply no predictive bias even though bias in measurement exists, while others imply both predictive bias and measurement bias (Millsap, 2007). To illustrate the first case, consider a model that permits the measurement intercepts and factor means to vary across groups, but assumes for all k,

$$\Lambda_k = \Lambda \qquad \Theta_{zk} = \Theta \qquad \Phi_k = \Phi. \tag{9.20}$$

This model implies slope invariance, but has no certain implications for invariance in regression intercepts. Specifically, the regression intercept in the kth group is

$$B_{0k} = (\tau_{yk} - \mathbf{B}_1'\tau_{zk}) + (\lambda_y - \mathbf{B}_1'\Lambda_z)\kappa_k. \tag{9.21}$$

For the two group case $(K = 2)$, the difference in intercepts between groups is

$$B_{01} - B_{02} = [(\tau_{y1} - \tau_{y2}) - \mathbf{B}_1'(\tau_{z1} - \tau_{z2})] + (\lambda_y - \mathbf{B}_1'\Lambda_z)(\kappa_1 - \kappa_2). \tag{9.22}$$

If the measurement intercepts are invariant but the factor means are not, we are back in the situation in Equations 9.18 and 9.19. If the measurement intercepts are not invariant, the situation is more complex. For example, suppose that the criterion measurement intercepts are invariant ($\tau_{yk} = \tau_y$), but the predictor intercepts vary across groups. Then assuming that $\mathbf{B}_1 > 0$, differences in the predictor measurement intercepts must be considered in comparison to the factor mean difference $(\kappa_1 - \kappa_2)$. If group one is the higher scoring group on $\mathbf{X}$ and there is a bias in favor of group one on the predictor measurement intercepts $(\tau_{z1} > \tau_{z2})$, this bias will operate against the factor mean difference in Equation 9.22, possibly leading to little or no group difference in regression intercepts B_{0k}. Under these conditions, we would find little or no predictive bias, even though measurement bias is present. The measurement bias here is manifested as an additive constant for one group's predictor scores. This group is given a systematic advantage on the predictor through this additive constant, but the prediction system would be viewed as unbiased by the usual standard of invariance in regression lines.

A numerical example may help to clarify the implications of the foregoing models. Consider a single predictor $(p = 1)$ and suppose that $r_{yz} = .5$, a level of association that is consistent with real prediction studies in college admissions and some employment domains. We will set the communality for the predictor test at .60 and at .42 for the criterion measure. The factor model parameter values are set as

$$\lambda_z = .6 \qquad \lambda_y = .4 \qquad \phi = 1.0 \qquad \theta_z = .24 \qquad \theta_y = .22. \qquad (9.23)$$

For the measurement intercepts and factor means, we will first examine the model in Equation 9.18 that assumes invariance in all measurement intercepts. Setting $\kappa_2 = 0$ and $\kappa_1 = .5$ gives a mean separation on the factor scores in the two populations of one-half standard deviation. We can calculate the common slope value for the two populations as

$$B_1 = \frac{\lambda_y \lambda_z \phi}{\lambda_z^2 \phi + \theta_z} = .4. \qquad (9.24)$$

Then the regression intercepts are found as

$$B_{0k} = (\tau_y - B_1 \tau_z) + (\lambda_y - B_1 \lambda_z)\kappa_k. \qquad (9.25)$$

We can set $\tau_z = 0$ and $\tau_z = .2$, giving

$$B_{0k} = (-.4(.2)) + (.4 - .4(.6))\kappa_k = .16\kappa_k - .08. \qquad (9.26)$$

This result leads to $B_{01} = 0$ and $B_{02} = -.08$. The difference in regression intercepts is therefore .08, with group one having the higher value. To get perspective on this intercept difference, the actual criterion mean difference between groups is $.4(.5) = .20$, and so about 40% of this mean difference remains between any two people from the different groups who have identical predictor scores. The use of a common regression line to predict Y from Z in this scenario would penalize members of the higher-scoring group one. No measurement bias exists in either the predictor or the criterion, and so measurement bias cannot explain the difference in regression intercepts. Instead, it can be argued that the group difference in intercepts is due to the nonzero unique variance in the predictor: $\theta_z > 0$. If $\theta_z = 0$, the regression intercepts become invariant because in that case (see Equation 9.24),

$$\lambda_y - B_1\lambda_z = \lambda_y - \left(\frac{\lambda_y}{\lambda_z}\right)\lambda_z = 0. \tag{9.27}$$

Note that $\theta_z > 0$ is possible even if the reliability of Z is perfect because the unique variance can include variance in addition to the measurement error variance, as discussed in Chapter 4. In other words, it is not only measurement error that creates the intercept difference, but rather all sources of variance that are irrelevant to the common factor underlying the predictor and criterion.

Next, we can consider the case in which the predictor measurement intercepts differ across groups. We define

$$\tau_{z1} = .2 \qquad \tau_{z2} = 0. \tag{9.28}$$

The higher scoring group one gets the higher measurement intercept as well here, and so the measurement bias favors group one. The group difference in the regression intercepts is found as

$$B_{01} - B_{02} = (\lambda_y - B_1\lambda_z)(\kappa_1 - \kappa_2) - B_1(\tau_{z1} - \tau_{z2}). \tag{9.29}$$

Substituting the parameter values into this equation leads to

$$B_{01} - B_{02} = (.4 - .4(.6))(.5) - .4(.2 - 0) = 0. \tag{9.30}$$

The regression intercepts are invariant, and so the regression lines are identical across groups. No predictive bias is present in this case. Systematic measurement bias favoring group one is present, however. The predictor means for the two groups are found as

$$\mu_{z1} = \tau_{z1} + \lambda_z\kappa_1 = .2 + .6(.5) = .50, \tag{9.31}$$

$$\mu_{z2} = \tau_{z2} + \lambda_z\kappa_2 = 0. \tag{9.32}$$

The groups differ by .50 in their means on the predictor, but 40% of this difference is due to the group difference in measurement intercepts. Given that the predictor shows no predictive bias, the predictor test might be used for selection purposes in an educational, employment, or clinical setting, even though one group is systematically favored by the test.

In the above example, the measurement intercept difference of .20 was chosen specifically to produce invariance in the regression intercepts. Other values for the measurement intercept difference would produce other effects on the regression intercepts. We can summarize the impact of the measurement intercept difference as follows:

$$\tau_{z1} - \tau_{z2} > .20 \qquad B_{01} - B_{02} < 0, \tag{9.33}$$

$$\tau_{z1} - \tau_{z2} = .20 \qquad B_{01} - B_{02} = 0, \tag{9.34}$$

$$\tau_{z1} - \tau_{z2} < .20 \qquad B_{01} - B_{02} > 0. \tag{9.35}$$

As noted here, when the measurement intercept difference becomes quite large, favoring the first group, the regression intercepts begin to be larger for group two. In this case, the use of a single regression line for both groups begins to penalize group two, as we would expect given the measurement bias. This effect does not appear, however, until the measurement intercept difference is quite large. Until that point, the measurement bias is veiled by the invariance in the regressions or by the regression intercepts that seem to penalize group one. If there is one lesson to be drawn from the intercept results in Equations 9.33 through 9.35, it is that the presence or absence of group differences in regression intercepts is not diagnostic for the presence or absence of measurement bias.

The previous numerical examples were for the $p = 1$ case, with a single predictor variable, but similar results can be formulated for $p > 1$ and a single factor. In this case, the effects of measurement intercept differences on the regression intercepts are more complicated because the differences are composited by the regression weights. With invariance for the criterion measurement intercepts, we have from Equation 9.22

$$B_{01} - B_{02} = (\lambda_y - \mathbf{B}'_1\mathbf{\Lambda}_z)(\kappa_1 - \kappa_2) - \mathbf{B}'_1(\tau_{z1} - \tau_{z2}). \tag{9.36}$$

The measurement intercept differences $(\tau_{z1} - \tau_{z2})$ are weighted by the elements of $\mathbf{B}_1$ and summed. If the measurement intercept differences have different signs, some cancellation will occur, and this may nearly eliminate the impact of the measurement intercepts on the regression intercepts. Many possibilities exist. A distinct advantage of the $p > 1$ case, however, is the ability to test the fit of the factor model that permits the measurement intercepts to vary. This test was not possible for the $p = 1$ case. The ability to test the model with varying intercepts will also permit estimation of the group difference in intercepts. Estimation of these group differences would be important for evaluating the potential impact of the measurement bias.

All of the results thus far have assumed that any measurement bias is represented by only group differences in measurement intercepts. Confining discussion to this limited form of measurement bias allows us to focus attention only on group differences in regression intercepts. If we expand discussion to permit group differences in other factor model parameters, we will also need to consider group differences in regression slopes, along with regression intercepts.

Consider the situation in which only factor means and variances are varying across groups, with all other factor model parameters invariant. For two groups, we have

$$\kappa_1 \neq \kappa_2 \qquad \phi_1 \neq \phi_2, \tag{9.37}$$

$$\Lambda_1 = \Lambda_2 \qquad \tau_1 = \tau_2 \qquad \Theta_1 = \Theta_2. \tag{9.38}$$

Technically, invariance in the criterion unique variances is not required, but we will retain this constraint in the following. This case represents invariance in the factorial sense: Only the distributions of the common factor scores are varying across groups. It can be shown that in this case, regression invariance will not hold (Millsap, 1995). The regression slopes will vary across groups, and, as a consequence, the regression intercepts are likely to vary as well. This situation is another case in which lack of predictive invariance arises for reasons that are unrelated to measurement bias. The only requirement here is that the variance in the factor scores varies across groups. Group differences in factor variances could arise for any number of reasons, such as selection processes that operate on common factors (see Chapter 4 for a discussion of selection).

Invariance in the regression slopes is not possible in the above scenario, but is mathematically possible if measurement bias is allowed. First, consider the situation in which group differences in predictor unique variances are permitted: $\Theta_{z1} \neq \Theta_{z2}$. We continue to assume invariance in factor pattern matrices and intercepts:

$$\Lambda_1 = \Lambda_2 \qquad \tau_1 = \tau_2. \tag{9.39}$$

In this case, it can be shown (Millsap, 1995) that invariance in regression slopes will hold if and only if

$$\frac{\phi_2}{\phi_1} = \frac{\lambda^{*\prime} \Theta \lambda^*}{\lambda^{*\prime} \lambda^*}. \tag{9.40}$$

Here $\lambda^* = \Theta_{z1}^{-1/2}\Lambda_z$ and $\Theta = \Theta_{z1}^{-1}\Theta_{z2}$. From this result, it is clear that while regression slope invariance is mathematically possible, it requires a proportionality condition that is highly unlikely to hold. Note that for the special case of $p = 1$, the above condition simplifies to

$$\frac{\phi_2}{\phi_1} = \frac{\theta_{z1}}{\theta_{z2}}. \tag{9.41}$$

Here it is more clearly seen that the required proportionality condition is unusual and cannot be routinely assumed to hold.

The conclusion implied by the above results is inescapable: under the single factor model for X with varying factor score means and variances, we expect to see invariant regression slopes only if the factor loadings vary across groups: $\Lambda_1 \neq \Lambda_2$. This fact suggests an inconsistency between predictive invariance and measurement invariance for the single factor model with group differences in factor variances. Empirical studies that support slope invariance in prediction do not thereby provide evidence for measurement invariance in this sense.

The Multiple Factor Case

We can extend discussion of the relationship between predictive invariance and measurement invariance to the case of multiple factors ($r > 1$) in the factor model. The multiple factors underlying X could take a variety of forms. One possibility could be a bifactor model structure in which one general factor affects all measures in X, and any additional factors only affect disjoint subsets of the $p + 1$ measures in X. Alternatively, there may be no general factor, with subsets of measures each forming separate factors. The results to be described here will make few assumptions about the configuration of the factor structures within each group, apart from invariance constraints. Sharper results may follow from specific assumptions about the factor structure.

We begin by again considering the case in which the only factor model parameters that vary across groups are the factor means: $\kappa_1 \neq \kappa_2$. In this multiple factor case, the factor means are arrayed in $r \times 1$ vectors κ_k. The ordering of these means need not be consistent across factors. For example, the factor mean for the first factor may be highest in group one, while the factor mean for the second factor may be highest in group two. In the case in which the factor means are all highest in a single group (e.g., $\kappa_1 > \kappa_2$), we can derive some clear implications for the regression intercepts B_{0k} and their ordering across groups. Suppose that $\kappa_1 > \kappa_2$ in the above sense. We further suppose that almost all other factor model parameters are invariant across groups or that

$$\Lambda_1 = \Lambda_2 \qquad \tau_1 = \tau_2 \qquad \Theta_{z1} = \Theta_{z2} \qquad \Phi_1 = \Phi_2. \qquad (9.42)$$

The only exception to this invariance, aside from the factor means, are the unique variances for the criterion measure Y, which are not required to be invariant for the results to follow. These assumptions imply that slope invariance holds: $\mathbf{B}_{1k} = \mathbf{B}_1$ for all k. In addition, we assume that the elements of λ_y are nonnegative, that the predictor factor pattern matrix Λ_z is full rank, that the diagonal elements of Θ_z are positive, and that Φ is positive definite. It can then be shown that

$$B_{01} > B_{02}. \qquad (9.43)$$

The group with the largest factor means will also have the largest regression intercept.

The above result is not an "if and only if" result, unlike the analogous results for the single factor case. In the multiple factor case, it may be possible for $B_{01} > B_{02}$ even if κ_1 does not have uniformly larger elements than κ_2. The model leading to the above result is testable, depending on the value of p in relation to r, the number of common factors. After imposing constraints needed for identification and assuming that the unique factor variances for the criterion are invariant, the degrees of freedom for the model with $K = 2$ groups can be shown to be

$$df = p^2 + p(3-r) + \frac{r^2 - 3r}{2} + 2. \qquad (9.44)$$

For $r = 1$, this df reduces to $p(p + 2)$, which is the df mentioned earlier for the single factor case. The df in Equation 9.44 will not be positive at all combinations of p and r. At $r = 3$, for example, we must have $p > 1$ if the df is to be positive. Rejection of the model in Equation 9.42 suggests that at least one of the invariance constraints is inappropriate. Respecification of the model to investigate which constraints might be producing the lack of fit will depend on the df, and whether the df is sufficient to evaluate weaker models.

The foregoing model permits no measurement bias. If we introduce measurement bias in the form of group differences in measurement intercepts, we can again find a situation in which both slope invariance and intercept invariance may hold. The regression intercept difference is now

$$B_{01} - B_{02} = [(\tau_{y1} - \tau_{y2}) - \mathbf{B}_1'(\tau_{z1} - \tau_{z2})] + (\lambda_y' - \mathbf{B}_1'\Lambda_z)(\kappa_1 - \kappa_2). \qquad (9.45)$$

Again assuming that the elements of $\mathbf{B}_1$ are not negative, if the criterion measurement intercepts are invariant, but the predictor measurement intercepts vary, many different scenarios for the regression intercepts are possible. If group one has both the largest measurement intercepts and the largest factor means, there could be little or no difference in regression intercepts between groups.

To illustrate this model, suppose that $p = 4$ with $r = 2$, so that two factors underlie $\mathbf{X}$. We will adopt the following parameter values:

$$\boldsymbol{\lambda}'_y = [.4 \quad 0] \qquad \Theta_y = .2237, \tag{9.46}$$

$$\boldsymbol{\Lambda}_z = \begin{bmatrix} .5 & 0 \\ .6 & 0 \\ 0 & .5 \\ 0 & .6 \end{bmatrix} \qquad \Theta_z = \begin{bmatrix} .2 & 0 & 0 & 0 \\ 0 & .2 & 0 & 0 \\ 0 & 0 & .2 & 0 \\ 0 & 0 & 0 & .2 \end{bmatrix}, \tag{9.47}$$

$$\Phi = \begin{bmatrix} 1 & .5 \\ .5 & 1 \end{bmatrix}. \tag{9.48}$$

It can be shown that the above values lead to a squared multiple correlation between Y and $\mathbf{Z}$ of .3196, with raw regression slopes of

$$\mathbf{B}_1 = \begin{bmatrix} .2335 \\ .2802 \\ .0355 \\ .0426 \end{bmatrix}. \tag{9.49}$$

We will set $\tau_{y1} = \tau_{y2} = 0$. We will also set $\kappa_2 = 0$ and $\tau_{z2} = 0$, while permitting κ_1 and τ_{z1} to be positive. We have

$$\boldsymbol{\lambda}_y - \boldsymbol{\Lambda}'_z \mathbf{B}_1 = \begin{bmatrix} .4 \\ 0 \end{bmatrix} - \begin{bmatrix} .2849 \\ .0433 \end{bmatrix} = \begin{bmatrix} .1151 \\ -.0433 \end{bmatrix}. \tag{9.50}$$

Suppose that $\kappa_1 = [.5 \quad .5]$. Then

$$(\boldsymbol{\lambda}'_y - \mathbf{B}'_1 \boldsymbol{\Lambda}_z)\kappa_1 = .0359. \tag{9.51}$$

Hence, if $B_{01} - B_{02} = 0$, we must have

$$\mathbf{B}_1' \boldsymbol{\tau}_{z1} = .0359. \tag{9.52}$$

Many choices are possible for $\boldsymbol{\tau}_{z1}$ here. One example would be

$$\boldsymbol{\tau}_{z1} = \begin{bmatrix} .030 \\ .030 \\ .080 \\ .416 \end{bmatrix}. \tag{9.53}$$

More generally, in this example, we can state the rules that specify the relation between B_{01} and B_{02} as a function of $\boldsymbol{\tau}_{z1}$:

$$B_{01} = B_{02} \quad \text{if } \mathbf{B}_1' \boldsymbol{\tau}_{z1} = .0359, \tag{9.54}$$

$$B_{01} > B_{02} \quad \text{if } \mathbf{B}_1' \boldsymbol{\tau}_{z1} < .0359, \tag{9.55}$$

$$B_{01} < B_{02} \quad \text{if } \mathbf{B}_1' \boldsymbol{\tau}_{z1} > .0359. \tag{9.56}$$

These results show that if $\boldsymbol{\tau}_{z1} - \boldsymbol{\tau}_{z2} = 0$, we will have $B_{01} > B_{02}$ as expected, given the group difference in factor mean vectors. Group one has the highest factor means. If $\boldsymbol{\tau}_{z1} \neq \boldsymbol{\tau}_{z2}$ so that measurement bias is present, there is no way of knowing the ordinal relation between B_{01} and B_{02} without knowing the measurement intercepts. Conversely, finding regression intercept differences empirically does not tell us about the group difference in the measurement intercepts.

The model in Equation 9.42 includes invariance constraints on all model parameters except the factor means. We now consider a weaker model that permits both the factor means and the factor covariance matrices $\boldsymbol{\Phi}_k$ to vary across groups. This model does not incorporate any measurement bias, unlike the model just considered. It can be shown (Millsap, 1995) that under this model, the regression slopes will be invariant if and only if

$$\mathbf{Db} = \mathbf{b}. \tag{9.57}$$

Here $\mathbf{D}$ is a diagonal matrix of eigenvalues in the spectral representation of

$$\mathbf{T}^{-1} \boldsymbol{\Phi}_1 \mathbf{T}^{-1'} = \mathbf{QDQ}'. \tag{9.58}$$

The matrix $\mathbf{T}$ is found through the triangular factoring $\mathbf{\Phi}_2 = \mathbf{TT'}$. The vector $\mathbf{b}$ is found as

$$\mathbf{b} = (\mathbf{D}^{-1} + \mathbf{H'H})^{-1}\mathbf{Q'T}, \tag{9.59}$$

$$\mathbf{H} = \mathbf{\Theta}_{z1}^{-1/2}\mathbf{\Lambda}_z\mathbf{T}. \tag{9.60}$$

This required condition is mathematically possible but highly unlikely, given that Equation 9.57 implies that all elements of $\mathbf{b}$ are zero except those that correspond to unit elements in $\mathbf{D}$. The implication is that if the factor covariance matrices vary across groups, slope invariance will almost surely not hold. As in the single factor case, there are a number of reasons why we might expect the factor covariance matrices to vary across groups.

Generalizations of the model just considered will require the introduction of measurement bias at some level. We have already considered a model that permits the measurement intercepts to vary. An alternative model would permit the unique factor covariance matrices $\mathbf{\Theta}_k$ to vary across groups, along with the factor means and the factor covariance matrices. We will retain the invariance constraints on the factor pattern matrices and measurement intercepts. In this situation, when will the groups have invariant regression slopes? It can be shown (Millsap, 1995) that the regression slopes are invariant if and only if the vector $\mathbf{b}$ in Equation 9.57 is an eigenvector corresponding to a unit eigenvalue of the matrix

$$\mathbf{DP\Omega P}^{-1}. \tag{9.61}$$

Here
   $\mathbf{D}$ is defined in Equation 9.58
   The matrix $\mathbf{\Omega}$ is diagonal
   $\mathbf{P}$ is nonsingular

with

$$\mathbf{P'(H'\Theta H)P} = \mathbf{\Omega} \qquad \mathbf{P'(H'H)P} = \mathbf{I}. \tag{9.62}$$

The matrix $\mathbf{H}$ was defined in Equation 9.60. The matrix $\mathbf{I}$ is an identity matrix. We also have

$$\mathbf{\Theta} = \mathbf{\Theta}_{zi}^{-1}\mathbf{\Theta}_{z2}. \tag{9.63}$$

The conditions required for slope invariance in this scenario are quite complex and, while mathematically possible, are unlikely to hold in real data. We can conclude that if both the factor covariance matrices and the unique factor covariance matrices vary over groups, slope invariance will not hold in general.

We have considered a variety of factor models, under varying numbers of variables p and numbers of factors r, for their implications for predictive invariance. We can summarize the findings first by saying that when a common factor model underlies $\mathbf{X}$, the presence or absence of regression invariance carries few implications for whether measurement bias is present. Consider the situation in which regression intercepts vary but regression slopes are invariant over groups. We have shown that this scenario could arise because (a) no measurement bias is present, and only factor means differ across groups, or (b) both factor means and measurement intercepts vary across groups, with the latter implying measurement bias. If the regression lines are identical across groups but the population means on $\mathbf{X}$ vary over groups (which is nearly always true in practice), the only scenario that explains this finding is one that permits both factor means and measurement intercepts to vary. Measurement bias again exists in this scenario. Hence, in this case, we can almost certainly infer that measurement bias is present. If we find that regression slopes vary across groups, many factor model scenarios are consistent with this situation, including some in which no measurement bias is present. The best option in ambiguous cases is to specify and test the proposed factor model directly, assuming that the values of p and r permit the model to be tested.

General Latent Variable Models

All of the preceding results have specified common factor models for $\mathbf{X} = (Y, \mathbf{Z})$ and have described the consequences for predictive invariance under varying levels of factorial invariance. The predictor and criterion scores in $\mathbf{X}$ are usually continuous or are discrete with a large number of possible values. Item response theory models do not offer much advantage in such cases. We can consider more general, nonparametric latent variable conditions that are relevant to predictive invariance.

Theorem 3.3 is relevant here. Changing notation to make the theorem more clear in the present context, consider the following statement of the theorem. Suppose that for all groups defined by $\mathbf{V}$,

$$P(Y \mid \mathbf{Z}, \mathbf{W}, \mathbf{V}) = P(Y \mid \mathbf{W}, \mathbf{V}). \tag{9.64}$$

Within any group, Y and $\mathbf{Z}$ are conditionally independent given $\mathbf{W}$. Here $\mathbf{W}$, $\mathbf{Z}$, and $\mathbf{V}$ can all be considered multivariate. Suppose also that

$$P(\mathbf{Z} \mid \mathbf{W}, \mathbf{V}) = P(\mathbf{Z} \mid \mathbf{W}), \tag{9.65}$$

$$P(Y \mid \mathbf{W}, \mathbf{V}) = P(Y \mid \mathbf{W}). \tag{9.66}$$

Both Y and $\mathbf{Z}$ are measurement invariant. Finally, suppose that neither $\mathbf{W}$ nor $\mathbf{Z}$ is independent of $\mathbf{V}$. In other words, there are group differences in the distributions of $\mathbf{W}$ and $\mathbf{Z}$. This will be true in nearly all investigations of measurement invariance. Then as shown in Chapter 3, it must be true that for at least some values of $\mathbf{Z}$,

$$P(Y \mid \mathbf{Z}, \mathbf{V}) \neq P(Y \mid \mathbf{Z}). \tag{9.67}$$

Predictive invariance cannot hold under these conditions, even though measurement invariance holds for both Y and $\mathbf{Z}$.

This theorem reveals a deep inconsistency between measurement invariance and predictive invariance in any situation involving (a) group differences in predictor and latent variable distributions, and (b) conditional or local independence as assumed by nearly all latent variable models. No other assumptions are required. No distributional assumptions are needed, and the dimension of $\mathbf{W}$ is not specified. The conditional independence assumption is relevant for the prediction context, where Y and $\mathbf{Z}$ are disjoint measures with no actual overlap.

The generality of the conditional independence theorem is an advantage because it does not require any specific latent variable model to underlie $\mathbf{X}$. On the other hand, the theorem is also not specific in describing the form of the violation of predictive invariance that might result from measurement invariance in $\mathbf{X}$. It is possible that the violation of predictive invariance is trivial from a practical standpoint. We will not be able to judge the practical significance of the violation without specifying a model, obtaining real data, and estimating some relevant parameters.

The theorem has a further important implication. Suppose that upon empirical investigation, we cannot find evidence of any violation of predictive invariance. If we conclude that predictive invariance does hold, we must then also conclude that measurement invariance fails to hold for Y, $\mathbf{Z}$, or both Y and $\mathbf{Z}$. In other words, predictive invariance in this situation implies that either the predictor or the criterion are biased as measures of $\mathbf{W}$. This inconsistency between predictive and measurement invariance was called the duality paradox in Millsap (1995).

The above results suggest that there are conditions under which it is possible to have both predictive invariance and conditional independence for $\mathbf{X} = (Y, \mathbf{Z})$. Specifically, suppose that conditional independence in Equation 9.64 holds and that we also have measurement invariance for Y in Equation 9.66. Suppose also that

$$P(\mathbf{W} \mid \mathbf{Z}, \mathbf{V}) = P(\mathbf{W} \mid \mathbf{Z}). \tag{9.68}$$

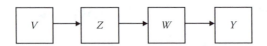

FIGURE 9.1
Path model with local independence for (Z, Y) and bias in Z.

Then it can be shown (Meredith & Millsap, 1992) that predictive invariance will hold. The condition in Equation 9.68 can be shown to imply that **Z** is biased as a measure of **W**. The condition in Equation 9.68 states that **W** and Y are conditionally independent given **Z**. One condition under which this condition might be sensible is when a formative measurement model holds for $(\mathbf{Z}, \mathbf{W})$, rather than the traditional reflective factor model (Bollen & Lennox, 1991). A path model representation of the resulting situation is shown in Figure 9.1 for the case in which all variables (Y, Z, W, V) are univariate. This scenario has appeared as a model in salary discrimination studies (McFatter, 1987; Millsap & Taylor, 1996). For the usual situation in which $(Y, \mathbf{Z})$ are each test scores or performance measures, this model seems unrealistic in its placement of **W** as formed by **Z**. A further problem is that in this scenario, group differences in **Z** exist that do not disappear once **W** is controlled. These differences will in turn affect any use of **Z** for selection or classification purposes, and the resulting impact may be hard to justify.

Conclusion

The purpose of this chapter has been to describe the implications of measurement bias for the use of tests in prediction across multiple populations. Differential prediction in this context refers to the moderation of the test's predictive properties by population membership. In psychological testing, differential prediction is usually equated with group differences in the linear regression relating the test to the criterion. To be more general, the concept of predictive invariance was here defined to parallel the earlier definition of measurement invariance in Chapter 3. The question then becomes how measurement bias is related to predictive bias, in both the general case and under specific measurement models and prediction methods. The case of linear regression was discussed extensively because this approach is commonly used. Similarly, the common factor model was a focus because it is a measurement model in frequent use. More general conditions were also considered. It was shown that under the usual local independence assumptions, a deep inconsistency exists between predictive invariance and measurement invariance for $(Y, \mathbf{Z})$.

The question of the relationship between measurement bias and predictive bias has not received much attention in the literature until recently

(Borsboom, Romeijn, & Wicherts, 2008; Bryant, 2004). Drasgow (1982) presented some conditions under which measurement bias might go undetected if test-criterion correlations were the focus of study. For many researchers, intuition would suggest that the presence of measurement bias should make predictive bias more likely, and hence that findings of predictive invariance should lead us to conclude that measurement invariance also holds. This "consistency" hypothesis may underlie viewpoints such as those in Jensen (1980), who stated that invariance in predictive relations between tests and criteria lend support for the factorial invariance of such tests. Similar ideas can be found in many other sources (Berk, 1982; Hunter, Schmidt, & Hunter, 1979; Hunter, Schmidt, & Rauschenberger, 1984; Murphy & Davidshofer, 1991; Sackett & Wilk, 1994; Shepard, 1982).

An interesting case study of the consistency viewpoint lies in the area of employment testing. Large meta-analytic studies of cognitive test correlations with performance criteria have been conducted in this domain, leading to the conclusion that across ethnic populations (and many other classifications as well), few if any real group differences exist in these correlations (Schmidt & Hunter, 1998). Few slope differences are found in empirical studies of differential prediction in this area (Gottfredson, 1994; Hartigan & Wigdor, 1989; Jensen, 1980; Sackett & Wilk, 1994; Schmidt et al., 1980). The general conclusion has been that at minimum, slope invariance holds across ethnic groups. It is also argued that a single common factor "g" underlies both test and job performance, accounting for a large share of the reliable variance in these measures (Gottfredson, 1988; Gottfredson & Crouse, 1986; Hunter, 1986; Ree & Earles, 1991; Ree, Earles, & Teachout, 1994; Schmidt, 1988; Thorndike, 1986). The "g" factor therefore accounts for most of the predictive power of cognitive tests in relation to job performance criteria. Finally, it is argued that ethnic group differences in test performance and job performance are largely due to differences in "g," rather than other influences such as measurement bias (Gottfredson; Jensen, 1985, 1986, 1992; Schmidt). The story that emerges from this body of research is then as follows. An invariant single factor model underlies both cognitive tests and job performance criteria across ethnic groups, and any systematic group differences on these measures are due to real group differences on that single factor. Furthermore, when these tests are used to predict job criteria, the regressions have essentially invariant slopes, and the correlations between the tests and criteria are invariant.

The results presented earlier in this chapter suggest that the above story is implausible. Under factorial invariance, slope invariance is possible only if the factor variances ϕ_k are also identical across groups. Given that mean differences on tests and criteria are observed and are believed to indicate population level differences, the above story suggests that the only factor model parameter that varies over groups is the mean of "g." It is unclear why we should expect differences in means but no differences in variances. In any case, the above model is directly testable using procedures discussed earlier, even if only a single predictor is used. Such tests would help settle the plausibility of the model just described in a way that continued empirical predictive studies cannot. As of this writing, no such tests of the model have been reported in the literature.

Group differences in regression intercepts with slopes that are invariant are consistent either with the highly constrained model just described or with one that permits group differences in measurement intercepts as well. Group differences in measurement intercepts are a form of measurement bias. If the possibility of bias is ignored, and the predictor test is used for prediction or selection purposes, what will happen? Suppose that the regression results reveal a larger regression intercept for the majority or reference group. A common regression line would then appear to penalize the reference group through under-prediction. Assuming that the difference in regression intercepts is not too large, we might then choose to go ahead and use a common line as a basis for selection of individuals, arguing that the resulting penalty to the majority group is ignorable. Hartigan and Wigdor (1989) noted empirical regression findings of this type. If in reality, the measurement intercepts vary across groups so that bias against the minority group is present, what would be the impact on selection?

This question does not appear to have received systematic study, a fact that is not surprising given the general view that group differences in factor structure in many applied settings are ignorable or do not exist. Millsap and Kwok (2004) investigated the impact of violations of factorial invariance on group differences in sensitivity, specificity, and positive predictive value (success ratio) for the test. Quantities such as sensitivity and specificity are more familiar to practitioners and less abstract than factor loadings. The motivation here is to understand whether measurement bias, if present, contributes significantly to inaccuracy in selecting people based on test scores. It may be true that measurement bias contributes little to inaccuracy under some conditions. Also, it is true that group differences in sensitivity, specificity, and positive predictive value will exist even if no measurement bias is present, given group differences in latent variable distributions (Borsboom et al., 2008). The question of interest is whether measurement bias worsens the inaccuracy to a meaningful degree.

The approach taken in Millsap and Kwok (2004) considered a single predictor test whose items fit a conventional single factor model in all groups. Measurement bias is represented as a violation of factorial invariance. It is assumed that a cutpoint on the test score distribution (the sum of the item scores) is established based on a desired percentile to be selected in the pooled population that combines all groups. An analogous cutpoint is then hypothesized for the factor scores, establishing the same percentile. Considering the bivariate distribution of test and factor scores, the two cutpoints create quadrants in this bivariate distribution. Sensitivity, specificity, and positive predictive value can then be calculated once the bivariate distributions for each separate group are located. In this way, one can treat any hypothetical scenario that combines group differences in factor means and variances, along with group differences in factor structure. The factor structure determines the relationship between the factor scores and the test scores through parameters that determine item and total test scores at any given factor score. The factor structure also determines the communality, or the correlation between factor and test scores. The hypothesized model can include varying degrees of measurement bias, ranging from none at all to large group differences in relevant parameters such as measurement intercepts or factor loadings. It then becomes possible to actually see what happens to sensitivity in the various groups, for example, as the degree of measurement bias grows or shrinks. The procedure requires some assumptions about the shape of the bivariate distributions. Bivariate normal distributions were used in Millsap and Kwok. Any plausible assumptions can be used, as long as it is possible to calculate the relevant accuracy measures. Given enough data, the bivariate distributions could even be based on real empirical studies.

The procedure in Millsap and Kwok (2004) addressed how measurement bias might affect the accuracy of selection, treated as a binary decision (e.g., select or not select). If a binary decision is the outcome of interest, this procedure may be useful. If the outcome of interest is an actual quantitative prediction for Y, we can quantify how systematic errors of prediction are affected by the absence or presence of measurement bias. For example, suppose that the predictions are generated using linear regression. From earlier results, we know how the regression equations are determined by the underlying factor model. For any given factor score, it is possible to calculate a prediction using a parameterization that either does or does not incorporate measurement bias. The impact of measurement bias can then be studied through comparisons of predicted scores with or without bias in measurement. This impact could then be summarized across the factor score distributions by group.

The results in this chapter suggest that anyone who is using psychological measures for predictive purposes in multiple populations should be concerned about the issue of measurement invariance. It is quite possible that there are no apparent group differences in the prediction model, even though the predictors Z or the criterion Y are biased in the measurement sense. In such situations, one might investigate measurement bias directly using the methods described in this book, or, at minimum, conduct sensitivity analyses tailored to the local situation as done in Millsap and Kwok (2004). Sensitivity analyses could take many other forms, depending on the type of measurement model considered appropriate for the measures at hand. None of these options will be pursued if researchers fail to consider the issue of measurement invariance, however. It is hoped that the results in this book will convince the reader of the importance of invariance in measurement.

References

Ackerman, T. A. (1992). A didactic explanation of item bias, item impact, and item validity from a multidimensional perspective. *Journal of Educational Measurement, 29*, 67–91.

Ackerman, T. A., & Evans, J. A. (1994). The influence of conditioning scores in performing DIF analyses. *Applied Psychological Measurement, 18*, 329–342.

Agresti, A. (2002). *Categorical data analysis* (2nd ed.). New York: Wiley-Interscience.

Agresti, A., & Yang, M. (1987). An empirical investigation of some effects of sparseness in contingency tables. *Computational Statistics and Data Analysis, 5*, 9–21.

Aguinis, H. (2004). *Regression analysis for categorical moderators.* New York: Guilford.

Ahmavaara, Y. (1954). The mathematical theory of factorial invariance under selection. *Psychometrika, 19*, 27–38.

Aitken, A. C. (1934). Note on selection from a multivariate normal population. *Proceedings of the Edinburgh Mathematical Society, 4*, 106–110.

Akaike, H. (1973). Information theory and an extension of the maximum likelihood principle. In B. N. Petrov & F. Csaki (Eds.), *Second international symposium on information theory* (pp. 26–281). Budapest: Akademiai Kiado.

Alexander, R. A., & DeShon, R. P. (1994). Effect of error variance heterogeneity on the power of tests for regression slope differences. *Psychological Bulletin, 115*, 308–314.

Alexander, R. A., & Govern, D. M. (1994). A new and simpler approximation for ANOVA under variance heterogeneity. *Journal of Educational Statistics, 19*, 91–101.

Algina, J. (1980). A note on identification in the oblique and orthogonal factor analysis models. *Psychometrika, 45*, 393–396.

Algina, J., & Penfield, R. D. (2009). Classical test theory. In R. E. Millsap & A. Maydeu-Olivares (Eds.), *The Sage handbook of quantitative methods in psychology* (pp. 93–122). London: Sage Publications.

Allen, N. L., & Holland, P. W. (1993). A model for missing information about the group membership of examinees in DIF studies. In P. W. Holland & H. Wainer (Eds.), *Differential item functioning* (pp. 241–252). Hillsdale, NJ: Erlbaum.

Allen, M. J., & Yen, W. M. (1979). *Introduction to measurement theory.* Florence, KY: Wadsworth.

Amemiya, T. (1985). *Advanced econometrics.* Cambridge, MA: Harvard University Press.

Andersen, E. B. (1970). Asymptotic properties of conditional maximum likelihood estimators. *Journal of the Royal Statistical Society, Series B, 32*, 283–301.

Andersen, E. B. (1973). A goodness of fit test for the Rasch model. *Psychometrika, 38*, 123–140.

Andersen, E. B. (1977). Sufficient statistics and latent trait models. *Psychometrika, 42*, 69–81.

Andersen, E. B. (1980). *Discrete statistical models with social science applications.* Amsterdam: North-Holland.

Anderson, T. W. (1984). *An introduction to multivariate statistical analysis* (2nd ed.). New York: Wiley.

Anderson, T. W., & Rubin, H. (1956). Statistical inference in factor analysis. In J. Neyman (Ed.), *Proceedings of the third Berkeley symposium on mathematical statistics and probability* (pp. 111–150). Berkeley, CA: University of California Press.

Andrich, D. (1978a). A rating formulation for ordered response categories. *Psychometrika, 43,* 561–573.

Andrich, D. (1978b). Application of a psychometric rating model to ordered categories which are scored with successive integers. *Applied Psychological Measurement, 2,* 581–594.

Andrich, D. (1985). A latent trait model for items with response dependencies: Implications for test construction and analysis. In S. E. Embretson (Ed.), *Test design: Developments in psychology and psychometrics* (pp. 245–275). Orlando, FL: Academic Press.

Andrich, D., & Luo, G. (1993). A hyperbolic cosine latent trait model for unfolding dichotomous single-stimulus responses. *Applied Psychological Measurement, 17,* 253–276.

Angoff, W. H. (1993). Perspectives on differential item functioning methodology. In P. W. Holland & H. Wainer (Eds.), *Differential item functioning* (pp. 3–23). Hillsdale, NJ: Erlbaum.

Ankenmann, R. D., Witt, E. A., & Dunbar, S. B. (1999). An investigation of the power of the likelihood-ratio goodness-of-fit statistic in detecting differential item functioning. *Journal of Educational Measurement, 36,* 277–300.

Arbuckle, J. L., & Wothke, W. (1999). *AMOS 4.0 user's guide.* Chicago: Smallwaters Corporation.

Archer, R. P., & Klinefelter, D. (1991). MMPI factor analytic findings for adolescents: Item and scale-level factor structures. *Journal of Personality Assessment, 57,* 356–367.

Arminger, G. (1995). Specification and estimation of mean structures: Regression models. In G. Arminger, C. G. Clogg & M. E. Sobel (Eds.), *Handbook of statistical modeling for the social and behavioral sciences* (pp. 77–183). New York: Plenum Press.

Babakus, E., Ferguson, C. E., & Jöreskog, K. G. (1987). The sensitivity of confirmatory maximum likelihood factor analysis to violations of measurement scale and distributional assumptions. *Journal of Marketing Research, 24,* 222–228.

Baker, F. B. (1992a). Equating tests under the graded-response model. *Applied Psychological Measurement, 16,* 87–96.

Baker, F. B. (1992b). *Item response theory: Parameter estimation techniques.* New York: Marcel Dekker.

Baker, F. B. (1993). EQUATE 2.0: A computer program for the characteristic curve method of IRT equating. *Applied Psychological Measurement, 17,* 20.

Baker, F. B., & Al-Karni, A. (1991). A comparison of two procedures for computing IRT equating coefficients. *Journal of Educational Measurement, 28,* 147–162.

Bartholomew, D. J. (1980). Factor analysis for categorical data. *Journal of the Royal Statistical Society, Series B, 42,* 293–321.

Bartholomew, D. J. (1981). Posterior analysis of the factor model. *British Journal of Mathematical and Statistical Psychology, 34,* 93–99.

Bartholomew, D. J. (1983). Latent variable models for ordered-categorical data. *Journal of Econometrics, 22,* 229–243.

Bartholomew, D. J. (1984). Scaling binary data using a factor model. *Journal of the Royal Statistical Society, Series B, 46,* 120–123.

Bartholomew, D. J. (1987). *Latent variable models and factor analysis.* London: Charles Griffin & Company.

Bartholomew, D. J. (1996). Comment on: Metaphor taken as math: Indeterminacy in the common factor model. *Multivariate Behavioral Research, 31,* 551–554.

Bartholomew, D. J., & Leung, S. O. (2002). A goodness-of-fit test for sparse 2^p contingency tables. *British Journal of Mathematical and Statistical Psychology, 55,* 1–15.

Barrett, P. (2007). Structural equation modeling: Adjudging model fit. *Personality and Individual Differences, 42,* 815–824.

Bartlett, M. S. (1950). Tests of significance in factor analysis. *British Journal of Psychology (Statistics Section), 3,* 77–85.

Basilevsky, A. (1994). *Statistical factor analysis and related methods: Theory and applications.* New York: Wiley.

Beguin, A. A., & Glas, C. A. W. (2001). MCMC estimation and some model-fit analyses of multidimensional IRT models. *Psychometrika, 66,* 541–562.

Bekker, P. A. (1986). A note on the identification of restricted factor loading matrices. *Psychometrika, 51,* 607–611.

Bekker, P. A., Merckens, A., & Wansbeek, T. J. (1994). *Identification, equivalent models, and computer algebra.* Boston: Academic Press.

Bekker, P. A., & ten Berge, J. M. F. (1997). Generic global identification in factor analysis. *Linear Algebra and Applications, 264,* 255–263.

Benjamini, Y., & Hochberg, Y. (1995). Controlling the false discovery rate: A practical and powerful approach to multiple testing. *Journal of the Royal Statistical Society, Series B, 57,* 289–300.

Bentler, P. M. (1990). Comparative fit indexes in structural models. *Psychological Bulletin, 107,* 238–246.

Bentler, P. M. (1995). *EQS structural equations program manual.* Encino, CA: Multivariate Software Inc.

Berk, R. A. (Ed.). (1982). *Handbook of methods for detecting test bias.* Baltimore: Johns Hopkins University Press.

Bernstein, I. H., & Teng, G. (1989). Factoring items and factoring scales are different: Spurious evidence of multidimensionality due to item categorization. *Psychological Bulletin, 105,* 467–477.

Beuducel, A., & Wittmann, W. (2005). Simulation study on fit indices in confirmatory factor analysis based on data with slightly distorted simple structure. *Structural Equation Modeling, 12,* 41–75.

Bickel, P. D., & Doksum, K. A. (1977). *Mathematical statistics: Basic ideas and selected topics.* San Francisco, CA: Holden-Day.

Birnbaum, M. H. (1979). Procedures for the detection and correction of salary inequities. In T. R. Pezzullo & B. F. Brittingham (Eds.), *Salary equity* (pp. 121–144), Lexington, MA: Lexington Books.

Bishop, Y. M. M., Feinberg, S. E., & Holland, P. W. (1975). *Discrete multivariate analysis.* Cambridge, MA: MIT Press.

Bloxom, B. (1972). Alternative approaches to factorial invariance. *Psychometrika, 37,* 425–440.

Bock, R. D. (1972). Estimating item parameters and latent ability when responses are scored in two or more nominal categories. *Psychometrika, 37,* 29–31.

Bock, R. D., & Aitkin, M. (1981). Marginal maximum likelihood estimation of item parameters: An application of the EM algorithm. *Psychometrika, 46*, 443–449.

Bock, R. D., Gibbons, R., & Muraki, E. (1988). Full-information item factor analysis. *Applied Psychological Measurement, 12*, 261–280.

Bollen, K. A. (1989). *Structural equations with latent variables.* New York: Wiley.

Bollen, K. A. (1996). An alternative 2SLS estimator for latent variable models. *Psychometrika, 61*, 109–121.

Bollen, K. A. (2001). Two-stage least squares and latent variable models: Simultaneous estimation and robustness to misspecifications. In R. Cudeck, S. Du Toit, & D. Sörbom (Eds.), *Structural equation modeling: Present and future* (pp. 119–138). Lincolnwood, IL: Scientific Software.

Bollen, K. A., & Jöreskog, K. G. (1985). Uniqueness does not imply identification. *Sociological Methods and Research, 14*, 155–163.

Bollen, K. A., & Lennox, R. (1991). Conventional wisdom on measurement: A structural equation perspective. *Psychological Bulletin, 110*, 305–314.

Bolstad, W. M. (2010). *Understanding computational Bayesian statistics.* Hoboken, NJ: Wiley.

Boomsma, A., & Hoogland, J. J. (2001). The robustness of LISREL modeling revisited. In R. Cudeck, S. Du Toit, & D. Sörbom (Eds.), *Structural equation modeling: Present and future* (pp. 139–168), Lincolnwood, IL: Scientific Software.

Borsboom, D. (2005). *Measuring the mind: Conceptual issues in contemporary psychometrics.* Cambridge: Cambridge University Press.

Borsboom, D., Romeijn, J. W., & Wicherts, J. M. (2008). Measurement invariance versus selection invariance: Is fair selection possible? *Psychological Methods, 13*, 75–98.

Bradlow, E. T., Wainer, H., & Wang, X. (1999). A Bayesian random effects model for testlets. *Psychometrika, 64*, 153–168.

Brennan, R. L. (2001). *Generalizability theory.* New York: Springer.

Browne, M. W. (1974). Generalized least squares in the analysis of covariance structures. *South African Statistical Journal, 8*, 1–24.

Browne, M. W. (1982). Covariance structures. In D. M. Hawkins (Ed.), *Topics in multivariate analysis* (pp. 72–141). Cambridge: Cambridge University Press.

Browne, M. W. (1984). Asymptotically distribution free methods in the analysis of covariance structures. *British Journal of Mathematical and Statistical Psychology, 37*, 62–83.

Browne, M. W., & Arminger, G. (1995). Specification and estimation of mean and covariance structure models. In G. Arminger, C. C. Clogg, & M. E. Sobel (Eds.), *Handbook of statistical modeling for the social and behavioral sciences* (pp. 185–249). New York: Plenum Press.

Browne, M. W., & Cudeck, R. (1993). Alternative ways of assessing model fit. In K. A. Bollen & J. S. Long (Eds.), *Testing structural equation models* (pp. 136–162). Newbury Park, CA: Sage Publications.

Bryant, D. U. (2004). *The effects of differential item functioning on predictive bias.* Unpublished doctoral dissertation, University of Central Florida, Orlando, FL.

Burnham, K. P., & Anderson, D. R. (1998). *Model selection and inference: A practical information-theoretic approach.* New York: Springer.

Buse, A. (1982). The likelihood ratio, Wald, and Lagrange multiplier tests: An expository note. *American Statistician, 36*, 153–157.

Butcher, J. N., Dahlstrom, W. G., Graham, J. R., Tellegan, A., & Kaemmer, B. (1989). *MMPI-2 manual for administration and scoring*. Minneapolis, MN: University of Minnesota.

Byrne, B. M., Shavelson, R. J., & Muthén, B. (1989). Testing for equivalence of factor covariance and mean structures: The issue of partial measurement invariance. *Psychological Bulletin, 105*, 456–466.

Cai, L. (in press). High dimensional exploratory item factor analysis by a Metropolis–Hastings Robbins-Monro algorithm. *Psychometrika, 75*, 33–57.

Cai, L., Maydeu-Olivares, A., Coffman, D., & Thissen, D. L. (2006). Limited information goodness of fit testing of item response theory models in sparse 2^p tables. *British Journal of Mathematical and Statistical Psychology, 59*, 173–194.

Camilli, G. (1992). A conceptual analysis of differential item functioning in terms of a multidimensional item response model. *Applied Psychological Measurement, 16*, 129–147.

Camilli, G., & Shepard, L. A. (1994). *Methods for identifying biased test items*. Thousand Oaks, CA: Sage Publications.

Camilli, G., & Smith, J. K. (1990). Comparison of the Mantel–Haenszel test with a randomized and a jackknife test for detecting biased items. *Journal of Educational Statistics, 15*, 53–67.

Campbell, D. T., & Fiske, D. W. (1959). Convergent and discriminant validation by the multitrait-multimethod matrix. *Psychological Bulletin, 56*, 81–105.

Candell, G. L., & Drasgow, F. (1988). An iterative procedure for linking metrics and assessing item bias in item response theory. *Applied Psychological Measurement, 12*, 253–260.

Carroll, J. B. (1945). The effect of difficulty and chance success on correlations between items and between tests. *Psychometrika, 26*, 347–372.

Carroll, J. B. (1983). The difficulty of a test and its factor composition revisited. In H. Wainer & S. Messick (Eds.), *Principles of modern psychological measurement*. Hillsdale, NJ: Erlbaum.

Cattell, R. B. (1944). "Parallel proportional profiles" and other principles for determining the choice of factors by rotation. *Psychometrika, 9*, 267–283.

Cattell, R. B. (1966a). *Handbook of multivariate experimental psychology*. New York: Rand McNally.

Cattell, R. B. (1966b). The scree test for the number of factors. *Multivariate Behavioral Research, 1*, 245–276.

Cattell, R. B. (1972). Real base, true zero factor analysis. *Multivariate Behavioral Research Monograph, 72–1*. Fort Worth, TX: Texas Christian University.

Cattell, R. B., & Cattell, A. K. S. (1955). Factor rotation for proportional profiles: Analytic solution and an example. *British Journal of Statistical Psychology, 8*, 83–92.

Chang, H. H., & Mazzeo, J. (1994). The unique correspondence of the item response function and the item category response functions in polytomously scored item response models. *Psychometrika, 59*, 391–404.

Chang, H. H., Mazzeo, J., & Roussos, L. (1996). Detecting DIF for polytomously scored items: An adaptation of the SIBTEST procedure. *Journal of Educational Measurement, 33*, 333–353.

Chou, C. P., & Bentler, P. M. (1995). Estimates and tests in structural equation modeling. In R. H. Hoyle (Ed.), *Structural equation modeling: Concepts, issues, and applications* (pp. 37–55). Thousand Oaks, CA: Sage Publications.

Chou, C. P., Bentler, P. M., & Satorra, A. (1991). Scaled test statistics and robust standard errors for non-normal data in covariance structure analysis: A Monte Carlo study. *British Journal of Mathematical and Statistical Psychology, 44,* 347–357.

Christensen, R. (1997). *Log-linear models and logistic regression.* New York: Springer.

Christoffersson, A. (1975). Factor analysis of dichotomized variables. *Psychometrika, 40,* 5–32.

Cleary, T. A. (1968). Test bias: Prediction of grades of Negro and white students in integrated colleges. *Journal of Educational Measurement, 5,* 115–124.

Cliff, N. (1979). Test theory without true scores? *Psychometrika, 44,* 373–393.

Cliff, N. (1989). Ordinal consistency and ordinal true scores. *Psychometrika, 54,* 75–91.

Cliff, N. (1993). What is and isn't measurement. In G. Keren & C. Lewis (Eds.), *A handbook for data analysis in the behavioral sciences: Methodological issues* (pp. 59–93). Hillsdale, NJ: Erlbaum.

Cliff, N., & Keats, J. A. (2003). *Ordinal measurement in the behavioral sciences.* Mahwah, NJ: Erlbaum.

Cochran, W. G. (1954). Some methods for strengthening the common χ^2 tests. *Biometrics, 10,* 417–451.

Cohen, A. S., & Kim, S. H. (1993). A comparison of Lord's χ^2 and Raju's area measures in the detection of DIF. *Applied Psychological Measurement, 17,* 39–52.

Cohen, A. S., & Kim, S. H. (1998). An investigation of linking methods under the graded response model. *Applied Psychological Measurement, 22,* 116–130.

Cohen, A. S., Kim, S. H., & Baker, F. B. (1993). Detection of differential item functioning in the graded response model. *Applied Psychological Measurement, 17,* 335–350.

Cohen, A. S., Kim, S. H., & Subkoviak, M. J. (1991). Influence of prior distributions on detection of DIF. *Journal of Educational Measurement, 28,* 49–59.

Cohen, A. S., Kim, S. H., & Wollack, J. A. (1996). An investigation of the likelihood-ratio test for detection of differential item functioning. *Applied Psychological Measurement, 20,* 15–26.

Collins, L. M., & Lanza, S. T. (2009). *Latent class and latent transition analysis: With applications in the social, behavioral, and health sciences.* New York: Wiley.

Coombs, C. H. (1964). *A Theory of data.* New York: Wiley.

Costa, P. T., Zonderman, A. B., McCrae, R. R., & Williams, J. B., Jr. (1985). Content and comprehensiveness in the MMPI: An item factor analysis in a normal adult sample. *Journal of Personality and Social Psychology, 48,* 925–933.

Crane, P. K., Gibbons, L. E., Jolley, L., & van Belle, G. (2006). Differential item functioning analysis with ordinal logistic regression techniques: DIFdetect and difwithpar. *Medical Care, 44*(Suppl. 3), S115–S123.

Crane, P. K., van Belle, G., & Larson, E. B. (2004). Test bias in a cognitive test: Differential item functioning in the CASI. *Statistics in Medicine, 23,* 241–256.

Cressie, N., & Holland, P. W. (1983). Characterizing the manifest probabilities of latent trait models. *Psychometrika, 48,* 129–141.

Cronbach, L. J., Gleser, G. C., Nanda, H., & Rajaratnam, N. (1972). *The dependability of behavioral measurements.* New York: Wiley.

Croon, M. (1990). Latent class analysis with ordered classes. *British Journal of the Mathematical Statistical Society, 43,* 171–192.

Cudeck, R. (1989). Analysis of correlation matrices using covariance structure models. *Psychological Bulletin, 105,* 317–327.

Curran, P. J., Bollen, K. A., Chen, F., Paxton, P., & Kirby, J. (2003). The finite sampling properties of the RMSEA: Point estimates and confidence intervals. *Sociological Methods and Research, 32*, 208–252.

Curran, P. J., Bollen, K. A., Paxton, P., Kirby, J., & Chen, F. (2002). The noncentral chi-square distribution in misspecified structural equation models: Finite sample results from a Monte Carlo simulation. *Multivariate Behavioral Research, 37*, 1–36.

Curran, P. J., West, S. G., & Finch, J. F. (1997). The robustness of test statistics to nonnormality and specification error in confirmatory factor analysis. *Psychological Methods, 1*, 16–29.

De Ayala, R. J. (2009). *The theory and practice of item response theory.* New York: Guilford.

Deshon, R. P. (2004). Measures are not invariant across groups without error variance homogeneity. *Psychology Science, 46*, 137–149.

DeShon, R. P., & Alexander, R. A. (1996). Alternative procedures for testing regression slope homogeneity when group error variances are not equal. *Psychological Methods, 1*, 261–277.

Divgi, D. R. (1985). A minimum chi-square method for developing a common metric in item response theory. *Applied Psychological Measurement, 9*, 413–415.

Dolan, C. V. (2009). Structural equation mixture modeling. In R. E. Millsap & A. Maydeu-Olivares (Eds.), *The Sage handbook of quantitative methods in psychology* (pp. 568–591). London: Sage Publications.

Donoghue, J. R., & Allen, N. L. (1993). Thin versus thick matching in the Mantel–Haenszel procedure for detecting DIF. *Journal of Educational Statistics, 18*, 131–154.

Donoghue, J. R., Holland, P. W., & Thayer, D. T. (1993). A Monte Carlo study of factors that affect the Mantel–Haenszel and standardization measures of differential item functioning. In P. Holland & H. Wainer (Eds.), *Differential item functioning* (pp. 137–166). Hillsdale, NJ: Erlbaum.

Donoghue, J. R., & Isham, S. P. (1998). A comparison of procedures to detect item parameter drift. *Applied Psychological Measurement, 22*, 33–51.

Dorans, N. J., & Holland, P. W. (1993). DIF detection and description: Mantel–Haenszel and standardization. In P. W. Holland & H. Wainer (Eds.), *Differential item functioning* (pp. 35–66). Hillsdale, NJ: Erlbaum.

Dorans, N. J., & Kulick, E. (1983). Assessing unexpected differential item performance of female candidates on SAT and TSWE forms administered in December 1977: An application of the standardization approach (RR-83-9). Princeton, NJ: Educational Testing Service.

Dorans, N. J., & Kulick, E. (1986). Demonstrating the utility of the standardization approach to assessing unexpected differential item performance on the Scholastic Aptitude Test. *Journal of Educational Measurement, 23*, 355–368.

Dorans, N. J., & Schmitt, A. P. (1993). Constructed response and differential item functioning: A pragmatic approach. In R. E. Bennett & W. C. Ward (Eds.), *Construction versus choice in cognitive measurement: Issues in constructed response, performance testing, and portfolio assessment* (pp. 135–165). Hillsdale, NJ: Erlbaum.

Dorans, N. J., Schmitt, A. P., & Bleistein, C. A. (1988). *The standardization approach to assessing differential speededness* (Research Report No. 88–31). Princeton, NJ: Educational Testing Service.

Douglas, J., Kim, H. R., & Stout, W. (1996). Item bundle DIF hypothesis testing: Identifying suspect bundles and assessing their DIF. *Journal of Educational Measurement, 33*, 465–484.

Douglas, J., Stout, W., & DiBello, L. (1996). A kernel smoothed version of SIBTEST with applications to local DIF inference and function estimation. *Journal of Educational and Behavioral Statistics, 21*, 333–363.

Drasgow, F. (1982). Biased test items and differential validity. *Psychological Bulletin, 92*, 526–531.

Drasgow, F. (1987). Study of the measurement bias of two standardized psychological tests. *Journal of Applied Psychology, 72*, 19–29.

Drasgow, F., Levine, M. V., & Williams, E. A. (1985). Appropriateness measurement with polychotomous item response models and standardized indices. *British Journal of Mathematical and Statistical Psychology, 38*, 67–86.

Dretzke, B. J., Levin, J. R., & Serlin, R. C. (1982). Testing for regression homogeneity under variance heterogeneity. *Psychological Bulletin, 91*, 376–383.

Duncan, O. D. (1984). Rasch measurement: Further examples and discussion. In C. F. Turner & E. Martin (Eds.), *Surveying subjective phenomena* (Vol. 2, pp. 367–403). New York: Russell Sage Foundation.

Dunn, J. E. (1973). A note on sufficiency condition for uniqueness of a restricted factor matrix. *Psychometrika, 38*, 141–143.

Edelen, M. O., Thissen, D., Teresi, J. A., Kleinman, M., & Ocepek-Welikson, K. (2006). Identification of differential item functioning using item response theory and the likelihood-based model comparison approach: Application to the Mini-Mental State Examination. *Medical Care, 44*, S134–S142.

Edwards, M. C. (2010). A Markov Chain Monte Carlo approach to confirmatory item factor analysis. *Psychometrika, 75*, 474–497.

Ellis, J. L., & Van den Wollenberg, A. L. (1993). Local homogeneity in latent trait models: A characterization of the homogeneous monotone IRT model. *Psychometrika, 58*, 417–429.

Embretson, S. E., & Reise, S. P. (2000). *Item response theory for psychologists.* Mahwah, NJ: Erlbaum.

Everitt, B. S. (1984). *An introduction to latent variable models.* London: Chapman & Hall.

Fan, X., & Sivo, S. A. (2005). Sensitivity of fit indices to misspecified structural or measurement model components: Rationale of the two-index strategy revisited. *Structural Equation Modeling, 12*, 343–367.

Finch, H. (2005). The MIMIC model as a method for detecting DIF: Comparison with Mantel–Haenszel, SIBTEST, and the IRT likelihood-ratio. *Applied Psychological Measurement, 29*, 278–295.

Fischer, G. H. (1968). *Psychologische Testtheorie.* Bern, Switzerland: Huber.

Fischer, G. H. (1995a). Some neglected problems in IRT. *Psychometrika, 60*, 459–487.

Fischer, G. H. (1995b). Deviations of the Rasch model. In G. H. Fischer & I. W. Molenaar (Eds.), *Rasch models: Foundations, recent developments, and applications* (pp. 15–38). New York: Springer.

Fischer, G. H., & Molenaar, I. W. (Eds.). (1995). *Rasch models: Foundations, recent developments, and applications.* New York: Springer.

Flanagan, D. P., McGrew, K. S., & Ortiz, S. O. (2000). *The Wechsler intelligence scales and Gf-Gc theory: A contemporary approach to interpretation.* Boston: Allyn and Bacon.

Flora, D. B., & Curran, P. J. (2004). An empirical evaluation of alternative methods of estimation for confirmatory factor analysis with ordinal data. *Psychological Methods, 9*, 466–491.

Flowers, C. P., Oshima, T. C., & Raju, N. S. (1999). A description and demonstration of the polytomous DFIT framework. *Applied Psychological Measurement, 23*, 309–326.

Flowers, L., Osterlind, S. J., Pascarella, E. T., & Pierson, C. T. (2001). How much do students learn in college?: Cross-sectional estimates using the College BASE. *Journal of Higher Education, 72*, 565–583.

Fox, J.-P., & Glas, C. A. W. (2001). Bayesian estimation of multilevel IRT models using Gibbs sampling. *Psychometrika, 66*, 271–288.

Fuller, W. A. (1987). *Measurement error models.* New York: Wiley.

Gelman, A., Carlin, J. B., Stern, H. S., & Rubin, D. B. (2003). *Bayesian data analysis.* New York: Chapman & Hall.

Geman, S., & Geman, D. (1984). Stochastic relaxation, Gibbs distributions and Bayesian restoration of images. *IEEE Transactions on Pattern Analysis and Machine Intelligence, 6*, 721–741.

Gibson, W. A. (1959). Three multivariate models: Factor analysis, latent structure analysis, and latent profile analysis. *Psychometrika, 24*, 229–252.

Glas, C. A. W. (1988). The derivation of some tests for the Rasch model from the multinomial distribution. *Psychometrika, 53*, 525–546.

Glas, C. A. W. (1989). *Contributions to estimating and testing Rasch models.* Doctoral thesis, University of Twente, Enschede.

Glas, C. A. W. (1999). Modification indices for the 2-pl and the nominal response model. *Psychometrika, 64*, 273–294.

Glas, C. A. W., & Ellis, J. L. (1994). *Rasch scaling program.* Groningen, The Netherlands: iecProGAMMA.

Glas, C. A. W., & Verhelst, N. D. (1995a). Testing the Rasch model. In G. H. Fischer & I. W. Molenaar (Eds.), *Rasch models: Foundations, recent developments, and applications* (pp. 69–95). New York: Springer.

Glas, C. A. W., & Verhelst, N. D. (1995b). Tests of fit for polytomous Rasch models. In G. H. Fischer & I. W. Molenaar (Eds.), *Rasch models: Foundations, recent developments, and applications* (pp. 325–352). New York: Springer.

Golembiewski, R. T., Billingsley, K., & Yeager, S. (1976). Measuring change and persistence in human affairs: Types of change demonstrated by OD designs. *Journal of Applied Behavioral Science, 12*, 133–157.

Gorsuch, R. L. (1983). *Factor analysis.* Mahwah, NJ: Erlbaum.

Gottfredson, L. S. (1988). Reconsidering fairness: A matter of social and ethical priorities. *Journal of Vocational Behavior, 33*, 293–319.

Gottfredson, L. S. (1994). The science and politics of race norming. *American Psychologist, 49*, 955–963.

Gottfredson, L. S., & Crouse, J. (1986). Validity versus utility of mental tests: Example of the SAT. *Journal of Vocational Behavior, 29*, 363–378.

Gregorich, S. E. (2006). Do self-report instruments allow meaningful comparisons across diverse population groups? Testing measurement invariance using the confirmatory factor analysis framework. *Medical Care, 44*, S78-S94.

Gulliksen, H. (1950). *Theory of mental tests.* New York: Wiley.

Gulliksen, H., & Wilks, S. S. (1950). Regression tests for several samples. *Psychometrika, 15*, 91–114.

Gustafsson, J. E. (1980). Testing and obtaining fit of data to the Rasch model. *British Journal of Mathematical and Statistical Psychology, 33*, 205–233.

Guttman, L. (1950). The basis for scalogram analysis. In S. A. Stoufer, L. Guttman, E. A. Suchman, P. L. Lazarsfeld, S. A. Star, & J. A. Clausen (Eds.), *Studies in social psychology in World War II: Vol. 4. Measurement and prediction* (pp. 60–90). Princeton, NJ: Princeton University Press.

Guttman, L. (1953). Image theory for the structure of quantitative variates. *Psychometrika, 18*, 277–296.

Guttman, L. (1954). Some necessary conditions for common-factor analysis. *Psychometrika, 19*, 149–161.

Guttman, L. (1955). The determining of factor score matrices with implications for five other basic problems of common-factor theory. *British Journal of Statistical Psychology, 8*, 65–81.

Guttman, L. (1992). The irrelevance of factor analysis for the study of group differences. *Multivariate Behavioral Research, 27*, 175–204.

Guttman, L., & Levy, S. (1991). Two structural laws for intelligence tests. *Intelligence, 15*, 79–103.

Haberman, S. J. (1977). Maximum likelihood estimates in exponential response models. *The Annals of Statistics, 5*, 815–841.

Haebara, T. (1980). Equating logistic ability scales by a weighted least squares method. *Japanese Psychological Research, 22*, 144–149.

Hambleton, R. K., & Swaminathan, H. (1985). *Item response theory: Principles and applications*. Boston: Kluwer-Nijhoff.

Hancock, G. R., & Samuelsen, K. M. (Eds.). (2008). *Latent variable mixture models*. Charlotte, NC: Information Age Publishing.

Hanson, B. A. (1998). Uniform DIF and DIF defined by differences in item response functions. *Journal of Educational and Behavioral Statistics, 23*, 244–253.

Harrison, D. (1986). Robustness of IRT parameter estimation to violations of the unidimensionality assumption. *Journal of Educational Statistics, 11*, 91–115.

Hartigan, J. A., & Wigdor, A. K. (Eds.). (1989). *Fairness in employment testing: Validity generalization, minority issues, and the General Aptitude Test Battery*. Washington, DC: National Academy Press.

Hastings, W. K. (1970). Monte Carlo sampling methods using Markov chains and their applications. *Biometrika, 57*, 97–109.

Hathaway, S. R., & McKinley, J. C. (1940). *The MMPI manual*. New York: The Psychological Corporation.

Hathaway, S. R., & McKinley, J. C. (1983). *The MMPI manual*. New York: The Psychological Corporation.

Hattie, J. (1985). Methodology review: Assessing unidimensionality of tests and items. *Applied Psychological Measurement, 9*, 139–164.

Hattie, J., Krakowski, K., Rogers, H. J., & Swaminathan, H. (1996). An assessment of Stout's index of essential unidimensionality. *Applied Psychological Measurement, 20*, 1–14.

Hauck, W. W. (1983). A note on confidence bands for the logistic response curve. *American Statistician, 37*, 158–160.

Heinen, T. (1996). *Latent class and discrete latent trait models: Similarities and differences*. Thousand Oaks, CA: Sage Publications.

Hemker, B. T., Sijtsma, K., Molenaar, I. W., & Junker, B. W. (1997). Stochastic ordering using the latent trait and the sum score in polytomous IRT models. *Psychometrika, 62,* 331–347.

Hoijtink, H. (1991a). *PARELLA: Measurement of latent traits by proximity items.* Leiden, The Netherlands: DWSO Press.

Hoijtink, H. (1991b). The measurement of latent traits by proximity items. *Applied Psychological Measurement, 15,* 153–169.

Hoijtink, H. (2009). Bayesian data analysis. In R. E. Millsap & A. Maydeu-Olivares (Eds.), *The Sage handbook of quantitative methods in psychology* (pp. 423–443). London: Sage Publications.

Holland, P. W. (1981). When are item response models consistent with observed data? *Psychometrika, 46,* 79–92.

Holland, P. W. (1990). On the sampling theory foundations of item response theory models. *Psychometrika, 55,* 577–601.

Holland, P. W., & Rosenbaum, P. R. (1986). Conditional association and unidimensionality in monotone latent variable models. *The Annals of Statistics, 14,* 1523–1543.

Holland, P. W., & Thayer, D. T. (1988). Differential item performance and the Mantel–Haenszel procedure. In H. Wainer & H. Braun (Eds.), *Test validity* (pp. 129–145). Hillsdale, NJ: Erlbaum.

Holland, P. W., & Wainer, H. (Eds.). (1993). *Differential item functioning.* Hillsdale, NJ: Erlbaum.

Horn, J. L. (1965). A rationale and test for the number of factors in factor analysis. *Psychometrika, 30,* 179–185.

Horn, J. L., & McArdle, J. J. (1992). A practical guide to measurement invariance in research on aging. *Experimental Aging Research, 18,* 117–144.

Horn, J. L., McArdle, J. J., & Mason, R. (1983). When is invariance not invariant: A practical scientist's look at the ethereal concept of factor invariance. *The Southern Psychologist, 1,* 179–188.

Hosmer, D. W., & Lemeshow, S. (2000). *Applied logistic regression* (2nd ed.). New York: Wiley-Interscience.

Howe, W. G. (1955). *Some contributions to factor analysis* (Report ORNL-1919). Oak Ridge, TN: Oak Ridge National Laboratory.

Hu, L., & Bentler, P. M. (1995). Evaluating model fit. In R. H. Hoyle (Ed.), *Structural equation modeling: Concepts, issues, and applications* (pp. 76–99). Thousand Oaks, CA: Sage Publications.

Hu, L., Bentler, P. M., & Kano, Y. (1992). Can test statistics in covariance structure analysis be trusted? *Psychological Bulletin, 112,* 351–362.

Humphreys, L. G. (1952). Individual differences. *Annual Review of Psychology, 3,* 131–150.

Humphreys, L. G. (1984). *A theoretical and empirical study of the psychometric assessment of psychological test dimensionality and bias* (ONR Research Proposal). Washington, DC: Office of Naval Research.

Humphreys, L. G. (1986). An analysis and evaluation of test and item bias in the prediction context. *Psychological Bulletin, 71,* 327–333.

Hunter, J. E. (1986). Cognitive ability, cognitive aptitudes, job knowledge, and job performance. *Journal of Vocational Behavior, 29,* 340–362.

Hunter, J. E., & Schmidt, F. L. (2000). Racial and gender bias in ability and achievement tests: Resolving the apparent paradox. *Psychology, Public Policy, and Law, 6*, 151–158.

Hunter, J. E., Schmidt, F. L., & Hunter, R. (1979). Differential validity of employment tests by race: A comprehensive review and analysis. *Psychological Bulletin, 86*, 721–735.

Hunter, J. E., Schmidt, F. L., & Rauschenberger, J. (1984). Methodological, statistical, and ethical issues in the study of bias in psychological tests. In C. R. Reynolds & R. T. Brown (Eds.), *Perspectives on bias in mental testing* (pp. 41–99). New York: Plenum Press.

Hurvich, C. M., & Tsai, C. L. (1989). Regression and time series model selection in small samples. *Biometrika, 76*, 297–307.

Ironson, G. H., & Subkoviak, M. (1979). A comparison of several methods of assessing item bias. *Journal of Educational Measurement, 16*, 209–225.

Jannerone, R. J. (1986). Conjunctive item response theory kernals. *Psychometrika, 51*, 357–373.

Jannerone, R. J. (1997). Models for locally dependent responses: Conjunctive item response theory. In W. J. Van der Linden & R. K. Hambleton (Eds.), *Handbook of modern item response theory* (pp. 465–479). New York: Springer.

Jennrich, R. I. (1978). Rotational equivalence of factor loading matrices with specified values. *Psychometrika, 43*, 421–426.

Jensen, A. R. (1980). *Bias in mental testing*. New York: Free Press.

Jensen, A. R. (1985). The nature of black–white differences on various psychometric tests: Spearman's hypothesis. *Behavioral and Brain Sciences, 8*, 193–219.

Jensen, A. R. (1986). G: Artifact or reality? *Journal of Vocational Behavior, 29*, 301–331.

Jensen, A. R. (1992). Spearman's hypothesis: Methodology and evidence. *Multivariate Behavioral Research, 27*, 225–233.

Jiang, H., & Stout, W. (1998). Improved Type I error control and reduced estimation bias for DIF detection using SIBTEST. *Journal of Educational and Behavioral Statistics, 23*, 291–322.

Johnson, J. H., Null, C. H., Butcher, J. N., & Johnson, K. N. (1984). Replicated item-level factor analysis of the full MMPI. *Journal of Personality and Social Psychology, 47*, 105–114.

Johnson, V. E., & Albert, J. H. (1999). *Ordinal data modeling*. New York: Springer.

Johnson, M. S., & Sinharay, S. (2005). Calibration of polytomous item families using Bayesian hierarchical modeling. *Applied Psychological Measurement, 29*, 369–400.

Jöreskog, K. G. (1971a). Statistical analysis of sets of congeneric tests. *Psychometrika, 36*, 109–133.

Jöreskog, K. G. (1971b). Simultaneous factor analysis in several populations. *Psychometrika, 36*, 409–426.

Jöreskog, K. G. (1979). A general approach to confirmatory factor analysis with addendum. In K. G. Jöreskog, D. Sörbom, & J. Magidson (Eds.), *Advances in factor analysis and structural equation models* (pp. 21–43). New York: Abt Associates.

Jöreskog, K. G. (1990). New developments in LISREL: Analysis of ordinal variables using polychoric correlations and weighted least squares. *Quality and Quantity, 24*, 387–404.

Jöreskog, K. G. (1993). Latent variable modeling with ordinal variables. In K. Haagen, D. J. Bartholomew, & M. Deistler (Eds.), *Statistical modeling and latent variables* (pp. 163–171). Amsterdam: North-Holland.

Jöreskog, K. G., & Moustaki, I. (2001). Factor analysis of ordinal variables: A comparison of three approaches. *Multivariate Behavioral Research, 36,* 347–387.

Jöreskog, K. G., & Sörbom, D. (2002). *LISREL 8.52 for Windows.* Lincolnwood, IL: Scientific Software.

Junker, B. W. (1993). Conditional association, essential independence, and monotone unidimensional item response models. *The Annals of Statistics, 21,* 1359–1378.

Kaiser, H. F. (1960). The application of electronic computers to factor analysis. *Educational and Psychological Measurement, 20,* 141–151.

Kamata, A., & Bauer, D. J. (2008). A note on the relation between factor analytic and item response theory models. *Structural Equation Modeling, 15,* 136–153.

Kaplan, D. (1988). The impact of specification error on the estimation, testing, and improvement of structural equation models. *Multivariate Behavioral Research, 23,* 69–86.

Kaplan, D. (1989). Model modification in covariance structure analysis: Application of the expected parameter change statistic. *Multivariate Behavioral Research, 24,* 285–305.

Kelderman, H. (1984). Loglinear Rasch model tests. *Psychometrika, 49,* 223–245.

Kelderman, H. (1989). Item bias detection using loglinear IRT. *Psychometrika, 54,* 681–697.

Kelderman, H. (1997). Loglinear multidimensional item response model for polytomously scored items. In W. J. Van der Linden & R. K. Hambleton (Eds.), *Handbook of modern item response theory* (pp. 287–304). New York: Springer.

Kelderman, H., & Macready, G. B. (1990). The use of loglinear models for assessing differential item functioning across manifest and latent examinee groups. *Journal of Educational Measurement, 27,* 307–327.

Kelderman, H., & Rijkes, C. P. M. (1994). Loglinear multidimensional IRT models for polytomously scored items. *Psychometrika, 59,* 147–177.

Kelderman, H., & Steen, R. (1988). LOGIMO: *A program for loglinear IRT modeling.* Enschede, The Netherlands: University of Twente.

Kim, H. R. (1994). *New techniques for the dimensionality assessment of standardized test data.* Unpublished doctoral dissertation, Department of Statistics, University of Illinois at Urbana-Champaign.

Kim, S., & Cohen, A. S. (1991). A comparison of two area measures for detecting differential item functioning. *Applied Psychological Measurement, 15,* 269–278.

Kim, S., & Cohen, A. S. (1992). Effects of linking methods on detection of DIF. *Journal of Educational Measurement, 29,* 51–66.

Kim, S., & Cohen, A. S. (1995). A minimum χ^2 method for equating tests under the Graded-Response model. *Applied Psychological Measurement, 19,* 167–176.

Kim, S., & Cohen, A. S. (1998). Detection of differential item functioning under the graded response model with the likelihood ratio test. *Applied Psychological Measurement, 22,* 295–303.

Kim, S., Cohen, A. S., & Kim, H. O. (1994). An investigation of Lord's procedure for differential item functioning. *Applied Psychological Measurement, 18,* 217–228.

Koehler, K. (1986). Goodness-of-fit tests for log-linear models in sparse contingency tables. *Journal of the American Statistical Association, 81*, 483–493.

Koehler, K., & Larntz, K. (1980). An empirical investigation of goodness-of-fit statistics for sparse multinomials. *Journal of the American Statistical Association, 75*, 336–344.

Kok, F. (1988). Item bias and test multidimensionality. In R. Langeheine & J. Rost (Eds.), *Latent trait and latent class models* (pp. 263–275). New York: Plenum Press.

Kolen, M. J., & Brennan, R. L. (2010). *Test equating, scaling and linking: Methods and practices* (2nd ed.). New York: Springer.

Kyngdon, A. (2008). The Rasch model from the perspective of the representational theory of measurement. *Theory and Psychology, 18*, 89–109.

Langeheine, R., & Rost, J. (Eds.). (1988). *Latent trait and latent class models*. New York: Plenum Press.

Lautenschlager, G. J., & Park, D. G. (1988). IRT item bias detection procedures: Issues of model misspecification, robustness, and parameter linking. *Applied Psychological Measurement, 12*, 365–376.

Lawley, D. N. (1943). A note on Karl Pearson's selection formulae. *Proceedings of the Royal Society of Edinburgh, 2*, 28–30.

Lawley, D. N., & Maxwell, A. E. (1973). Regression and factor analysis. *Biometrika, 60*, 331–484.

Lazersfeld, P. F. (1950a). The logical and mathematical foundation of latent structure analysis. In S. Stouffer (Ed.), *Measurement and prediction* (pp. 362–412). Princeton, NJ: Princeton University Press.

Lazersfeld, P. F. (1950b). The interpretation and mathematical foundation of latent structure analysis. In S. Stouffer (Ed.), *Measurement and prediction* (pp. 413–472). Princeton, NJ: Princeton University Press.

Lazersfeld, P. F., & Henry, N. W. (1968). *Latent structure analysis*. Boston: Houghton-Mifflin.

LeckLiter, I. N., Matarazzo, J. D., & Silverstein, A. B. (1986). A literature review of factor analytic studies of the WAIS-R. *Journal of Clinical Psychology, 42*, 332–342.

Lee, S. Y. (1981). A Bayesian approach to confirmatory factor analysis. *Psychometrika, 46*, 153–160.

Lee, S. Y. (2007). *Structural equation modeling: A Bayesian approach*. Hoboken, NJ: Wiley.

Lee, S. Y., Poon, W. Y., & Bentler, P. M. (1989). Simultaneous analysis of multivariate polytomous variates in several groups. *Psychometrika, 54*, 63–73.

Lee, S. Y., Poon, W. Y., & Bentler, P. M. (1992). Structural equation models with continuous and polytomous variables. *Psychometrika, 57*, 89–105.

Lee, S. Y., & Song, X. Y. (2002). Bayesian selection on the number of factors in a factor analysis. *Behaviormetrika, 29*, 23–39.

Lewis, C. L. (1993). A note on the value of including the studied item in the test score when analyzing test items for DIF. In P. Holland & H. Wainer (Eds.), *Differential item functioning* (pp. 317–319). Hillsdale, NJ: Erlbaum.

Lehmann, E. L. (1986). *Testing statistical hypotheses* (2nd ed.) London, U.K.: Chapman & Hall.

Li, H., & Stout, W. (1995). *Assessment of unidimensionality for mixed polytomous and dichotomous item data: Refinements of Poly-DIMTEST*. Paper presented at the annual meeting of the National Council on Measurement in Education, San Francisco, CA.

Li, H., & Stout, W. (1996). A new procedure for detection of crossing DIF. *Psychometrika, 61,* 647–677.

Lim, R. G., & Drasgow, F. (1990). Evaluation of two methods for estimating item response theory parameters when assessing differential item functioning. *Journal of Applied Psychology, 75,* 164–174.

Linacre, J. M. (2001). *A user's guide to WINSTEPS/MINISTEPS.* Chicago: Winsteps.com

Linn, R. L. (1978). Single-group validity, differential validity, and differential prediction. *Journal of Applied Psychology, 63,* 507–512.

Linn, R. L. (1984). Selection bias: Multiple meanings. *Journal of Educational Measurement, 21,* 33–47.

Linn, R. L., Levine, M. V., Hastings, C. N., & Wardrup, J. L. (1981). An investigation of item bias in a test of reading comprehension. *Applied Psychological Measurement, 5,* 159–173.

Long, J. S. (1997). *Regression models for categorical and limited dependent variables.* Thousand Oaks, CA: Sage Publications.

Longford, N. T. (1995). *Models for uncertainty in educational testing.* New York: Springer.

Longford, N. T., Holland, P. W., & Thayer, D. T. (1993). Stability of the MH D-DIF statistics across populations. In P. W. Holland & H. Wainer (Eds.), *Differential item functioning* (pp. 171–196). Hillsdale, NJ: Erlbaum.

Lord, F. M. (1980). *Applications of item response theory to practical testing problems.* Hillsdale, NJ: Erlbaum.

Lord, F. M., & Novick, M. R. (1968). *Statistical theories of mental test scores.* Reading, MA: Addison-Wesley.

Lord, F. M., & Pashley, P. J. (1988). *Confidence bands for the three-parameter logistic item response curve* (ETS Research Report 88-67). Princeton, NJ: Educational Testing Service.

Loyd, B. H., & Hoover, H. D. (1980). Vertical equating using the Rasch model. *Journal of Educational Measurement, 17,* 179–193.

Lubke, G. H., & Dolan, C. V. (2003). Can unequal residual variances across groups mask differences in residual means in the common factor model? *Structural Equation Modeling, 10,* 175–192.

Lubke, G. H., & Muthén, B. O. (2004). Applying multi-group confirmatory factor models for continuous outcomes to Likert scale data complicates meaningful group comparisons. *Structural Equation Modeling, 11,* 514–534.

MacCallum, R. C. (1986). Specification searches in covariance structure modeling. *Psychological Bulletin, 100,* 107–120.

MacCallum, R. C. (2009). Factor analysis. In R. E. Millsap & A. Maydeu-Olivares (Eds.), *The Sage handbook of quantitative methods in psychology* (pp. 123–147). London: Sage Publications.

MacCallum, R. C., Browne, M. W., & Sugawara, H. M. (1996). Power analysis and determination of sample size for covariance structural modeling. *Psychological Methods, 1,* 130–149.

MacCallum, R. C., Roznowski, M., & Necowitz, L. B. (1992). Model modifications in covariance structure analysis: The problem of capitalization on chance. *Psychological Bulletin, 111,* 490–504.

Magnus, J. R., & Neudecker, H. (1988). *Matrix differential calculus with applications in statistics and econometrics.* New York: Wiley.

Mantel, N. (1963). Chi-square tests with one degree of freedom: Extensions of the Mantel–Haenszel procedure. *Journal of the American Statistical Association, 58*, 690–700.

Mantel, N., & Haenszel, W. (1959). Statistical aspects of the analysis of data from retrospective studies of disease. *Journal of the National Cancer Institute, 22*, 719–748.

Maraun, M. (1996). Metaphor taken as math: Indeterminacy in the factor analysis model. *Multivariate Behavioral Research, 31*, 517–538.

Marco, G. L. (1977). Item characteristic curve solutions to three intractable testing problems. *Journal of Educational Measurement, 14*, 139–160.

Marsh, H. W. (1998). The equal correlation baseline model: Comment and constructive alternatives. *Structural Equation Modeling, 5*, 78–86.

Marsh, H. W., Hau, K. T., & Wen, Z. (2004). In search of the golden rules: Comment on hypothesis-testing approaches to setting cutoff values for fit indexes and dangers in overgeneralizing Hu and Bentler's (1999) findings. *Structural Equation Modeling, 11*, 320–341.

Martin, J. K., & McDonald, R. P. (1975). Bayesian estimation in unrestricted factor analysis: A treatment for Heywood cases. *Psychometrika, 40*, 505–517.

Martin-Löf, P. (1973). *Statistiska Modeller* [Statistical Models]. Aneckningar frän seminarier lasaret 1969–1970, utarbetade av Rolf Sundberg. Obetydligt ändrat nytryck, Oktober 1973. Stockholm: Institut för Försäkringsmatematik och Matematisk Statistisk vid Stockholms Universitet.

Masters, G. N. (1982). A Rasch model for partial credit scoring. *Psychometrika, 47*, 149–174.

Masters, G. N. (1985). A comparison of latent-trait and latent-class analyses of Likert-type data. *Psychometrika, 50*, 69–82.

Masters, G. N., & Wright, B. D. (1997). The partial-credit model. In W. J. Van der Linden & R. K. Hambleton (Eds.), *Handbook of modern item response theory* (pp. 101–121). New York: Springer.

Maydeu-Olivares, A. (2001a). Limited information estimation and testing of Thurstonian models for paired comparison data under multiple judgement testing. *Psychometrika, 66*, 209–228.

Maydeu-Olivares, A. (2001b). Multidimensional item response theory modeling of binary data: Large sample properties of NOHARM estimates. *Journal of Educational and Behavioral Statistics, 26*, 49–69.

Maydeu-Olivares, A. (2005). Linear item response theory, nonlinear item response theory, and factor analysis: A unified framework. In A. Maydeu-Olivares & J. J. McArdle (Eds.), *Contemporary psychometrics* (pp. 73–100). Mahwah, NJ: Erlbaum.

Maydeu-Olivares, A., & Joe, H. (2005). Limited and full information estimation and goodness-of-fit testing in 2^n contingency tables: A unified framework. *Journal of the American Statistical Association, 100*, 1009–1020.

Maydeu-Olivares, A., & Joe, H. (2006). Limited information goodness-of-fit testing in multidimensional contingency tables. *Psychometrika, 71*, 713–732.

McArdle, J. J., & Cattell, R. B. (1994). Structural equation models of factorial invariance in parallel proportional profiles and oblique confactor problems. *Multivariate Behavioral Research, 29*, 63–113.

McCauley, C. D., & Mendoza, J. (1985). A simulation study of item bias using a two-parameter item response model. *Applied Psychological Measurement, 9,* 389–400.

McCullagh, P., & Nelder, J. A. (1989). *Generalized linear models* (2nd ed.). London: Chapman & Hall.

McDonald, R. P. (1974). The measurement of factor indeterminacy. *Psychometrika, 39,* 203–222.

McDonald, R. P. (1981). The dimensionality of tests and items. *British Journal of Mathematical and Statistical Psychology, 34,* 100–117.

McDonald, R. P. (1985). *Factor analysis and related methods.* Hillsdale, NJ: Erlbaum.

McDonald, R. P. (1989). An index of goodness-of-fit based on non-centrality. *Journal of Classification, 6,* 97–103.

McDonald, R. P. (1997). Normal ogive multidimensional model. In W. J. Van der Linden & R. K. Hambleton (Eds.), *Handbook of item response theory* (pp. 258–269). New York: Springer.

McDonald, R. P. (1999). *Test theory: A unified treatment.* Mahwah, NJ: Erlbaum.

McDonald, R. P., & Ahlawat, K. S. (1974). Difficulty factors in binary data. *British Journal of Mathematical and Statistical Psychology, 27,* 82–99.

McDonald, R. P., & Krane, W. R. (1977). A note on local identifiability and degrees of freedom in the asymptotic likelihood ratio test. *British Journal of Mathematical and Statistical Psychology, 30,* 198–203.

McDonald, R. P., & Krane, W. R. (1979). A Monte Carlo study of local identifiability and degrees of freedom in the asymptotic likelihood ratio test. *British Journal of Mathematical and Statistical Psychology, 32,* 121–132.

McDonald, R. P., & Marsh, H. W. (1990). Choosing a multivariate model: Non-centrality and goodness-of-fit. *Psychological Bulletin, 107,* 247–255.

McDonald, R. P., & Mok, M. C. (1995). Goodness-of-fit in item response models. *Multivariate Behavioral Research, 30,* 23–40.

McFatter, R. M. (1987). Use of latent variable models for detecting discrimination in salaries. *Psychological Bulletin, 101,* 120–125.

McKelvey, R. D., & Zavoina, W. (1975). A statistical model for the analysis of ordinal level dependent variables. *Journal of Mathematical Sociology, 4,* 103–120.

McKinley, R., & Mills, C. (1985). A comparison of several goodness-of-fit statistics. *Applied Psychological Measurement, 9,* 49–57.

McLaughlin, M. E., & Drasgow, F. (1987). Lord's chi-square test of item bias with estimated and with known person parameters. *Applied Psychological Measurement, 11,* 161–173.

Mead, R. (1976). *Assessment of fit of data to the Rasch model through analysis of residuals.* Unpublished Doctoral Dissertation, University of Chicago.

Meijer, R. R., & Sijtsma, K. (2001). Methodology review: Evaluating person fit. *Applied Psychological Measurement, 25,* 107–135.

Mellenbergh, G. J. (1989). Item bias and item response theory. *International Journal of Educational Research, 13,* 127–143.

Mellenbergh, G. J. (1994). Generalized linear item response theory. *Psychological Bulletin, 115,* 300–307.

Meredith, W. (1964). Notes on factorial invariance. *Psychometrika, 29,* 177–185.

Meredith, W. (1965). Some results based on a general stochastic model for mental tests. *Psychometrika, 30,* 419–440.

Meredith, W. (1993). Measurement invariance, factor analysis, and factorial invariance. *Psychometrika, 58,* 525–543.

Meredith, W., & Millsap, R. E. (1992). On the misuse of manifest variables in the detection of measurement bias. *Psychometrika, 57,* 289–311.

Messick, S. (1989). Validity. In R. L. Linn (Ed.), *Educational measurement* (pp. 13–103). Washington, DC: American Council on Education and National Council on Measurement in Education.

Metropolis, N., Rosenbluth, A. W., Rosenbluth, M. N., Teller, A. H., & Teller, E. (1953). Equations of state calculations by fast computing machines. *Journal of Chemical Physics, 21,* 1087–1091.

Michell, J. (1990). *An introduction to the logic of psychological measurement.* Hillsdale, NJ: Erlbaum.

Michell, J. (1999). *Measurement in psychology: A critical history of a methodological concept.* New York: Cambridge University Press.

Miller, T., Spray, J., & Wilson, A. (1992). *A comparison of three methods for identifying nonuniform DIF in polytomously scored test items.* Paper presented at Psychometric Society meeting, Columbus, OH.

Millsap, R. E. (1995). Measurement invariance, predictive invariance, and the duality paradox. *Multivariate Behavioral Research, 30,* 577–605.

Millsap, R. E. (1997). Invariance in measurement and prediction: Their relationship in the single-factor case. *Psychological Methods, 2,* 248–260.

Millsap, R. E. (1998). Group differences in regression intercepts: Implications for factorial invariance. *Multivariate Behavioral Research, 33,* 403–424.

Millsap, R. E. (2001). When trivial constraints are not trivial: The choice of uniqueness constraints in confirmatory factor analysis. *Structural Equation Modeling, 8,* 1–17.

Millsap, R. E. (2007). Invariance in measurement and prediction revisited. *Psychometrika, 72*(4), 461–473.

Millsap, R. E. (2008). Model-implied invariance in psychometrics: Be skeptical when theory suggests data are not needed. *Measurement: Interdisciplinary Research and Perspectives, 6,* 195–197.

Millsap, R. E., & Everson, H. T. (1991). Confirmatory measurement model comparisons with latent means. *Multivariate Behavioral Research, 26,* 479–497.

Millsap, R. E., & Everson, H. T. (1993). Methodology review: Statistical approaches for assessing measurement bias. *Applied Psychological Measurement, 17*(4), 297–334.

Millsap, R. E., & Hartog, S. B. (1988). Alpha, beta, and gamma change in evaluation research: A structural equation approach. *Journal of Applied Psychology, 73,* 574–584.

Millsap, R. E., & Kwok, O. (2004). Evaluating the impact of partial factorial invariance on selection in two populations. *Psychological Methods, 9,* 93–115.

Millsap, R. E., & Meredith, W. (1989). *The detection of DIF: Why there is no free lunch.* Paper presented at the annual meeting of the Psychometric Society, University of California-Los Angeles, July 7–9, 1989.

Millsap, R. E., & Meredith, W. (1992). Inferential conditions in the statistical detection of measurement bias. *Applied Psychological Measurement, 16,* 389–402.

Millsap, R. E., & Meredith, W. (2007). Factorial invariance: Historical perspectives and new problems. In R. Cudeck & R. MacCallum (Eds.), *Factor analysis at 100* (pp. 131–152). Mahwah, NJ: Erlbaum.

Millsap, R. E., & Taylor, R. (1996). Latent variable models in the investigation of salary discrimination: Theory and practice. *Journal of Management, 22,* 653–673.

Millsap, R. E., & Yun-Tein, J. (2004). Assessing factorial invariance in ordered-categorical measures. *Multivariate Behavioral Research, 39,* 479–515.

Mislevy, R. J. (1986). Recent developments in the factor analysis of categorical variables. *Journal of Educational Statistics, 11,* 3–31.

Mislevy, R. J., & Bock, R. D. (1993). *BILOG-3 Item analysis and test scoring with binary logistic models.* Mooresville, IN: Scientific Software.

Mokken, R. J. (1971). *A theory and procedure of scale analysis, with applications in political research.* New York/Berlin: Walter de Gruyter-Mouton.

Mokken, R. J. (1997). Nonparametric models for dichotomous responses. In W. J. van der Linden & R. K. Hambleton (Eds.), *Handbook of modern item response theory* (pp. 351–367). New York: Springer.

Mokken, R. J., & Lewis, C. (1982). A nonparametric approach to the analysis of dichotomous item responses. *Applied Psychological Measurement, 6,* 417–430.

Molenaar, I. W. (1983). Some improved diagnostics for failure of the Rasch model. *Psychometrika, 48,* 49–72.

Molenaar, I. W. (1997). Nonparametric models for polytomous responses. In W. J. Van der Linden & R. K. Hambleton (Eds.), *Handbook of modern item response theory* (pp. 369–380). New York: Springer.

Molenaar, P. C. M., & Von Eye, A. (1994). On the arbitrary nature of latent variables. In A. Von Eye & C. C. Clogg (Eds.), *Latent variables analysis* (pp. 226–242). Thousand Oaks, CA: Sage Publications.

Mulaik, S. A. (2009). *Foundations of factor analysis* (2nd ed.). Boca Raton, FL: Chapman & Hall/CRC.

Mulaik, S. A., & McDonald, R. P. (1977). The effect of additional variables on factor indeterminacy in models with a single common factor. *Psychometrika, 43,* 177–192.

Mulaik, S. A., & Millsap, R. E. (2000). Doing the four-step right. *Structural Equation Modeling, 7,* 36–73.

Muraki, E. (1992). A generalized partial credit model: Application of an EM algorithm. *Applied Psychological Measurement, 16,* 159–176.

Murphy, K. R., & Davidshofer, C. O. (1991). *Psychological testing: Principles and applications.* Englewood Cliffs, NJ: Prentice Hall.

Muthén, B. O. (1978). Contributions to factor analysis of dichotomized variables. *Psychometrika, 43,* 551–560.

Muthén, B. O. (1984). A general structural equation model with dichotomous, ordered categorical and continuous latent variable indicators. *Psychometrika, 49,* 115–132.

Muthén, B. O. (1989). Latent variable modeling in heterogeneous populations. *Psychometrika, 54,* 557–585.

Muthén, B. O., & Christoffersson, A. (1981). Simultaneous factor analysis of dichotomous variables in several groups. *Psychometrika, 46,* 407–419.

Muthén, B. O., du Toit, S. H. C., & Spisac, D. (in press). Robust inference using weighted least squares and quadratic estimating equations in latent variable modeling with categorical and continuous outcomes. *Psychometrika.*

Muthén, B. O., & Hofacker, C. (1988). Testing the assumptions underlying tetrachoric correlations. *Psychometrika, 53,* 563–578.

Muthén, B. O., & Kaplan, D. (1992). A comparison of some methodologies for the factor analysis of non-normal Likert variables: A note on the size of the model. *British Journal of Mathematical and Statistical Psychology, 45,* 19–30.

Muthén, B. O., & Yang Hsu, J. W. (1993). Selection and predictive validity with latent variable structures. *British Journal of Mathematical and Statistical Psychology, 46,* 255–271.

Muthén, L., & Muthén, B. O. (1998–2006). *Mplus User's Guide* (4th ed.). Los Angeles, CA: Muthén & Muthén.

Muthén, B. O., & Satorra, A. (1995). Technical aspects of Muthén's LISCOMP approach to the estimation of latent variable relations with a comprehensive measurement model. *Psychometrika, 60,* 489–503.

Nagayama-Hall, G. C., Bansal, A., & Lopez, I. R. (1999). Ethnicity and psychopathology: A meta-analytic review of 31 years of comparative MMPI/MMPI-2 research. *Psychological Assessment, 11,* 186–197.

Nandakumar, R. (1991). Traditional dimensionality versus essential dimensionality. *Journal of Educational Measurement, 28,* 99–117.

Nandakumar, R. (1993a). Assessing essential unidimensionality of real data. *Applied Psychological Measurement, 17,* 29–38.

Nandakumar, R. (1993b). Simultaneous DIF amplification and cancellation: Shealy–Stout's test for DIF. *Journal of Educational Measurement, 30,* 293–311.

Nandakumar, R. (1994). Assessing latent trait unidimensionality of a set of items—comparison of different approaches. *Journal of Educational Measurement, 31,* 1–18.

Nandakumar, R., & Stout, W. (1993). Refinements of Stout's procedure for assessing latent trait dimensionality. *Journal of Educational Statistics, 18,* 41–68.

Nandakumar, R., Yu, F., Li, H. H., & Stout, W. (1998). Assessing unidimensionality of polytomous data. *Applied Psychological Measurement, 22,* 99–115.

Narayanan, P., & Swaminathan, H. (1994). Performance of the Mantel–Haenszel and simultaneous item bias procedures for detecting differential item functioning. *Applied Psychological Measurement, 20,* 315–338.

Narayanan, P., & Swaminathan, H. (1996). Identification of items that show nonuniform DIF. *Applied Psychological Measurement, 20,* 257–274.

Neisser, U., Boodoo, G., Bourchard, T. J., Boykin, A. W., Brody, N., Ceci, S. J., Halpern, D. F., Loehlin, J. C., Perloff, R., Sternberg, R. J., & Urbina, S. (1996). Intelligence: Knowns and unknowns. *American Psychologist, 51,* 77–101.

Nering, M. L., & Ostini, R. (2010). *Handbook of polytomous item response theory models.* New York: Routledge.

Neyman, J., & Scott, E. L. (1948). Consistent estimates based on partially consistent observations. *Econometrika, 16,* 1–32.

Novick, M. R. (1966). The axioms and principle results of classical test theory. *Journal of Mathematical Psychology, 3,* 1–18.

Nunnally, J. C. (1978). *Psychometric theory* (2nd ed.). New York: McGraw-Hill.

Olsson, U. (1979). Maximum likelihood estimation of the polychoric correlation coefficient. *Psychometrika, 44,* 443–460.

Olsson, U., Drasgow, F., & Dorans, N. J. (1982). The polyserial correlation coefficient. *Psychometrika, 47,* 337–347.

Oort, F. J. (1998). Simulation study of item bias detection with restricted factor analysis. *Structural Equation Modeling, 5,* 107–124.

Orlando, M., & Thissen, D. (2000). Likelihood-based item-fit indices for dichotomous item response theory models. *Applied Psychological Measurement, 24,* 50–64.

Orlando, M., & Thissen, D. (2003). Further investigation of the performance of S-X2: An item fit index for use with dichotomous item response theory models. *Applied Psychological Measurement, 27,* 289–298.

Oshima, T. C. & Miller, M. D. (1990). Multidimensionality and IRT-based invariance indices: The effect of between group variation in trait correlations. *Journal of Educational Measurement, 27,* 273–283.

Oshima, T. C., Raju, N. S., & Flowers, C. P. (1997). Development and demonstration of multidimensional IRT-based internal measures of differential functioning of items and tests. *Journal of Educational Measurement, 34,* 253–272.

Osterlind, S. J., Robinson, R. D., & Nickens, N. M. (1997). Relationship between collegians' perceived knowledge and congeneric tested achievement in general education. *Journal of College Student Development, 38,* 255–265.

Overton, R. C. (2001). Moderated multiple regression for interactions involving categorical variables: A statistical control for heterogenous variance across two groups. *Psychological Methods, 6,* 218–233.

Park, D. G. (1988). *Investigations of item response theory bias detection.* Unpublished Doctoral Dissertation, University of Georgia, Athens.

Park, D. G., & Lautenschlager, G. J. (1990). Improving IRT item bias detection with iterative linking and ability scale purification. *Applied Psychological Measurement, 14,* 163–173.

Pashley, P. J. (1992). Graphical IRT-based DIF analyses. ERIC document ED385576.

Patz, R., & Junker, B. (1999a). Applications and extensions of MCMC in IRT: Multiple item types, missing data, and rated responses. *Journal of Educational and Behavioral Statistics, 24,* 342–366.

Patz, R., & Junker, B. (1999b). A straightforward approach to Markov chain Monte Carlo methods for item response models. *Journal of Educational and Behavioral Statistics, 24,* 146–178.

Pearson, K. (1902). On the influence of natural selection on the variability and correlation of organs. *Philosophical Transactions of the Royal Society A, 200,* 1–66.

Pearson, E. S., & Wilks, S. S. (1933). Methods of statistical analysis appropriate for *k* samples of two variates. *Biometrika, 25,* 353–378.

Perline, R., Wright, B. D., & Wainer, H. (1979). The Rasch model as additive conjoint measurement. *Applied Psychological Measurement, 3,* 237–255.

Peterson, D. W. (1986). Measurement error and regression analysis in employment cases. In D. H. Kaye & M. H. Aicken (Eds.), *Statistical methods in discrimination litigation* (pp. 107–131). New York: Dekker.

Peterson, N. S., & Novick, M. R. (1976). An evaluation of some models for culture-fair selection. *Journal of Educational Measurement, 13,* 3–29.

Pfanzagl, J. (1971). *Theory of measurement.* New York: Wiley.

Philips, A., & Holland, P. W. (1987). Estimation of the variance of the Mantel–Haenszel log-odds-ratio estimate. *Biometrics, 43,* 425–431.

Pike, G. (1992). The components of construct validity: A comparison of two measures of general education outcomes. *Journal of General Education, 41,* 130–160.

Poon, W. Y., Lee, S. Y., Afifi, A. A., & Bentler, P. M. (1990). Analysis of multivariate polytomous variates in several groups via the partition maximum likelihood approach. *Computational Statistics and Data Analysis, 10,* 17–27.

Post, W. J. (1992). *Nonparametric unfolding models: A latent structure approach.* Leiden, The Netherlands: DSWO Press.

Potthoff, R. F. (1966). *Statistical aspects of the problem of biases in psychological tests.* (Institute of Statistics Mimeo series 479). Chapel Hill, NC: University of North Carolina-Chapel Hill.

Quiroga, A. M. (1992). *Studies of the polychoric correlation and other correlation measures for ordinal variables.* Unpublished doctoral dissertation, Acta Universitatis Upsaliensis.

Raju, N. S. (1988). The area between two item characteristic curves. *Psychometrika, 56,* 365–379.

Raju, N. S. (1990). Determining the significance of estimated signed and unsigned areas between two item response functions. *Applied Psychological Measurement, 14,* 197–207.

Raju, N. S., Bode, R. K., & Larsen, V. S. (1989). An empirical assessment of the Mantel–Haenszel statistic for studying differential item performance. *Applied Measurement in Education, 2,* 1–13.

Raju, N. S., Steinhaus, S. D., Edwards, J. E., & DeLassio, J. (1991). A logistic regression model for personnel selection. *Applied Psychological Measurement, 15,* 139–152.

Raju, N. S., Van der Linden, W. J., & Fleer, P. F. (1995). IRT-based internal measures of differential functioning of items and tests. *Applied Psychological Measurement, 19,* 353–368.

Ramsay, J. O. (1991). Kernal smoothing approaches to nonparametric item characteristic curve estimation. *Psychometrika, 56,* 611–630.

Ramsay, J. O. (1997). A functional approach to modeling test data. In W. J. Van der Linden & R. K. Hambleton (Eds.), *Handbook of modern item response theory* (pp. 381–394). New York: Springer.

Ramsay, J. O., & Silverman, B. W. (1997). *Functional data analysis.* New York: Springer.

Ramsay, J. O., & Winsberg, S. (1991). Maximum marginal likelihood estimation for semiparametric item analysis. *Psychometrika, 56,* 365–379.

Rao, C. R. (1973). *Linear statistical inference and its applications.* New York: Wiley.

Rasch, G. (1960). *Probabilistic models for some intelligence and attainment tests.* Copenhagen, Denmark: Danish Institute for Educational Research.

Rasch, G. (1961). On general laws and the meaning of measurements in psychology. *Proceedings of the IV Berkeley symposium on mathematical statistics and probability* (Vol. IV, pp. 321–333). Berkeley, CA: University of California Press.

Reckase, M. D. (1997). The past and future of multidimensional item response theory. *Applied Psychological Measurement, 21,* 25–36.

Reckase, M. D. (2009). *Multidimensional item response theory.* New York: Springer.

Reddon, J. R., Marceau, R., & Jackson, D. N. (1982). An application of singular value decomposition to the factor analysis of MMPI items. *Applied Psychological Measurement, 6,* 275–283.

Ree, M. J., & Earles, J. A. (1991). Predicting training success: Not much more than *g*. *Personnel Psychology, 44,* 321–332.

Ree, M. J., Earles, J. A., & Teachout, M. S. (1994). Predicting job performance: Not much more than *g*. *Journal of Applied Psychology, 79*, 518–524.

Reise, S. P., & Flannery, W. P. (1996). Assessing person fit on measures of typical performance. *Applied Measurement in Education, 9*, 9–26.

Reise, S. P., Widaman, K. F., & Pugh, R. H. (1993). Confirmatory factor analysis and item response theory: Two approaches for exploring measurement invariance. *Psychological Bulletin, 114*, 552–566.

Reiser, M. (1996). Analysis of residuals for the multinomial response model. *Psychometrika, 61*, 509–528.

Reiser, M., & Vandenberg, M. (1994). Validity of the chi-square test in dichotomous variable factor analysis when expected frequencies are small. *British Journal of Mathematical and Statistical Psychology, 47*, 85–107.

Rensvold, R. B., & Cheung, G. W. (2001). Testing for metric invariance using structural equation models: Solving the standardization problem. In C. A. Schriesheim & L. L. Neider (Eds.), *Research in management* (Vol. 1, pp. 25–50). Greenwich, CN: Information Age Publishing.

Rigdon, E. E. (1998a). The equal correlation baseline model for comparative fit assessment in structural equation modeling. *Structural Equation Modeling, 5*, 63–77.

Rigdon, E. E. (1998b). The equal correlation baseline model: A reply to Marsh. *Structural Equation Modeling, 5*, 87–94.

Rigdon, E. E., & Ferguson, C. E. (1991). The performance of the polychoric correlation coefficient and selected fitting functions in confirmatory factor analysis with ordinal data. *Journal of Marketing Research, 28*, 491–497.

Rindskopf, D. (2009). Latent class analysis. In R. E. Millsap & A. Maydeu-Olivares (Eds.), *The Sage handbook of quantitative methods in psychology* (pp. 199–215). London: Sage Publications.

Riordan, C. R., Richardson, H. A., Schaffer, B. S., & Vandenberg, R. J. (2001). Alpha, beta, and gamma change: A review of past research with recommendations for new directions. In L. L. Neider & C. Schreisheim (Eds.), *Equivalence in measurement* (pp. 51–98). Greenwich: Information Age Publishing.

Roberts, J. S., & Laughlin, J. E. (1996). A unidimensional item response model for unfolding responses from a graded disagree–agree response scale. *Applied Psychological Measurement, 20*, 231–255.

Robins, J., Breslow, N., & Greenland, S. (1986). Estimators of the Mantel–Haenszel variance consistent in both sparse data and large-strata limiting models. *Biometrics, 42*, 311–323.

Roff, M. (1936). Some properties of the communality in multiple factor theory. *Psychometrika, 1*, 1–6.

Rogers, H. J., & Swaminathan, H. (1993). A comparison of the logistic regression and Mantel–Haenszel procedures for detecting differential item functioning. *Applied Psychological Measurement, 17*, 105–116.

Rosenbaum, P. R. (1984). Testing the conditional independence and monotonicity assumptions of item response theory. *Psychometrika, 49*, 425–435.

Rosenbaum, P. R. (1988). Item bundles. *Psychometrika, 53*, 349–359.

Roussos, L., & Stout, W. (1996a). A multidimensionality-based DIF analysis paradigm. *Applied Psychological Measurement, 20*, 355–371.

Roussos, L., & Stout, W. (1996b). Simulation studies of the effects of small sample size and studied item parameters on SIBTEST and Mantel–Haenszel Type I error performance. *Journal of Educational Measurement, 33*, 215–230.

Rozeboom, W. W. (1996). What might common factors be? *Multivariate Behavioral Research, 31*, 637–650.

Rudner, L. M., Getson, P. R., & Knight, D. L. (1980). Biased item detection techniques. *Journal of Educational Statistics, 5*, 213–233.

Sackett, P. R., Borneman, M., & Connelly, B. S. (2008). High-stakes testing in education and employment: Evaluating common criticisms regarding validity and fairness. *American Psychologist, 65*, 215–227.

Sackett, P. R., Schmitt, N., Ellington, J. E., & Kabin, M. B. (2001). High-stakes testing in employment, credentialing and higher education: Prospects in a post-affirmative action world. *American Psychologist, 56*, 302–318.

Sackett, P. R., & Wilk, S. L. (1994). Within-group norming and other forms of score adjustment in preemployment testing. *American Psychologist, 49*, 929–954.

Samejima, F. (1969). Estimation of ability using a response pattern of graded scores. *Psychometrika Monograph No. 17.*

Samejima, F. (1972). A general model for free-response data. *Psychometrika Monograph No. 18.*

Samejima, F. (1974). Normal ogive model on the continuous response level in the multidimensional latent space. *Psychometrika, 39*, 111–121.

Samejima, F. (1997). Graded response model. In W. J. Van der Linden & R. K. Hambleton (Eds.), *Handbook of modern item response theory* (pp. 85–100). New York: Springer.

Samuelsen, K. M. (2008). Examining differential item functioning from a latent mixture perspective. In G. R. Hancock & K. M. Samuelsen (Eds.), *Latent variable mixture models.* (pp. 177–197). Charlotte, NC: Information Age Publishing.

Satorra, A. (2000). Scaled and adjusted restricted tests in multi-sample analyses of moment structures. In D. D. H. Heijmans, D. S. G. Pollack, & A. Satorra (Eds.), *Innovations in multivariate statistical analysis: A festschrift for Heinz Neudecker* (pp. 233–247). Dordrecht, The Netherlands: Kluwer Academic Publishers.

Satorra, A., & Bentler, P. M. (1988). Scaling corrections for chi-square statistics in covariance structure analysis. *Proceedings of the Business and Economic Statistics Section of the American Statistical Association, 36*, 308–313.

Satorra, A., & Bentler, P. M. (1994). Corrections to test statistics and standard errors on covariance structure analysis. In A. von Eye & C. C. Clogg (Eds.), *Latent variables analysis* (pp. 399–419). Thousand Oaks, CA: Sage Publications.

Scheines, R., Hoijtink, H., & Boomsma, A. (1999). Bayesian estimation and testing of structural equation models. *Psychometrika, 64*, 37–52.

Scheuneman, J. D. (1987). An experimental exploratory study of the causes of bias in test items. *Journal of Educational Measurement, 24*, 97–118.

Schmidt, F. L. (1988). The problem of group differences in ability test scores in employment selection. *Journal of Vocational Behavior, 33*, 272–292.

Schmidt, F. L., & Hunter, J. E. (1998). The validity and utility of selection methods in personnel psychology: Practical and theoretical implications of over 85 years of research findings. *Psychological Bulletin, 124*, 262–274.

Schmidt, F. L., Pearlman, K., & Hunter, J. E. (1980). The validity and fairness of employment and educational tests for Hispanic Americans: A review and analysis. *Personnel Psychology, 33,* 705–724.

Schmitt, N. (1982). The use of analysis of covariance structures to assess beta and gamma change. *Multivariate Behavioral Research, 17,* 343–358.

Schönemann, P. H. (1971). The minimum average correlation between equivalent sets of uncorrelated factors. *Psychometrika, 36,* 21–30.

Schulman, R., & Haden, R. (1975). A test theory for ordinal measurements. *Psychometrika, 40,* 455–472.

Scott, J. T. (1966). Factor analysis and regression. *Econometrika, 34,* 552–562.

Segall, D. O. (1983). Test characteristic curves, item bias, and transformation to a common metric in item response theory: A methodological artifact with serious consequences and a simple solution. Unpublished manuscript, Department of Psychology, University of Illinois, Urbana-Champaign.

Shapiro, A. (1985). Identifiability of factor analysis: Some results and open problems. *Linear Algebra and Its Applications, 70,* 1–7.

Shealy, R., & Stout, W. (1993a). An item response theory model for test bias and differential test functioning. In P. Holland & H. Wainer (Eds.), *Differential item functioning* (pp. 197–240). Hillsdale, NJ: Erlbaum.

Shealy, R., & Stout, W. (1993b). A model-based standardization approach that separates true bias/DIF from group differences and detects test bias/DIF as well as item bias/DIF. *Psychometrika, 58,* 159–194.

Shepard, L. A. (1982). Definitions of bias. In R. A. Berk (Ed.), *Handbook of methods for detecting test bias* (pp. 9–30). Baltimore: Johns Hopkins University Press.

Shepard, L. A., Camilli, G., & Averill, M. (1981). Comparison of procedures for detecting test-item bias with both internal and external ability criteria. *Journal of Educational Statistics, 6,* 317–375.

Shepard, L. A., Camilli, G., & Williams, D. M. (1984). Accounting for statistical artifacts in item bias research. *Journal of Educational Statistics, 9,* 93–128.

Shepard, L. A., Camilli, G., & Williams, D. M. (1985). Validity of approximation techniques for detecting item bias. *Journal of Educational Measurement, 22,* 77–105.

Shi, J. Q., & Lee, S. Y. (1998). Bayesian sampling-based approach for factor analysis models with continuous and polytomous data. *British Journal of Mathematical and Statistical Psychology, 51,* 233–252.

Sijtsma, K. (1998). Methodology review: Nonparametric IRT approaches to the analysis of dichotomous item scores. *Applied Psychological Measurement, 22,* 3–31.

Sijtsma, K., & Junker, B. W. (1996). A survey of theory and methods of invariant item ordering. *British Journal of Mathematical and Statistical Psychology, 49,* 79–105.

Sijtsma, K., & Molenaar, I. W. (2002). *Introduction to nonparametric item response theory.* Thousand Oaks, CA: Sage Publications.

Sinharay, S. (2005). Assessing fit of unidimensional item response theory models using a Bayesian approach. *Journal of Educational Measurement, 42,* 375–395.

Sinharay, S., Johnson, M. S., & Stern, H. S. (2006). Posterior predictive assessment of item response theory models. *Applied Psychological Measurement, 30,* 298–321.

Somes, G. W. (1986). The generalized Mantel–Haenszel statistic. *American Statistician, 40,* 106–108.

Song, X. Y., & Lee, S. Y. (2001). Bayesian estimation and test for factor analysis model with continuous and polytomous data in several populations. *British Journal of Mathematical and Statistical Psychology, 54*, 237–263.

Sörbom, D. (1974). A general method for studying differences in factor means and factor structure between groups. *British Journal of Mathematical and Statistical Psychology, 27*, 229–239.

Spearman, C. (1904). The proof and measurement of association between two things. *American Journal of Psychology, 15*, 72–101.

Spearman, C. (1907). Demonstration of formulae for true measurement of correlation. *American Journal of Psychology, 18*, 161–169.

Spearman, C. (1913). Correlations of sums and differences. *British Journal of Psychology, 5*, 417–426.

SPSS Inc. (2008). *SPSS Statistics 17.0 Release 17.0.1* Chicago, IL: SPSS Inc.

Stark, S., Chernyshenko, O. S., & Drasgow, F. (2004). Examining the effects of differential item (functioning and differential) test functioning on selection decisions: When are statistically significant effects practically important? *Journal of Applied Psychology, 89*, 497–508.

Stark, S., Chernyshenko, O. S., & Drasgow, F. (2006). Detecting differential item functioning with confirmatory factor analysis and item response theory: Toward a unified strategy. *Journal of Applied Psychology, 91*, 1291–1306.

Steele, C. M., & Aronson, J. (1995). Stereotype threat and the intellectual test performance of African-Americans. *Journal of Personality and Social Psychology, 69*, 797–811.

Steenkamp, J. E. M., & Baumgartner, H. (1998). Assessing measurement invariance in cross-national consumer research. *Journal of Consumer Research, 25*, 78–90.

Steiger, J. H. (1990). Structural model evaluation and modification: An interval estimation approach. *Multivariate Behavioral Research, 25*, 173–180.

Steiger, J. H. (1998). A note on multiple sample extensions of the RMSEA fit index. *Structural Equation Modeling, 5*, 411–419.

Steiger, J. H., & Fouladi, R. T. (1997). Noncentrality interval estimation and the evaluation of statistical models. In L. L. Harlow, S. A. Mulaik, & J. H. Steiger (Eds.), *What if there were no significance tests?* (pp. 251–257). Mahwah, NJ: Erlbaum.

Steiger, J. H., & Lind, J. M. (1980). *Statistically based tests for the number of common factors*. Paper presented at the annual meeting of the Psychometric Society, Iowa City, IA.

Steiger, J. H., & Schönemann, P. H. (1978). A history of factor indeterminacy. In S. Shye (Ed.), *Theory construction and data analysis in the behavioral sciences* (pp. 136–178). San Francisco: Jossey-Bass.

Steiger, J. H., Shapiro, A., & Browne, M. W. (1985). On the multivariate asymptotic distribution of sequential chi-square statistics. *Psychometrika, 50*, 253–263.

Stevens, S. S. (1946). On the theory of scales of measurement. *Science, 103*, 667–680.

Stewart, J. R. (1974). Factor analysis and rotation of the 566 MMPI items. *Social Behavior and Personality, 2*, 147–156.

Stocking, M. L., & Lord, F. M. (1983). Developing a common metric in item response theory. *Applied Psychological Measurement, 7*, 201–210.

Stone, C. A. (2000). Monte Carlo based null distribution for an alternative goodness-of-fit test statistic in IRT models. *Journal of Educational Measurement, 37*, 58–75.

Stone, C. A., & Hanson, M. A. (2000). The effect of errors in estimating ability on goodness-of-fit tests for IRT models. *Educational and Psychological Measurement, 60*, 974–991.

Stone, C. A., & Zhang, B. (2003). Assessing goodness of fit of item response theory models: A comparison of traditional and alternative procedures. *Journal of Educational Measurement, 4*, 331–332.

Stout, W. (1987). A nonparametric approach for assessing latent trait dimensionality. *Psychometrika, 52*, 589–617.

Stout, W. (1990). A new item response theory modeling approach with applications to unidimensionality assessment and ability estimation. *Psychometrika, 55*, 293–325.

Stout, W., Habing, B., Kim, H. R., Roussos, L., Zhang, J., & Douglas, J. (1996). Conditional covariance-based nonparametric multidimensionality assessment. *Applied Psychological Measurement, 20*, 331–354.

Stout, W., Li, H., Nandakumar, R., & Bold, D. (1997). MULTISIB: A procedure to investigate DIF when a test is intentionally two-dimensional. *Applied Psychological Measurement, 21*, 195–213.

Stuart, A., & Ord, K. J. (1991). *Kendall's advanced theory of statistics: Vol. 2. Classical inference and relationship*. New York: Oxford University Press.

Subkoviak, M. J., Mack, J. S., Ironson, G. H., & Craig, R. (1984). Empirical comparison of selected item bias detection procedures with bias manipulation. *Journal of Educational Measurement, 21*, 49–58.

Sugiura, N. (1978). Further analyses of data by Akaike's information criterion and the finite corrections. *Communication in Statistics: Theory and Methods, A(7)*, 13–26.

Suppes, P., & Zanotti, M. (1981). When are probabilistic explanations possible? *Synthese, 48*, 191–199.

Swaminathan, H., & Rogers, H. J. (1990). Detecting differential item functioning using logistic regression procedures. *Journal of Educational Measurement, 27*, 361–370.

Sympson, J. B. (1978). A model for testing with multidimensional items. In D. J. Weiss (Ed.), *Proceedings of the 1977 computerized adaptive testing conference* (pp. 82–98). Minneapolis, MN: Psychometric Methods Program, Department of Psychology, University of Minnesota.

Takane, Y., & de Leeuw, J. (1987). On the relationship between item response theory and factor analysis of discretized variables. *Psychometrika, 52*, 393–408.

Tanaka, J. S. (1993). Multifaceted conceptions of fit in structural equation models. In K. A. Bollen & J. S. Long (Eds.), *Testing structural equation models* (pp. 10–39). Newbury Park, CA: Sage Publications.

Tatsuoka, K. K. (1996). Use of generalized person-fit indices, zetas for statistical pattern classification. *Applied Measurement in Education, 9*, 65–75.

The Oxford English Dictionary (1989), 2nd ed. [CD-ROM] Oxford, U.K.: Oxford University Press.

Thissen, D. (1982). Marginal maximum likelihood estimation for the one-parameter logistic model. *Psychometrika, 47*, 201–214.

Thissen, D. (1991). MULTILOG: Multiple Category Item Analysis and Scoring Using Item Response Theory. Chicago, IL: Scientific Software International Inc.

Thissen, D. (2001). IRTLRDIF v2.06: Software for the Computation of the Statistics Involved in Item Response Theory Likelihood-Ratio Tests for Differential Item Functioning. Available Online: http://www.unc.edu//dthissen//dl.html

Thissen, D., & Steinberg, L. (1984). Taxonomy of item response models. *Psychometrika, 51*, 567–578.

Thissen, D., & Steinberg, L. (2009). Item response theory. In R. E. Millsap & A. Maydeu-Olivares (Eds.), *The Sage handbook of quantitative methods in psychology* (pp. 148–177). London: Sage Publications.

Thissen, D., Steinberg, L., & Gerrard, M. (1986). Beyond group-mean differences: The concept of item bias. *Psychological Bulletin, 99*, 118–128.

Thissen, D., Steinberg, L., & Wainer, H. (1988). Use of item response theory in the study of group differences in trace lines. In H. Wainer & H. Braun (Eds.), *Test validity* (pp. 147–169). Hillsdale, NJ: Erlbaum.

Thissen, D., Steinberg, L., & Wainer, H. (1993). Detection of differential item functioning using the parameters of item response models. In P. Holland & H. Wainer (Eds.), *Differential item functioning* (pp. 67–113). Hillsdale, NJ: Erlbaum.

Thissen, D., & Wainer, H. (1990). Confidence envelopes for item response theory. *Journal of Educational Statistics, 15*, 113–128.

Thomson, G. H., & Lederman, W. (1939). The influence of multivariate selection on the factorial analysis of ability. *British Journal of Psychology, 29*, 288–305.

Thorndike, R. L. (1986). The role of general ability in prediction. *Journal of Vocational Behavior, 29*, 332–339.

Thurstone, L. L. (1947). *Multiple factor analysis*. Chicago: University of Chicago Press.

Tjur, T. (1982). Connection between Rasch's item analysis model and a multiplicative Poisson model. *Scandinavian Journal of Statistics, 9*, 23–30.

Tryon, R. C. (1957). Reliability and behavior domain validity: Reformulation and historical critique. *Psychological Bulletin, 54*, 229–249.

Uttaro, T., & Millsap, R. E. (1994). Factors influencing the Mantel–Haenszel procedure in the detection of differential item functioning. *Applied Psychological Measurement, 18*, 15–25.

Vale, C. D. (1986). Linking item parameters onto a common scale. *Applied Psychological Measurement, 10*, 333–344.

Vandenberg, R. J., & Lance, C. E. (2000). A review and synthesis of the measurement invariance literature: Suggestions, practices, and recommendations for organizational research. *Organizational Research Methods, 3*, 4–70.

Van der Linden, W. J., & Hambleton, R. K. (Eds.). (1997). *Handbook of modern item response theory*. New York: Springer.

Van den Wollenberg, A. L. (1979). *The Rasch model and time limit tests*. (Doctoral Thesis) Nijmegen, the Netherlands: University of Nijmegen.

Van den Wollenberg, A. L. (1982). Two new test statistics for the Rasch model. *Psychometrika, 47*, 123–139.

Verhelst, N. D., & Eggen, T. J. H. M. (1989). *Psychometrische en statistische aspecten van peilingsonderzoek* [Psychometric and statistical aspects of assessment research] (PPON-rapport, 4). Arnheim, The Netherlands: CITO.

Verhelst, N. D., & Glas, C. A. W. (1995). The one parameter logistic model. In G. H. Fischer & I. W. Molenaar (Eds.), *Rasch models: Foundations, recent developments, and applications*. (pp. 215–237). New York: Springer.

Verhelst, N. D., Glas, C. A. W., & Van der Sluis, A. (1984). Estimation problems in the Rasch model: The basic symmetric functions. *Computational Statistics Quarterly, 1*, 245–262.

Verhelst, N. D., Glas, C. A. W., & Verstralen, H. H. F. M. (1994). *OPLM: Computer program and manual*. Arnheim, The Netherlands: CITO.

Wainer, H. (1993). Model-based standardized measurement of an item's differential impact. In P. W. Holland & H. Wainer (Eds.), *Differential item functioning* (pp. 123–135). Hillsdale, NJ: Erlbaum.

Wainer, H., Bradlow, E. T., & Wang, X. (2007). *Testlet response theory and its applications*. New York: Cambridge University Press.

Wainer, H., & Kiely, G. L. (1987). Item clusters and computerized adaptive testing: A case for testlets. *Journal of Educational Measurement, 24*, 185–201.

Wainer, H., Sireci, S. G., & Thissen, D. (1991). *Differential testlet functioning: Definitions and detection* (Research Report No. 91-21). Princeton, NJ: Educational Testing Service.

Wainer, H., & Thissen, D. (1996). How is reliability related to the quality of test scores? What is the effect of local dependence on reliability? *Educational Measurement: Issues and Practice, 15*, 22–29.

Wald, A. (1943). Tests of statistical hypotheses concerning several parameters when the number of observations is large. *Transactions of the American Mathematical Society, 54*, 426–482.

Waller, N. G. (1999). Searching for structure in the MMPI. In S. E. Embretson & S. L. Hershberger (Eds.), *The new rules of measurement: What every psychologist and educator should know* (pp. 185–217). Mahwah, NJ: Erlbaum.

Waller, N. G., & Meehl, P. E. (1998). *Multivariate taxometric procedures: Distinguishing types from continua*. Thousand Oaks, CA: Sage Publications.

Waller, N. G., Thompson, J. S., & Wenk, E. (2000). Using IRT to separate measurement bias from true group differences on homogeneous and heterogeneous scales: An illustration with the MMPI. *Psychological Methods, 5*, 125–146.

Wang, W. C. (2004). Effects of anchor item methods on detection of differential item functioning within the family of Rasch models. *Journal of Experimental Education, 72*, 221–261.

Wang, W. C., & Yeh, Y. L. (2003). Effects of anchor item methods on differential item functioning detection with the likelihood-ratio test. *Applied Psychological Measurement, 27*, 479–498.

Warm, T. A. (1978). *A primer of item response theory* (Technical Report No. 941078). Washington, DC: U.S. Coast Guard Institute.

Weeks, J. P. (2010). plink: IRT separate calibration linking methods (R package). URL http://cran.r-project.org/web/packages/plink/index.html

Wenk, E. (1990). *Criminal careers: Criminal violence and substance abuse (final report)*. Washington, DC: Department of Justice, National Institute of Justice.

Wicherts, J. M., Dolan, C. V., & Hessen, D. J. (2005). Stereotype threat and group differences in test performance: A question of measurement invariance. *Journal of Personality and Social Psychology, 89*, 696–716.

Widaman, K. F., & Reise, S. P. (1997). Exploring the measurement invariance of psychological instruments: Applications in the substance abuse domain. In K. J. Bryant, *Alcohol and substance use research* (pp. 281–324). Washington, DC: American Psychological Association.

Williams, J. S. (1978). A definition for the common factor analysis model and the elimination of problems of factor indeterminacy. *Psychometrika, 43*, 293–306.

Williams, V. S. L. (1997). The "unbiased" anchor: Bridging the gap between DIF and item bias. *Applied Measurement in Education, 10*, 253–267.

Wilson, E. B. (1928). On hierarchical correlation systems. *Proceedings of the National Academy of Sciences, 14*, 283–291.

Wirth, R. J., & Edwards, M. C. (2007). Item factor analysis: Current approaches and future directions. *Psychological Methods, 12*, 58–79.

Woods, C. M. (2006). Ramsay-curve item response theory to detect and correct for nonnormal latent variables. *Psychological Methods, 11*, 253–270.

Woods, C. M. (2007). Ramsay-curve IRT for Likert-type data. *Applied Psychological Measurement, 31*, 195–212.

Woods, C. M. (2008). Likelihood-ratio DIF testing: Effects of nonnormality. *Applied Psychological Measurement, 32*, 511–526.

Woods, C. M. (2009). Empirical selection of anchors for tests of differential item functioning. *Applied Psychological Measurement, 33*, 42–57.

Woods, C. M., & Thissen, D. (2006). Item response theory with estimation of the latent population distribution using spline-based densities. *Psychometrika, 71*, 281–301.

Wright, D. J. (1986). An empirical comparison of the Mantel–Haenszel and standardization methods of detecting differential item performance (Statistical Report No. SR-86-99A). Princeton, NJ: Educational Testing Service.

Wright, B. D., Mead, R., & Draba, R. (1976). Detecting and correcting item bias with a logistic response model (Research Memorandum No. 22). Department of Education, Statistical Laboratory, Chicago: University of Chicago.

Wright, B. D., & Panchapakesan, N. (1969). A procedure for sample-free item analysis. *Educational and Psychological Measurement, 29*, 23–48.

Yang Hsu, J. W. (1995). Sampling behavior in estimating predictive validity in the context of selection and latent variable modeling: A Monte Carlo study. *British Journal of Mathematical and Statistical Psychology, 48*, 75–97.

Yen, W. M. (1981). Using simulation results to choose a latent trait model. *Applied Psychological Measurement, 5*, 245–262.

Yoon, M., & Millsap, R. E. (2007). Detecting violations of factorial invariance using data-based specification searches: A Monte Carlo study. *Structural Equation Modeling, 14*, 435–463.

Yuan, K. H. (2005). Fit indices versus test statistics. *Multivariate Behavioral Research, 40*, 115–148.

Yuan, K. H., & Bentler, P. M. (2004). On the chi-square difference and z tests in mean and covariance structure analysis when the base model is misspecified. *Educational and Psychological Measurement, 64*, 737–757.

Zhang, J., & Stout, W. (1999). The theoretical DETECT index of dimensionality and its application to approximate simple structure. *Psychometrika, 64*, 213–249.

Zieky, M. (1993). Practical questions in the use of DIF statistics in item development. In P. W. Holland & H. Wainer (Eds.), *Differential item functioning* (pp. 337–364). Hillsdale, NJ: Erlbaum.

Zimowski, M., Muraki, E., Mislevy, R. J., & Bock, R. D. (2003). BILOG-MG Vers. 3.0. Mooresville, IN: Scientific Software.

Zumbo, B. D. (1999). *A handbook on the theory and methods of differential item functioning (DIF): Logistic regression modeling as a unitary framework for binary and Likert-type (ordinal) item scores.* Ottawa, ON: Directorate of Human Resources Research and Evaluation, Department of National Defense.

Zwick, R. (1990). When do item response function and Mantel–Haenszel definitions of differential item functioning coincide? *Journal of Educational Statistics, 15,* 185–197.

Zwick, R., Donoghue, J. R., & Grima, A. (1993). Assessing differential item functioning in performance tasks. *Journal of Educational Measurement, 30,* 233–251.

Zwick, R., & Thayer, D. T. (1994). Evaluating the magnitude of differential item functioning in polytomous items. *Journal of Educational Statistics, 21,* 187–201.

Zwick, R., Thayer, D. T., & Lewis, C. (1999). An empirical Bayes approach to Mantel–Haenszel DIF analysis. *Journal of Educational Measurement, 36,* 1–28.

Zwick, R., Thayer, D. T., & Lewis, C. (2000). Using loss functions for DIF detection: An empirical Bayes approach. *Journal of Educational and Behavioral Statistics, 25,* 225–247.

Zwick, R., Thayer, D. T., & Mazzeo, J. (1997). Descriptive and inferential procedures for assessing DIF in polytomous items. *Applied Measurement in Education, 10,* 321–344.

Author Index

A

Ackerman, T.A., 18, 47, 54, 57, 148, 243–244
Afifi, A.A., 126, 132
Agresti, A., 181, 183, 236, 247–248, 250, 252, 255–256, 262–263
Aguinis, H., 284
Ahlawat, K.S., 121
Ahmavaara, Y., 73, 114
Aitken, A.C., 114–115
Aitkin, M., 32, 122, 165
Akaike, H., 100
Albert, J.H., 166, 263
Alexander, R.A., 284
Algina, J., 30, 79
Al-Karni, A., 212
Allen, M.J., 30
Allen, N.L., 44, 242
Amemiya, T., 194, 202
Andersen, E.B., 37, 155, 162, 177–178, 195–197, 205
Anderson, D.R., 100
Anderson, T.W., 40, 79, 103, 130
Andrich, D., 22, 24, 37, 155–156
Angoff, W.H., 4, 8
Ankenmann, R.D., 199–201
Arbuckle, J.L., 90
Archer, R.P., 143
Arminger, G., 32, 36, 73, 91, 122, 126, 133–134, 186, 250
Aronson, J., 18, 55
Averill, M., 219

B

Babakus, E., 121
Baker, F.B., 147, 208–210, 212–213, 222
Bansal, A., 143
Barrett, P., 98
Bartholomew, D.J., 32, 34, 36, 41–42, 61, 122–123, 131–132, 154, 181, 185

Bartlett, M.S., 186
Basilevsky, A., 32
Bauer, D.J., 154, 185
Baumgartner, H., 50, 102, 105
Beguin, A.A., 166
Bekker, P.A., 79
Benjamini, Y., 173
Bentler, P.M., 90, 94–95, 99, 126, 132–133, 138
Berk, R.A., 5, 234, 301
Bernstein, I.H., 121
Beuducel, A., 98
Bickel, P.D., 61
Billingsley, K., 45
Birnbaum, M.H., 287
Bishop, Y.M.M., 252, 255–256
Bleistein, C.A., 245
Bloxom, B., 78, 114–115
Bock, R.D., 32, 37, 122, 131, 165, 167, 181, 183–184, 220
Bode, R.K., 242
Bolt, D., 276
Bollen, K.A., 40, 79, 83–84, 92, 98, 127, 300
Bolstad, W.M., 92
Boodoo, G., 5
Boomsma, A., 91–92
Borneman, M., 5
Borsboom, D., 5–6, 9–10, 30, 39, 301–302
Bourchard, T.J., 5
Boykin, A.W., 5
Bradlow, E.T., 20, 147, 166
Brennan, R.L., 21, 29, 213
Breslow, N., 237
Brody, N., 5
Browne, M.W., 32, 36, 73, 89–91, 97–98, 122, 126, 133–134, 186
Bryant, D.U., 301
Burnham, K.P., 100
Buse, A., 197
Butcher, J.N., 141, 143
Byrne, B.M., 51, 102, 107

Subject Index